HIROSHIMA IN AMERICA

HIROSHIMA

IN AMERICA

FIFTY YEARS
OF DENIAL

Robert Jay Lifton & Greg Mitchell

A GROSSET/PUTNAM BOOK
PUBLISHED BY G. P. PUTNAM'S SONS NEW YORK

Excerpt from "Apocalyptic Narrative," from Apocalyptic Narrative, by Rodney Jones, © 1993 by Rodney Jones, reprinted by permission of Houghton Mifflin Co. All rights reserved.

Excerpt from The Price of Vision: The Diary of Henry A. Wallace, edited by John Morton Blum, © 1971 by the Estate of Henry A. Wallace and John Morton Blum, reprinted by permission of Houghton Mifflin Co. All rights reserved.

Excerpt from The Nuclear Delusion, by George Kennan, © 1982 by George Kennan, reprinted by permission of Pantheon Books.

Excerpts from "The Testimony of Light" and "The Garden," from The Angel of History, by Carolyn Forché, © 1994 by Carolyn Forché, published in 1994 by HarperCollins. Reprinted by permission of the author.

Excerpt from "Nagasaki, Uncle Walt, the Eschatology of America's Century," from American Noise, by Campbell McGrath, © 1993 by Campbell McGrath, first published by The Ecco Press in 1993. Reprinted by permission.

Excerpt from "Sunset Blossoms Snow," from Hiroshima Flows Through Us, by Brown Miller, © 1977 by Brown Miller, first published by Cherry Valley Editions in 1977. Reprinted by permission of the author.

Excerpt from "Ground Zero," by Sharon Doubiago, from Psyche Drives the Coast: Poems, 1976–1987, © 1990 by Sharon Doubiago, published by The Empty Bowl Press. Reprinted by permission of the author.

Excerpt from Advertisements for Myself, by Norman Mailer, © 1959 by Norman Mailer. Reprinted by permission of Wylie, Aitken & Stone, Inc.

Excerpt from Dawn Over Zero: The Story of the Atomic Bomb, by William L. Laurence, © 1946 by William L. Laurence, first published in 1946 by Greenwood Press.

A GROSSET/PUTNAM BOOK
PUBLISHED BY G. P. PUTNAM'S SONS
Publishers Since 1838
200 Madison Avenue
New York, NY 10016

Copyright © 1995 by Robert Jay Lifton and Greg Mitchell

Frontispiece photo courtesy of UPI/BETTMANN

Book design by Gretchen Achilles

Library of Congress Cataloging-in-Publication Data

Lifton, Robert Jay, date.
Hiroshima in America : fifty years of denial / by Robert Jay
Lifton and Greg Mitchell.
p.   cm.
ISBN 0-399-14072-7
1. Hiroshima-shi (Japan)—History—Bombardment, 1945—Influence.
2. Atomic bomb victims—Japan. 3. Hiroshima-shi (Japan)—History—
Bombardment, 1945—Moral and ethical aspects. 4. World war,
1939–1945—United States. I. Mitchell, Greg. II. Title.
D767.25.H6L42 1995   95-13734 CIP
940.54'25—dc20

Printed in the United States of America

1 3 5 7 9 10 8 6 4 2

This book is printed on acid-free paper. ♾

FOR THE SURVIVORS—
JAPANESE AND AMERICAN

*Power over life and death—
don't be proud of it.
Whatever they fear from you,
you'll be threatened with.*

SENECA

Contents

Contents

PART III
Memory and Witness—Struggles with History

PART IV
Hiroshima's Legacy—Moral, Psychological, Political

ACKNOWLEDGMENTS

As this book took hold of us, and we followed its trails, we intensified our dialogue with each other and with our friends and colleagues. Michael Flynn became a combination of research assistant and intellectual adviser in ways that greatly deepened and broadened the enterprise. Charles Strozier also contributed much on multiple levels from beginning to end.

We were especially fortunate to receive guidance from two of the leading historians on matters pertaining to Hiroshima: Barton Bernstein and Martin Sherwin. Bernstein's careful reading of the entire manuscript was a collegial act of the greatest generosity. Sherwin taught us much about the Smithsonian controversy and, more importantly, about the responsibility and intellectual possibilities of the historian.

Lucy Silva prepared much of the final manuscript while keeping its authors in line. Our agents, Sarah Lazin and Lynn Nesbit, offered both strong support and good advice. We are grateful also in various important ways to Jo Becker, John Bedway, Kai Bird, Dan Ellsberg, Kai Erickson, Jon Herskovitz, Sheila Hamanaka, Erwin Knoll, Eric Markusen, Philip Nobile, Michael Perlman, and Lawrence Wittner.

For invaluable interviews and conversations: Erik Barnouw, McGeorge Bundy, Theodore Conant, Gerald Holton, Philip Morrison, David Reisman, and Herbert Sussan. We would also like to express our thanks to the Harry S. Truman Library Institute, which provided a research grant, and the staff of the Truman Library, especially Dennis Bilger and Liz Safly; to Ned Comstock of the Cinema-Television Library at the University of Southern California; and to the Hiroshima International Cultural Foundation.

Betty Jean Lifton and Barbara Bedway were an essential part of both the dialogue and the writing process, even as they lovingly sustained us. Natasha Karen Lifton, Kenneth Jay Lifton, and Jennifer Mitchell also made special contributions.

Jane Isay, our editor at Grosset/Putnam, has been more than remarkable in helping us to cast and recast central themes of the book, in helping us to deepen our own collaboration and then joining it, and in combining warm friendship with wise editorial discipline. Kate Murphy has been a key figure in keeping the entire process moving in a more or less orderly fashion.

INTRODUCTION
THE RAW NERVE

You cannot understand the twentieth century without Hiroshima. Each of us has lived there, studied the effects of the atomic bomb, and written extensively about it. In that way, we have attempted to explain what happened to the city on August 6, 1945, and what is still happening to many of the survivors there. That experience led us to explore what happened to America as a consequence of Hiroshima—both the bomb's existence in the world, and our having used it.

This subject is charged with emotion. When the atomic bomb was dropped over Hiroshima, Americans felt both deep satisfaction and deep anxiety, and these responses have coexisted ever since. Fifty years later, Americans continue to experience pride, pain, and confusion over the use of the atomic bomb against Japan. Part of each of us wishes to believe that the decision to use the bomb was reasonable and justified, but another part remains uncomfortable with what we did.

It has never been easy to reconcile dropping the bomb with a sense of ourselves as a decent people. Because this conflict remains unresolved it continues to provoke strong feelings. There is no historical event Americans are more sensitive about. Hiroshima remains a raw nerve.

We decided to look underneath that raw nerve, at its sources—historical and psychological—and consequences. This time we wanted to explore what has happened in our own country. Our focus in this book is not what occurred in Japan on August 6, 1945, but rather its impact on America in the fifty years since. We examine the manipulations and distortions that surround the use of the bomb: the mythology Americans have constructed around Hiroshima, and its cost to ourselves and to the world.

This is the story of how one country, our country, dealt with the Hiroshima bomb, before and after its use, and how this led to profound conflict and uneasiness, causing us to embrace the weapons that terrify us. Hiroshima can be a window of truth not only to our past and current nuclear dilemmas, but also to the broader confusions of our time.

The Hiroshima raw nerve was responsible for the recent dispute that erupted over an exhibit at the National Air and Space Museum in Washington, D.C. Officials called the exhibit—scheduled to mark the fiftieth anniversary of the atomic bombings—the most divisive ever attempted at any of the Smithsonian Institution's national museums.

Curators planned to put on display the *Enola Gay,* the plane that carried the first atomic bomb over Japan, and designed an exhibit around it that would fully explore the decision to use the bomb, and its effects. They would present both the justifications for, and doubts about, the atomic attack, based on the latest scholarship; and they would not flinch from showing what happened at ground zero. Soon, veterans' groups were claiming that the planned exhibit was pro-Japanese and dishonored U.S. servicemen. Newspaper editorials charged the Smithsonian with "political correctness," and columnist George Will accused the curators of being anti-American. Both houses of Congress passed resolutions condemning the exhibit.

Yielding to pressure, the museum made massive deletions and revisions in the script for the show, culminating in a two-day negotiating session with representatives of the American Legion. What emerged was an exhibit that endorsed in every detail the official version of Hiroshima that has endured since 1945: The atomic bombings were necessary to prevent an invasion of Japan and save up to a million American lives. Now historians and disarmament activists were angry. A delegation of scholars, including the authors of this book, met with the museum director to protest the censorship, labeling it "historical cleansing" and "patriotic correctness." Peace activists scheduled protests to greet the opening of the exhibit.

Finally, on January 30, 1995, the Smithsonian announced that it was, in effect, canceling the exhibit. Now there would be displayed only the plane, a plaque, and a tape of the flight crew recounting the mission. Hiroshima would be excluded altogether.

Another controversy erupted over plans by the U.S. Postal Service to issue a stamp bearing an image of the mushroom cloud, to commemorate the use of the bomb against Japan. The A-bomb stamp was canceled, but America's nerve endings appear more sensitive to Hiroshima than ever. Half a century ago something revolutionary happened, and it changed everything. But instead of attempting to come to terms with the atomic bombing, on all its levels of meaning, Americans continue to treat Hiroshima, above all else, as a threat to our national self-image.

Why does Hiroshima still matter, now that the Cold War has ended and the Soviet Union no longer exists as a nuclear threat? Here we would stress that nuclear danger has by no means disappeared, that tens of thousands of nuclear warheads remain in the world, often under less control than in the past. The danger of nuclear proliferation is greater than ever; the bomb may soon be in the hands of reckless leaders or terrorist groups. Since Nagasaki, nuclear weapons have not been exploded in a war, but they have nearly been used on a number of occasions. We can hardly put permanent faith in the mixture of restraint and good fortune that has prevailed. Nuclear weapons are still the ultimate threat, in ways that can be traced back to Hiroshima.

Hiroshima set a precedent for the use of the weapon—an example that continues to be widely endorsed. As long as we continue to defend and justify the Hiroshima model we risk making that kind of decision again. But there is another reason why Hiroshima matters. We believe that Americans need to confront Hiroshima and fill in the blanks in history, because no matter what we think of dropping the bomb, it has affected us deeply. Our present historical moment cries out for candor. Around the world, previously suppressed experience has been uncovered, notably in Russia and Eastern Europe. America has had its own revelations of suppressed history in connection with the Vietnam war, the Iran-Contra affair, and most recently, radiation experiments conducted by the government and the military (which originated in the secrecy surrounding the Hiroshima bomb). Americans are increasingly aware of the value of such confrontations for our political, ethical, and psychological well-being.

To be sure, no country ever fully confronts its own history, least of all when morally vulnerable. Japan, for example, has been deeply divided over coming to terms with its brutal behavior prior to, and during, World War II. Some Japanese justify this avoidance by pointing to what America did in Hiroshima and Nagasaki—just as some Americans point to Japanese silence about its atrocities as a reason to minimize or justify the atomic bombings. Other voices in both countries recognize that nobody benefits from, and everyone is endangered by, such suppression.

The end of the Cold War enables us to look more clearly at the world. We need no longer be blinded by the polarization that so consumed and distorted all perceptions. We believe there is a yearning, conscious or unconscious, on the part of Americans, and most other people in the world, to have the burden of nuclear weapons—their past use, near-use and potential use—lifted from them. There is a wish to step out of the nuclear narrative for good. We believe that nuclear threat can never be truly eradicated without first coming to terms with Hiroshima.

The atomic bomb was used in the late stages of a long and dehumanizing war, and our enemies likely would have used it against us. "America was not morally unique—just technologically exceptional," historian Barton Bernstein has observed. Nuclear weapons pose a problem for everyone, but because America got there first our relationship to the bomb has been particularly painful. Our choice today is between perpetuating a mind-set that allows another Hiroshima—or creating one that prevents that outcome and enhances human life.

Hiroshima is not just an event of the past but a source of vital insight for the future. Yet few Americans know the full story of either the decision to use the bomb or its human effects. This is partly due to misleading official statements and government secrecy. But the most compelling reason for the failure to confront Hiroshima is our disinclination to do so—a collective form of psychic numbing.

From the moment the American public learned of the use of the bomb and caught glimpses of its devastating power, we have been struggling with what to do with that knowledge and those images. There was an almost immediate awareness that the weapon represented a new totality of destruction from which no one was safe. "Seldom, if ever, has a war ended leaving the victors with such a sense of uncertainty and fear," radio commentator Edward R. Murrow observed, "with such a realization that the future is obscure and that survival is not assured."

But very quickly, there was an impulse of a different kind, what we perceive as a "wrong turning," an effort on the part of officials to justify the use of the bomb on ethical grounds, to hide its grotesque effects on people, and to deny the weapon's revolutionary significance. "This is the story of a pride that begot blindness," Lewis Mumford observed in 1948. It represented an inability to confront the full truth of Hiroshima, an insufficient recognition in our policies and our attitudes that nothing was the same after Hiroshima—that human survival was now at issue. The wrong turning reflected, and contributed to, Cold War fears, leading to a fateful embrace of nuclear weapons and an arms race with the Soviet Union that drained America, economically and psychologically, for decades.

Hidden from the beginning, Hiroshima quickly disappeared into the depths of American awareness. As early as 1946, the writer Mary McCarthy was calling Hiroshima "a hole in human history." Thirty years later, physicist Ralph Lapp, who worked on the atomic bomb, asked, "If the memory of things is to deter, where is that memory? Hiroshima has been taken out of the American conscience, eviscerated, extirpated." Whatever our avoidance and numbing, Americans remain haunted by the atomic bombings, all the more so because they remain obscure, distant, and mysterious, and because they were our doing.

What is remarkable is that the terms of the Hiroshima debate have changed so little since August 1945.

From the start, Americans were not shown the human effects of the bomb. This reinforced the psychological resistance to taking in the horror of Hiroshima. Nearly fifty years later, the same impulses were at play in the Smithsonian dispute. Curators, under pressure, removed from the exhibit nearly every photograph of dead or badly injured Japanese civilians. There remains today a reluctance to face squarely what America did, or excuse it, perhaps even wish it away.

That there was no alternative to dropping atomic bombs on two Japanese cities remains an article of faith. For years opinion polls consistently found public support for the use of the bomb by better than two-to-one margins. Those who present arguments to the contrary are often denounced as "revisionists" or accused of "revising history"—as if history is something static and new facts and interpretations are necessarily wrong, even unpatriotic. A congressman critical of the original plans for the Smithsonian exhibit condemned museum officials, explaining, "Their job is to tell history, not rewrite it." *What* history? Whose version of history?

Significantly, a recent Gallup poll (announced in March 1995) suggests, if not a change of heart, at least a reopening of the issue in the minds of many Americans. While 44 percent of those surveyed said they "would have dropped the atomic bomb" on Hiroshima, 49 percent would have "tried some other way" to force the Japanese to surrender. It seems clear that Americans are much more uncomfortable about what happened at Hiroshima than generally assumed.

In this book we examine the psychological and ethical impact of the Hiroshima bomb on Americans, and our struggles with and against what we call the "official narrative." A narrative is a story, a series of events told in a way that renders them coherent and thereby conveys some form of meaning. What the Hiroshima narrative conveys is the justification, even wisdom, of our use of the atomic bomb to save lives and end the war.

Struggles with the Hiroshima narrative have to do with a sense of meaning in a nuclear age, with our vision of America and our sense of ourselves. The poet Richard Hugo has observed: "The world never learns. History has a way of making the past palatable, the dead/a dream. . . ." Yet Hiroshima casts a shadow on every aspect of our personal and collective existence.

Most books about the atomic bomb and Hiroshima climax on August 6, 1945. Our book begins there, with Truman's announcement of the invention of the bomb and its use against Japan, which set the tone for the official narrative that followed.

Just three weeks earlier America had successfully tested an atomic device at the Trinity site in New Mexico. On July 26, the U.S. and Great Britain issued the Potsdam Declaration, demanding that Japan surrender unconditionally at once or else face swift and certain ruin by unidentified means. Two days later, the Japanese rejected the ultimatum, and President

Truman ordered the bomb used against the enemy as soon as possible. At fifteen minutes past eight on the morning of August 6 (Hiroshima time), one American plane dropped one bomb on one Japanese city, killing 100,000 people immediately, and fatally injuring at least 50,000 others. In his announcement, Truman began the process of justifying the bombing and shielding Americans both from the human effects of the bomb and its implications for the future.

From that beginning, we look at the "wrong turning" in the years immediately following the use of the bomb against Japan. Instead of viewing Hiroshima as an ethical crisis and a harbinger of danger, Americans became entranced by the bomb, drawn to its destructive power. We also reveal, from personal interviews and considerable original research, what could be called the Hiroshima cover-up—the suppression of evidence (including articles, photographs, and film footage) that showed the human consequences of the Hiroshima bomb.

Only after exploring America's early response to Hiroshima do we, in Part II, examine Truman's decision to use the bomb. This reverses the chronology, but in that way we are able to mirror how Americans actually experienced Hiroshima—first, what they were told, and then what really happened. We undertake not just historical analysis (based on the latest evidence) but a psychological study of the decision process, and especially of Harry Truman within that process. Carrying the story forward again, we then study Truman's defense of the Hiroshima decision in the many years that followed. We believe that no such evaluation of Truman and Hiroshima has been attempted before, and that a surprising portrait emerges.

In Part III, we examine how Americans have struggled with Truman's decision, and the Hiroshima narrative, ever since. This includes American presidents, journalists and historians, scientists, war veterans and peace activists. The nearly half century of struggle with the Hiroshima narrative culminated in the fierce controversy surrounding the Smithsonian exhibit, which we explore in detail.

Then, in our concluding section, we examine how the psychological sequence of the use of the bomb, and America's response to it, left its mark on all that followed. We consider the grave, and little recognized, costs of Hiroshima: nuclear entrapment, moral inversion, national self-betrayal, enduring patterns of secrecy and numbing, deep cultural confusions, and the fear of futurelessness.

But our conviction, finally, is that we need not be permanently bound to that legacy. By confronting it, and exploring what it has done to living in the late twentieth century, we embark on a path of renewal.

PART I

Explaining Hiroshima—
The Official Narrative

CHAPTER 1

THE ANNOUNCEMENT

On August 6, 1945, President Truman faced the task of telling the world that America's crusade against fascism had culminated in exploding a revolutionary new weapon of extraordinary destructive power over a Japanese city. It was vital that this event be understood as a reflection of dominant military power and at the same time consistent with American decency and concern for human life. Everyone involved in preparing the presidential statement sensed that the stakes were high, for this marked the unveiling of both the atomic bomb and the official narrative of Hiroshima.

When the astonishing news emerged that morning, it took the form of a routine press release, eleven hundred and sixty words long. President Truman was at sea a thousand miles away, returning from Potsdam. Shortly before eleven o'clock, an information officer from the War Department arrived at the White House bearing bundles of press releases. A few minutes later, assistant press secretary Eben Ayers began reading the president's announcement to about a dozen members of the Washington press corps. The atmosphere was so casual, and the statement so momentous, that the reporters had difficulty grasping it. "The thing didn't penetrate with most of them," Ayers later remarked. Finally, they rushed to call their editors, and at least one reporter found a disbeliever at the other end of the line.

The first few sentences of the statement set the tone:

> Sixteen hours ago an American airplane dropped one bomb on Hiroshima, an important Japanese Army base. That bomb had more power than 20,000 tons of TNT. It had more than two thousand times the blast power of the British "Grand Slam" which is the largest bomb ever yet used in the history of warfare.
>
> The Japanese began the war from the air at Pearl Harbor. They have been repaid many fold. And the end is not yet. With this bomb we have now added a new and revolutionary increase in destruction to supplement the growing power of our armed forces. In their present form these bombs are now in production and even more powerful forms are in development.
>
> It is an atomic bomb. It is a harnessing of the basic power of the universe. The force from which the sun draws its powers has been loosed against those who brought war to the Far East.

Although details were modified at the last moment, Truman's four-page statement had been crafted with considerable care over many months. If use of the atomic bomb was inherent in its invention, an announcement of this sort was inevitable. Only the timing was in doubt.

Several drafts of the document were prepared by aides to General Leslie R. Groves, director of the Manhattan Project, and Secretary of War Henry L. Stimson. The manuscript was adjusted again after the spectacularly successful test of the first atomic device at the Trinity site in mid-July, to give it what Stimson called more "pep." Stimson finished the revisions on July 31 and dispatched an aide, manuscript in hand, to Potsdam, where Truman was meeting with the leaders of Great Britain and the Soviet Union. "The reason for the haste," Stimson advised Truman in a cover note, "is that I was informed only yesterday that, weather permitting, it is likely that the weapon will be used as early as August 1. . . ." Truman immediately approved a final draft and the next day sailed for home.

For several hours after the atomic bomb exploded over Hiroshima on the evening of August 5, General Groves, from his office at the Pentagon, frantically attempted to determine the results. Reports from the Pacific suggested that the blast had met all expectations, but Hiroshima was now shrouded in dust and smoke, and it was impossible to determine the extent of the damage. As written, the Truman document declared with apparent pride that the target had been destroyed, but Groves put off its release as long as possible, eager to confirm the damage. Observing this, General George C. Marshall, the military chief of staff, asked him to guard against expressing too much satisfaction in the statement, noting the likelihood of a large number of Japanese casualties. Groves replied by invoking the memory of the Bataan death march, when thousands of American prisoners were killed by the Japanese.

Finally, fearing that Tokyo radio would beat President Truman to the punch—reducing the impact of his announcement—Henry Stimson ordered the statement released. Groves deleted all claims of destruction and added two details in the opening sentence: the number of hours that had elapsed since the bombing and the name of the stricken city.

From its very first words, the official narrative was built on a half-truth. Hiroshima did contain an important military base, used as a staging area for Southeast Asia. As many as forty thousand enemy soldiers may have been stationed there at the time. But the bomb had been aimed at the center of a city of 350,000, a continuation of the American policy of bombing civilian populations in Japan to undermine the morale of the enemy. Significantly, the phrase "Japanese Army base" was not included in any draft of the statement and was apparently inserted by Groves at the last minute— possibly without Truman's knowledge—when he learned that the bomb had found its target.

Until that moment no one knew for certain that the weapon would work. A massive civilian death toll had always seemed likely; only now was it a reality. Referring to the city as a military base obscured the nature of the casualties. Should the Japanese still fail to surrender, Truman warned, the bomb would be used against other military targets: "We shall destroy their docks, their factories, and their communications."

The emphasis on the bomb's explosive force, followed by a blunt reference to Pearl Harbor, expressed dominant power and triumphal revenge. The authors of the Truman statement, however, faced a problem of rendering the unimaginable in concrete terms. At first they settled on TNT equivalency, based on the unexpectedly high yield of the Trinity test. But the image was abstract. Few Americans had a sense of what one ton of TNT could accomplish, let alone twenty thousand tons. So, in the final draft, they inserted another analogy: that of a single, very powerful bomb—the British "Grand Slam." The new weapon was two thousand times more potent than *that*.

Because the president in this statement would make no reference to radiation effects, the imagery of just a bigger bomb prevailed. His startling revelation—"It is an atomic bomb"—did not appear until paragraph three. Truman properly described the new weapon as "revolutionary" but only in regard to the destruction it could cause, failing to mention its most distinctive new feature: radiation.

Unlike other epochal military triumphs, the Hiroshima mission involved no fierce fighting by brave soldiers led by wise and courageous generals. The showdown was decidedly technological and one-sided, involving only a handful of American airmen. It lacked a human dimension. But there was a battle for Truman to point to—a "battle of the laboratories" with Nazi Germany, which "held fateful risks for us as well as the battles of the air, land and sea." The generals in this struggle were the scientists and industrialists who created the Hiroshima bomb and the foot soldiers were the 125,000 workers who constructed it.

"We won the greatest scientific gamble in history," Truman announced. It was "the greatest achievement of organized science in history." Harnessing "the basic power of the universe" granted omnipotence to those who possessed it. Truman's reference to "even more powerful forms" of the bomb in development could be interpreted not only as a warning to the Japanese but also to the world.

How did Truman justify dropping the bomb? He first cited vengeance for Pearl Harbor. Only much later in the statement did he point out that the enemy had rejected the Potsdam ultimatum of July 26 calling for unconditional surrender, which was meant "to spare the Japanese people from utter destruction." By asking Americans to be "grateful to Providence" that the Axis powers did not get the bomb first, Truman was suggesting that the use of such a weapon by a decent people against an evil enemy was morally acceptable. Nowhere in the statement did he mention what would soon become and long remain the cornerstone of official justification: the claim that the use of the bomb saved many American lives.

Throughout the text, the imagery was technocratic and triumphal: in the stark announcement of a new weapon and its destructive force, the narrow condemnation of the enemy (several mentions of Pearl Harbor), and the assertion of unlimited American power. There were no dead anywhere. The statement was upbeat, as Stimson and Truman wished, with little of the sense of tragic responsibility that would soon pervade discussion of the bomb. It was devoid of dread. Only faintly, in announcing that the U.S. would maintain a curtain of secrecy around "atomic energy," did it recognize the threat the new weaponry posed to the human future. Instead, Truman hailed atomic power as a potential energy source—after "a long period" of intensive research—and suggested that it "can become a powerful and forceful influence toward the maintenance of world peace." Yet this promise of renewal seemed almost laconic, more of a distraction from the weapon's horror than a felt promise of national rebirth.

The themes of Truman's statement—military necessity, American decency, scientific and industrial achievement, and an embrace of the weapons as a near-mystical force that confers omnipotence—would reverberate long afterward in official and unofficial rhetoric. Born in the intensity and distortion that characterize wartime, these themes have continued to dominate peacetime discourse about Hiroshima and the bomb.

CHAPTER 2

THE OFFICIAL STORY UNFOLDS

Truman's announcement initiated the Hiroshima narrative, but the official story expanded and evolved by the hour.

Many Americans first heard the news from the radio, which broadcast the text of Truman's statement shortly after its release. The afternoon newspapers reported the story under banner headlines: "ATOM BOMB, WORLD'S GREATEST, HITS JAPS," "JAP CITY BLASTED BY ATOMIC BOMB," "ATOM BOMB ON JAPAN!" Few of the articles were accompanied by photographs. The Pentagon had released no pictures, so most of the newspapers relied on maps of Japan with Hiroshima circled.

Initial reports were based solely on the Truman announcement, a longer statement by Secretary of War Stimson, and a bulletin from the Pentagon revealing that "an impenetrable cloud of dust and smoke" over Hiroshima interfered with an assessment of damage. Many accounts highlighted the president's claim of an explosive force equivalent to twenty thousand tons of TNT. This probably led most Americans to conclude that the atomic bomb "was essentially an addition to the gunpowder family, a kind of super-blockbuster," Daniel Lang of the *New Yorker* later observed.

News of the atomic bombing spread so fast that, by evening, radio commentators assumed that most listeners were already aware of it. Some of their observations transcended Truman's announcement in significant ways, suggesting that the public imagination was outrunning the official story. Contrasting emotions of gratification and anxiety had already emerged. Lowell Thomas proudly proclaimed on CBS radio that Hiroshima had been completely devastated. Don Goddard of ABC, perhaps after consulting an atlas, revealed that the target was not simply a military base but a city the size of Denver. "For all we know, we have created a Frankenstein," H. V. Kaltenborn warned, striking an ominous chord Truman had ignored. "We must assume that with the passage of only a little time, an improved form of the new weapon we use today can be turned against us."

Most Americans recognized immediately that the new bomb would shorten the war. No one felt more grateful than soldiers in the Pacific. "We whooped and yelled like mad, we downed all the beer we'd been stashing away," one later recalled. "We shot bullets into the air and danced between the tent rows, because this meant maybe we were going to live, and not as cripples."

When Ray Bradbury, a young science fiction writer, saw the headlines, riding a bus in Los Angeles, his reaction was: "Yes, of course, so it's here!" Bradbury knew this day would come, for he had pondered the splitting of the atom for years. For some Americans, however, the immediate reaction was one of discomfort, even revulsion. When Lewis Mumford, the cultural critic, heard the report over the radio at his home in upstate New York his immediate reaction was "almost physical nausea," he wrote in his notes two days later. Mumford felt the bomb's power was "too absolute to be entrusted" to human beings and the very fact that we had used it was proof that we were "neither intelligent enough nor morally sound enough to be in charge of this weapon."

It was the playwright Maxwell Anderson, however, who best expressed the conflicting emotions many Americans felt. "My first reaction was an obvious one," he told a reporter a few days later. "I have two sons in the service, and I hoped the bomb would help shorten the war. But at the same time," he continued, "I felt a great apprehensiveness. This new bomb, you know, is a very dangerous plaything for civilization."

The Official Story

It wasn't until the following morning, August 7, that a detailed account of the atomic bomb, and the Hiroshima mission, reached the public. Nearly all the newspaper and radio stories were based on fourteen separate press releases distributed by the Pentagon several hours after the president's announcement. Like Truman's statement, these documents had been carefully prepared and revised over a period of months. One man, working for General Groves, wrote a majority of the reports, which hailed the decision to build the bomb and heralded "the birth of a new age—The Age of Atomic Energy." Groves would later reflect, with satisfaction, that "most newspapers published our releases in their entirety. This is one of the few times since government releases have become so common that this has been done."

The articles disclosed, among other things, the genesis of the bomb project, the story of the first atomic chain reaction, and the test of the new weapon at the Trinity site (described as "unprecedented, magnificent, beautiful, stupendous and terrifying"). Each of these events, taken separately, would have dominated the news had they been reported when they actually occurred. Now they were all emerging at the same moment—from the same office at the Pentagon.

The story was too overwhelming for the public to absorb at once: fantastic atomic theory, a secret nuclear industry employing tens of thousands of workers, a cast of characters with unfamiliar names like Oppenheimer and Groves and Tibbets—as well as the first confirmed reports of "terrific damage" in Hiroshima. Taken together it represented, according to the Pentagon, a "fabulous achievement"—not only the means to "save thousands of American lives" (an argument Truman neglected) but an invention for the future "immeasurably more important than the discovery of electricity or any of the other great discoveries. . . ." Readers faced an unprecedented array of articles, ten or more in each newspaper, with startling headlines like: "Basic Force of Universe Unleashed," "Atom Bombs Made In 3 Hidden Cities," "New Age Ushered," "Billowing Fire Ball Dims Sun In Desert Test," "New Epoch in Science, War," "Japs Admit Great Atomic Bomb Damage."

Photographs, however, were still at a premium. One of the few visual images made available to the press by General Groves was a picture of himself studying a wall map of Japan. Another was an aerial photograph of the Manhattan Project facility at Hanford, Washington. These were not dynamic images, so newspapers improvised. The *San Francisco Chronicle* published a photograph of the British "Grand Slam" bomb under the heading "Multiply This by Two Thousand!" Several of the Hearst newspapers printed a cartoon showing Uncle Sam blasting a stereotypical buck-toothed "Jap" with the "Sun's Power" of an atomic bomb. The Hearst syndicate also distributed a picture of a small hydroelectric power station in Hiroshima which it claimed "may have been the primary target of the new atomic bombers."

As it happens, the power plant, on the outskirts of Hiroshima, was untouched by the bombing, but the journalists could not have known that. They had to rely completely on information from the military. Since neither the inventors of the bomb, nor those who had decided to use it, were available for interviews, press coverage amounted to little more than rewrites of War Department documents extolling the bomb.

General Groves left nothing to chance. Before Hiroshima, he had prepared an order prohibiting U.S. commanders in the field from commenting on the atomic attacks without clearance from the War Department. "We didn't want MacArthur and others saying the war could have been won without the bomb," Groves later explained. Indeed, MacArthur and many of the other commanders believed the bomb was not needed to end the war.

In orchestrating the official story of Hiroshima, as in so many aspects of the bomb, General Groves played a central role. Back in March, he had sought permission to hire a "suitable newspaperman" to serve as a kind of "pool correspondent." Reporters near the bomb plants were starting to poke around, and Groves feared "serious breaks" after the first test of the bomb in the New Mexico desert that summer.

Even if secrecy held, the new weapon would come under tremendous scrutiny after it was used against Japan. At that point, Groves warned in an internal memo, "the project will be subject to harassing investigation, official inquiries. . . . and all the miscellany of crackpots, columnists, commentators, political aspirants, would-be authors and world savers." Truman would disclose preliminary information but "the follow-up stories and comments . . . could well be ruinous. At that time, it may be necessary to control the situation by the issuance of carefully written press releases." From that moment on, control of nuclear commentary would be the government's goal.

The Manhattan Project already had a public-relations staff, but Groves sought a respected journalist who would supply a seemingly "more objective touch" and add authority to the press releases. An associate recommended William L. Laurence, Pulitzer Prize–winning science reporter for the *New York Times*. Less than a month later, meeting secretly at the *Times*, Groves found Laurence eager to take the job.

Laurence brought to any project what *Times* editor Turner Catledge once called an "unquenchable, boyish enthusiasm for his job." But this was something special. Laurence considered the atomic bomb the discovery of the century and believed that no greater honor could come to any newspaperman than creating the War Department's official press releases. He could write whatever he wanted, with only two provisos: the reports were subject to approval by Groves and Stimson; and they would be stamped Top Secret and locked in a vault, awaiting the end of the war or the use of the bomb, whichever came first.

That day arrived on August 6. The official material would indeed "control the situation," as Groves had hoped, thanks in no small part to the celebratory yet highly credible quality of Laurence's press releases. In one of these documents Laurence would coin the expression "the Atomic Age," and it was he, perhaps more than anyone, who set the tone for the entire era.

One of the few articles to appear in the nation's newspapers on August 7 that Laurence may not have conceived himself was an item in the *Times* identifying him as the man behind "the pounds of official reports and bales of War Department 'handouts' designed to enlighten laymen on the working of the atomic bomb. . . ." Like the bomb itself, Laurence had been something of an official secret, and like so much else surrounding the weapon his role could only be revealed after its use.

The Spokesman

In William Laurence the atomic bomb elite found an even better spokesman than they could have anticipated. His intense and creative contributions to the emerging narrative powerfully influenced the way Americans came to perceive Hiroshima. His sensibility, derived from the flow of his life, and especially from his attitude toward both history and science, was remarkably attuned to a glorification of the bomb as an expression of what he termed "atomic energy."

Laurence, always fascinated by Einstein's theories, had first written about atomic energy in 1929, "long before it was more than a gleam in a scientist's eye," as he put it. His first encounter with the bomb occurred in 1939 at a conference of the American Physical Society, at which he heard a group of leading physicists discuss "a revolutionary discovery—uranium fission." At the end of the meeting, with some agitation, he asked Enrico Fermi and Niels Bohr, "Does all this add up to an atomic bomb?" According to his later account they both looked "startled," and Fermi answered that "theoretically" it could be "possible someday" but not for twenty-five years or so. The answer did not satisfy Laurence, who commented, "Maybe Hitler will make one in much less time."

He came from the encounter "a frightened man" and started a one-man campaign as "a journalistic Paul Revere" to alert America to the danger. First he wrote a series of articles on the possibility of such a bomb in the *New York Times* in May 1940. When that did not create a wave of concern he submitted a sensational article to the *Saturday Evening Post,* warning of reports that "by direct order of Hitler . . . some 200 of Germany's greatest scientists were concentrating all their joint energies" on making the bomb. That turned out to be an exaggeration, and Laurence could not have known that Roosevelt had already activated a modest American bomb project (initiated by Leo Szilard with the help of Albert Einstein).

Nearly five years later, looking for some form of "active war service," Laurence enthusiastically responded to Groves's invitation to work on the secret military project. For Laurence the next four months was a thrilling adventure of an almost supernatural kind: "Thus began my journey through Atom Land-on-Mars . . . by July 12, 1945, I had been with the

Atomic Bomb Project (Manhattan District) a little over two months, Atomic Time, the equivalent of a lifetime or more in non–atomic calendar time. I'd flown more than 35,000 miles and had visited all the secret plants, which at that time no one mentioned by name—Oak Ridge, Hanford, Los Alamos; the Martian laboratories at Columbia, Chicago, and California universities. I had seen things no human eye had seen before, things no one had ever thought possible." Part of the adventure was the secrecy itself. The contents of his wastebasket would be collected every night and burned.

His sense of the reactor at Hanford was of "mighty cosmic forces" at work. He wrote to his New York editor: "The story is much bigger than I could imagine, fantastic, bizarre, fascinating and terrifying. When it breaks it will be an Eighth Day wonder, a sort of Second Coming of Christ yarn. . . . the world will not be the same after the day of the big event. . . ."

"Genesis" is what Laurence called the portion of his book *Dawn Over Zero* that covers the Trinity test and the events leading up to it. That biblical imagery of new life, of a primal beginning, dominates Laurence's response. It was a moment of transcendence, exciting and mysterious: "I watched the birth of the era of atomic power from the slope of a hill in the desert land of New Mexico." He was awed by both the occasion and the great scientists—in this setting, one might say priests—in whose company he found himself. Laurence also took pride in the element of risk. On the list of proposed articles he prepared for Groves was "Eyewitness account of test in New Mexico," and he added in parentheses: "provided eyewitness survives." He so valued atomic bombs and their use in the war that, when first told of the planned Trinity test, he asked: "You're going to waste an atomic bomb on American soil? If you have a bomb, why not drop it on Japan right off and end the war? What's the sense of wasting a good bomb?"

In his memorable description of the Trinity explosion, Laurence combined Genesis-like imagery with religious awe that included worshipful feelings toward the bomb itself:

And just at that instant there rose from the bowels of the earth a light not of this world, the light of many suns in one. It was a sunrise such as the world had never seen, a great green super-sun climbing in a fraction of a second to a height of more than eight thousand feet, rising ever higher until it touched the clouds, lighting up earth and sky all around with a dazzling luminosity.

Up it went, a great ball of fire about a mile in diameter, changing colors as it kept shooting upward, from deep purple to orange, expanding, growing bigger, rising as it expanded, an elemental force freed from its bonds after being chained for billions of years. For a fleeting instant the color was unearthly green, such as one sees only in the corona of the sun during a total eclipse. It was as though the earth had opened and the skies had split. One felt as though one were present at the moment of creation when God said: "Let there be light."

To the scientists' pre-Trinity uncertainty—"Will it work?"—Laurence gave a mystical answer that extends far beyond the question:

With the flash came a delayed roll of mighty thunder heard, just as the flash was seen, for hundreds of miles. The roar echoed and reverberated from the distant hills and the Sierra Oscura range nearby, sounding as though it came from some supramundane source as well as from the bowels of the earth. The hills said yes and the mountains chimed in yes. It was as if the earth had spoken and the suddenly iridescent clouds and sky had joined in one affirmative answer. Atomic energy—yes. It was like the grand finale of a mighty symphony of the elements, fascinating and terrifying, uplifting and crushing, ominous, devastating, full of great promise and great forebodings.

Nothing could be more revealing, however, than the contrast between his reaction and that of George Kistiakowsky, the scientist who had a major role in the building of the bomb. "To Dr. Kistiakowsky the bursting of the first atomic bomb was 'the nearest thing to Doomsday,' " Laurence reported. "To me, who saw the same thing, the spectacle meant the birth of a new world." Indeed Laurence thought that Trinity "may turn out to be the greatest moment in history."

Laurence emphasized his personal sense of transcendence: "We were really transported to another planet, to another civilization." He frequently used words like *spectacle* and *drama* to describe what he found himself in the middle of, and he spoke of "the elemental flame," or the "first fire ever made on earth that did not have its origin in the sun." He again invoked his favorite god: "Prometheus had broken his bonds and brought a new fire down to the earth."

But one of the most remarkable images of all had to do with reconstructing bomb imagery to represent an ultimate symbol of human freedom: ". . . the mountain that grows above the clouds took the form for a fleeting instant of a gigantic Statue of Liberty, its arm raised to the sky, symbolizing the birth of a new freedom for man." Laurence was surely not wrong in claiming that not only he but many others at Trinity, including Oppenheimer, had some kind of religious experience. But his own could be characterized as the most passionate form of conversion—or reconversion—to nuclearism, to the worship of a revolutionary instrument of destruction.

Laurence was excited at the expectation of joining what became the Hiroshima mission: "I had a fairly good notion that I was to be privileged to be an eyewitness of the dropping of the first atomic bomb just as I had witnessed the first test in New Mexico." And: "I was going to fly with the most powerful weapon in existence." He arrived on Tinian too late to join the mission, but on that Pacific island he was able to observe the final preparations, including the bomb assembly.

It was the weapon itself that moved him most. "Being close to it and watching it as it was being fashioned into a living thing so exquisitely shaped that any sculptor would be proud to have created it, one somehow crossed the borderline between reality and non-reality and felt oneself in the presence of the supranatural," he wrote. "Could it be that this innocent-looking object, so beautifully designed, so safe to handle, could in much less time than it takes to wink an eye annihilate an entire city and its population? Could that comparatively little thing produce the flash of many suns and make the earth tremble for many miles?"

Laurence described the "curious sensation," the following day, of hearing the news of Truman's atomic-bomb announcement while "watching the atomists working on the assembly of the second atomic bomb . . . The world's greatest story was being broadcast, and mine had been the honor, unique in the history of journalism, of preparing the War Department's official press release for world-wide distribution. No greater honor could have come to any newspaperman, or anyone else for that matter."

The Nagasaki run for Laurence was a consummation of his passion for the weapon: "Until then I didn't know whether my entire connection with the atomic bomb would have been a sort of glorious journalistic striptease —that I had seen everything but missed the climactic point." During flight preparations, Laurence proudly held in his hand the thirteen pounds of material that contained the critical mass of plutonium for the bomb, commenting that "if you were to take the slightest amount of it inside, you would die a horrible death."

He decided to make his story a running account of the mission as it occurred. The first sentence—"We are on our way to bomb the homeland of Japan, in a formation equivalent to 2,000, and possibly 4,000 B-29 superbombers"—set the tone for his "I was there" (or "I am here!") account. He later revealed his sense of drama and personal omnipotence, even divinity, as he contemplated the destruction of a Japanese city:

> As I was writing, there again came a strange sort of interference by destiny because . . . the primary target was a town called Kokura. And I was ruminating. It was early morning; it was dark; and I was thinking of the town of Kokura being asleep and all the inhabitants having gone to bed, men, women, and children. . . . they were like a fatted calf, you know, saved for the slaughter. And so they were absolutely a peaceful city. . . . and they had been going to bed, going about their jobs night after night, month after month, week after week, year after year. *And here I am. I am destiny. I know. They don't know. But I know that this was their last night on earth.* I felt that the likelihood was that Kokura would be completely wiped off the face of the earth. I was thinking: there's *a feeling of a human being, a mere mortal, a newspaper man by profession, suddenly has the knowledge which has been given to him, a sense—you might say—of divinity.* I know that in a few hours you won't be there any more. . . . I realized also that . . . Kokura might be spared. . . . So here again destiny in the form of maybe a breeze

of wind, you know, would decide whether or not one town would be wiped out and another one spared or visa versa. [Italics added.]

This principle of "destiny" enabled him to suppress concerns about the bomb's victims: "You feel that sense of compassion, and then you say again, 'You had nothing to do with it. This determination, this destiny, has been decided on long ago by forces much greater than any human decision can make or influence.'" Interspersed were references to Nagasaki as a military target—as a "great industrial and shipping center" and a city "making weapons of war for use against us." Impulses of revenge for Japanese war-making and atrocities served to protect him from concerns about civilian victims: "Does one feel any pity or compassion for the poor devils about to die? Not when one thinks of Pearl Harbor and of the Death March on Bataan."

Once more, over Nagasaki, Laurence gave us a description of the explosion that combined awe, infatuation, and worship of a "living" entity. He spoke of "the giant flash that . . . flooded our cabin with intense light . . . a pillar of purple fire . . . a living thing, a new species of being, born right before our incredulous eyes. . . ."

He admitted that he had "mixed emotions" about Nagasaki and experienced a "certain tinge of regret that it had to be done," as he had seen photos of Hiroshima and knew this bomb to be even more powerful. But even twenty years later he justified the Nagasaki bomb by explaining that "we had given the Japanese at least two days in which to take action against their military, to arouse public opinion and all. Nothing happened."

Because of censorship and bureaucratic confusion, Laurence's story on Nagasaki was not published until a month later. But as we have seen, many other stories he had written while working with the Manhattan Project were published in newspapers almost immediately after Truman's announcement. The difficulty for Laurence was that his name was not associated with them. Although the handouts given to journalists were identified as written by him, "they proceeded to take my stories and just rewrite them or patch them together." Either the stories would bear the name of some other journalist or else have no byline at all—so that "I had the curious experience of watching my own story in my own paper with the byline of somebody else."

Laurence was particularly proud of his contribution to the official announcements by Truman and Stimson. The president's statement, he claimed, "I had written as far back as two months before it actually happened." Laurence had, in fact, written an early draft, but when that statement was shown to the top advisory panel on the bomb, the so-called Interim Committee, James Conant, a leading member, considered it "too detailed, highly exaggerated, even phoney." The committee decided upon a shorter announcement to be "reworked" by an aide to Stimson. Expunged from the final statement was much of Laurence's rhetoric about Prometheus, and about "this great marvelous new continent of atomic power" offering "a new Promised Land of wealth, health, and happiness for all mankind . . . a new era of prosperity such as the world has never seen."

In mid-August, just after the surrender, he was about to leave for Hiroshima and Nagasaki to observe the damage, when he heard that the *New York Times* wanted him back immediately. This was "one of my greatest disappointments" because he had been given the "biggest assignment any reporter could have and I wasn't given the opportunity to do the mopping up." But upon returning to the *Times,* he wrote a ten-part series about the bomb and potential developments in atomic energy. He considered these articles to constitute "the story of the century," and he won his second Pulitzer Prize for them. While they tended to downplay the dangers of radiation, the articles, as a later commentator put it, were "an emotional celebration of the science, engineering, and industry behind the bomb, couched in superlatives that left the dilemmas favored by civic journalism far behind."

Certain themes predominate in Laurence's relationship to the bomb, themes that are psychological as well as historical. The first is his personal merger with the weapon, a breakdown of boundaries between man and bomb to the extent that each came to represent—to support, enhance, and speak for—the other. This merger evolved over time and had much to do with Laurence's role as official spokesman. But he was chosen for that role because of his prior interest in the weapon, his scientific knowledge and passion as well as his apocalyptic imagination—so that "When the time came to choose someone to tell the story of the actual use of atomic energy and warfare . . . it was inevitable that I should get the part."

Concerning the Nagasaki flight, he said: "We were all playing a part on a tremendous stage, the stage of history, outside of space and time you might even say, in which forces that had been working for thousands of years had finally come to a culminating point." While each of us seeks connections with forces larger than ourselves as a way of experiencing a sense of immortality, in Laurence's case we may speak of immortality *hunger*. His merger with the bomb was a merger with ultimate forces that control human events, so that again during that flight he could say: "Here I am. I am destiny." Crucially, Laurence placed science at the heart of his own immortality hunger and the world's "destiny." More than that, he celebrated, indeed embodied, the marriage of science and the bomb.

His visionary embrace of science and sense of destiny also served the psychological purpose of helping him suppress the human effects of the weapon he so extolled. When he asks himself "How does a human being feel carrying the most destructive weapon in history, a weapon that you know is going to kill maybe a hundred thousand, maybe two hundred thousand human beings . . . and you think of thousands of little children who certainly had nothing to do with the war . . . ," his answer is: "As you look back at it, you try to rationalize a thing like that. You are in it. You say it's one of the inevitables of history; there is nothing you can do about it to change it. . . . that somehow human beings become like automatons—they play the part but nevertheless it's a part written for them by some external force which they are just playing out." Now destiny erases individual responsibility. But his expression "You *try* to rationalize a thing like that" suggests that at least a glimmer of doubt, of compassion, breaks through the numbing.

Nineteen years after participating in the mission to drop the second atomic bomb on Nagasaki, Laurence recalled how, in making notes during the course of the flight, he "thought about the strange destiny that has taken me from a little village in Lithuania to the United States, an immigrant boy, through Harvard College, through the First World War as a soldier in France, and again through many strange struggles and vicissitudes and here I am over the skies of Japan in what may be the last scene of the greatest war in history and as the official observer of that final act." What Laurence called "destiny" was, indeed, a remarkable confluence of life experiences.

Laurence was born in 1888 in an isolated Jewish village in Lithuania that was in his words "completely out of space and time"—without electricity or running water. He was first a Talmudic student but rebelled against his father's religious orthodoxy and became a "rabid atheist," but was later to transfer his spiritual passion to science. Restless and seeking to extricate himself from his obscure environment, he was drawn to radical movements and took part in the 1905 uprisings in Russia, throwing bricks and narrowly escaping arrest. When the revolution failed, he decided to embark for the United States and managed, later in 1905, to be smuggled across the border from Russia to Germany in a barrel.

Arriving in America, he changed his name from Leid Sieu to William (for Shakespeare) Leonard (for Leonardo da Vinci) Laurence (for the name of the street he came to live on in Roxbury, Massachusetts). He learned English quickly and won a scholarship to Harvard. He studied physics and chemistry and, later, philosophy and drama.* Long interested in writing and journalism, the young Laurence had difficulty obtaining employment both before and following World War I, even after obtaining a law degree. He was hired as a reporter by the *New York World,* and in 1930 he became a science reporter for the *New York Times.* He saw himself as one of a "new breed" who no longer treated scientists as "freaks of nature" or as "odd balls, queer ducks who talked this strange, queer language," which had been frequently the journalistic custom. Laurence took them and their work seriously, making use of his own scientific background.

With justification, Laurence considered himself a pioneer among science writers, the "true descendants of Prometheus"; their task was to "take the fire from the scientific Olympus, the laboratories and universities, and bring it down to the people." He was fond of invoking such mythological language as part of his particular version of a religion of science. It involved both radical faith in science as a form of deliverance and a mystical relationship to the cosmos.

In certain ways, W. L. Laurence can be seen as a representative twentieth-century American living out a successful immigrant experience of dislocation, hard work, and achievement. His journey from medieval

---

* *Among the younger students he tutored in chemistry was James Conant.*

Lithuania to the skies over Nagasaki suggests the protean flexibility of the twentieth-century self. But Laurence was far from typical in the intensity of his life journey: in the added incentive, as a Jew who lost family members in the Holocaust, to contribute whatever he could to the defeat of fascism; in the extremity of his mystical religion of science and particularly atomic science; in his equation of the atomic-bomb achievement with scientific utopia and his own psychological merger with the bomb; and in his destiny-laden immortality hunger. These latter traits have been widespread over the course of this century, but rarely have they been combined in such an ideal way for a prospective atomic-bomb spokesman. His personal blend of psychological, intellectual, and historical exposures brought him to a task that he, undoubtedly a decent human being, carried out all too well.

CHAPTER 3

FIRST BREAKS IN THE NARRATIVE

The Truman announcement and the flood of material from the War Department firmly established the Hiroshima narrative. It would not take long, however, for breaks in the official story to appear.

At first, journalists had to follow where the Pentagon led. Wartime censorship remained in effect, and there was no way any reporter could reach Hiroshima for a look around. One of the few early stories that did not come directly from the military was a wire service report filed by a journalist traveling with the president aboard the *Augusta*. Approved by military censors, it went beyond, but not far beyond, the measured tone of the president's official statement. It depicted Truman, his voice "tense with excitement," personally informing his shipmates about the atomic attack. "The experiment," he announced, "has been an overwhelming success."

The sailors were said to be "uproarious" over the news. "I guess I'll get home sooner now," was a typical response. Nowhere in the story, however, was there a strong sense of Truman's reaction. Missing from this account was his exultant remark when the news from the Pacific first reached the ship: "This is the greatest thing in history!"

On August 7, military officials finally confirmed that Hiroshima had been devastated: at least 60 percent of the city wiped off the map. They offered no casualty estimates, emphasizing instead that the obliterated area housed major industrial targets. The Air Force provided the newspapers with an aerial photograph of Hiroshima, with most of the city visible within a circle that marked the "maximum radius of damage." Significant targets were identified by name. For anyone paying close attention there was something troubling about this picture. Of the thirty targets, only four were specifically military in nature. Industrial sites consisted of three textile mills.*

On Guam, weaponeer William S. Parsons and *Enola Gay* pilot Paul Tibbets calmly answered reporters' questions, limiting their remarks to what they had observed after the bomb exploded. Some of the images they used, such as "a mushroom of boiling dust," were already growing familiar, thanks to W. L. Laurence's widely quoted press release on Trinity. Parsons revealed that the bomb had hit its target "right on the button." Asked how he felt about the people down below at the time of detonation, Parsons said that he experienced only relief that the bomb had worked and might be "worth so much in terms of shortening the war."

Almost without exception newspaper editorials endorsed the use of the bomb against Japan. Many of them sounded the theme of revenge first raised in the Truman announcement. Others pointed out that the bomb "differs in degree, but not in kind, from the other instruments of warfare in common use," as the *Hartford Courant* put it. Most of them emphasized that using the bomb was merely the logical culmination of war. "However much we deplore the necessity," the *Washington Post* observed, "a struggle to the death commits all combatants to inflicting a maximum amount of destruction on the enemy within the shortest span of time." The *Post* added that it was "unreservedly glad that science put this new weapon at our disposal before the end of the war."

Referring to American leaders, the *Chicago Tribune* commented: "Being merciless, they were merciful." A drawing in the same newspaper pictured a dove of peace flying over Japan, an atomic bomb in its beak.

· · ·

* Indeed, a U.S. survey of the damage, not released to the press, found that less than 10 percent of the city's manufacturing, transportation, and storage facilities had been damaged.

At the same time, however, the first non-official news reports began to break into print, including graphic accounts of casualties, a subject ignored in the War Department's briefings. Tokyo radio called Hiroshima a city of the dead with corpses "too numerous to be counted . . . literally seared to death," according to a United Press report. It was impossible to "distinguish between men and women." Those caught outside by the blast were burned alive, while those indoors were crushed by falling buildings. Medical aid was hampered by the fact that all the hospitals in the city were in ashes. The Associated Press carried the first eyewitness account, attributed to a Japanese soldier who had crudely described the victims (over Tokyo radio) as "bloated and scorched—such an awesome sight—their legs and bodies stripped of clothes and burned with a huge blister. . . ."

Americans who came across these reports were thrust briefly into the reality of atomic warfare—if this information could be believed. The *New York Times* observed that the Japanese were "trying to establish a propaganda point that the bombings should be stopped." The Hearst newspapers published a cartoon showing a hideous, apelike "Jap" rising out of the ruins of Hiroshima screaming at Americans, "They're Not Human!"—with the caption *Look who's talking.*

But in quoting from Tokyo radio, newspapers introduced their readers to a disturbing point of view: the atomic bombing was not an act of deliverance blessed by the Almighty but a "crime against God and man"; not a legitimate part of war but something "inhuman," a cruel "atrocity," and a violation of international law, specifically Article 22 of the Hague Convention which outlawed attacks on defenseless civilians. The Japanese also compared the bomb to the use of poison gas, a weapon generally considered taboo. It was this very analogy many American policy makers and scientists had feared as they contemplated using the bomb.

Other condemnations appeared as the War Department's grip on the story weakened slightly. "All the evidence points to the fact that the use of this bomb was unnecessary," said Robert M. Hutchins, chancellor of the University of Chicago, and therefore America had "lost its moral prestige." The *New York Herald-Tribune* found "no satisfaction in the thought that an American air crew had produced what must without doubt be the greatest simultaneous slaughter in the whole history of mankind," likening it to the "mass butcheries of the Nazis or of the ancients."

A leading religious body in America, the Federal Council of

Churches, urged that the U.S. drop no more atomic bombs on Japan, in a statement issued by two of its leaders, G. Bromley Oxnam and John Foster Dulles. "If we, a professedly Christian nation, feel morally free to use atomic energy in that way, men elsewhere will accept that verdict," they argued. "Atomic weapons will be looked upon as a normal part of the arsenal of war and the stage will be set for the sudden and final destruction of mankind." To refuse to use additional weapons would be viewed not as evidence of weakness, they wrote, but of "moral and physical greatness."

By the time their statement was issued on August 9 the bomb had already been used again.

From the beginning, the official narrative provoked a profoundly divided response. Relatively few found fault with the use of the bomb; it was the fact of the bomb that produced fears. America had won the race for the bomb but it "may yet reap the whirlwind," Hanson Baldwin, military analyst for the *New York Times,* declared. The *Chicago Tribune* called the atomic bomb the greatest scientific achievement in history but "it may also mean the obliteration of the civilization that makes such discoveries possible."

President Truman, meanwhile, had returned to Washington looking tanned and fit after a long sea voyage. Cabinet members and presidential aides greeted him at the White House just before midnight on August 7. Truman suggested they join him upstairs in his study for a drink, where he analyzed the Potsdam conference and rated the men he met there. He seemed to be "favorably impressed" with Stalin as someone who talked straight and could be "depended upon," Eben Ayers recorded in his diary.

When several guests started to leave, Truman asked, "What's the hurry?" A couple of his aides stayed behind to chat with the president awhile longer. One of them later revealed that during the entire time the atomic bomb was not mentioned even once. "Now, that may seem strange —it does to me now," Eben Ayers said later. A pattern of personal, and collective, distancing had begun.

The following morning, the president was back at his desk ready for work. He "showed his pleasure at the success" of the atomic bombing but was concerned about the "possible effects" of further development of the weapon, Ayers observed. Truman seemed worried about "the attitude of the pope concerning the bomb development" and "was troubled as to how to reach the pope to reassure him." Someone mentioned that Archbishop Spellman of New York might agree to serve as intermediary. (Truman would confer with Spellman three days later.) Later, Henry Stimson showed the president the first aerial photos of Hiroshima after the bombing. Truman "mentioned the terrible responsibility that such destruction placed upon us here and himself," Stimson observed in his diary. Within hours the plutonium bomb was dropped over Nagasaki.

Interest in Hiroshima receded as other events in the Pacific war, as well as speculation about a Japanese surrender, took center stage. On August 9, the top two headlines on the front page of the *New York Times* announced the Soviets' declaration of war against Japan. Not until line three did this message appear: "ATOM BOMB LOOSED ON NAGASAKI." The target of the second attack, a city of 270,000 people, was described, variously, as a naval base, an industrial center, or a vital port for military shipments and troop embarkation. A United Press story affirmed that the U.S. military "long suspected" that the few remaining ships in the Japanese fleet "might be lurking" there (although, as it turns out, they were not).

On the evening of August 9, President Truman spoke directly to the public for the first time since his return. A reported 41.5 million Americans tuned in. Truman's radio speech, delivered the day after Nagasaki and four days following Hiroshima, was primarily a report on Potsdam. He opened with images of Berlin as a "ghost city" and thanked God that America had been spared such devastation. After speaking for several more minutes, he came to the atomic bombings. "Having found the bomb, we have used it," Truman declared—an odd choice of words, suggesting a technological imperative. Yet the president wanted everyone to know that using the bomb was "not lightly undertaken." Explaining the motivation, he mentioned Pearl Harbor, the brutal treatment of American prisoners, and other Japanese atrocities. Only then did he cite the goal of saving the lives of "thousands and thousands of Americans."

Confronting the rumors of mass casualties that were just emerging, Truman emphasized, as he had in his first announcement, that the Hiroshima bomb had been dropped on a military base, not a large city. "That was because we wished in the first attack to avoid, in so far as possible, the killing of civilians," he explained. Such restraint would soon disappear if the "Japs" did not surrender, for the U.S. planned to target "war indus-

tries" and "unfortunately thousands of civilian lives will be lost." By implication, the civilian death toll in the first two atomic bombings was low.

Truman also seemed concerned about public fears of the long-term
threat posed by the bomb, a subject passed over lightly in his August 6
announcement. At the last moment his speechwriters inserted in his
August 9 address the following sentence: "I realize the tragic significance
of the atomic bomb." This was undoubtedly meant to assure the American
people that their president was not oblivious to the dangers posed by this
instrument of mass killing. The United States had emerged from the war
"the most powerful nation, perhaps, in all history," Truman observed, but
one saddled with the "awful responsibility" of being the "trustees" of the
bomb. Yet, he added, America should bear the burden of the bomb gladly.
"We thank God it has come to us," Truman declared, "instead of to our
enemies; and we pray that He may guide us to use it in His ways and for
His purposes."

The Truman radio address re-asserted the Hiroshima story he had established on August 6. It capped a three-day period when the atomic bomb
dominated the news as few developments had done before, and as the
bomb itself would never do again. On August 10, when a tentative Japanese surrender offer appeared, the bomb moved to the sidelines. "Atomic
bomb is likely to be forgotten in [the] U.S. along with the war itself," one
magazine predicted. Newspapers were filled with reports of premature
victory celebrations and speculation about the postwar economy. "No one
is trying to assess the relative influence of the atomic bomb and the Russian declaration of war in bringing about the Japanese offer of surrender,"
Edward R. Murrow declared on the radio. "People are content to leave
that argument to the historians."

Controversy raged concerning the Japanese emperor: Should he be
retained on the throne or tried as a war criminal? This was no small matter,
because the U.S. had demanded unconditional surrender before using the
bomb and before Russia had entered the war. According to a Gallup poll,
70 percent of the public advocated punishing Hirohito—by exile, impris-
onment, or execution. Germany had accepted unconditional surrender
three months earlier, and the public expected no less of Japan. While the
surrender debate played out in the press, the public remained unaware of
the behind-the-scenes drama at the White House which featured a presi-

dent, more troubled by the use of atomic bombs than he revealed in public, under pressure to use more of them.

Many Americans were clamoring for continued atomic attacks to secure an unconditional surrender. A woman in Indianapolis who had lost a son in the Pacific cried: "I'd like to fly over there and drop more bombs myself." Senator Richard B. Russell of Georgia, in a letter to Truman, wondered why the U.S. appeared to be backing off, "after the blood, treasure and enterprise of the American people have given us the upper hand." Truman informed Russell that he was not going to order any more atomic attacks if he could help it. Although the Japanese were "beasts," Americans should not "act in the same manner" as the enemy, "wiping out whole populations." This gave every indication that Truman—contrary to his continued use of the phrase "military base" to describe the city of Hiroshima—was well aware that the bomb had killed tens of thousands of civilians.

Truman knew that another bomb would be ready in a little more than a week; and among the targets for the next attack were cities four to ten times larger than Hiroshima and Nagasaki. He had personally directed the use of the first bomb on Japan, but as part of that order other bombs were to be utilized as they became available, without requiring additional approval. The Nagasaki bomb had simply been delivered when ready, on an accelerated schedule promoted by General Groves that gave the Japanese little time to respond to the first attack. This may have surprised even the president.

On August 10, Henry Stimson suggested a bombing halt, citing (according to one of those present) "the growing feeling of apprehension and misgiving as to the effect of the atomic bomb even in our own country." Later that day, Truman announced to his cabinet that he had prohibited the use of additional atomic bombs without his consent. Truman probably experienced some discomfort at how closely the second atomic strike had followed the first. Now he decided that if there was to be another atomic attack he would authorize it expressly, with full respect for the human consequences.

Four days later, with the Japanese surrender not yet in hand, Truman's patience was wearing thin. He "sadly" told British officials, according to one internal report, "that he now had no choice but to drop an atomic bomb on Tokyo."

• • •

Like Truman, many of the Manhattan Project scientists were finding that the consequences of atomic warfare were harder to accept in reality than in theory. When General Groves called Robert Oppenheimer at Los Alamos on August 6 to congratulate him, the following conversation occurred:

> *Groves:* Apparently it went with a tremendous bang.
> *Oppenheimer:* When was this, was it after sundown?
> *Groves:* No, unfortunately, it had to be in the daytime on account of security of the plane and that was left in the hands of the Commanding General over there. . . .
> *Oppenheimer:* Right. Everybody is feeling reasonably good about it and I extend my heartiest congratulations. It's been a long road.

This exchange is revealing in several respects. Oppenheimer's report that the scientists only felt "reasonably" pleased reflects questions some scientists had been raising at Los Alamos for months concerning the use of the bomb and mass killing. Also, Oppenheimer seemed to indicate that he believed the target would be bombed after dark, not at 8:15 in the morning. At night, workers and students would have been at home, shielded at least partly from the heat and radiation produced by the atomic explosion. Eight o'clock in the morning was rush hour in Hiroshima, and Oppenheimer would have sensed immediately what a bomb drop at that moment meant in terms of casualties—and what it signified about our intentions. Groves agreed that this was unfortunate and eagerly assigned responsibility for the daytime attack, which he had long advocated, to another general.

The news from Washington was relayed to the other Los Alamos scientists via loudspeaker with these words: "One of our units has just been successfully dropped on Japan." (There was no mention of the words *bomb* or *weapon.)* The place went up "like we'd won the Army-Navy game," according to one observer. The scientists had worked hard and well together; this was their moment of triumph. Edward Teller, walking from his apartment to a lab, passed a colleague sitting in a jeep, a huge smile on his face. "One down!" the scientist called to Teller. A few minutes later, Oppenheimer was greeted as a hero by a cheering, foot-stomping crowd assembled at the camp theater. He responded by clasping his hands over his head in a victory salute.

Otto Frisch, the physicist, found the carryings-on rather "ghoulish." Later he recalled feeling "unease, indeed nausea," when he saw that many of his friends were rushing to the telephone to book tables at the LaFonda Hotel in Santa Fe, "in order to celebrate." Frank Oppenheimer, physicist and brother of Robert Oppenheimer, at first felt relieved that the Hiroshima bomb was "not a dud." Then he felt depressed about the loss of life. "We had somehow always thought it would not be dropped on people," he later said.

A party called to mark the occasion at Los Alamos that evening fizzled. Few couples danced; most of the scientists, perhaps regretting their show of emotion that afternoon, sat around talking quietly among themselves. Robert Oppenheimer shared with a colleague a telex he had received from Washington: damage reports from Hiroshima. Growing increasingly depressed, the two men left the party. On his way home, Oppenheimer spied one of his young scientists throwing up in the bushes (the incident would be recounted often) and thought to himself: *The reaction has begun.*

Another leading physicist, Leo Szilard, who had provided the initial impetus for inventing the weapon, had reacted months earlier, submitting a petition to the president seeking to avoid using the bomb against Japanese cities. Now from Chicago he wrote to a friend that dropping the bomb was "one of the greatest blunders of history," both from a "practical point of view" and "from the point of view of our moral position. . . . It is very difficult," Szilard observed, "to see what wise course of action is possible from here on."

A few days later Oppenheimer screened for Los Alamos scientists aerial footage of what was left of Hiroshima. No one spoke. Hans Bethe, the physicist, felt shock at the damage and pity for the victims. It was one thing to imagine the blast; to witness the actual results left "an awful impression," he later explained. "We were really horrified." Bethe resolved that the weapon must never be used again.

Four days after the attack on Hiroshima, Ernest O. Lawrence, inventor of the cyclotron, arrived at Los Alamos expecting to find Oppenheimer in a triumphant mood, only to discover that he felt guilt ridden and depressed. It was the day after Nagasaki, and the Los Alamos scientists (even many of those who felt Hiroshima was justified) were taking it badly. Some would later use the words *sick* or *nausea* to describe their reaction to Nagasaki. Oppenheimer wondered aloud if the living at Hiroshima and

Nagasaki might envy the dead. It was something almost everyone would eventually say.

Public Reactions

On August 14, Japan capitulated, agreeing to surrender, but with its emperor retained. Diplomacy still ended the war. Truman called the surrender "unconditional" anyway, and the press did not challenge him. This proved, as historian Barton Bernstein has pointed out, that the government could manipulate public opinion by both retreating from unconditional surrender—and denying it. (Arthur Krock's report in the *New York Times,* for example, opened with: "Japan today unconditionally surrendered. . . .") With victory in hand, few Americans protested the keeping of the emperor. V-J Day had finally arrived. This meant that Hiroshima would fade as America plunged headlong into the postwar era. Despite a few breaks in the official story, the War Department had effectively managed the news media, thanks to its control over information, a generally acquiescent press, and the national euphoria over an impending surrender.

Americans listened to the radio broadcasts, read the newspapers, viewed the first pictures of the mushroom cloud, and pondered the editorials.* But what did they actually make of the atomic bombings in August 1945? It is difficult to say. For one reason, we were not polled as relentlessly or rigorously as we are today. Also, it is hard to separate personal emotions about the use of a weapon of mass destruction from what seemed the end result: the surrender of Japan. For nearly everyone, joy over the end of the war overwhelmed moral qualms.

Concerning one group of Americans it is easy to generalize. Most servicemen in the Pacific, and those who expected to be sent there soon, viewed the bombing of Japan as their personal salvation—an obvious and natural reaction. Later, as veterans, they would play a pivotal role in de-

---

* Audiences in movie theaters watched a newsreel of Truman reading his announcement of the attack on Hiroshima, shot on board the Augusta on August 6. For this filming, Truman had taken a pencil and personally reedited the statement, adding more than to the stated cost of the bomb project—"more than *two billion dollars.*" Now that the bomb had been used, and with success, that investment was no longer something to fret about, but celebrate.

fending the Hiroshima narrative—for these were the lives reputedly saved by the bomb, and over the years their survival would be invoked as reason enough to have used the weapon. "We were playing a lottery," John Ciardi, a bomber pilot in the Pacific (later a poet) recalled. "A certain number of planes had to be lost. You were just hoping that by blind chance yours would not be. When news of the atom bomb came—we didn't know what it was—we won the lottery. Hey, we're gonna get out of here!"

With Japan's surrender, the bomb appeared to fulfill its promise as the winning weapon. "Thank God for the atomic bomb," a serviceman from Mississippi wrote *Life* magazine. William Styron, then a Marine officer slated to lead a rifle platoon in the invasion, would recall that he felt "ecstatic" to have "an almost tactile burden of insecurity and dread" lifted from his shoulders.

Americans back home also felt grateful for the bomb. A Roper poll found that more than 50 percent supported exactly what Truman did—and an additional 23 percent regretted that the U.S. did not get a chance to use "many more of the bombs before Japan had a chance to surrender." A Gallup survey in mid-August discovered that 85 percent endorsed the use of the bomb, and only 10 percent disapproved, with pollsters noting "hardly any difference of opinion by sex, age, or education."

The approval rating was so resounding that most scholars have failed to probe further. But other, largely unexamined, polls raise fascinating questions. A Gallup survey in August 1945, for example, found that by a margin of 69 to 17 percent those polled thought it was a "good thing," not a "bad thing," that the atomic bomb was developed. But then, asked if they thought it "likely" that "some day experiments in smashing atoms will cause an explosion which will destroy the entire world," the results were surprising: a sizable number (27 percent) said "yes." Many of the same people who endorsed the invention and use of the bomb nevertheless felt it would "likely" destroy the world. This reflected the seemingly contradictory emotions of approval and fear the bomb evoked, a combination that has continued to disturb and confuse Americans ever since.

It is not hard to fathom why the atomic bombings drew such overwhelming support. Indeed, it is difficult to imagine otherwise. The bomb meant victory—an association that would endure. The known good the bomb had already seemed to accomplish (the end of the war) outweighed what it might one day cause (the end of the world). Added to this were the elements of racism (strong on both sides) and revenge. Images of Pearl Harbor were still vivid. Years of considering the "Japs" fanatics and savages, perhaps even subhuman, would have made the death toll at Hiroshima and Nagasaki easier to accept.

There were other factors. Since the fall of Germany, the notion of unconditional surrender had become a popular concept. Pre-Hiroshima surveys showed that Americans wanted the Pacific war to end with the Japanese homeland in ruins, its people subjugated, an American occupation force in place. Also, faith in our political and military leaders had never been higher, and anything they did to bring the conflict to a close was not likely to be challenged. In addition, the creation of the atomic bomb produced a groundswell of pride in American technology and our can-do spirit.

Somewhere in this psychological mix was an irrevocable belief in American virtue. Our aims in this war were pure, meaning we could occasionally use inhuman instruments—such as the flamethrower—to rout the enemy. Few voices had been raised against our strategic bombing in Europe, which resulted in the deaths of tens of thousands of civilians in Dresden and other cities, or the firebombing of Japan, which killed hundreds of thousands more. On the morning of August 6, before the Hiroshima story broke, a page-one headline in the *Atlanta Constitution* read: "580 B-29S RAIN FIRE, TNT ON 4 MORE DEATH-LIST CITIES." There is no record of readers expressing outrage.

Unquestionably, every American—policy maker, military leader, and average citizen alike—had been brutalized by the war. Death by bullet, bayonet, or bomb had come to tens of millions, causing those who remained among the living to harden their hearts or turn away in horror. But it is too easy, as many have done, to leave it at that, for the American public was never exposed to the full effects and intent of the air war. The United States had "never previously made war against women and children," the historian William O'Neill has observed. Strategic bombing of cities, therefore, was said to be aimed at industrial and military targets; civilian casualties were officially ignored or downgraded. Americans did not learn that as many as 100,000 had been killed in the March 9, 1945, firebombing of Tokyo until three weeks after Hiroshima, when a witness, a Danish diplomat, described the attack over ABC radio.

It is certainly true that, in the moral realm, there was a symbiotic relationship between strategic bombing and atomic bombing. One helped justify the other. But one must distinguish between the general response to total war—calloused resignation—and specific approval of the mass killing of civilians from the air, which was never quite the case with Americans. That is why President Truman, while privately fretting about destroying "whole populations," publicly described the city of Hiroshima as a "military base."

A Time for Reflection

By mid-August, the surprise and excitement that greeted Truman's announcement had passed. A time for reflection had arrived. Just at this moment, the first post-Hiroshima issues of national magazines appeared. Much of what their writers had to say was original, thoughtful, even prescient. They sought meaning in the creation and use of the bomb that had been hidden by the cascade of clichés. These commentaries centered on four themes: the sustained shaking of foundations, the threat to the continuation of the human species, the "splitting" of the mind (no less than the atom), and questions of justification and guilt directly related to the use of the bomb against Japan.

In conveying a shaking of foundations, *Time* magazine wrote of the bomb—the author turned out to be staff writer James Agee—that "relative to it, the war itself shrank to minor significance"; that it left us "still, as in the aftershock of a great wound, bemused and only semi-articulate"; and that it "split open the universe and revealed the prospect of the infinitely extraordinary." In the *Saturday Review,* Norman Cousins spoke of "a primitive fear, the fear of the unknown, the fear of forces man can neither channel nor comprehend . . . the fear of irrational death." E. B. White, in a *New Yorker* "Talk of the Town" article, observed: "For the first time in our lives, we can feel the disturbing vibrations of complete human readjustment." These commentaries suggested that the bomb imposed a sudden new human dislocation—extreme, probably permanent, and not quite knowable.

A second theme, the threat to the human future, was inseparable from the constantly reiterated dimensions of the Hiroshima and Nagasaki bombs. In *U. S. News,* editor David Lawrence described how "A single airplane riding high in the stratosphere, unobserved and undetected . . . can appear suddenly over London or Washington or Detroit or Pittsburgh or any city in a peaceful area and destroy human lives by the hundreds of thousands in just a few seconds." Hanson Baldwin, the respected military journalist, made this vision even darker in *Life* when he warned of "a fresh page in military history . . . the coupling of atomic energy explosives (destructive power) with rocket propulsion (range)."

The third theme was again sounded by James Agee when he wrote, "All thoughts and things were split." The individual psyche was said to be divided, the collective human future fractured. There was hope that "the discovery which had done most to end the worst of wars might also, quite conceivably, end all wars—if only man could learn its control and use," Agee wrote. But there were also, elsewhere in *Time,* searing forebodings: "Man had been tossed into the vestibule of another millennium. It was wonderful to think of what the Atomic Age might be, if man was strong and honest. But at first it was a strange place, full of weird symbols and the smell of death."

When it came to the fourth theme, a moral judgment about the use of the bomb against Japan, commentaries were most divergent, and perhaps most passionate. *Time* magazine (again Agee) expressed a fairly typical view in stating that "the sudden achievement of victory was a mercy, to the Japanese no less than to the United Nations, but mercy born of a ruthless force beyond anything in human chronicle." The suggestion of guilt was eloquent but diffuse: "[T]he demonstration of power against living creatures instead of dead matter created a bottomless wound in the living conscience of the race."

This juxtaposition of awe and questioning on one hand, and emphasis upon the saving of lives on the other, occurred frequently. Freda Kirchwey in the *Nation* found "no answer" to the argument that "the loss of life on both sides would have been many times greater if the atomic bomb had not been used." Richard Strout (writing as "TRB") in the *New Republic* suggested that "it could justly be argued that in the short-range view [the bomb] shortened the war and saved lives, though from the longer view we may all regret that it was ever employed. . . . Personally, I am sick and tired of decisions like this being made in secret." The *New Yorker* pointed out that the argument that atomic energy was "so fearsome" that no nation would "dare unleash it" was "fragile" because "one nation (our own) has already dared take the atom off its leash, has dared crowd its luck, and not for the purpose of conquering the world, merely to preserve liberty."

Among the few voices expressing direct moral outrage at the American use of the bomb, three rang loud and clear—and were never fully forgettable.

Virtually the only commentator to focus on the bomb's radiation effects, Dwight Macdonald, in his leftwing journal *politics,* decried the dropping of "half-understood poisons" on a civilian population. That so few protested this act signaled America's "decline to barbarism." Macdonald noted the "flimsiness" of the stated justifications for using the bomb, such as punishing an aggressor and saving American lives, and argued that *"any* atrocious action, absolutely *any* one, could be excused on such grounds."

David Lawrence, the conservative columnist, called his first polemic in *U.S. News* "What Hath Man Wrought!" With more than mere irony, he declared that "We—the great, idealistic, humane democracies on the so-called civilized side—began bombing men, women and children in Germany. Last week we reached the climax—we destroyed hundreds of thousands of civilians in Japanese cities with the new atomic bomb." However we rejoice in victory, he went on, ". . . we shall not soon purge ourselves of the feeling of guilt which prevails among us. Military necessity will be our consistent cry in answer to criticism, but it will never erase from our minds the simple truth that we, of all civilized nations, though hesitating to use poison gas, did not hesitate to employ the most destructive weapon of all times indiscriminately against men, women and children. What a precedent for the future we have furnished to other nations even less concerned than we with scruples or ideals!" He added: "Surely we cannot be proud of what we have done. If we state our inner thoughts honestly, we are ashamed of it."

Perhaps his most powerful commentary, a week later, entitled "A Curious Chronology," consisted of a list of quotations outlawing or protesting war against civilians, including the Hague conventions of 1899 and

1907, official American condemnations of Japanese bombings of Chinese civilians ("the public opinion in the United States regards such methods as barbarous"), President Roosevelt's statement in 1939 warning of "the ruthless bombing from the air of civilians [which has] sickened the hearts of every civilized man and woman"—and finally, Truman's speech on August 9, in which he reaffirmed that "the first atomic bomb was dropped on Hiroshima, a military base. . . ."

A similar moral outrage emerged in a very different place, the liberal Catholic magazine, *Commonweal*. Victory in the war, it argued, "is defiled. . . . the name Hiroshima, the name Nagasaki are names for American guilt and shame." Japan had already been annihilated, was offering no opposition, and "then, without warning an American plane dropped the atomic bomb on Hiroshima . . . without warning we dropped it into the middle of a city and then without warning we dropped it into the middle of another city. . . . to secure peace, of course. To save lives, of course. After we had brought indescribable death to a few hundred thousand men, women and children, we said that this bomb must remain always in the hands of peace-loving peoples." We had placed ourselves in the realm of evil aggressors, so that when international law returned, "Germans, Japanese and Americans will remember with horror the days of their shame."

Later, at the end of August, *Commonweal* found it "disturbing that there has been so little public protest" in America about our use of the bomb. The editorial expressed doubts about the claim of saving American lives, adding that "even assuming that it did save many lives, this should be balanced against the number of lives in the future which its use by us placed in jeopardy." And if this is done, "we are confronted with an obligation to condemn what we ourselves did, an obligation to admit that our victory has been sadly sullied not only because we used this weapon but because we have tacitly acceded to its use."

In terms of moral judgment, then, we may say that the major impulse was to seek *some* justification for use of the bomb—usually in the form of the claim of lives saved—but that underneath any such justification lay deep layers of uneasiness, and moral scruples taking shape anywhere from mild doubts to enraged, ethical condemnation. *Life* magazine, for example, observed that "Prometheus, the subtle artificer and friend of man, is still an American citizen" but also recognized that there was some truth in the claim by a distinguished Japanese Christian that our cruelty in using the weapon exceeded that of Genghis Khan. "From the very concept of strate-gic bombing," the essay explained, "all the developments—night, pattern, saturation, area, indiscriminate—have led straight to Hiroshima, and Hiro-shima was and was intended to be almost pure *Schrecklichkeit* [terror]." After that damning acknowledgment, the subsequent call to "the individ-ual conscience" as "our sole safeguard against the very real danger of a reversion to barbarism" seemed less than convincing. More persuasive was the added comment that "we are in a strange new land."

CHAPTER 4

SECRECY AND SUPPRESSION

Near the end of 1945, *Fortune* magazine analyzed a recent survey of American attitudes about the bomb. "We know what the atomic bombs did to Hiroshima and Nagasaki," the editors observed. "What did they do to the American mind?" The premise was flawed, however, for Americans did not fully "know what the atomic bombs did" to the two Japanese cities. This was partly due to psychological resistance, but it was also the result of secrecy, distortion, and suppression that would persist, and have profound effects, for decades.

Of the hundreds of early articles about Hiroshima, one had a particularly disturbing impact. Dr. Harold Jacobson, a physicist in New York, wrote a story for the Hearst news service predicting that Hiroshima would remain contaminated by radiation for seventy years. Anyone who chose to inhabit, or even visit, the city would "become infested with secondary radiation" and "die in the same way victims of leukemia die." Rain would "pick up the lethal rays" and carry them to the rivers and the sea, killing all water life. The city would resemble nothing so much as "our conception of the moon" well into the next century. Some of the Hearst papers carried the story on their front page on August 8. The article was extraordinary on two counts: No one else was alerting the world to the bomb's insidious radiation effects, and the author, identified as a Manhattan Project scientist, appeared credible.

While Jacobson exaggerated wildly, his inaccurate projections led to official denials that were themselves misleading. And the intensity of that response suggests that he had struck a nerve. The Pentagon distributed a memo to the press claiming there was "no basis" for Jacobson's speculations and called on Robert Oppenheimer to refute them. Analysis of data from the Trinity site led Oppenheimer to assert that there was "no appreciable radioactivity on the ground at Hiroshima and what little there was decayed very rapidly." The War Department emphasized that Jacobson's connection to the Manhattan Project was marginal.

But the incident did not end there. Military officials visited Jacobson at his office in New York and informed him that he could be prosecuted under the Espionage Act; as a Manhattan Project scientist he had been pledged to secrecy. Jacobson collapsed and was taken home by a physician. There he was questioned for several hours by FBI agents. Afterward, he attempted to clarify his position. He explained that the article was based on his own assumptions, not "confidential" information, and confessed that he was "surprised and pleased" to learn that the Trinity bomb left no trace of radioactivity.

A few days later a Tokyo news service (citing the original Jacobson article) warned that Hiroshima might be uninhabitable for seventy years. The report caused many Hiroshima residents to flee in panic and discouraged medical teams from entering the city. Jacobson's claims might not have been taken seriously in Japan except for one fact: thousands who had survived the atomic bombings without serious injury were now suffering from a mysterious disease. "Many of those who received burns cannot survive the wounds because of the uncanny effects which the atomic bomb produces on the human body," a Japanese wire service reported. "Even those who received minor burns, and looked quite healthy at first, weakened after a few days for some unknown reason."

Two days later, Tokyo radio described a "ghost parade" of the living doomed to die. The death toll among the tens of thousands of survivors was soaring. Relief workers and relatives of victims who came to the city immediately after the bombing had also become ill. This suggested that lingering radioactivity in the air and soil—"residual" or "secondary" radiation—was the cause.

As with the Jacobson story, the American response was swift. Officials identified as "experts on Japanese propaganda" told the press that these "abstract" theories may be nothing more than an attempt to "capitalize on the horror of atomic bombing in an effort to win sympathy from their conquerors." Behind the scenes, however, the military was considering the issue of radiation quite seriously. The Pentagon's censorship office had deleted two-thirds of a *Philadelphia Bulletin* article which revealed that radioactivity from the July 16 test had spread to small towns surrounding the Trinity site.

General Groves, meanwhile, had ordered a deputy to visit Japan shortly after the surrender and secure scientific and technical information about the effects of the bomb. The top priority of the mission: to "make certain that no unusual hazards were present in the bombed cities" that might harm American troops when they arrived in a few weeks. Although Groves asserted that "Japanese casualties from radioactivity were unlikely," he believed it was "most important, for the future of atomic bomb work as well as for historical reasons, that we determine the facts."

Radiation and Poison Gas: "Get the Anti-Propagandists Out"

Already, in ways that would be crucial, the radiation issue was becoming deeply confused, which meant that it could be readily manipulated.

That radiation could kill was nothing new. Precautions had long been taken in administering X rays. Workers who painted radium numbers on wristwatches had been dying for decades. But according to official statements, radioactivity associated with the atomic bomb was unpredictable, even unknowable; no one was inclined to say that it might cause ill effects. "The questions raised are all new," the *New York Times* cautioned.

In fact, the bomb makers recognized the dangers of radiation well before the atomic attack. Otto Frisch, the pioneering fission expert who later worked at Los Alamos, wrote in a 1939 report: "Owing to the spreading of radioactive substances with the wind, the bomb could probably not be used without killing large numbers of civilians. . . ." The threat to the American flight crew who would drop the bomb was considered carefully. Oppenheimer wrote a memo recommending that "for radiological reasons no aircraft should be closer than 2½ miles to the point of detonation" and "aircraft must avoid the cloud of radioactive materials." Radiation "emitted in detonation" would "of course" have an effect on those on the ground—then it would form a cloud which would disperse after a few hours. But if it rained, or if the explosion *caused* rain, much of the radiation, Oppenheimer warned, would come down to earth in the vicinity of the target. (Indeed, this would happen at Hiroshima.)

Before the Trinity test, calculations suggested that fallout posed a threat to those living downwind from the site. A lot would depend on which way the wind blew. General Groves rejected a proposal to evacuate or alert nearby residents in advance, thereby establishing a precedent for secrecy overriding safety that would survive long after the end of the war. Nothing was to interfere with setting off the bomb. When two physicians on Oppenheimer's staff proposed an evacuation, Groves replied, "What are you, Hearst propagandists?"

Soon after the shot went off at Trinity just before dawn on July 16, scientists monitored some alarming evidence. They had predicted that radiation would diminish to harmless levels three miles from the test site. Instead, it was settling to earth in a band thirty miles wide by one hundred miles long. One of the scientists found a paralyzed mule twenty-five miles from ground zero. Still, it could have been worse. The radioactive cloud had drifted over sparsely populated areas. "We were just damn lucky," the head of radiological safety for the test confessed later. "All I could think of was, my God, all that radioactivity up there has got to come down somewhere."

The local press knew nothing about the fallout, but some reporters were curious about the earth tremors and the flash of light. Groves released a statement—written by W. L. Laurence—announcing that an ammunition dump had exploded. The press did not question it. Secrecy was so important to Groves that when the shock wave from the Trinity blast reached his trench his first words were: "We must keep this whole thing quiet."

In the following weeks, ranchers discovered that dozens of cattle had odd burns and were losing their fur. Lansing Lamont, in his book on the Trinity test, observed that the "specter of endless lawsuits haunted the military." Oppenheimer ordered health reports from the test held in strictest secrecy. Not a word about fallout, or any of its effects, would appear in W. L. Laurence's widely quoted August 6 press release on the Trinity test. Fallout was absent in every account of the aftermath of the Hiroshima bomb. Of all the secret aspects of the bomb considered too sensitive for public consumption, fallout was perhaps the most sensitive of all.

Even as the scientists celebrated their success at Alamogordo the first radioactive cloud was drifting eastward over America, depositing fallout along its path. When Americans found out about this, three months later, the word came not from the government but from the president of the Eastman Kodak Company in Rochester, New York, who wondered why some of his film was fogging and suspected radioactivity as the cause.

One reason the atomic bombs were exploded high over Hiroshima and Nagasaki rather than close to the ground—as at Trinity—was to disperse the gamma rays and minimize the effects of radiation. The major reason for detonating the bomb at 1,800 feet, however, was to maximize the area that would be devastated by the blast and burn effects. Strategists, in other words, were not concerned so much with how many would be killed by the bomb but with how they would die.*

With blast and burn, death would come quickly and in a manner associated with conventional bombing. But radiation symbolized the special horror of the new weapon and introduced an element of moral ambiguity. It seemed comparable to the effects of poison gas, which warring nations had stockpiled but generally refused to use. Like poison gas, radiation caused invisible contamination. It left behind in the body some unfathomable substance that might strike you down, months or even years later. Unease about radiation probably contributed to underestimating its effects—and undoubtedly to the official denial of those effects when they actually occurred.

Planners recognized that the atomic bomb was vulnerable on this

---

* According to one of Groves's top aides, the U.S. was more concerned about the effects of radiation on Americans than on Japanese. "We wanted little or no residual radiation," he wrote, "because we hoped that our troops would soon occupy the city and we did not want to endanger them."

score. One of the few who opposed using the bomb for this reason, Truman's chief of staff, Admiral William D. Leahy, placed the bomb in "the same category" as poison gas. " 'Bomb' is the wrong word to use for this new weapon," Leahy would later observe. "It is not a bomb. It is not an explosive. It is a poisonous thing that kills people by its deadly radioactive reaction. . . ."

Reports of death by radiation in Japan complicated the Hiroshima story. As they celebrated the Japanese surrender, most Americans seemed to accept as necessary the instantaneous killing of tens of thousands of the enemy. But now the end-of-the-war euphoria was starting to wear off, just as reports of thousands of additional deaths from a cruel and lingering illness surfaced.

On August 24, General Leslie Groves received a telex from Los Alamos indicating that the project staff was "much concerned about Japanese broadcasts claiming murderous delayed radioactive effects at Hiroshima." Groves replied that he considered the reports a "hoax or propaganda." The top radiation specialist at Los Alamos also used the word *hoax* in reassuring the staff that the Japanese accounts "did not correspond to any experience known here."

Fearing that reporters would soon be seeking his official response to the Japanese claims, Groves telephoned Lieutenant Colonel Charles Rea, a doctor at Oak Ridge Hospital, and began reading excerpts from the Tokyo broadcasts, as reported by the Associated Press. Transcripts of this remarkable conversation reveal both men bluntly expressing their views at the outset. Rea called the death by radiation theory "kind of crazy," and Groves responded with a bit of black humor: "Of course, it's crazy—a doctor like me can tell that."

But Groves knew it wasn't "crazy." Perhaps that is why he seemed agitated as he read passages from the Japanese reports and solicited Rea's expert opinion. Groves's pride in the bomb's destructive power vied with his uneasiness about what it did to human beings. He did not want to believe what he could not quite dismiss. Groves even wondered if there was "any difference between Japanese blood and others." Both men ultimately seized upon the idea that everything was attributable to burns. The shared psychological maneuver was one of not only denying the truth of what the Japanese were reporting but also suppressing their own partial belief that the claimed radiation effects were real.

"I think it's good propaganda," Rea observed. "The thing is, these people got good and burned—good thermal burns."

Groves replied, "Of course, we are getting a good dose of propaganda." But Rea, deep down, knew there was more to it than that, for he responded: "Of course those Jap scientists over there aren't so dumb either. . . . They evidently know what the possibility is." Yet he reassured Groves that the Japanese claims were false, because "after all, it's a very poorly controlled experiment." In a second conversation with Groves later that day, Rea admitted, "We do know what some of these effects are" but concluded: "I think you had better get the antipropagandists out."

Five days later, Groves visited Oak Ridge, where he called the Japanese accounts of radiation disease pure propaganda. "The atomic bomb is not an inhuman weapon," he told reporters.

Groves and others involved in the bomb project would later argue that the reports from Japan had caught them by surprise, for they had expected that virtually everyone exposed to lethal doses of radiation would die from other causes first. (As one physicist explained, "Any person with radiation damage would have been killed with a brick first.") But Groves's top aide, Kenneth D. Nichols, would admit in his memoirs in 1987 that "we knew that there would be many deaths and injuries caused by the radiation as well as by heat and blast."

At Ground Zero: Censorship and Keeping a Secret

Until late August, little was known for certain about conditions on the ground in Hiroshima and Nagasaki, beyond hazy reconnaissance photographs and unconfirmed (and highly suspect) reports from the enemy about the actual effects of the bomb. But with General MacArthur's arrival at Yokohama on August 28, it was only a matter of time before American reporters entered Hiroshima and Nagasaki.

Whether they would be allowed to disclose freely what they discovered was another matter. President Truman had declared an end to wartime censorship in the United States on August 15, but articles and photographs documenting the "employment" of the atomic bomb remained under strict review. General MacArthur, in addition, had instituted his own censorship apparatus and notified reporters arriving in Japan that Hiroshima and Nagasaki were off limits. They could witness the Japanese surrender on board the *Missouri* in Tokyo Bay on September 2, then be escorted, if they wished, on a tour of prisoner-of-war camps in northern Japan.

Of several hundred Western reporters in Japan in early September only two chose to defy restrictions and travel on their own to the atomic cities.

One was the Australian war correspondent Wilfred Burchett. He set out from Tokyo for Hiroshima by train on the morning of September 2. Burchett, who had written dispatches glorifying the firebombing of Japanese cities, was simply looking for a scoop. (Only later did he become known for his pro-Soviet views.) The following morning he encountered in Hiroshima what he later described as a "death-stricken alien planet." He noticed a dank, sulfurous smell; people hurried past, white masks covering their noses and mouths.

Burchett was taken directly to one of the few hospitals left standing (although badly damaged) in the city. Its director, Michihiko Hachiya, later known in America as author of *Hiroshima Diary*, felt certain that what he called "radiation sickness" was real. Shortly after the bombing he had observed that one in five patients developed purple skin hemorrhages; some were also losing their hair. Many had white-cell counts about one-tenth the normal number. "Some toxic substance must be responsible," Dr. Hachiya wrote in his diary. About three weeks later, these patients began to die, and the death rate rose as each day passed.

In the half-standing hospital, Burchett found patients strewn about on the floor, suffering from the final stages of radiation disease, evidenced by fever, nausea, gangrene, and the halos of hair that surrounded their heads on the mats where they lay. The reporter pulled out his typewriter and, sitting on a chunk of rubble near the hypocenter, composed his historic article, which began:

In Hiroshima, 30 days after the first atomic bomb destroyed the city and shook the world, people are still dying, mysteriously and horribly—people who were uninjured in the cataclysm—from an unknown something which I can only describe as the atomic

plague. . . . I write these facts as dispassionately as I can in the
hope that they will act as a warning to the world. . . .

Just as Burchett was finishing his story, a group of journalists on an Air
Force charter landed just outside Hiroshima. Included in this group were
Bill Lawrence of *The New York Times,* Homer Bigart of the New York
Herald-Tribune, reporters for AP and the Hearst news service, photographers for the U.S. Strategic Bombing Survey, and an official censor. According to Burchett's later account, the reporters were not happy to
discover they had been scooped. He told one of the visitors, "The real
story is in the hospitals." After just a few hours they were ready to leave
and Burchett asked one of the officials to carry a copy of his article to
Tokyo. The request was denied.

That evening, Burchett managed to transmit his story to a colleague in
Tokyo, who eased it through the censorship office mainly intact, perhaps
because it was written for a British publication. Two days later, on September 5, it ran on the front page of the *London Daily Express* under the
headline "THE ATOMIC PLAGUE." Burchett credited his editor with displaying
extraordinary courage in publishing the article. Great Britain, after all, had
helped build the bomb.

On the same day Burchett's article appeared in England, Bill Lawrence's account of his visit to Hiroshima arrived on the front page of the
New York Times. Lawrence was a twenty-nine-year-old war correspondent
and near-namesake of Manhattan Project publicist and fellow *Times*man
William L. Laurence. Years later, historians would continually confuse the
two journalists, ascribing one man's work to the other. (Bill Lawrence
would later become a familiar figure on American television as White
House correspondent for ABC News during the 1960s.)

His story from Hiroshima was datelined September 3 but labeled "Delayed," suggesting that it had been held up in the censorship office for a
day. The tone of the Lawrence article was reserved, compared to
Burchett's cautionary account. In certain respects, however, the *Times*
story duplicated Burchett's piece, including a depiction of the enormity of
the destruction and the report of at least one hundred new deaths a day
from a mysterious ailment. Clearly, Lawrence was left shaken by his tour of
the ruins. Yet his honest and occasionally moving report built to a tri-
umphalist conclusion:

Here is the final proof of what the mechanical and scientific genius of America has been able to accomplish in war through the invention of the airplane, especially the B-29 Superfortress, and the atomic bomb. It should be the last evidence needed to convince any doubter of the need to retain and perfect our air offense and defense lest the fate of Hiroshima be repeated in Indianapolis or Washington or Detroit or New York.

Other accounts added little to Lawrence's story. This could be expected, since the correspondents arrived together, interviewed many of the same people, and left together after only a few hours. Each report testified to the devastation, and each introduced one or two haunting new images.

What appears odd, however, is that not a single article described conditions in hospitals or indicated that the reporters had seen any of the gravely injured patients. Yet in his memoirs (published in 1972), Bill Lawrence would reveal that on that day, "We talked with dying Japanese in the hospitals." Were the reporters disinclined to cover this angle—or prevented from doing so? It is hard to imagine that they did not want to write about it. The condition of these patients had been the subject of worldwide speculation for the past two weeks. Reporters were brought face-to-face with the evidence—yet nothing appeared in print.*

Whatever else can be said about these articles, they would remain the only accounts by American reporters from Hiroshima for many months. According to Lawrence's memoir, "General MacArthur's men were hopping mad" about the junket to Hiroshima. To prevent a re-occurrence, they cut off supplies of gasoline to planes that might make another such mission possible. But, as we will see, MacArthur did not stop there.

The *Daily Press* had allowed newspapers around the world to reprint Wilfred Burchett's article, which made it an international sensation. Bill Lawrence's story in the *New York Times* was less candid but more credible. Clearly, American officials had a public-relations problem on their hands. The lid on Hiroshima was starting to come off.

On September 5, the day the Burchett and Lawrence articles appeared, General MacArthur ordered all American reporters out of Tokyo. Isolated

---

* *Gay Talese would later refer to Bill Lawrence as "an aggressive reporter who could keep a secret."*

and closely watched in nearby Yokohama, they would not be able to rush off on their own for Hiroshima and Nagasaki. Just as the order came down, however, a second reporter was making his way independently to one of the atomic cities.

After years of covering the Pacific war, George Weller of the *Chicago Daily News* had no use for what he later called "General MacArthur's censors, his public relations officers and his military police." Censorship, he felt, was prolonged "long after the slightest pretext for it existed," and he was appalled by "the conformists" of his own profession who went along with the guided tours of prison camps, "away from where the war had been decided a month before." So, on September 5, Weller jumped at a chance to cover the one officially approved story to the south—a visit to a kamikaze base in Kyushu. Weller noted on a map that it was connected by railroad to Nagasaki.

The next day Weller shook off his Army escort at the kamikaze base, and slipped into Nagasaki. In many ways, his experience duplicated that of Wilfred Burchett in Hiroshima, except that he had the city to himself for three days, not one, before the junketing reporters arrived. But Weller made one mistake that Burchett avoided: He sent his lengthy report directly to MacArthur's headquarters in Tokyo for clearance. This would be the last he ever saw of it. It would never appear in print in any form, despite the fact that Weller felt rather dispassionate about (and indeed, endorsed) the atomic bombings. Weller had bluntly described the physical and medical effects of the Nagasaki bomb but "eschewed all horror angles," he later recalled. By sending his story directly to the censorship office he felt he was giving the MacArthur command "the least possible excuse to hold up my research."

Weller would later summarize his experience in two words. Referring to MacArthur's censors, he wrote: "They won."

"Public-Relations Work"

The Pentagon had not yet issued an estimate of Japanese casualties in Hiroshima and Nagasaki. An Air Force public-relations officer urged General Curtis LeMay to suppress any figures on civilians killed, as it would, he feared, "make us look like barbarians. . . ." LeMay should release the figures "at the right time," he advised, and that time would be after the U.S. collected "atrocity stories about what Japs did to our B-29 crews when they were shot down."

On September 5, the same day that the first articles from Hiroshima appeared, Secretary of State James Byrnes released a report of more than two hundred atrocities committed by the Japanese during the war. Included were stories of American airmen and soldiers decapitated, buried alive, even eaten by the enemy. Intended or not, the connection to the horror stories coming out of Hiroshima was clear enough, as *Time* magazine observed:

> In a week when the first U.S. newsmen entered Hiroshima and Nagasaki and made plain to U.S. readers the appalling devastation of those cities, the State Department issued a formal report on atrocities committed by the Japanese. The timing was not missed by many readers.

A confluence of events on September 9 suggests that American officials, right up to the White House, had indeed initiated a public-relations campaign to counter the first articles from Hiroshima.

The War Department, after weeks of delay, finally allowed the *New York Times* to publish W. L. Laurence's exultant first-person account of the Nagasaki bombing mission. The same day, Laurence happened to be touring the Trinity test site with Leslie Groves and Robert Oppenheimer. The top-secret area finally had been opened to journalists—in response to a suggestion from the White House two weeks earlier. President Truman's secretary, Charles G. Ross, had sent an extraordinary memo to the War Department urging the military to recruit a group of reporters to explore the test site. "This might be a good thing to do in view of continuing propaganda from Japan," Ross wrote. A Pentagon official replied that this was "perfectly agreeable" to the War Department and suggested that Ross get in contact with General Groves.

Now Groves was personally escorting some of the newsmen near ground zero. His driver, a twenty-nine-year-old soldier named Patrick Stout, spent several minutes in the crater of the blast and was photographed, smiling.

Laurence's account of this visit (delayed three days due to a censorship review) disclosed quite frankly why he and thirty other journalists had been invited: to "give lie to" Japanese propaganda "that radiations were responsible for deaths even after" the Hiroshima attack. General Groves had expressly asked the reporters to assist him in this effort, and they did not disappoint him. Geiger counters showed that surface radiation, after nearly two months, had "dwindled to a minute quantity, safe for continuous human habitation," Laurence asserted. He did introduce one bit of contrary information: the reporters had been advised to wear canvas overshoes to protect against radiation burns.

But Laurence was keeping a lot to himself. He was the only reporter who knew about the fallout scare surrounding the Trinity shot: the paralyzed mule, scientists in jeeps chasing a radioactive cloud, Geiger counters clicking off the scale. Here was the nation's leading science reporter, severely compromised, not only unable but disinclined to reveal all he knew about the potential hazards of the most important scientific discovery of his time.

The press tour had "an oddly reassuring effect," the *New York Times* observed in an editorial. The bomb was "bad enough" but not "as bad as it was painted." *Life* magazine concluded, on the basis of this visit, that only "a few" Japanese could have died from immediate exposure to radiation, and "none died from radioactivity afterward." This led *Life* to declare that "Japanese in Hiroshima and Nagasaki had died within the grotesque legality of wartime killing." The poison gas connotations had been quieted.*

Across the Pacific, on September 9, Bill Lawrence was patrolling the ruins of Nagasaki. When his report appeared the following morning it was clear that in the five days since his vivid evocation of Hiroshima he had moved much closer to the official version of events. Lawrence declared that he was now convinced that "horrible as the bomb undoubtedly is, the Japanese are exaggerating its effects in an effort to win sympathy for themselves in an attempt to make the American people forget the long record of cold-blooded Japanese bestiality."

---

* Later, a scientist informed the soldier who stood in the crater, Patrick Stout, that he had been exposed to dangerous levels of radioactivity. Twenty-two years later Stout became ill and was diagnosed with leukemia. The military, apparently acknowledging radiation as the cause, granted him "service-connected" disability compensation. Stout died in 1969.

And so on a single day two *New York Times* reporters were escorted by the military to sites thousands of miles apart over which atomic devices had exploded—and each provided reassuring testimony about the human effects of those weapons. On this same noteworthy day, September 9, investigators would offer the first expert American opinion from the third atomic landmark: Hiroshima.

General Thomas F. Farrell, sent by General Leslie Groves, arrived in Hiroshima on September 8, with chief radiologist Stafford Warren, two physicists from Los Alamos (Philip Morrison and Robert Serber), and eight other scientists. They had been ordered to return to Tokyo the following day with preliminary findings. Groves apparently was in a rush to control the potential damage caused by the first articles from Hiroshima. How objectively did Farrell approach his inquiry? A member of the research team later revealed that Farrell had instructed him that "our mission was to prove that there was no radioactivity from the bomb."

Investigators visited a shed erected amid the rubble for a briefing by Japan's leading radiation expert, Masao Tsuzuki. A few days earlier, when Philip Morrison met Tsuzuki in Tokyo, the professor had given him a copy of a 1926 paper describing his famous radiation experiments on rabbits. "Ah, but the *Americans*—they are wonderful," Tsuzuki said, slapping Morrison's thigh. "It has remained for them to conduct the *human experiment!*"

Now, in Hiroshima, Tsuzuki appeared deeply worried about the rising toll of bomb victims. He suggested that perhaps the bomb had released some form of "poison gas" in addition to radiation, something that could cause fatal injuries if inhaled. Farrell, alarmed, asked one of the scientists to assure Tsuzuki that this was not possible. Then he ordered the investigators to grab their Geiger counters and get some readings. Tsuzuki, meanwhile, led members of the study team on a tour of hospitals. They were troubled by his excitable, accusatory behavior. Pointing at one woman he announced: "Gamma rays. Nothing to be done about it. She'll be dead this evening or tomorrow. That's what an atomic bomb does." Visiting a laboratory, he picked up a brain removed from one of the victims and said, "Yesterday it was rabbits, today it's Japanese."

That night, Farrell returned to Tokyo and filed a report with General Groves, who immediately announced to the press that if any Japanese had died from exposure to radiation "the number was very small" and could be partially attributed to poor Japanese medical care. Vegetation was growing in Hiroshima, and radiation levels were so low "you could live there forever."

A few months later Daniel Lang of the *New Yorker* would call the Farrell mission "an unusual mixture of tourism, scientific exploration and public-relations work." Radiation effects threatened "the humaneness of American methods of warfare," and so the U.S. Army, "sensitive to such criticism, felt called upon to prove as soon as possible that the new bombs were entitled to the same degree of respect accorded by the civilized world to rockets, mines, incendiaries, and sixteen-inch shells." As Morrison explained to Lang: "A fine moral point was involved."

Three days after completing his preliminary survey, General Farrell held a press conference at the Imperial Hotel in Tokyo, which brought the early radiation story to a climax. Farrell, who privately described himself as Leslie Groves's "handyman" and "alter ego," questioned the accuracy of Japanese reports of 70,000 to 100,000 killed in Hiroshima and Nagasaki and categorically denied that the bomb produced a lingering form of radiation. He emphasized that "no poison gases were released." This was technically accurate, but metaphorically false. Farrell admitted that some were now dying due to exposure to gamma rays on August 6 (just as the Japanese had been reporting from the start), but this was virtually overlooked in press coverage that focused on his disavowal of "poison gas." Profound fear had led to exaggerations, and American spokesmen seized upon them to minimize actual effects.

Yet the American experts had only examined a small part of Hiroshima and hadn't even reached Nagasaki (where a different kind of atomic device, made with plutonium not uranium, had exploded with even greater force). They had not yet traced the path of fallout downwind or studied the reported high levels of radiation in local reservoirs and in areas where "black rain" fell. Privately, Manhattan Project officials knew that the question of residual radiation was far from settled. Leslie Groves, in fact, informed the Joint Chiefs that "any conclusions" on that matter "should be postponed until the data is in."

An official line had now been set: recognize the delayed effects of radiation but describe the number of Japanese victims as "some" or "a few." Here it is impossible to distinguish willful deceit from a wishful rush to judgment. By November, chief radiologist Stafford Warren was telling Congress that 7 to 8 percent of all deaths in Hiroshima had been caused by radiation. Several months later the U.S. Strategic Bomb Survey would put this figure at "no less than" 15 to 20 percent—that is, at least 20,000 fatalities—with an equal number suffering severe illness.

The Farrell press conference completed a frenzied week of public relations, managed by the War Department in Washington and occupation head-quarters in Tokyo. Farrell had charged that the Japanese "told the truth but not the whole truth" about radiation effects. That was accurate, but of course this was the American policy as well.

Near the end of the Farrell press conference, a dramatic confrontation occurred. Wilfred Burchett had just returned to Tokyo from Hiroshima. Alerted by a colleague, he arrived at the press briefing ill and unwashed. Challenging Farrell's claim that no danger of radiation remained, Burchett related how a Japanese guide had taken him to a stream on the outskirts of the city. Fish would swim only so far, then turn belly-up and die. "I'm afraid you've fallen victim to Japanese propaganda," Farrell responded. The briefing broke up, and Burchett was taken to a hospital, where it was discovered that his white blood cell count was below normal.

With this, press coverage of the bomb's effects in Japan virtually ceased for several months. It may be only coincidence, but it was precisely at this moment that President Truman, at the suggestion of General Groves, sent an unusual request, "in confidence," to American editors and broadcasters. Truman, in the interest of "the highest national security," asked the media not to publish information on a wide range of matters related to the bomb, including its "operational use," "without first consulting with the War Department."

When he emerged from the hospital a few days later, Wilfred Burchett discovered that his camera containing film shot in Hiroshima was missing, and that General MacArthur had ordered him expelled from Japan. By this point, MacArthur's office in Tokyo was playing a central role in control-ling the news from Hiroshima.

One story in particular had the potential to create a public-relations nightmare. When the American occupying force arrived in Hiroshima it learned that several, and perhaps a dozen or more, American prisoners had been killed by the American bomb. A Japanese military policeman was twice called to MacArthur's headquarters to confirm the report, and the remains of some of the American airmen were found. The shocking discovery was kept hidden from the press, however. Families of the victims were told that the men had died in Japan, but Hiroshima was not mentioned.*

MacArthur was just as concerned about the flow of information within Japan. He ordered Japanese newspapers to submit articles and photographs to a censorship board prior to publication. On September 19, a sweeping press code was issued. It included numerous principles that would prohibit virtually any reports from Hiroshima. Further, Japanese newspapers were forbidden to reveal that they were being subjected to censorship. Readers, therefore, might believe they were getting the complete story of the atomic bombings when they were not.

Book censorship was established shortly thereafter. Japanese scientists studying the effects of the atomic bomb also had to submit their papers to the censorship board for review, where they would be held indefinitely. This discouraged vital research. Dr. Tsuzuki, the radiation authority, would come into conflict with American officials over this edict, calling it "unforgivable" to restrict scientific investigation and publication while people were dying from a mysterious new disease.

Censorship would not end until October 1949, and scientific papers could not be freely published for two years after that. During this period the atomic bomb was virtually a forbidden subject in Japan. Between 1945 and 1948 only four books and one collection of poetry about the bomb were published in Japan. A renowned account of the bombings, *The Bells of Nagasaki*, by Takashi Nagai, was published in 1949 (after a two-year delay) only after he added a section on Japanese atrocities in Manila. Even books by Americans ran afoul of Occupation guidelines. Publication of John Hersey's *Hiroshima* in Japan was held up for more than two years, and permitted only after the Authors League of America protested. Commenting on this controversy, General MacArthur declared that those who claimed that censorship existed in Japan were engaged in "a maliciously

---

* The truth, in the form of declassified War Department documents, did not emerge for more than thirty years. Even then, the Pentagon was so sensitive on this issue that for some time it continued to deny that American POWs had been killed in Hiroshima.

false propaganda campaign." Monica Braw, in her book on the Occupation, recently observed:

> Censorship not only deleted certain facts, it hindered atomic bomb survivors from speaking out about their experiences, experiences that they alone had and that would have helped the rest of mankind understand what the world had come to. They could not or would not speak, out of deference to the Americans, out of fear, or because they did not want trouble. Through censorship, Japan was closed to the world . . . One is hard put not to agree with the Japanese historian Seiji Imahori, who said that by silencing the voice of the atomic bomb survivors "an important possibility to decisively influence the world situation was lost."

Hiding Half the Picture

Shortly after the Occupation began, a Japanese research council dispatched a film unit to Hiroshima and Nagasaki to record the physical and medical effects of the bomb. It was under the direction of Akira Iwasaki, whose antimilitarist views had landed him in Japanese prison during the war. On October 17, 1945, when the film crew was halfway through its project, one of its cameramen was arrested by American military police in Nagasaki. They instructed Iwasaki to stop all shooting and seized his footage. Two days later, Occupation officials banned all filming in Hiroshima and Nagasaki and ordered anyone who had shot any footage to submit it to American headquarters.

The one exception to this order: an American film project under the direction of Lieutenant Daniel McGovern of the U.S. Strategic Bombing Survey. McGovern had advised his superiors that the initial footage shot by the Japanese was "irreplaceable" and of "inestimable value" to those in charge of America's atomic program, because "the conditions under which it was taken will not be duplicated until another atomic bomb is released under combat conditions." He hired Iwasaki and his film crew to shoot thousands of additional feet of 35mm black-and-white footage. Then the Japanese helped edit and caption the material for a nearly three-hour documentary entitled *The Effects of the Atomic Bombs Against Hiro-shima and Nagasaki.*

The finished film was shipped to the U.S. on May 5, 1946, with much fanfare in the American press. Then it disappeared: declared Top Secret and locked in a vault. The film was never shown to the American public, and was not returned to the Japanese until the late 1960s.

It is not hard to imagine why American officials were uncomfortable with the footage shot by Iwasaki. The Japanese newsreel team had gone into hospitals to document the burn and radiation effects. They not only photographed a burned-out trolley car, but the rows of bodies and bones that surrounded it. Even the footage of strictly physical phenomena featured troublesome imagery: radioactive sand clogging wells used for drinking water; dead stalks of rice seven miles from the hypocenter; the silhouette of a painter on a ladder, his brush outstretched, permanently etched onto the surface of a concrete wall by the flash of the bomb.

Yet this film would not be seen by anyone (outside the military) for decades. During this period few Americans were exposed to visual evidence of what the bomb did to human beings. Indeed, virtually no one in the United States or Japan even knew of the existence of the landmark footage. Finally, the Japanese government learned of the film and asked the U.S. to return it. A headline in the *New York Times* read: " '45 Japanese Film of Hiroshima Suppressed by U.S. for 22 Years." The Pentagon sent a copy of the footage to Japan in 1968.

When Eric Barnouw, the noted authority on documentary film, heard about this he asked the Pentagon if he could view the footage. Barnouw was shaken by what he saw. "It was a revelation," he later observed, "showing how little we understood about the effects of these weapons. . . . Why, and by what right, was the footage declared secret? It contained no military information, the supposed basis for such a classification." After a year of editing, Barnouw produced a somber, sixteen-minute film, entitled *Hiroshima/Nagasaki: August 1945,* with eloquent, understated narration. A screening in New York drew wide press coverage, and orders for the film started pouring in from libraries, colleges, and churches.

The Iwasaki film wasn't the only historic footage suppressed. Just as the Japanese filmmakers were completing their work in early 1946, an American crew was shooting color film in Hiroshima and Nagasaki, also under the supervision of Lieutenant Daniel McGovern. They captured images of human misery even more shocking than the Japanese footage; only color film could do justice to the grotesque nature of the flash burns. This was the only color footage shot in Hiroshima and Nagasaki, yet it too would be stamped Top Secret by the U.S. military and remain hidden for more than three decades, despite (as we will see in Part III) the strenuous efforts of one of the filmmakers to win its release.

Daniel McGovern, who personally delivered all of this footage to the Pentagon in June 1946, would later express annoyance that both the Japanese and American films had been kept hidden for so long. When asked in 1983 (by one of the authors of this book) why this had happened, McGovern explained: "The AEC, the Pentagon and Manhattan Project people wanted it buried. I was told by these people 'hell no and damn no'—they did not want it shown. They were fearful because of the horror it contained. I was told that under no circumstances would it be released. They didn't want that material shown, because it showed effects on men, women and children." In McGovern's view, "they didn't want that material out because they were sorry for their sins—and because they were working on new nuclear weapons."

From the very start, the visual record of the atomic bombing would be limited to structural effects, while the human dimension would be evaded or ignored. For several weeks after Hiroshima—before MacArthur landed —the only available image was the mushroom cloud. It was frightening but detached from anything human on the ground. At the end of August, when American planes started flying low over Hiroshima and Nagasaki, the first photographs of the ruins appeared, and they were certainly stark: a few concrete buildings and charred trees punctuating a flat, eerily empty landscape.

Still, these photos hardly did justice to the catastrophe. None of them showed the entire area of devastation, just one quadrant. Newspapers and magazines were carrying similar shots of the incinerated section of Tokyo. There was no way of knowing that much of Tokyo remained standing while nearly all of Hiroshima had been destroyed. When the *New York Herald-Tribune* published pictures of Hiroshima and Tokyo adjacent to each other it was hard to tell them apart, except that the rubble in Hiroshima seemed more pulverized.

A few days later, magazines and newspapers published the first photographs taken on the ground. The only people who appeared in them were walking on desolate roads that cut through the rubble—testimony to the living, not the dead. *Life* presented photos of factory ruins, twisted trees, and telephone poles, and a skeleton of a city bus blown "clear across" the city by a "freak of the atomic blast." Henry Luce once described the "power of a picture" in an increasingly technical and complicated world as the ability "to capture an event, distill an emotion, amaze, inspire, instruct, and even repulse." Yet *Life*'s photographs from Hiroshima did not succeed completely in any of those ways. Although the images were human scale, they lacked evidence of human destruction. Hiroshima was simply, as *Life* put it, a "still stinking junk-pile." There were no injured Japanese in these photographs, no doctors and nurses treating the ill and wounded, no funeral pyres, no one mourning. Even the physical ruins featured in the photographs were less than fully representative (no schools, hospitals, or homes were included).

It wasn't that *Life* was squeamish. In August it had published a gruesome series of photos of a Japanese soldier in Borneo set on fire by a flamethrower. But in that instance only one person died, it was a combatant not a civilian, and the wielder of the weapon was Australian not American.

Apparently, even President Truman was shielded from witnessing the full human effects of the bomb. Hap Arnold, commanding general of the Army Air Forces, sent to the president an album of photographs from the atomic cities. Truman thanked him personally for doing this. Most of the pictures, however, were aerial shots. Just four were taken at ground level, and in these pictures none of the Japanese, walking amid the rubble, appeared badly injured.

Indeed, it would be years until Americans saw—or were allowed to see —any Hiroshima images that put a human face on the consequences of the bombing. *(Life* would later admit that for years this meant that "the world . . . knew only the physical facts of atomic destruction.") That this was not accidental can be observed in the experience of Yoshito Matsushige, a photographer for a Hiroshima newspaper. He took the only pictures in the city on the day of the bomb. That night, with his house in ruins and Hiroshima smoldering all around him, he washed his film in an irradiated creek and hung it out to dry on the burned branch of a tree.

Two of his photographs, taken just hours after the blast, reveal a shattered group of survivors on a bridge leading to the center of the city. A policeman pours cooking oil on the arms of several teenagers to treat their burns. Over the bridge, in the distance, a menacing tornado of smoke and fire seems to be advancing. There are no corpses in these photographs, yet they capture the horror of the atomic bomb far better than images of blackened trees or twisted girders. That is because the people in Matsushige's photos are not only feeling the effects of the blast—they are still experiencing the bomb itself. The weapon has not yet finished with them or their city. The fear and confusion etched on their faces says more about the human response to the monstrous unknown than any editorial or essay. The viewer is on that bridge to Hiroshima, three hours after the bomb fell, staring into the terror. The photos are so affecting because all of us in a sense have been standing on that same road ever since.

When the American occupiers arrived in Hiroshima they confiscated Matsushige's photographs—and pictures taken by others in the city since August 6. But Matsushige managed to keep some of the negatives, made a few pirate prints, and gave them to American correspondents returning to the States, assuming their editors would be only too happy to publish them. Yet despite the undeniable power and uniqueness of the photos, they would not appear in America until September 1952. *Life* would publish them that year under the headline "WHEN ATOM BOMB STRUCK—UNCENSORED." These and other "stark" pictures taken by Japanese photographers "had been suppressed by jittery U.S. military censors through seven years of the Occupation," *Life* revealed.

Hiroshima Hits Home

The Japanese were not the only ones suffering from health defects caused by the atomic bomb, and the suppression of evidence about those effects.

On September 21, 1945, the *New York Times* published a brief Associated Press article headlined: "Atomic Bomb Worker Died 'From Burns.' " Officials at Los Alamos had revealed that six days earlier a "worker" had died "from burns in an industrial accident." His name was Harry Daghlian, age twenty-four, identified only as an instructor at Purdue University who had joined the bomb project in November 1943. There was no information about the nature of the "industrial accident," when it had occurred, or why the fatality was being reported five days later.

This wire service report marked the only mention of the incident in the American media. Only years later would details of the accident emerge. Harry Daghlian, in fact, was no mere industrial "worker" but a physicist intimately involved with the bomb project, who had helped assemble the core of the Trinity bomb. Daghlian worked at what was known as the Omega Site, where technicians experimented with pushing hemispheres of plutonium together, then waited for a chain reaction to begin. The trick, of course, was not to let the chain reaction get out of hand. That was why this row of buildings was distant from the main facility at the laboratory.

On the evening of August 21, Harry Daghlian was conducting an experiment at the Omega Site when he dropped a thirteen-pound tungsten brick on top of a small structure enclosing a sphere of plutonium that had already gone critical. In a panic, he attempted to bring the reaction under control by tipping over the table, but it refused to move. Finally, with his bare hands, he tore away the bricks surrounding the plutonium, allowing the neutrons to escape, and the reaction stopped.

Within hours, Daghlian felt sick and went to the hospital. Over the following days, he exhibited many of the symptoms of radiation disease being reported in Japan (and dismissed as propaganda by General Groves and others). Los Alamos now had a victim of its own. Anyone who doubted the stories of lingering death by radiation in Hiroshima and Nagasaki could have watched it transpire right at Los Alamos.

The Daghlian accident was perceived by some of the scientists as retribution, "a means by which those who had created this new horror were at last confronted with the fruits of their labors," a writer later observed. Daghlian would hang on for twenty-four days. Within five hours of his death the government would present his mother a life insurance check for $10,000, perhaps hoping to forestall legal action. Suppression of the cause of death was so complete that nine months later, when Daghlian's former boss, Louis Slotin, died after a similar accident, *Time* magazine referred to *Slotin* as "the first peacetime victim of nuclear fission."

On May 21, 1946, Slotin was experimenting at the Omega site with one of the plutonium cores soon to be shipped to the Pacific for the Bikini tests when the accident occurred. (A screwdriver he was using slipped.) Slotin and seven others were immediately hospitalized. Scientists flew in from all over the country to monitor the condition of each of the men. Photographers snapped pictures. Like the victims in Hiroshima and Nagasaki the eight Americans would be studied, but the Los Alamos victims were unique in that their radiation exposure was "pure," without the complicating effects of an explosive burst.

Phil Morrison stayed at Slotin's bedside. Calculations showed that Slotin had received about the same radiation dose as those standing a mile from the hypocenter in Hiroshima. Three days after the accident, the Army prepared a press release, similar to the one that distorted the Daghlian incident. Morrison threatened to expose the real cause of the accident (and its effects) "as a symbol of responsibility," he later observed. There was "no military reason" to suppress the accident, but officials wanted to make "more bombs" and "were concerned about people's fear of radiation," Morrison told us.

The Army hastily rewrote the release, revealing that Slotin had been working with fissionable materials, and was "possibly" exposed to radiation at dangerous levels. To render the incident heroic, the release reported that he had prevented even greater injury to fellow scientists by halting the chain reaction with his bare hands, obscuring the fact that Slotin had performed the fatal experiment in a reckless fashion. Eight days after the accident, many of Slotin's colleagues attended a cocktail party for visiting dignitaries at Los Alamos, but no mention of the accident was permitted. The following day Slotin died. Leslie Groves credited Slotin with saving lives, and *Time* hailed him as the "Hero of Los Alamos." The accident was publicly forgotten, but not by the scientists who had witnessed its human effects firsthand.

In these ways an official policy of obscuring the truth about radiation was established. For decades this form of secrecy would have tragic implications for more than half a million workers in the nuclear weapons industry, for residents of communities adjoining those installations, for the more than 250,000 soldiers subjected to fallout from nuclear tests or exposed to radiation in postwar Hiroshima and Nagasaki, and for the thousands of thousands of people who lived downwind from the Nevada test site.

This pattern was also grimly evident in confirmation from the Department of Energy, beginning in 1993, of radiation experiments conducted on thousands of Americans, many without their consent. A recently declassified AEC memo, sent to doctors at Oak Ridge and dated April 17, 1947, contains a haunting directive: "It is desired that no document be released which refers to experiments with humans and might have adverse effect on public opinion or result in legal suits. Documents covering such field work should be classified 'Secret.' " Most of this "field work" (as we will explore later) occurred in the late 1940s and the 1950s. Even as Harry Daghlian lay dying, secret experiments were already taking place, involving injections of small amounts of plutonium and uranium.

A study would later show that of two hundred letters to the editor—a rough guide to public awareness and concern—published in major newspapers in the United States in the months following Hiroshima not one mentioned radiation.

CHAPTER 5

RESTRAINING THE SCIENTISTS

In the first weeks after Hiroshima, scientists who helped build the bomb, and knew more about its destructive power than anyone, gained prominence but played only a limited part in the emerging public debate over atomic policy. Statements by activist scientists raising questions about the use of the first bombs, and the military's inclination to build more of them, were classified top secret. Leo Szilard would later observe that for weeks following Hiroshima the scientists were not allowed to express a public opinion "on the political implications of the bomb."

During the same period, as we have seen, eyewitness stories, visual images, and reports of radiation disease in Hiroshima were suppressed or distorted. General Leslie Groves spoke urgently and often about the need to build better bombs. He asserted that "the people of the United States would be committing suicide if work on atomic energy was not continued." Prefiguring a character in *Dr. Strangelove*, Groves told Congress in a smooth monotone that forty million Americans might perish in an atomic attack but survivors would retaliate and win the war. He also testified that he had been told by doctors that radiation sickness did not cause "undue suffering. In fact, they say it is a very pleasant way to die." All of this angered the activist scientists, who believed that the press and the public considered Groves the spokesman for everyone who helped make the bomb.

The scientists, nevertheless, had conflicting emotions. I. I. Rabi described them as "frankly pleased, terrified, and to an even greater extent embarrassed. . . ." What they felt was not a consuming sense of guilt—most believed the end of the war justified the Hiroshima (if not the Nagasaki) bombing—but rather "an intensely personal experience of the reality of evil," as one close observer described it. As days passed, their qualms about perfecting the weapon grew so strong that Robert Oppenheimer would inform Washington that as a group they did not wish to be asked to work on the bomb against the dictates of their hearts. "When the Japanese surrendered we did not stop our production of atomic bombs," Leo Szilard pointed out. "On what cities do we intend to drop those bombs?"

Many scientists searched, with the same zeal that produced the weapon, for a way to prevent a nuclear arms race. Laura Fermi, wife of Enrico, felt they "assumed for themselves the responsibility for Hiroshima and Nagasaki, for the evils that atomic power might cause anywhere." They formed organizations at each of the Manhattan Project sites and began drafting memos. The Association of Los Alamos Scientists was known, fittingly, as ALAS. Most of the statements were loosely based on the still-classified Franck report, written by scientists in June, which had called use of the bomb against Japan "inadvisable" without a prior demonstration, and warned of a postwar arms race.

Crafted by many hands, the scientists' statements nevertheless had three common themes: it was futile to try to keep the bomb "secret," it was impossible to develop a defense against it, and an arms race was inevitable without international controls. One other aspect the statements shared: none specifically took issue with the decision to use the bomb against Japan. Scientists were too divided on this question to speak as one. (A survey of atomic scientists in September 1945 found that 42.5 percent felt that a demonstration shot should have been tried first or that the bomb should not have been used at all.) Virtually none of the scientists chose to speak out individually. To do so at that time would have been unpopular and might have damaged their political message. As their new publication, *The Bulletin of Atomic Scientists,* later put it, dropping the bomb on Japan "was water over the dam, and there appeared to be no reason to risk disagreements on past events when groups of scientists were all united on what the future developments should be." Focusing on the future also meant not dwelling on their personal involvement in the devastation already caused by the bomb.

One scientist with a history of independent behavior did attempt to provoke a public debate over Hiroshima. When he learned of the atomic attack on Japan, Leo Szilard immediately asked A. H. Compton, director of the Metlab at the University of Chicago, for permission to release a petition he had circulated among Manhattan Project scientists in July. Szilard planned to have it published in *Science* magazine. The petition had asked President Truman not to use the bomb against the Japanese without explicit warning, "based purely on moral considerations," and was signed by sixty-eight Chicago scientists. Szilard had given it to Compton to give to the president. Compton had passed it along to General Groves, who made sure Truman never saw it.

On August 7, Compton agreed to the release, but the Army overruled him, and instructed Szilard not to publish it. Groves ordered the document reclassified "secret," even though it contained no military or technical information. The Army claimed that the document suggested that the Manhattan Project had been plagued with dissension and "fundamental differences in point of view"—an implication "which, if released at this time," might well harm the national interest.

Szilard wrote the White House appealing for the release of the petition. The military responded by threatening to have Szilard fired from his job at the University of Chicago and prosecuted under the Espionage Act.

President Truman was about to introduce his atomic-energy bill in Congress, and officials advised scientists to conceal their policy proposals as "a matter of political expediency," according to one of the activists. The War Department, to enforce this edict, classified the statement by the Los Alamos scientists as a state paper, prohibiting its release. The explanation: only after Truman announced his atomic policy in October would a free debate begin. The public, meanwhile, could not know that scientists felt any misgivings about the use of the bomb against Japan, or had privately issued dire warnings about the future. In a powerful column, Hanson

New York Times's military editor, complained that five weeks
e Hiroshima and "nothing has been done about the atomic

The great surge of public awe of overwhelming interest and international concentration has slackened; the iron of public opinion,
which was malleable, is settling now into the cold mould of the
old order. What was needed to accompany the atomic bomb was
some action in the political and moral and psychological fields as
dramatic and as tremendous as the achievement of atomic fission.
That no such action has yet been taken is the world's loss—and
America's loss.

Robert Oppenheimer submitted a key policy document to the War
Department, summarizing the sentiment emerging from the laboratories.
Scientists had come to certain "general conclusions" with "profound"
implications for the future. There was no way the U.S. could maintain
absolute hegemony in this field. More effective bombs could be built, but
this would not prevent war or promote security. Therefore, international
control of the atom must be pursued. The scientists, Oppenheimer explained, would "be most happy" if their views were brought to the attention of the American public.

But Secretary of State Byrnes informed Oppenheimer, through an
aide, that the call for international agreements was "not practical." He
advised Oppenheimer "and the rest of the gang" to pursue their work on
atomic weapons with "full force." The goal was "to keep ahead of the
race." The scientists' document, needless to say, was not released to the
public.

Truman Responds: The Arms Race Is On

Byrnes had supplanted Stimson (who was about to retire) as Truman's
closest adviser on the bomb. He was about to open talks with the Soviets
and opposed any positive approach to Stalin. Byrnes believed that the
Russians "were only sensitive to power," Henry Stimson observed in his

diary, and with the bomb "in his hip pocket he felt he was in a far better position to come back with tangible accomplishments even if he did not threaten anyone expressly with it."

Stimson, in contrast, embraced some of the scientists' sentiments. Shortly after the Japanese surrender, Stimson and John J. McCloy, assistant secretary of war, shared what the latter would describe as "long and painful thoughts about the atomic triumph." They speculated that the central problem facing mankind was not the Soviet dictatorship but the atomic bomb. Rather than wield the bomb as a club, the U.S. could use it to reduce the Soviets' hostility and perhaps prevent them from fueling an atomic arms race.

The Soviets were already deeply suspicious of America's aims. "Hiroshima has shaken the whole world," Stalin had told his chief scientist, Igor Kurchatov. "The balance has been destroyed." Now Stimson proposed meeting distrust with candor.

On September 12, he presented to Truman a memo he had drafted with McCloy. Stimson called for the U.S. to continue to press for democratic reforms within the Soviet Union, but "we should not delay our approach to Russia in the matter of the atomic bomb. . . . For if we fail to approach them now and merely continue to negotiate with them, having this weapon rather ostentatiously on our hip, their suspicions and their distrust of our purposes and motives will increase." This would "stimulate feverish activity" on the part of the Soviets in developing the bomb, leading to an arms race "of a rather desperate character." Unlike Byrnes, Stimson recognized that the U.S. did not have to wear the bomb on its hip; the message of Hiroshima was clear enough.

Dean Acheson, undersecretary of state, produced a thoughtful document supporting Stimson, arguing that the advantage of being ahead in an atomic arms race "is nothing compared with not having the race." Across the ocean, however, Byrnes was already drawing on the bomb's power in his meetings with the Soviets. Truman sent a cable: "Give 'em hell and stand your guns." The Soviets did not respond favorably. Afterward, Byrnes complained that the Soviets "don't scare."

The Army's control over the Manhattan Project scientists continued as weeks passed. When physicist Samuel K. Allison complained in a speech about the secrecy—and referred to the "tragedy" of Nagasaki, the first such public condemnation of that bombing—General Groves sent his top aide to Chicago to order him to be quiet. Ten days later, columnist Dorothy Thompson reported Allison's comment about Nagasaki and wondered why the scientists' views could only reach the public through the back door. Finally, the activists wrote a letter of protest to the War Department, complaining that the "policy of abridging free expression. . . . interferes, we believe, with the development of an intelligent public opinion and policy based upon the pertinent facts in a situation of transcendent importance for the future of this country."

Scientists, marginalized in the post-Hiroshima policy debate, believed they would finally be heard when the president revealed his atomic policy in early October. And, indeed, Truman asserted in his statement that controlling the weapon was urgent and "discussions" must begin immediately with other nations so that "cooperation might replace rivalry in the field of atomic power." But was this just rhetoric? As much as he claimed to agree with Stimson, Truman inwardly sympathized with Byrnes and others who opposed cooperating with the Soviets.

This became apparent on October 8 when Truman, during an informal press conference at Reelfoot Lake, Tennessee, declared that if the Soviets wished to "catch up with us" on the bomb, "they will have to do it on their own hook, just as we did." *Time* magazine complained that the president was treating the bomb with "an oddly offhand air," choosing a bull session with reporters at a fishing lodge, against a background of bourbon and poker, to make this pronouncement. A few days after that, a longtime friend asked the president if "the armaments race" was on, and Truman answered yes, vowing that the U.S. "would stay ahead."

And so, in the end, Truman had sided with Byrnes, Groves, and Congress—not Stimson, Acheson, and the activist scientists. Soon the Soviets would denounce the American policy with a new phrase, "atomic diplomacy," and vowed to continue working on their own bomb (which they were in any case inclined to do).

The activists were also angered by the president's domestic proposal, drafted by the War Department and put forward as the May-Johnson bill. Among other things, it emphasized military uses, and control, of atomic energy. An Atomic Energy Commission could bar any information it desired to keep secret, with stiff penalties for violations. To make matters worse, the administration tried to push the bill through Congress with only a one-day hearing. Representative Helen Gahagan Douglas charged that scientific experts had been forbidden to speak although "they alone can tell us what is fully in store."

The scientists, who had patiently waited for a chance to air their views, were outraged. Their protests forced the hearings to resume, and several of the activists, including Leo Szilard, were called to testify. They feverishly expanded their lobbying activities and formed their first national organization, the Federation of Atomic Scientists. Suddenly, the activists' warnings filled the pages of magazines and newspapers. Truman threw his support to a new bill that provided for civilian control of atomic energy. But, in a sense, all this came too late. As Hanson Baldwin had observed, the moment of prime public concern about the bomb, and Hiroshima, had passed. The White House and Congress had long since seized political control of the bomb.

The Scientists' Heresy: "Read, Discuss, Act!"

Without publicly criticizing the decision to use the bomb against Japan, the scientists nevertheless had created a kind of nuclear heresy that threatened the official narrative. Hiroshima was born of secrecy; they were for openness. Hiroshima suggested that atomic energy could be used as a military weapon; they were for peaceful applications only. Hiroshima represented the advantage of being ahead in an arms race; they were for international control.

Of the leading scientists, few felt more conflicted than Robert Oppenheimer. In a letter to E. O. Lawrence, Oppenheimer expressed "a profound grief, and a profound perplexity about the course we should be following." He compared working on atomic weapons to perfecting poison gases after World War I but affirmed that the scientists would "of course. . . . earnestly do whatever was really in the national interest." This fit the pattern of Oppenheimer's relationship with the bomb: a special combination of nuclearism, personal anguish, and compliance. His chosen role as "inside scientist" would not end until he began to question the dangers of nuclearism in opposing the hydrogen bomb.

Many of the leading scientists shared much of Oppenheimer's outlook. Harold Urey, after calling strongly for controlling the bomb, advised Congress that if negotiations failed, "we must make atomic bombs, we must make them larger, we must make them efficient . . . We can and must devise means for delivery of such bombs to possible future enemies."

In mid-October, Oppenheimer retired as director of Los Alamos, on a day that celebrated the lab's achievements. Each worker received a silver pin stamped with a large "A" and a small "bomb." Oppenheimer, characteristically, cast doubt on their accomplishments. "If atomic bombs are to be added as new weapons to the arsenals of a warring world, or to the arsenals of nations preparing for war," he remarked in a short speech, "then the time will come when mankind will curse the names of Los Alamos and of Hiroshima."

Three days later, Oppenheimer met with Henry Wallace in Washington. That evening in his diary Wallace wrote:

> I never saw a man in such an extremely nervous state as Oppenheimer. He seemed to feel that the destruction of the entire human race was imminent. . . . He has been in charge of the scientists in New Mexico and says that the heart has completely gone out of them there; that all they think about now are the social and economic implications of the bomb and that they are no longer doing anything worthwhile on the scientific level. . . . He says that Secretary Byrnes' attitude on the bomb has been very bad. . . . He thinks the mishandling of the situation at Potsdam has prepared the way for the eventual slaughter of tens of millions or perhaps hundreds of millions of innocent people.

Wallace concluded his diary entry with this observation: "The guilt consciousness of the atomic bomb scientists is one of the most astounding things I have ever seen."

Throughout the long autumn of testifying, petitioning, and lobbying in Washington, D.C., Hiroshima was rarely mentioned in the press, except in passing. When the Pentagon's junkets to Hiroshima ended in September,

American reporters in the Far East either lost interest or surrendered in the face of restrictions from MacArthur's office. The Hiroshima decision remained largely unexamined, and the radiation scare had dissipated.

Still, anti-bomb sentiment was growing, thanks largely to the atomic scientists. A slim paperback called *One World or None,* put out by the Federation of Atomic Scientists, received favorable reviews and sold 100,000 copies. It included seminal writings by Einstein, Oppenheimer, Morrison, Szilard, and others, divided into two sections: the danger of atomic war and what to do about it. Contributors generally agreed that world government was the answer. Paul Boyer has described the book's message as "Read, discuss, act!"

The same combination of urgency and optimism fueled the scientists' unlikely, but significant, involvement with the first Hollywood movie about Hiroshima and the bomb, *The Beginning or the End.* Indeed, the inspiration for the film came directly from the scientists' movement. A few weeks after the Hiroshima attack, Dr. Edward Tomkins, an Oak Ridge chemist, wrote to one of his former high-school students, actress Donna Reed, expressing surprise that Hollywood did not already have a movie about the birth of the atomic age in the works. He wondered if the film industry wanted to "tell the people of the world some inherent facts about the bomb they should know." The actress's husband, Hollywood agent Tony Owen, told Sam Marx, a producer at Metro-Goldwyn-Mayer, about the letters. Marx sold the idea for a movie to the head of the studio, Louis B. Mayer, who called it "the most important story" he would ever film.

When Marx and Owen arrived at Oak Ridge in early November 1945, Tomkins greeted them with these words: "We are very happy you are here. We hope you can soon tell the world the meaning of this bomb, because we are scared to death!" Then the two men, along with Tomkins, went to Washington, where they won the approval of the Federation of Atomic Scientists. Their mission culminated in a meeting with President Truman at the White House. After describing his own experience with the bomb, Truman said: "Make your film, gentlemen, and put this message into your picture—tell the men and women of the world that they are at the beginning, or the end."

"Mr. President, you have just chosen the title of our film," Sam Marx replied.

Encouraged by this response, the scientists played an important role in shaping the early scenarios for the movie, which raised questions about the use of the bomb. Rather than condescend to Hollywood, the activists took *The Beginning or the End* seriously, knowing it could "fix a pattern of history in the minds of the American people," as Vannevar Bush put it. The scientists had once put faith in officials to handle the bomb wisely and with restraint, and to communicate their concerns to the public. Disillusioned with Washington, some of the scientists now turned to Hollywood to carry their message.

What they did not know was that an MGM official, following the meeting at the White House, had assured Truman that the film would be made "always within the bounds of governmental approval." This essentially gave the White House a veto over the final script. It seemed that the president, in naming the film, had staked something of a claim to it. General Groves, in addition, had secretly demanded and received the right of script approval—along with $10,000 in cash. The scientists had suddenly lost control of what they considered their picture. Groves and Truman would, indeed, intervene, ordering crucial revisions in the original script (as we explore later), transforming the scientists' cautionary tale into a ringing endorsement of the Hiroshima narrative.

During the same period, the scientists cooperated with the making of a *March of Time* film short re-enacting the opening of the atomic age. Military and government officials insisted on a positive treatment of the Hiroshima decision. The scientists inserted a plea for international control, and many felt so strongly about the propaganda value of the film, which was called *Atomic Power!*, that they agreed to play themselves in the re-enactments—even though they must have known they would look awkward, even ridiculous.

Once again, for the cameras, Szilard helped Einstein write his pivotal letter to Roosevelt (sparking America's atomic program) and Oppenheimer lectured at Los Alamos. James Conant and Vannevar Bush somberly shook hands in the desert—actually, the dirt-covered floor of a warehouse in Harvard Square—after the successful Trinity test. In reviewing the film short, *Time* magazine recalled that W. L. Laurence had described a quite different scene at Trinity: the bomb makers performing a "primordial fire dance" in celebration. But "history—or rather the human ability to stare history straight in the eyes—is not yet tough enough to endure that sight," *Time* concluded.

CHAPTER 6

A COUNTER-NARRATIVE EMERGES

Near the end of 1945 the first elements of a sustained challenge to the Hiroshima narrative finally appeared. In the nine months that followed, a coherent counter-narrative gradually emerged, threatening to undermine the official story.

Only one witness testifying before Congress in the autumn of 1945 insisted on a human-centered Hiroshima perspective. Philip Morrison, the young Cornell physicist who had accompanied General Farrell's first mission to Hiroshima, shared the concerns of the activist scientists. In his testimony in early December, he simply related what he had seen in Hiroshima, along with articulate commentary.

His statement—widely covered by the press, recorded for the radio, and reprinted in many magazines—had considerable impact because the effects of the bomb had largely disappeared from public consciousness. Little had been revealed since General Farrell's statements in September minimizing radiation effects and loss of life in the Japanese cities. Major Alexander de Seversky, an American airplane designer, had gained wide publicity (through press conferences and an article in *Reader's Digest)* when he denounced "hysterical" appraisals of the bomb's power. It would take hundreds of A-bombs to destroy a city like New York, he projected. After visiting Hiroshima he declared that "nothing happened" there which indicated that the atomic bomb was a revolutionary weapon: Two hundred B-29s laden with incendiaries could have done the job just as well.

Now here was Philip Morrison, a gifted writer and speaker, providing what *Newsweek* called "a terrifying eyewitness account" of "transcendent importance." His description of the Hiroshima holocaust ranged from the particular to the general to the universal. Describing the victims, he observed that many had "literally crawled out of the wrecks of their homes relatively uninjured. But they died anyway. They died from a further effect, the results of radiumlike rays emitted in great number from the bomb at the instant of the explosion. . . . I am not a medical man, but like all nuclear physicists I have studied this disease a little. It is a hazard of our profession. With the atomic bomb, it became epidemic."

Placing this horror in the context of a devastated city, he forced the reader to confront not only mass extermination but perhaps the nearly equal horror of surviving an atomic attack. Eighty percent of all the physicians and nurses in Hiroshima had been killed or disabled. "With the fire stations wrecked and firemen burned, how control a thousand fires?" Morrison asked. "With the doctors dead and the hospitals smashed, how treat a quarter of a million injured?"

But what Morrison really wanted to communicate was the sense that the atomic bomb was "not merely a new weapon: it is a revolution in war. . . . War can now destroy not cities, but nations." He brought this warning chillingly to life with the following passage:

A Japanese official stood in the rubble and said to me: "All this from one bomb; it is unendurable." We learned what he meant. The cities of all Japan had been put to flame by the great flights of B-29s from the Marianas. But at least there was warning, and a sense of temporary safety. The thousand-bomber raids were not concealed; they even formed a pattern of action which the war-wise Japanese could count on. But now every hour of every day above any Japanese city there might be one American plane. And one bomber could now destroy a city. The alert would be sounded day and night. Even if the raiders were over Fukuoka, you, in Sendai, a thousand miles north, must still fear death from a single plane. This is unendurable.

In February 1946, the *New Republic* printed Morrison's testimony almost in its entirety. The same week, *Time* magazine published what it called "an extraordinary document, the first detailed account of the atomic bombing of Hiroshima." It was authored by the Reverend John A. Siemes, a German priest who resided at a mission in Hiroshima. His simple act of witness, first written for a Jesuit magazine, personalized many of the graphic details in Morrison's testimony (and prefigured the more celebrated account in John Hersey's *Hiroshima)*. Soon it was excerpted in several prominent magazines.

Siemes recalled that in the days after the bomb struck, "funeral processions passed our house from morning to night, bringing the deceased to a small valley near by. There the dead were burned. People brought their own wood and themselves did the cremation. Late at night, the little valley was lit up by the funeral pyres." Only at the very end did this professor of philosophy probe the meaning of what he had experienced, but he did so memorably.

We [survivors] have discussed among ourselves the ethics of the use of the bomb. Some condemned its use on a civil population. Others were of the view that in total war there was no essential difference between civilians and soldier, and that the bomb itself was an effective force, warning Japan to surrender and thus to avoid total destruction. It seems logical to me that he who supports total war in principle cannot complain of a war against civilians. The crux of the matter is whether total war in its present form is justifiable, even when it serves a just purpose. Is it not attended by material and spiritual evils which far exceed whatever the good that might result? When will our moralists give us a clear answer to this question?

As if responding to Siemes's plea, moralists were about to try. One of them was Lewis Mumford, who in August had lamented that humankind was not morally sound enough to handle the new weapon. He organized a petition campaign calling for dismantling all existing atomic bombs, canceling all scheduled tests, and submitting the weapon to U.N. control. He sent personal letters to President Truman and General Eisenhower pleading his case. Mumford had lost a son during the war and felt that unless the bomb could be defused, the Allied victory, and his son's death, would be in vain.

What resulted was one of the classic texts of the period, "Gentlemen: You Are Mad!," a short essay published by *Saturday Review* in late winter of 1946. It opened sensationally: "We in America are living among madmen." The chief madmen went under the title general, senator, scientist, secretary of state, even president. "Without a public mandate of any kind, the madmen have taken it upon themselves to lead us by gradual stages to that final act of madness which will corrupt the face of the earth and blot out the nations of men, possibly put an end to all life on the planet itself." What they call national security was really "organized suicide."

How did the madmen get away with it? "There is a reason: we are madmen, too. . . . Our failure to act is the measure of our madness. . . . We know that the madmen are still making these machines, and we do not even ask them for what reason, still less do we bring their work to a halt." The only ones who showed "a normal awareness of danger" were the scientists, and they had only been permitted by "their keepers" to send their messages of warning "in scattered fragments. . . . For the President, the generals, the admirals, and the administrators have lied to us about their infernal machine: they have lied by their statements and even more they have lied by their silences."

What was to be done about it? "While the whole world writhes in a spasm of madness, let us in America be mad with a method, mad with a purpose. Let us say No to the atomic bomb rather than say No to life." Although he never mentioned Hiroshima by name, Mumford demanded that our leaders call together the people of the world and show them "our guilty hands, our hands already stained with a madman's blood, still clenched in a madman's purpose. . . ."

Building a Case: Moral and Military

It is hard to say what immediate impact the scattered voices of conscience had. Many Americans remained deeply worried about the atomic bomb; indeed, one anthropologist asserted that the country was still in the grip of a "fear psychosis." But postwar society, seeking a respite from mass slaughter in all its forms, was not ready to reconsider the atomic bombings.

Not a single *New York Times* reporter, for example, visited Hiroshima from September 5, 1945 (when Bill Lawrence left), until the following February. More than five months had passed, but that second junket, which included the *Times*'s Lindesay Parrott, was chillingly similar to the first: the military taking a tightly controlled group of reporters on a brief tour of the ruins. Parrott's report emphasized that Hiroshima looked like just another bombed-out city. It was rebuilding rapidly, and the correspondents and army officers "had constantly to remind themselves" that Hiroshima had been hit by a very special bomb. A group of badly injured survivors in a hospital "seemed rather proud" of the "distinguished attention" they received from the reporters—"and all these injuries are now apparently curing."

Coverage of Hiroshima focused almost exclusively on rebuilding and regeneration: flower gardens amid the rubble. According to a typical media account, "Hiroshima prayed for the dead—but also held bargain sales and dances." Children in Hiroshima, it was said, loved Americans even more than youngsters elsewhere. *Time* quoted a schoolboy telling a visitor, "American soldier good. Americans number one." The boy's mother and sister had been killed by the bomb.

Back in America, Hiroshima was more often celebrated than lamented. A re-enactment of the atomic bombings (narrated by Edward G. Robinson) climaxed a Tribute to Victory program at the Los Angeles Coliseum. One hundred thousand cheered as a B-29, tracked by searchlights, skimmed over the top of the stadium. As it roared away, a terrific explosion shook the ground, and a mushroom-shaped cloud of smoke erupted. The *Los Angeles Times* called it "an almost too-real depiction of devastation."

But soon, questioning the morality of the Hiroshima attack would receive a public airing that surpassed all that preceded it. Until then, the voices proclaiming Hiroshima a sin (such as *Commonweal* and Dwight MacDonald) were nearly all on the margins of moral and political life in America. But now a mainstream organization joined in, and it made front-page news.

From the start, ethical expressions about Hiroshima came mainly from church leaders and church publications, but no high-level religious body officially condemned the atomic attacks.* On March 5, 1946, however, the Federal Council of Churches released a powerful report, signed by twenty-two prominent Protestant religious leaders, unsparing in its criticism of the Hiroshima and Nagasaki bombings:

> We would begin with an act of contrition. As American Christians, we are deeply penitent for the irresponsible use already made of the atomic bomb. We are agreed that, whatever be one's judgment of war in principle, the surprise bombings of Hiroshima and Nagasaki are morally indefensible. They repeated in a ghastly form the indiscriminate slaughter of noncombatants that has become familiar during World War II. They were loosed without specific warning, under conditions which virtually assured the deaths of 100,000 civilians.

The churchmen argued that Japan was already defeated and that a demonstration shot should have been attempted. The use of the bomb may have shortened the war somewhat but "the moral cost was too high" and would "affect gravely the future of mankind."

As the nation that first used the weapon, "we have sinned grievously against the laws of God and against the people of Japan. Without seeking to apportion blame among individuals we are compelled to judge our chosen course inexcusable." The report condemned the Allies' incendiary raids with equal force but argued that this precedent did not make Hiroshima any more acceptable. Yet Americans might still deliver a positive message for the future, first by offering a "convincing expression" of repentance and then by helping to rebuild Hiroshima and Nagasaki. The

---

* *Bishop G. Bromley Oxnam and John Foster Dulles of the Federal Council of Churches, who had pleaded that no further bombs be used against Japan after Hiroshima, expressed "profound thankfulness" to President Truman a few days later for using the bomb only once more. This, they argued, showed a "self restraint which greatly increases our moral authority in the world. Also, we have given a practical demonstration of the possibility of atomic energy bringing war to an end."*

council also called on the U.S. to halt production of atomic weapons and to declare that it would never be the first to use them in battle.

Response from those who participated in the Hiroshima decision came quickly. Arthur H. Compton, a minister's son, sent a letter to Bishop Oxnam, a council leader, expressing his grave concern over the call for abandoning atomic weapons. God had fought on our side during the war, he argued, "supplying free men with weapons that tyranny could not produce." Now the U.S. had the "inescapable obligation to keep these weapons ready for the protection of freedom in a warlike world. This is a duty God demands of those who claim the right to live in peace and freedom."

James B. Conant also expressed alarm. He had expected the Hiroshima decision to be denounced by "professional pacifists" but was shocked to learn of an attack from the Protestant center. Reinhold Niebuhr, the theologian whose "conservative realism" he greatly admired, was among the sponsors of the council's report. In a forceful letter of protest to Niebuhr, Conant insisted that the bomb's use was "part and parcel" of the war effort, no different morally from the destruction of other Japanese cities.

Niebuhr responded with a conciliatory letter, indicating that most of his fellow signees would have supported use of the bomb against Japan if proper warnings had failed and an invasion was about to begin. But, raising a crucial point, he instructed Conant that there was "too general a disposition to disavow guilt because on the whole we have done good—in this case defeated tyranny." He endorsed the council's call for contrition "because I thought it important from the Christian standpoint to admit the moral ambiguity of all righteous people in history, who are, despite the good they do, involved in antecedent and in marginal guilt."

The Council of Churches' action seemed to prod a number of church leaders who had been silent on this subject. Fulton J. Sheen, then a monsignor at Catholic University, declared that the attack on Hiroshima was contrary to moral law, for it failed to make the moral distinction between civilians and the military. The claim of killing to save lives "was precisely the argument Hitler used in bombing Holland . . . Once the primary consideration is the winning of a war without regard to the justice of war, then all men are reduced to vermin and all appeals to justice are voided."

David Lawrence, the conservative columnist who had raised many of these moral issues shortly after the bombings, spoke out again, reprinting the Council of Churches' report in his magazine *U.S. News* and endorsing its call for contrition. The sin of organized murder is as bad as the sin of individual murder, Lawrence observed. Nations, like individuals, "must live with their consciences once a war is ended." Americans should rebuild Hiroshima to re-establish a spiritual foundation—and to purge their minds of the feeling of guilt "that sooner or later must envelop more and more of us as we learn what the weapons we created really did to innocent men, women and children."

This response by religious leaders to the moral issues raised by Hiroshima might have been expected. But the next assault on the official narrative was a surprise, coming from an unexpected source: a commission supervised by the military.

With Germany defeated, President Truman ordered an impartial group of investigators to survey the effectiveness of the American air war in Europe. The U.S. Strategic Bombing Survey would conclude, surprisingly, that it was a failure: the damage to the German economy proved less than it cost to inflict it. In the fall of 1945 the investigators—some one thousand strong—were sent to Japan, led by vice chairman Paul Nitze. This group of engineers, doctors, architects, and other professionals probed the physical effects of the atomic bombings, shot thousands of feet of motion-picture film, and studied the Japanese surrender.

John Kenneth Galbraith, a young economist, was one of the twelve directors of the survey. Galbraith had long considered the bombing of cities an "appalling business" and felt anyone with any sensitivity would feel the same way. Learning of the existence of the atomic bomb before Hiroshima, he had strongly hoped the barbaric new weapon wouldn't work. Nitze, on the other hand, considered the bomb just another weapon and sought to demystify it. He argued that B-29s loaded with incendiaries could have matched what the A-bomb had done. (This neglected the effects of radiation, of course.) What most impressed Nitze was that some Japanese who happened to be in bomb shelters when the atomic weapons went off had survived the blast.

Yet when the survey was complete, Nitze and Galbraith agreed: American bombing, as in Germany, had failed to win the war. Rather it was a combination of factors, including crushing military defeats in the Pacific, the naval blockade of the Japanese mainland, and Russia's declaration of war, that produced the surrender. A key conclusion in the official report has been cited by critics of the Hiroshima decision ever since:

> Based on a detailed investigation of all the facts, and supported by the testimony of the surviving Japanese leaders involved, it is the Survey's opinion that certainly prior to 31 December 1945, and in all probability prior to 1 November 1945, Japan would have surrendered even if atomic bombs had not been dropped, even if Russia had not entered the war, and even if no invasion had been planned or contemplated.

An equally unambiguous statement has not been quoted nearly as often: "The Hiroshima and Nagasaki bombs did not defeat Japan, nor by the testimony of the enemy leaders who ended the war did they persuade Japan to accept unconditional surrender." The emperor and his top ministers "had decided as early as May of 1945 that the war should be ended even if it meant acceptance of defeat on allied terms." At best, the report declared, the atomic attacks combined to "expedite the peace."*

In the early summer of 1946 the Strategic Bombing Survey briefly attracted media attention. The indefatigable David Lawrence reprinted the entire atomic bomb report of over sixteen pages in *U.S. News.* But after a few days, its moment passed. Hanson Baldwin of the *New York Times* proclaimed that it had "received far too little attention," considering that it refuted "so many 'facts' and theories." Deliberate or not, the timing of the report almost guaranteed that its impact would be diminished: It was released just hours before the first explosion of an atomic bomb since Nagasaki.

A Mixed Message from Bikini

Less than a year after successfully exploding an atomic device three times over land, the United States tested it two more times at sea over a guinea-

---

* *Another 1946 report for the War Department—not made public until 1989—went even further in declaring that Japanese leaders were looking for a "pretext" to surrender and that the Soviet entry into the war would have almost certainly provided it.*

pig fleet at Bikini atoll in the Pacific. The tests in July 1946 were greeted with skepticism from the start. Some feared a global catastrophe caused by tidal waves or a fissure in the earth's crust. Others objected to the removal of 167 Bikinians from their Pacific isle. The military operation, involving 42,000 participants, would be costly, an estimated one hundred million dollars.

Many argued with the timing: just two weeks after the U.S. presented the so-called Baruch Plan to the United Nations. "So we strive to save civilization, and we learn how to wreck it, all on the same weekend," one radio commentator observed. The Baruch plan called for the Soviet Union immediately to halt its atomic program, and after an international system of safeguards was in place, the U.S. would start dismantling its stockpile. The Soviets wanted this sequence to be reversed. Citing the Bikini tests, *Pravda* charged that the U.S. did not believe in restricting the bomb, but rather in perfecting it.

The bomb's three earlier explosions had been kept secret, so this display would be "its first public appearance on the world stage," as W. L. Laurence put it. The Pentagon deployed a command ship just for journalists and photographers. Norman Cousins, one of the correspondents on the press ship, was among the few junketeers who criticized the experiment. He decried the test as "authorized insanity." Yet Cousins felt some good might come out of it.

> It may be that we have forgotten too much since Hiroshima. It may be that the world is in need of periodic reminders, however costly. It may even be that a real disaster at Bikini could serve as the equivalent of another war which the world apparently needs, but cannot afford, before it will be ready to take the long step in its political evolution to organized world law.

But when the big day came, Test Able seemed to many a disappointment, even a dud. A fleet of eighty-seven guinea-pig ships was arrayed around Bikini Lagoon, but the weapon was dropped two miles off target and sank only two boats immediately. On board the press ship the most common response was: "Is that all?" A reporter said to Norman Cousins, "I was just thinking that the next war's not going to be so bad after all."

Indeed, the general tenor of the media coverage was that the bomb had been "oversold"—it was merely another weapon. The atomic bomb, Cousins affirmed, was "no longer a novelty on the face of the earth, no longer a phenomenon. After four bombs, the mystery dissolves into a pattern. By this time, there is almost a standardization of catastrophe." A-bomb advocates, on the other hand, were pleased that realism was replacing emotionalism. This meant that all future tests, as *Time* put it, would be met not with fear but only "curiosity."

Three weeks later, however, the second experiment, Test Baker, restored the bomb to its rightful place as a revolutionary weapon. This time the bomb was exploded underwater, almost directly beneath the target ships. This did three things: it immediately sank several huge ships and tossed a battleship into the air; the mushroom cloud, fed by foam and water, formed a stupendous cap three miles across—a pictorial masterpiece; and much of the moisture in the cloud fell back to sea, coating the fleet with a frightful layer of radioactivity.

Of ninety-two ghost ships, all but nine were either sunk, damaged, or heavily contaminated. After eleven days had passed and many of the target ships were still too hot with radiation to board, the admiral who commanded the tests declared: "This is a form of poison warfare." (He hastened to add that this did not apply to the atomic attacks on Japan, where most of the victims died from other causes.) An official report referred to the ships as "radioactive stoves" that would have "burned all living things aboard them with invisible and painless but deadly radiation." A few days later radioactive particles from the test were detected above San Francisco; a few days after that, over Paris.

The press generally paid the Baker bomb the respect it deserved. "It was Bikini, rather than Hiroshima and Nagasaki, that first brought the issue of radioactivity compellingly to the nation's consciousness," Paul Boyer has observed. W. L. Laurence, who had complained that his colleagues minimized the results of Test Able, felt redeemed by Test Baker. Yet he feared it was not enough. He recalled how the world had once "stood in awe of this new cosmic force," but having lived "with a nightmare for nearly a year, the average citizen is now only too glad to grasp at the flimsiest means that would enable him to regain his peace of mind."

Perhaps the ultimate distortion at Bikini was that no humans died during the tests (although many U.S. servicemen were exposed to harmful levels of radiation and likely suffered ill effects later). But only days after Test Baker, a remarkable work of reporting would restore to public consciousness not only the subject of Hiroshima but the reality of the human costs of the bomb.

Hersey's "Hiroshima"

When a new issue of the *New Yorker* arrived at the very end of August it seemed no different from any other. The cover featured a generic picnic scene. But quickly subscribers must have recognized that something was odd about this issue: there was no "Talk of the Town"; there were no cartoons. The entire issue was devoted to a "Reporter at Large" feature, sixty-eight pages long, titled simply "Hiroshima." It was written by war correspondent John Hersey, who at the age of thirty-one had already won a Pulitzer Prize for his novel *A Bell for Adano*.

In a note introducing the article the editors explained that they had taken this extraordinary step based on "the conviction that few of us have yet comprehended the all but incredible destructive power of this weapon, and that everyone might well take time to consider the terrible implications of its use." From Hersey's first sentence, it was clear that this was going to be a Hiroshima story like no other:

> At exactly fifteen minutes past eight in the morning, on August 6, 1945, Japanese time, at the moment when the atomic bomb flashed above Hiroshima, Miss Toshiko Sasaki, a clerk in the personnel department of the East Asia Tin Works, had just sat down at her place in the plant office and was turning her head to speak to the girl at the next desk.

The article had been months in the making. Hersey had discussed writing something about Hiroshima in a talk with a *New Yorker* editor, William Shawn (it is unclear who proposed the idea first). Hersey imagined an article documenting the power of the bomb and the destruction it caused to a city. But as he thought more about it, "I felt I would like to write about what happened not to buildings but to human beings," he explained later, "and I cast about for a way to find a form for that."

En route to the Far East, Hersey discovered Thornton Wilder's *The Bridge of San Luis Rey,* which explored a disaster in Peru through the eyes of a handful of victims. Hersey sensed this might be the best way to personalize the "terribly complicated" Hiroshima story. When he arrived in Hiroshima in April 1946 he interviewed several dozen survivors, before settling on six who were not at all representative: two Christian ministers, two doctors, and two working women (a secretary and a seamstress). Yet their stories were powerful, and their movements in the shattered city occasionally crossed, one of the requirements the author had set.

Hersey completed the research in just three weeks and was "terrified all the time," he later explained. He had seen the ruins of war many times before, most recently in Tokyo, but Hiroshima was different: "These ruins had been created by one instrument in one instant. And that was a terrifying notion. If I felt that coming there eight months later, what must the feelings of the people who were there at the time have been?" It was this "struggling effort to understand what they must have felt that produced whatever I was able to produce."

He prepared his article as a four-part series. William Shawn, who edited it closely, proposed running it in one issue so that reader interest would not flag. According to one report, Harold Ross, the *New Yorker* editor, believed that Hersey's sympathetic treatment of the bomb's victims might seem to some a trifle anti-American, so he asked him to insert an explanation of why the U.S. dropped the bomb. (It is hard to identify this addition, unless it is the very brief mention that Hiroshima had been an "inviting target" because of its military installation.)

The article caused an immediate sensation. All copies sold out on newsstands. The mayor of Princeton, New Jersey, asked every citizen to read it. The entire thirty-thousand-word story was read over the ABC radio network on four consecutive evenings, and many stations repeated the programs due to popular demand. The *New Yorker* was flooded with requests for extra copies; Albert Einstein wanted a thousand. Newspapers clamored for reprint rights, which Hersey granted with two conditions: that the proceeds go to the Red Cross and that the article not be abridged. Columnists and editors, most of whom had expressed strong support for the use of the bomb, nevertheless praised the article, many calling it the best reporting job of its time.* The *New York Times* declared that every American "who has permitted himself to make jokes about atom bombs, or who has come to regard them as just one sensational development that can now be accepted as part of civilization . . . ought to read Mr. Hersey." The editorial reminded readers that the "disasters at Hiroshima and Nagasaki were our handiwork," and that the crucial argument that the bomb was desirable because it saved more lives than it took might appear unsound after reading Hersey.

Others felt that the power of the article derived from what anthropologist Ruth Benedict called its "handwriting on the wall" aspect. Indeed, the entire article was a rebuke to the growing sentiment in some quarters —after the Bikini tests—that the bomb's effects were not all they were cracked up to be. Among other things, Hersey chronicled death-by-radiation, and specifically endorsed the Strategic Bombing Survey's estimate that this caused at least 20 percent of the casualties.

How did the millions of average Americans who read the article or heard it on the radio respond? An analysis of letters to the *New Yorker* revealed that most were terribly moved. A college student wrote, "I had never thought of the people in the bombed cities as individuals." Many mentioned that they were ashamed of what America had done. A young scientist, who had been proud of his work for the Manhattan Project, revealed that he wept as he read the article and was "filled with shame to recall the whoopee spirit" with which he and others had received the news of the bombing.

It appeared that "Hiroshima" might provoke widespread re-thinking of the wisdom, and the meaning, of the decision to use the bomb. Ever since August 1945 public debate had centered on what to do with the next bombs, not what had been done with the first ones. Now Hiroshima as a horrific historical event, not merely a rhetorical device, had re-emerged. Atomic scientists who had never before addressed the Hiroshima decision were now speaking out. Albert Einstein commented that the bomb probably was used primarily to end the Pacific war before Russia got into it.

Not everyone responded the same way to the article. "I read Hersey's report," one subscriber wrote the *New Yorker*. "It was marvelous. Now let

---

* *Two months later, "Hiroshima" was published in book form and became an immediate best-seller.*

us drop a handful on Moscow." Public criticism, however, came mainly from some who felt Hersey had not gone far enough. The *New York Times* ran what it called a "minority opinion" editorial, which charged that Hersey had merely "given us a picture of war's horrors as the world has long known them, rather than a picture of the unprecedented horrors of atomic warfare." Pain, panic, heroism, cruelty—these are the staples of war going back to the crossbow and arrow. What was missing in Hersey was a sense of scale, for "the special horror of the atom bomb is precisely in its direful arithmetic." The figure *100,000* indicating the number killed in a day conveyed more about the meaning of Hiroshima than any evocative anecdote.

Dwight Macdonald and Mary McCarthy, two early critics of the use of the bomb, were more caustic. Macdonald despised the article's "suave, toned-down, underplayed kind of naturalism," its "moral deficiency" in vision, its "antiseptic" prose. He wished Hemingway, with his more imaginative and vivid style, could have written it. Naturalism, he suggested, was no longer adequate "either esthetically or morally, to cope with the modern horrors."

Mary McCarthy went even further. Hersey had actually minimized the atomic bombing by treating it like an earthquake or hurricane or some other natural disaster, which offers to the journalist "a wealth of human interest stories" and "true-life narratives of incredible escapes." This made Hiroshima seem "familiar and safe, and so, in the final sense, boring." Focusing on "busy little Japanese Methodists" and other survivors was "an insipid falsification of the truth of atomic warfare"; to do the story justice, Hersey "would have had to interview the dead." Hersey also failed to enter "the moral world" and confront "the question of intention and guilt —which is what made Hiroshima more horrifying, to say the least, than the Chicago Fire. . . ."

Nothing MacDonald and McCarthy wrote was exactly wrong. What they missed was what Georges Bataille referred to as Hersey's "sensory representation of the cataclysm." Hersey had deliberately established a dispassionate tone. He did this, he later explained, so that he would not become a mediator in this story, allowing the reader to experience the atomic bombing as directly as possible. Paul Boyer has observed that Hersey's achievement was in transforming the sinister Japs "back into Japanese"—human beings. Hersey also described the full range of the bomb's effects, including radiation disease, in a way that average Americans might finally comprehend.

It is hard to say what effect "Hiroshima" may have had on those close to the bomb project. General Thomas Farrell felt so alarmed that he urged Bernard Baruch to propose an article to the *New Yorker* about six POWs in Japan—their mistreatment and about how *they* felt about the A-bomb. "We all exhausted ourselves" reading the article, McGeorge Bundy, who at that time was helping Stimson write his memoirs, recently recalled.

On the other hand, it is doubtful that President Truman read the piece at all. Six weeks after publishing the article, *New Yorker* editor Harold Ross sent Truman's secretary, Charles G. Ross, a few copies of the issue and asked if it was true (as he had been told by a Washington correspondent) that the president "has not heard of the article." He enclosed a recent item from Leonard Lyons's gossip column, which portrayed a visitor to the White House asking Truman if he had read John Hersey's "Hiroshima piece," with the president responding: "What was that?"

Secretary Ross immediately informed editor Ross that while he had read the Hersey piece and found it "magnificent," the president "may or may not" have read it. In any case, he would bring the article to Truman's attention. This did not satisfy the *New Yorker* editor. Harold Ross informed the White House that the magazine planned to reprint the Leonard Lyons item with a snappy *New Yorker* rejoinder (no doubt critical of Truman). "There is, of course, a feeling of holy zeal about the Hiroshima piece in this office," he explained, "and a hope that the leaders of all countries will read it."

A few days later, secretary Ross informed the editor that Truman had said he was "glad to have" the Hiroshima piece. Although there was no indication that Truman had actually read the story, editor Ross must have felt he had prodded as hard as he could, for he informed the White House that he had "killed" the Leonard Lyons item.

Although there was no official, high-level response to the Hersey article, behind the scenes it caused a considerable stir, not so much for its direct effects but its residual influence. Norman Cousins, predictably, played an essential part.

Just as he had done when he heard Truman's announcement on August 6, 1945, Cousins responded to reading John Hersey's article by immediately sitting down and writing an editorial for the *Saturday Review*. A year earlier he had not contested the Hiroshima decision, choosing (like so many others) to focus on the implications of the bomb. Cousins remained alarmed about America's atomic policy, describing it as one of "drift, default, and decay," but increasingly he questioned the decision to drop the bomb. Back in June he had brought to a popular audience for perhaps the first time the argument that the use of the bomb was essentially an "exercise in power politics," aimed as much at the Soviets as the Japanese —"to knock Japan out before Russia came in."

Now, his latest editorial captured, in little more than six hundred words, the essence of a Hiroshima counter-narrative that had been gathering depth and power for the past nine months. He called it "The Literacy of Survival." Cousins asserted that the significance of the "Hiroshima" phenomenon was not in the importance of Hersey's article (which he compared to Pliny writing about the eruption of Vesuvius) but in the way the reaction to the story indicated that "most Americans have not as yet recognized the implication set by us in unleashing atomic warfare." He then posed a series of questions for his readers, each an arrow aimed at the heart of the official narrative:

> Do we know, for example, that many thousands of human beings in Japan will die of cancer during the next few years because of radioactivity released by the bomb? Do we know that the atomic bomb is in reality a death ray, and that the damage by blast and fire may be secondary to the damage caused by radiological assault upon human tissue? Have we as a people any sense of responsibility for the crime of Hiroshima and Nagasaki? Have we attempted to press our leaders for an answer concerning their refusal to heed the pleas of the scientists against the use of the bomb without a demonstration? . . . And now that we have learned from a Navy spokesman that Japan was ready to quit even before Hiroshima, what happens to the argument that numberless thousands of American lives were saved?

Cousins concluded by calling for a halt to normal activity—"which is to say, a moratorium on trivia in order to acquire a basic literacy" on the moral and political implications of Hiroshima and other aspects of the atomic age. (A similar sentiment would inspire the moratoria and teach-ins opposing the Vietnam war.) If this did nothing else, Cousins observed, "it might at least enable the American people to recognize a crisis when they see one and are in one."

His moratorium idea was never pursued, but Cousins's probing questions provoked an immediate, and fateful, response in official circles.

James B. Conant, upon reading Cousins's editorial, called Vannevar Bush, another atomic-bomb pioneer, to discuss it. Both Cousins and Hersey emphasized the horrors of Hiroshima rather than putting the use of the bomb in context, Conant believed. On September 23, he sent a lengthy letter to Henry Stimson's former assistant Harvey Bundy, along with a clipping of the Cousins article. "I am considerably disturbed about this type of comment which has been increasing in recent days," Conant wrote, recognizing that the counter-narrative was gathering momentum. Warning of a potential "distortion of history" if these views went unchallenged, Conant proposed that it was of "great importance to have a statement of fact issued by someone who can speak with authority."

One person came immediately to mind: "There is no one who can do this better than Mr. Stimson."

CHAPTER 7

REASSERTING THE NARRATIVE:
THE STIMSON ARTICLE

Thoughtful, persistent questions about the Hiroshima decision had finally emerged, but in the space of a few weeks in the winter of 1947 they would be largely put to rest. A highly influential magazine article, along with a well-placed letter from the president, would reassert the official narrative so effectively it would remain virtually unchallenged for decades. The key characters were Harry Truman, Henry Stimson, and McGeorge Bundy. The catalyst, however, was James Bryant Conant.

James Conant's remarkable September 23, 1946, letter to Harvey Bundy, calling for a high-level response to the emerging counter-narrative, revealed not only his personal motives but the significance of what was at stake in the growing Hiroshima debate. He was far from alone in his concern. At almost the same moment, Bernard Baruch privately railed against Admiral William Halsey, who had recently declared that Japan was attempting to surrender at the time of the Hiroshima attack but the American scientists "had a toy and wanted to try it out." Baruch charged that this gave "aid and comfort to the minority in this country who seek to weaken our national security by putting America in the wrong on moral grounds in the eyes of the world."

In the following months the official reaction would take many forms, even a Hollywood film, *The Beginning or the End*. But an article written by Henry Stimson, inspired by James Conant, would prove by far the most significant. Indeed, its influence endures to this day.

Criticism of the Hiroshima decision was no longer limited to "professional pacifists," Conant observed in his letter to Harvey Bundy. Others were now "taking up the theme." Among those he cited were Norman Cousins and Admiral Halsey. This drumbeat of criticism, Conant wrote, threatened to repeat "the fallacy which occurred after World War I" when "so-called intellectuals who taught in our schools and colleges" asserted that the U.S. had wrongly entered that conflict. Now, he warned, the argument of Cousins and others might be embraced by educators and passed along to succeeding generations. He emphasized that "a small minority, if it represents the type of person who is both sentimental and verbally minded and in contact with our youth" could create "a distortion of history."

Conant asked Bundy to suggest to Henry Stimson that he write a short article "clarifying what actually happened with regard to the decision to use the bomb against the Japanese." He added that Vannevar Bush agreed with this idea.

What particularly troubled Conant was the growing perception that scientists had opposed the use of the bomb before Hiroshima. He stressed that Stimson must reveal that scientific leaders "raised no protest" and that they even participated in targeting discussions. Stimson should also declare that a demonstration shot was "not realistic," and denounce the "Monday morning quarterbacking" which held that Japan was about to surrender anyway. "At the same time," he added, "the statement should be largely factual and not an attempt to argue too much as to the military necessity for the bomb." For his part, Conant professed to be "quite unrepentant" about advocating the atomic attacks.

In closing, Conant suggested that they talk about all this over lunch, because it was "a matter of real importance and considerable urgency."

Conant and Concealment

The Conant letter suggests the extent to which America's finest minds contributed not only to the atomic bombings but to creating and maintaining an official version of Hiroshima that discouraged genuine reflection.

Conant was one of the few Americans who could be considered a "Renaissance man." An outstanding chemist, he became president of Harvard at the age of forty and was America's leading educational reformer and spokesman. After the war, he played a central role as an adviser on nuclear weapons policies and was a consistent advocate of international control. But whatever his accomplishments and contradictions, this brilliant advocate of free inquiry in the pursuit of knowledge came to play a major part in the containment of Hiroshima truths.

Conant himself was deeply implicated in the creation and use of the bomb. Starting in 1941, he had served as Vannevar Bush's deputy on the atomic bomb program at the National Defense Research Committee. He was the person most extensively involved in evaluation of "people, projects, and prospects," the one whose detailed memos largely determined what Bush would convey to the president. Conant did not help initiate the bomb project, but he was to become a key figure both in advocating that the bomb be used and how it would be used—against a heavily populated city.

It was at Conant's suggestion that the Interim Committee, which advised Stimson on atomic policy, established that the most desirable target for the bomb "would be a vital war plant . . . closely surrounded by workers' houses." The use of this ultimate euphemism can be understood as a direct reflection, in Conant and others, of an unyielding commitment both to the weapon and to a concept of American decency. The same conflict can be observed in Conant's immediate reaction to the success of the Trinity test: he found it horrifying but greeted it joyously. Minutes later, when the physicist Samuel Allison anxiously exclaimed, "My God, the Army's going to take this thing and fry Jap women and children with it!" Conant calmly replied: "Well, would you rather fry Jap women and children or lose a million men invading Japan?" (Two of his sons were stationed in the Pacific.)

After Hiroshima, Conant said and wrote little about the use of the bomb, an indication of the extent to which he must have numbed himself to the bomb's human effects. Yet whatever his distancing from Hiroshima, he reportedly made a telling comment about the bomb—"I'm sorry it worked"—as he waited with other high-level officials to meet with President Truman at the White House a few days after Hiroshima. The remark was consistent with a private note Conant had written two years earlier, indicating that he and the other scientists hoped "the thing won't work" —but they had to "make sure" that it wouldn't before abandoning the effort. It was also an expression of the uneasiness with which he bore his advocacy of the bomb's use.

From the beginning of his involvement with the atomic project, Conant was preoccupied with how people would respond to the existence and use of the bomb. He was concerned about both its immediate impact and the judgment of history, and he was never free from some worry about how he himself would be judged. In March 1945 he expressed the fear that there would be "almost public hysteria" if the government did not properly prepare Americans for the testing and use of the bomb. He compared the average citizen to a "patient" suffering from diabetes whom one had to scare sufficiently "to make him obey the dietary rules"; but if frightened too much, "despondency might set in—hysteria if you will— and the patient might overindulge in a mood of despair, with probably fatal consequences."

When questions about the Hiroshima bombing arose, Conant's response could be swift and agitated, as in the case of his letter to Reinhold Niebuhr. The official narrative, as Conant understood it, was that "if the American people would stay tough in regard to the use of the bomb" chances for peace and control of the weapon were good; but if "the propaganda against the use of the atomic bomb" went uncontested, our strength in having the bomb would be undermined.

Conant was also partly motivated by wishing to defend science and his fellow scientists. Following World War I, he had been struck by the attack on chemists who, like Conant, participated in making poison gas. But there was something more personal involved. A grotesque incident had occurred in Conant's life soon after he was awarded his chemistry Ph.D. from Harvard in 1916. He joined two other chemists in a business venture of manufacturing benzoic acid, which had high value as a preservative.

This led to tragedy: a large explosion killed one of his partners as well as two employees, and temporarily blinded the third partner. Conant was not at the scene, having accepted an instructorship at Harvard. But he revealed his guilt over having "deserted a post of danger" and for deficiencies in the plant's procedures that he considered "no one's fault except my own."

His way of responding to the matter had great significance for his later behavior. His experience with applied chemistry "should have discouraged me for a lifetime," he recalled later. But within eighteen months he was involved in the war effort, developing a new manufacturing process for a poison gas. The central psychological pattern here seems to be one of fending off the experience of guilt with a massive suppression of feeling; then the embracing of a new enterprise that is even more dangerous—and of still another kind of suppression, that of the moral consequences of the new enterprise.

Like many other chemists of the time, Conant had moved rather readily into work on poison gases. He took a leading role in supervising a top-secret project for mass-producing the deadly substance lewisite. While doing this work, Conant only rarely heard questions of morality raised. "To me," he later wrote, "the development of new and more effective gases seemed no more immoral than the manufacture of explosives and guns." This kind of logic led Conant, here and subsequently, to a stance of justification. When World War I was over, he was critical of chemists from Allied countries who viewed German and Austrian scientists as "tainted with war guilt"—his stance psychologically necessary, of course, in the face of his own activities.

Conant undoubtedly experienced his wartime work with poison gas as a personal triumph. His sense of self became centered not only on science but on science bound up with government and its advanced weaponry and wartime requirements—that is, science bound up with power. It has been said accurately that World War I was a "chemists' war" and World War II a "physicists' war." Conant was to be the American scientist who most intensely encompassed—indeed, whose life was shaped by—the revolutionary weaponry of both of these science-propelled wars.

Following Hiroshima, according to his son, Conant feared an all-out attack on science of a kind that would do harm to himself, people he had recruited for war work, and America at large. Ted Conant also associated his father's "gloominess" about the future with his need to defend actions concerning the bomb: the fear that Americans would become both "terri-fied" and "very angry" and would turn on those who made the weapon "without understanding from his point of view why it was necessary."

A characteristic feature of James Conant's role in defending the Hiro-shima decision in the autumn of 1946 was his capacity to channel and transform his anger over the rise of a counter-narrative into a carefully crafted plan that included the idea of an article, the ideal person to write it, and much of the content of the essay, as well as its tone and style. Never had Conant's talent for manipulating men and history been more on dis-play—a talent that contributed greatly to his enormous accomplishments as well as to his control over personal psychological conflicts.

"History with a Purpose"

It was obvious why Conant would identify Henry Stimson, who had just completed fifty years of public service, as the ideal spokesman for the official narrative. A lifelong Republican who had served two Democrats as secretary of war, Stimson was almost universally venerated. Still, Conant's letter to Harvey Bundy betrayed a certain lack of confidence that Stimson could carry out this assignment without considerable help. Conant virtu-ally outlined the article, and his tone suggested that the project would be highly collaborative.

Just in case Stimson refused, Conant asked Karl T. Compton, presi-dent of MIT and a member of the Interim Committee, to write a similar article. Compton had just returned from Hiroshima convinced that the bomb had saved millions of lives, Japanese and American. He eagerly complied with Conant's request and quickly sent him a draft. Meanwhile, Conant went to Stimson's home on Long Island for lunch and convinced him to accept the challenge. McGeorge Bundy, a junior fellow at Harvard (and Harvey Bundy's son), could assist him.

Soon Stimson was complaining about the assignment, confiding to a friend that he was the "victim" selected by Conant to defend the Hiro-shima decision. John J. McCloy, who claimed he knew Stimson "as well as any man alive," later observed that even though he agreed to write the pivotal essay defending the decision, "I know in his soul there were doubts. He lay awake at night before the decision [to drop the bomb] thinking about the consequences of dropping it on a civilian target, a city of that size."

McGeorge Bundy solicited drafts of the proposed article from, among others, his father, Leslie Groves, former Stimson aide George Harrison, and Interim Committee secretary Gordon Arneson. War Department historian Rudolph Winnacker provided essential facts. Stimson admitted that the essay was "the product of many hands," and the article, although still unwritten, had taken on the character of an official state paper. McGeorge Bundy and Stimson were not starting from scratch, however. Over several months they had been discussing the Hiroshima decision in collaborating on Stimson's memoirs. Now they had to hone their arguments and those submitted by others into a powerful, cohesive, and (more than anything) convincing six-thousand-word article.

What role did President Truman play in this process? After all, he had more at stake than any other individual.* Truman urged Stimson to write an article setting the record straight on Hiroshima—but it is not exactly clear when, or in what form, he did that. His request almost certainly came *after* Conant's initial approach to Stimson. In any case, it is significant that the same thought occurred to Truman at virtually the same time.

The first draft submitted to McGeorge Bundy came from his father, Harvey. Along with Conant's suggestions, it laid the groundwork for the article, placing a strong (if misleading) emphasis on the Interim Committee's "lengthy deliberations" on whether the bomb should be used, including "extended discussions" of "alternatives." Ultimately the decision to drop was based primarily on saving American lives, Bundy wrote.

On November 6, General Groves offered his draft, explaining that more than ever he believed such an article was necessary. Groves claimed to have spent "considerable time" on the draft yet welcomed "any alterations," as if the article were his, not Stimson's—as indeed it partly was. Groves painted a picture of thoughtful men exercising great care in making a wise decision. Characteristically, Groves took extensive credit, claiming that he, "perhaps more than any other man," had the opportunity "to

---

* *His approval rating, measured by the Gallup poll, which stood at 82 percent shortly after Hiroshima, now was 48 percent.*

consider in detail the potentialities and implications of the new weapon, not only from the military and national, but also from the social and international, point of view."

At the end of November, Stimson and McGeorge Bundy, after reviewing all this advice (and more), produced their own draft and sent it to Conant for his comments. Conant sent back what he called a "mutilated manuscript" along with an eight-page memo. He insisted that the article stick to a "mere recital of facts" and asked Bundy to eliminate every instance where Stimson "appears to be arguing his case or justifying his decision." A factual approach would appeal to skeptical readers and also make it "very hard for anyone on the other side to challenge this article."

There was another, unstated reason to avoid the appearance of advocacy. The Stimson article was "history with a purpose," Barton Bernstein has observed, yet the aim of the committee that produced it "was to conceal much of the purpose."

Turning to substance, Conant proposed a crucial deletion. He asked Bundy to eliminate any discussion of the pre-Hiroshima attempts by Stimson and others to modify the unconditional surrender demand and allow Japan to keep its emperor. Advocates of this step believed it might provoke surrender (possibly before the bomb was ready to be used). Conant told Bundy that introducing "the problem of the Emperor diverts one's mind from the general line of argumentation," and would therefore be "unnecessary and unwise."

On the other hand, Conant suggested adding a section explaining why the U.S. rejected the idea of a demonstration shot—that is, displaying the bomb's power to the Japanese before dropping it on the center of a city. The absence of an advance warning to Japan troubled the "people we are trying to impress with this article," Conant observed. He felt so strongly about this that he wrote the insert himself (and it later appeared almost verbatim in the published article).

What was most surprising, and ultimately troubling, about this sequence, Louis Menand recently observed, "was not that a statesman [Stimson] should wish to fix the record to reflect most favorably on himself. . . . What is remarkable is that the president of the country's leading institution of liberal learning, having set in motion a process leading to the publication of the facts about an event, should intervene in order to censor details he judged it undesirable for the public to learn."

A few days later, McGeorge Bundy told Conant he was "delighted" with the suggestions, and within two weeks he sent him a revised draft. This time Conant notified Stimson of his approval—most of his suggested changes had been made—and urged him to publish the article as soon as possible since there continued to be a "great deal of misinformation widely circulated" about the decision to use the bomb.

Henry Stimson's former assistant, Felix Frankfurter, suggested submitting the essay to *Life* magazine because of its wide circulation, but James Conant advocated *Harper's;* it had a serious tone and a readership that included many of those educators likely to pass along to the next generation the wrong message about Hiroshima. Conant's advice won out, as usual. *Harper's* not only offered to make the Stimson piece its cover story for February; it would allow other publications to reprint the article without charge, securing the mass readership desired.

By this time, however, Henry Stimson's qualms about the article had resurfaced. "I have rarely been connected with a paper about which I have so much doubt at the last moment," Stimson told a friend. "I think the full enumeration of the steps in the tragedy will excite horror among friends who heretofore thought me a kindly minded Christian gentleman but who will, after reading this, feel I am cold blooded and cruel."

Karl Compton's article (also inspired by Conant), entitled "If the Atomic Bomb Had Not Been Used," had just appeared in the December issue of the *Atlantic.* It was much shorter than Stimson's manuscript but covered some of the same ground. Still, it did not have the authority and gravity of the Stimson piece. Compton offered a new justification for the atomic bombings: if Japan had not surrendered, the typhoon that struck Okinawa in October 1945 would have hit the U.S. invasion forces "with a military disaster comparable to Pearl Harbor."

What limited the impact of the *Atlantic* article was that Compton lacked Stimson's standing. James Conant told Stimson that he was "the only one" who could answer the critics persuasively, and Felix Frankfurter urged him to move forward immediately. The longer "sloppy sentimentality" is "allowed to make its way," Frankfurter observed, "the more difficult it is to overtake it." Perhaps the most prescient comment came from Stimson's successor at the War Department, Robert Patterson, who pointed to the article's value as "source material" for future historians.

It was President Truman, however, who guaranteed there would be no last-minute retreat. On the final day of 1946 he reminded Stimson of his previous request that he write an article exposing the "procedure" that was followed before the bomb was dropped. "I think you know the facts of the whole situation better than anybody and I would like for you to straighten out the record on it," Truman wrote, apparently unaware that the article was already in the final editing stages. If Stimson did not feel duty bound to go ahead with the story before, he surely did now.

Truman appeared most concerned about allegations that the decision had been reached "hurriedly and without consideration," and related his recollections in brief. Seeking partnership in justification, he pointedly asked Stimson to "remember our conversation in Potsdam" when they decided that the bomb should be targeted on a city engaged "almost exclusively" in war work.

Stimson responded by telling Truman that he hoped his story would answer the "Chicago scientists" and "satisfy the doubts of the rather difficult class of the community which will have charge of the education of the next generation, namely educators and historians." As the article went to press, Stimson sent a copy of the manuscript to Henry Luce, hoping to inspire coverage in *Time* and *Life*.

By the time *Harper's* published his article, Henry Stimson seemed pleased that he had weathered the assignment. He informed Karl Compton that in their separate articles they each aimed to slay "the same ghosts" conjured up by the "uninformed and damaging criticism" of the Hiroshima decision. "I hope that together we may have done something to bring it to an end," Stimson wrote.

Little did Stimson know that President Truman would soon join them in that quest. With the President's permission, the *Atlantic* published a letter Truman wrote to Karl Compton after reading his article. This was highly unusual, as the Truman message had not been sent to the editor but to an author; the magazine, of course, understood that it could reap considerable publicity in publishing the letter. Truman called the Compton piece "the first sensible statement I have seen on the subject," with one *caveat:* it had understated his own responsibility in dropping the bomb ("the final decision had to be made by the President"). Then he added:

The Japanese were given fair warning and were offered the terms, which they finally accepted, well in advance of the dropping of the bomb. I imagine the bomb caused them to accept the terms.

This is a convincing argument, except for one detail: the terms offered to the Japanese "well in advance" in the Potsdam ultimatum did not include keeping the emperor. Truman's statement was a confabulation, as we shall later discuss. But it could seem convincing, as few Americans by this time recalled the terms of the proposed Japanese surrender. They were likely—and had a psychological need—to believe that their president was providing an accurate version of events.

As the *Atlantic* hoped, the Truman letter drew wide attention. The president had confronted Hiroshima so rarely for the record that his brief note to Compton was considered newsworthy.

Reducing the Critics to Silence

The Stimson article, published at the end of January 1947, caused a sensation nearly akin to that produced by John Hersey's "Hiroshima," and partly for the same reason: its calm, dispassionate, narrative voice. The *Harper's* cover line—"Henry L. Stimson Explains Why We Used the Atomic Bomb"—promoted it as definitive. Yet the real reason for its popularity rested on its behind-the-scenes revelations. It disclosed, for the first time, the key dates and meetings, the steps in the decision process, and the names of all the men who participated. Stimson even reprinted a couple of his memos to the president. This was intimate history.

Radio coverage was broad and favorable. Commentators treated the *Harper's* article not as advocacy but as statement of fact, just as Conant had hoped. Many newspapers, including the *Washington Post,* reprinted the entire article, and others quoted from it at length, often on the front page. A United Press dispatch, widely published, called it a "historic article"— with the ink on that issue of *Harper's* barely dry. The news peg for their story was: *nine* men made the decision to use the bomb. This elevated the eight members of the Interim Committee—a panel whose central role the public was learning about for the first time—to nearly the same level of responsibility as the president. The United Press story also emphasized Stimson's assertion of American lives saved: over one million, by far the highest estimate yet offered.

Editorials praised the essay. The *New York Times* linked it to Truman's letter in the *Atlantic* but called the appearance of the two documents "coincidence." Few analysts wondered why the Truman, Stimson, and Compton documents were written, according to Barton Bernstein, "whether their appearance at virtually the same time might be more than serendipity, or whether they were conceived with some larger purposes in mind."

The *New York Times,* over the past eighteen months, had expressed some misgivings about the Hiroshima decision. Now all doubts disappeared. The editors found the reasoning of Truman and Stimson "irrefutable" and their justifications "unchallengeable," and in a neat summary of the pivotal argument observed that "by sacrificing thousands of lives" the atomic bomb "saved millions." The New York *Herald-Tribune,* after endorsing the *Harper's* essay, expressed in just five haunting words exactly what Stimson and Truman—and Conant and Bundy and Compton—had accomplished. "So much for the past," the editorial declared.

Just days after Stimson's article appeared, the new Atomic Energy Commission met for virtually the first time. The United States, at this point, had exactly thirteen atomic bombs in its arsenal, none of them functional. At this crucial meeting, according to the minutes, "Discussion of the relative emphasis on *weapons* and *reactors* followed, with rather general final agreement that *weapons* were of first priority." Maximum effort would be devoted to developing and testing new devices, including the hydrogen bomb; on rebuilding Los Alamos; and on increasing production of raw materials for bombs.

Robert Oppenheimer, who had argued for peaceful uses of atomic energy, nevertheless went along with the decision, telling the group: "It seems to me that the heart of the problem has been reached with surprising speed: The making of atomic weapons is something to which we are now committed."

Support for the *Harper's* article arrived almost every day in Henry Stimson's mail. Included were positive notes from Ralph Bard, the lone Interim Committee critic of the decision; and from W. A. Higinbotham of the Federation of American Scientists. McGeorge Bundy, who was back in Boston, told Stimson that their article had been read by everyone he knew, "and it seems to have covered the subject so well that I find no follow-up work needed." Then he added, whimsically: "This is of particular interest in the case of one or two of my friends who certainly fall in Mr. Conant's unkindly classification of the 'verbal-minded'—I think we deserve some sort of medal for reducing these particular chatterers to silence."

Truman told Stimson he had clarified the issue "very well," and Karl Compton called the article "a highly needed finishing touch" to eliminate further criticism of the decision. Dean Acheson told Stimson it "was badly needed and . . . superbly done," and James Byrnes expressed the hope that it might "stop some of the idle talk." James Conant in public appearances recommended the article to his audiences without disclosing that he had inspired, edited, and partly written it.

In a letter to Stimson, Conant revealed a previously hidden motivation for attempting to block criticism of the Hiroshima decision. He asserted that "if the propaganda against the use of the atomic bomb had been allowed to grow unchecked, the strength of our military position by virtue of having the bomb would have been correspondingly weakened, and with this weakening would have come a decrease in the probabilities of an international agreement for the control of atomic energy." This was an argument that required more explanation, which Conant supplied.

> I am firmly convinced that the Russians will eventually agree to the American proposals for the establishment of an atomic energy authority of worldwide scope, *provided* they are convinced that we would have the bomb in quantity and *would be prepared to use it without hesitation* [our italics] in another war.

This explanation is fascinating on several levels. It points to a disturbing reason for maintaining the official Hiroshima narrative: not merely to provide the right message to future Americans but to impart the proper lesson to the Soviets, immediately. Conant was concerned about the credibility of America's threats (implied or explicit) to use its atomic arsenal "without hesitation" should that be required. If American officials admitted that they acted rashly in regard to Hiroshima—or simply allowed criticism of the decision to go unanswered—the Soviets might get the wrong idea about our intentions and our resolve. The enemy must remain convinced that American leaders had a clear conscience regarding Hiroshima and viewed the atomic bomb as just another weapon, tactically and morally. Like General Groves, Conant viewed the Stimson article not just as a defense of past events but as a facilitator of future action.

A few months later, Conant told a secret gathering of military officers at the National War College that he wished a top U.S. "official source" would announce that if war occurred and it was "militarily advisable," the first thing we would do is to start dropping atomic bombs. The *Harper's* article, Conant said, had "helped a great deal" in rallying public support for such a policy. "You have to get the past straight," he advised, "before you do much to prepare people for the future."

Praise for the *Harper's* essay ran so wide and deep that James Conant was startled when he received a letter from an old friend in Chicago, a lawyer, who confessed that not even Stimson had convinced him of the morality of the decision. Dropping the bomb on cities, he wrote, violated "every human instinct of many civilized people" and signified "acceptance of the Nazi philosophy" in this matter. What really alarmed Conant, however, was his friend's claim that most of the Chicago scientists now agreed with him.

Conant asked Robert Oppenheimer, who was back at Berkeley, to investigate this assertion. "As you know," Conant explained, in one of the understatements of the atomic age, "I feel that a great deal turns on this point in regard to the future." Oppenheimer eventually replied that while some highly vocal scientists opposed the Hiroshima decision, the majority "feel about things very much as you and I do."

The Argument That Would Endure

Most of those responding favorably to Stimson's article judged it for what he said, not what he omitted, but a closer look at each is highly revealing.

Since the Stimson essay would serve as the basic text for historians and journalists for decades, it is useful to summarize its argument step-by-step:

1. At no time prior to the use of the bombs did Roosevelt or Truman, or any other "responsible member of the government," ever indicate that the bomb, when ready, should not be used. The bomb was considered "as legitimate as any other" deadly weapon of war.

2. The Interim Committee, after frank discussions with its Scientific Panel, adopted the following recommendations for the president on June 1, 1945: the bomb should be used against Japan as soon as possible; it should be used on a "dual target"—a military installation surrounded by houses and buildings; it should be used without prior warning. Only a "tremendous shock" would "extract a genuine surrender from the Emperor. . . . For such a purpose the atomic bomb was an eminently suitable weapon."

3. The only member of the committee who dissented was Undersecretary of the Navy Ralph Bard, and his objection was limited to the lack of warning. The committee "carefully considered" a demonstration shot in an uninhabited area but discarded the idea as "impractical" and risky. Since the bomb had only been tested once, there was a real possibility that the demonstration would be "a dud," which would damage the surrender effort. "Furthermore, we had no bombs to waste. It was vital that a sufficient effect be quickly obtained with the few we had." The Scientific Panel advised that it could *"propose no technical demonstration likely to bring an end to the war; we see no acceptable alternative to direct military use."* (Stimson carefully noted: "Italics mine.")

4. Japan had sought a negotiated surrender, but its proposals were "vague" and far from unconditional. There was no indication of a weakening of Japanese military resolve. "A great military force" of five million men and five thousand suicide aircraft belonged "to a race which had already amply demonstrated its ability to fight literally to the death."

5. On July 2, 1945, Stimson urged the president to send a "last chance" ultimatum to Japan before using the bomb. The Potsdam ultimatum was offered on July 26 and rejected by the Japanese two days later. Therefore, bombs were dropped on Hiroshima and Nagasaki. These two cities were "active working parts of the Japanese war effort," one "an army center," the other "naval and industrial."

6. After Nagasaki, "we waited for a result. We waited one day." The

"controlling factor in the final Japanese decision to accept our terms of surrender was the atomic bomb." The incendiary raids on Tokyo caused greater damage and more casualties than the Hiroshima bombing, but the bomb was more than a military tool—"it was a psychological weapon." The Japanese surrender proved that the bomb "served exactly the purpose we intended."

7. The face of war is death. But the decision to drop the bombs on Japan was "our least abhorrent choice" (this would become an oft-quoted phrase). It stopped the fire raids and prevented a great clash of armies. "The destruction of Hiroshima and Nagasaki put an end to the Japanese war."

Stimson, Bundy, and Conant had fine-tuned the official narrative in a coherent form that would endure. The *Harper's* essay *became* the Hiroshima narrative. It expressed themes that would become familiar to generations of Americans, including a surrender that prevented a million U.S. casualties. Its claim: The atomic bombings did not merely quicken but caused the end of the war.

But as significant as what Stimson disclosed is what he omitted (as we will explore further in Part II). He made no mention of the role the Soviet Union's entry into the Pacific war—and postwar concerns about the Russians—played in the decision to use the bomb. He did not describe the attempt by Acting Secretary of State Joseph C. Grew to end the war (before the use of the bomb) by modifying the surrender terms, an effort that Stimson for a time supported. And he did not admit his own misgivings about the firebombing of Japanese cities—which would have called into question his moral defense of the atomic attacks.

He also failed to refer to an important reason for dropping the bomb explicitly mentioned to him by Conant, Harvey Bundy, and Groves: to persuade the world "that the saving of civilization in the future would depend on a proper international control of atomic energy" (as Bundy put it). It is a strange omission, in that *all* his top advisers for the article endorsed it. Stimson did too, privately admitting that using a horribly destructive weapon "was the only way to awaken the world to the necessity of abolishing war altogether." One is left to conclude that the architects of the article decided at some point that this psychological rationale ranged too far from "military necessity."

Because it would prove to be the keystone of all future justifications of the bombings, the question of how Stimson arrived at his figure for U.S. casualties is an important one—especially since many Americans mistakenly read "casualties" as "deaths." He wrote:

> We estimated that if we should be forced to carry this [invasion] plan to its conclusion, the major fighting would not end until the latter part of 1946, at the earliest. I was informed that such operations might be expected to cost over a million casualties, in American forces alone.

Stimson did not disclose who "informed" him of this. In fact, as we will see, official estimates for the Joint Chiefs were much lower. But until the mid-1980s, Stimson's figure was rarely challenged. Over the years President Truman even upgraded his own estimate to approximate Stimson's number.

This indicates how completely the *Harper's* essay was regarded as authoritative. Stimson himself would offer in 1948 an explanation for why this would be so. "History," he wrote, "is often not what actually happened but what is recorded as such."

Aftermath

Shortly after his article appeared, Henry Stimson and McGeorge Bundy returned to work on the memoir they would call *On Active Service in Peace and War*. Stimson received a letter that was noteworthy for being one of the few that took issue with his *Harper's* essay. Joseph C. Grew, a longtime friend, complained that Stimson had ignored the pre-Hiroshima debate over keeping the emperor—a thorny issue deleted at Conant's insistence. Grew told Stimson that he "and a good many others" would always feel that if Truman had assured the Japanese earlier about the status of the emperor "the atom bomb might never have had to be used at all . . . [and] the world would have been the gainer."

Grew's complaint hit home, for Stimson respected his knowledge of Japan; he was a former ambassador to that country. (In fact, Stimson "understood that Grew might well be right," McGeorge Bundy told us recently.) Completing work on their book, Stimson and Bundy inserted a new section. The authors not only described Grew's efforts to provoke an early Japanese surrender but acknowledged that Stimson "wholly agreed" with him and attempted to convince Truman to keep the emperor. They even admitted that "history might find that the United States, by its delay in stating its position, had prolonged the war." (General MacArthur made precisely the same point in a later conversation with Norman Cousins.)

This reveals how restricted Stimson and Bundy must have felt in writing the *Harper's* essay, with Conant and others reading drafts and strongly suggesting revisions. In their own book they felt relatively free to write what they pleased—for example, describing Stimson's anguish over the Tokyo firebombings. The book had nowhere near the impact of the article, however, and it is infrequently referred to today.

Bundy recently told us that the two men took a more "historical" approach in the book while the article was an "argument"—a "lawyer's brief" with Stimson himself as the client. The *Harper's* essay, Bundy explained, simply covered why the U.S. "did what we did," not "whether we should have done better." (This statement, of course, reflects the essential difference in viewpoint between defenders and critics of the Hiroshima decision.) Bundy also told us that it was "perfectly clear" that if the arguments for not using the bomb against Japan "had worked in 1945," they would have reinforced later arguments about not using the bomb again.

On Active Service also provided tantalizing hints, missing in the article, of how the Russians factored into the decision. It revealed that as early as April 1945 it was apparent that "the crucial questions in American policy toward atomic energy would be directly connected with Soviet Russia." Later, American leaders greeted the news of the successful Trinity test with "unconcealed satisfaction," believing the bomb would give the West a badly needed "equalizer" to Soviet aggression. But Stimson and Bundy left the implication of this attitude vague and unresolved.

Years later historians learned why: important passages in the book had been deleted by the authors before publication.

The original draft of the book included Stimson's September 11, 1945, memo to the president which (as we have seen) called for a direct approach to the Soviet Union to forestall an atomic arms race. It also described what inspired that memo: Stimson's belief that the State Department tended "to think of the bomb as a diplomatic weapon." Some of the men in charge

"were eager to carry the bomb for a while as their ace-in-the-hole. . . .
American statesmen were eager for their country to browbeat the Russians
with the bomb 'held rather ostentatiously on our hip.' "

Had these sentences appeared in the book, Barton Bernstein believes,
they might well have raised "unnerving insights for careful readers. . . .
If Byrnes had embraced the general tactics of atomic diplomacy so soon
after Hiroshima and Nagasaki, as the draft asserted, some readers might
have wondered whether these anti-Soviet aims had antedated the atomic
bombings and possibly even influenced the decision to drop the bomb on
Japan." It might also have undercut the determination of Stimson, Conant,
Truman, and others "to persuade Americans that the A-bomb decision
had been judiciously conceived, morally inspired, and undoubtedly necessary."

But these passages did not appear. Before publication, Stimson and
Bundy sent this section to George C. Marshall, who had recently replaced
Byrnes as secretary of state. The authors did not want anything they wrote
concerning 1945 to cause diplomatic problems for the U.S. in 1948 and
beyond. Marshall agreed that this was a sensitive issue and suggested they
send the chapter to George Kennan, policy planner at the State Department and pseudonymous author (as "X") of a celebrated recent article
calling for "containment" of the Soviets.

The critical passages outraged Kennan. He informed the authors that
they had it all wrong: No high American official had ever considered, let
alone made use of, atomic diplomacy.* Kennan issued a stern warning:

> I am afraid that if these statements were now to appear in an
> official biography of Mr. Stimson, a part of the reading public
> might conclude that the hope of influencing Russia by the threat
> of atomic attack had been, and probably remained, one of the
> permanently motivating elements of our foreign policy. Such an
> impression would play squarely into the hands of the Communists
> who so frequently speak of our "atomic diplomacy" and accuse us
> of trying to intimidate the world in general by our possession of
> the bomb.

---

* *A duplicitous statement, as Bernstein has pointed out, since Kennan himself in late 1946 advocated the use of
implicit atomic threats to encourage the Russians to accept the Baruch Plan.*

Bundy and Stimson knew that what they had written was factually accurate. But, as Bernstein notes, they also understood "that the real issue was not historical accuracy but the need for political correctness: The truth would embarrass the United States." And so they deleted the troublesome passages from the book. It would take another eighteen years for the Soviet angle as a consideration in the decision to drop the bomb on Japan to receive serious attention.

Looking back from the vantage point of the 1990s, James G. Hershberg, in his recent biography of James Conant, considered the significance of what occurred in the winter of 1947. "The crisis had passed," he observed. "The vast majority of public opinion still stood firmly behind U.S. atomic policy and its decision to use the weapons on Japan." The Compton article, and especially the Stimson essay, "helped to project the image of U.S. officials, military leaders, and Manhattan Project participants as decent, humane, patriotic, and compassionate; the image of President Truman as careful, informed, and deliberate in his decision to use the bomb; and the image of the United States as sincerely desirous of achieving peaceful control of the atom as a basis for world peace—but willing, if necessary, to use the weapon again to defeat aggression."

After studying recent opinion polls, one researcher observed in mid-1947 that on the whole "the threat of the bomb does not greatly preoccupy the people." Media coverage of the issue subsided. Robert Oppenheimer observed a "surprising lack, both quantitatively and in discernment, in the public discussion of atomic energy." Lewis Mumford denounced the "moral inertness" of the American people for ignoring the scientists' pleas. Leo Szilard wrote in 1947 that nothing much could be achieved "now or in the very near future until such time as the people of this country understand what is at stake. . . . Maybe God will work a miracle. . . ." Albert Einstein, too, felt bleak. "The public," he observed, "having been warned of the horrible nature of atomic warfare, has done nothing about it, and to a large extent has dismissed the warning from its consciousness." One major reason for this, of course, was that hardening Cold War attitudes and fear of the Soviets understandably caused many Americans to embrace for protection the very weapons we feared.

The scientists' movement went into decline, then disarray. "The predicted race of atomic armaments . . . is upon us," one of the activists wrote, the same month the Stimson article appeared. Many of the activists returned to weapons work. Leslie Groves gloated, commenting that after months as outsiders the scientists' "feet began to itch" and they returned to the fold "because it was just too exciting."

The impact of John Hersey's article and book had dimmed. Part of this was due to the effective argument of necessity raised by Stimson, Truman, and Compton. It is also possible, as Paul Boyer suggests, that Hersey had provided "less a stimulus to action than a cathartic end point." More likely the influence of the Hersey report was (and is) considerable, but it has always been only a part of a larger American consciousness dominated by numbing and resistance to Hiroshima truths.*

The Stimson article was the culmination of a powerful collective rear-guard action on the part of the atomic-bomb decision-makers to maintain their control over that consciousness. In the process, they rendered the American people still more passive and numbed toward the revolutionary weapons-world taking shape.

Returning to the Decision

In explaining to the American public why the atomic bombs were dropped on Japan, the Stimson and Compton articles, and Truman's letter to the *Atlantic,* were substantially in agreement. Where they differed dramatically was in apportioning responsibility for the final decision to use the weapon. This created a tantalizing mystery still alive today.

The Hiroshima debate was smothered so quickly that no one seemed to recognize the internal inconsistencies. Karl Compton failed even to mention Truman in his article and implied that Stimson, the Joint Chiefs, and General Marshall had dictated the decision. Stimson did not credit Marshall or the Joint Chiefs at all and accepted a major share of the responsibility himself—while acknowledging the president's "final responsibility." Truman rather belligerently took full credit, both in his letter to Compton and (as we will later see) in the final editing of the MGM

---

* *Twenty-four years after the Stimson article appeared, in 1971, a Harris poll found 64 percent supporting the use of the bomb and 21 percent opposed. The same poll in 1982 showed little change.*

atomic-bomb film, *The Beginning or the End*. Oddly, none of them paid much attention to General Groves or James Byrnes—individuals many historians now believe influenced the decision as much as anyone.

There was vast disagreement on the role of the Interim Committee. In his December 31, 1946, letter to Stimson, Truman had difficulty recalling who had served on it. Karl Compton barely mentioned it, and despite being a member of the committee he claimed he was "without responsibility for any of the decisions" that led to Hiroshima. Obviously, he felt the committee's role was minor. Stimson, on the other hand, placed considerable weight on the committee's recommendations. He claimed that one of the reasons it was established was to help *make* the decision. But some historians strongly dispute this, claiming that Stimson misrepresented the panel's rubber-stamp role. The mystery deepens if one considers that when Stimson mentioned the Interim Committee in a letter to Truman just days before Hiroshima, he felt he had to remind him that it had been "appointed with your approval, to study various features of the development and use of the atomic bomb."

This raises many questions. Clearly, as we will soon see, President Truman made the ultimate decision. But who played the strongest role in shaping that decision: Stimson, the Interim Committee, Byrnes, Groves, or Truman himself? Surely each played a part. But who had the firmest hand in directing (or manipulating) the decision? Or was it, as many allege, a "non-decision"—simply letting the atomic attacks happen? Why, then, did Truman, for the rest of his life, claim complete credit?

To explore these questions, we need to go back to the process by which the Hiroshima decision was made. "No single individual," Henry Stimson wrote at the start of his essay, "can hope to know exactly what took place in the minds of all of those who had a share in these events." But when we examine the decision process, we encounter psychological forces that are both troubling and crucial to understand today. We, in fact, encounter nothing less than a set of models for decision making—and for what has happened to America, and the world, in what we call the nuclear age.

PART II

MAKING AND DEFENDING THE DECISION—
HARRY TRUMAN'S TRAGEDY

CHAPTER 1

INFLUENCING TRUMAN—
THE PSYCHOLOGICAL FIELD

*135 days after
Roosevelt's death
analysis and justification
were detonated over
Hiroshima*

—BROWN MILLER,
"Sunset Blossoms Snow"

Harry S. Truman was a good man, a loving man, who made a decision to use the cruelest weapon in human history on a heavily populated city and then spent much of his remaining years defending that decision. It is not true, as many say, that he made no decision at all, that he merely got out of the way. But he was thrust into unfamiliar territory whose charged atmosphere was an enormous barrier to any other course. Truman, we believe, experienced an *atrocity-producing situation,* a psychological and political environment structured so as to motivate the average person to engage in slaughter, in this case an unprecedented dimension of slaughter. It is also true that, however pressured, one is personally responsible for such decisions. But the intent here is not to condemn Truman. It is rather to explore his dilemmas and actions within an atrocity-producing situation, so that we might be better able to resist our own capacity to create such conditions and leaders who behave as Truman did.

For Truman also became, over a period of twenty-seven years (all but seven and a half of them in retirement), America's premier spokesman on the atomic bombings. Whenever new information appeared, or a reporter or visitor raised questions, Truman would eagerly respond with an intense, often compelling, expression of personal justification. As the president who made the decision, he was listened to more than anyone else; he remained the voice of the official narrative.

A distinguished historian described Truman as "one of the most conscientious, dynamic and (within his horizons) clearsighted presidents we have ever had," praising the "statesmanlike insight, energy, and courage" he brought to every crisis. But a key for us here is that parenthetical phrase, "within his horizons." Those horizons were by no means claustrophobic; they had opened out considerably, often impressively, from narrow regional beginnings. But they were not broad enough to provide the extraordinary wisdom quite suddenly, one may say unfairly, demanded by the arrival, in wartime, of the atomic age.

Would anyone in Truman's place have been able to muster greater wisdom? We will leave that difficult question for now. What we can say is that this quintessential exemplar of Americana with a nineteenth-century sensibility could hardly be prepared for the genuinely revolutionary, world-encompassing, mid–twentieth century problem he faced. We need to examine Truman's decision in the light of all that influenced it at the time, including his struggles and relationships as president and commander in chief during the last months of a terrible war, and consider the psychological traits and historical images he brought to his ordeal. We will then see Truman emerge neither as hero nor villain, and certainly not as the model of control and country wisdom (enshrined in the misleading saying "The buck stops here!"), but as a tragic figure unable and unwilling to recognize, to touch emotionally, either his own tragedy or the human tragedy of the atomic bombings. Both his decision and his insistently hermetic defense of it have had extreme consequences for Americans as well as Japanese, and indeed for all others.

There was a decision, then, but it was not made at a particular moment and was not the product of a single mind. Rather, it resulted from a series of choices, of prior decisions, made by individuals and groups involved in a bomb-centered process. They created a psychological field—a flow of feeling, of intellectual calculations and passionate emotions, which often seemed amorphous and yet moved consistently in a fateful direction. Many different currents entered into that flow, currents having to do with war and peace, science and technology, national and international concerns, and psychological attractions and fears.

Harry Truman was thrust into the center of a dynamic process that could seem irresistible and was at the same time deeply confusing. Leslie Groves would later claim that Truman was merely, in the famous phrase, "like a little boy on a toboggan." But while Truman experienced strong bureaucratic and psychological momentum—and recognized certain bene- fits in using the bomb—shifts in events and attitudes around him did create the possibility of reversing that momentum and choosing other options. His decision was prefigured but not foreclosed. In the end he decided to use atomic weapons on undefended cities because he was drawn to their power, and because he was afraid *not* to use them.

Groves and the Secret Megamachine

With Franklin D. Roosevelt's death (on April 12, 1945), Harry Truman suddenly became the responsible leader in a terrifying, near-mystical psy- chological realm that he had no role in creating. The momentum toward using the bomb existed well before the weapons were even built. Oppen- heimer later claimed that "the decision was implicit in the project," but given the nature of the project, the momentum was highly secret.

For scientists and political and military leaders, it was infinitely more comfortable to focus on the bomb's technical requirements and strategic military use than to permit oneself to imagine the awesomely grotesque effects it would have on other human beings. In his diary, Stimson referred to the weapon as "the thing," "the gadget," "the dire," "the dreadful," "the terrible," "the awful," "the diabolical," or "the secret." As the high government official in closest touch with the bomb's development and its destructive power, Stimson needed these terms not only for military se- crecy but for his own psychological comfort, for sustaining his own psychic numbing and protecting himself from unacceptable ideas and im- ages. For those more on the periphery of the secret, the numbing came more easily. But for Truman, suddenly confronted with both the bomb and his presidential responsibility to deal with it, numbing had to be some- thing on the order of an emergency maneuver.

The secret momentum was bound up with the vast dimensions of the Manhattan Project. That energy derived in part from the fear that the Nazis would make use of advanced German physics to acquire the bomb first. Seen from the beginning as producing the weapon to "win the war," the enterprise took on its own technological and organizational dynamism as it became an atomic version of what Lewis Mumford called a "megamachine."

The embodiment of that megamachine was Leslie R. Groves, the aggressively dedicated, efficient, dictatorial Army general who was able to extend his administration of the project into vigorous policy influence at the highest levels. "There wasn't anything I didn't interfere with," he later asserted. Only Groves had direct, continuous, and authoritative contact with both the scientists working on the bomb and the decision makers who were going to determine its use. From his original charge to construct the facilities and set up the organization for making the bomb, Groves expanded his sense of mission to attempt to build the weapon in the shortest possible time, use it against the enemy, and thereby end the war. Not surprisingly, Groves developed a strong proprietary attitude toward the bomb, like a possessive father bent on displaying to the maximum the special talent of his offspring.

When Truman received his first full briefing on the bomb from Stimson and Groves, thirteen days after taking office, it was Groves who prepared a detailed memo on the weapon and explained its main features. Truman could hardly have known at the time that Groves closely manipulated all facets of the atomic environment. Respectful of scientific talent but often contemptuous toward idiosyncratic scientists—whom he once called a "collection of crackpots"—Groves imposed on them a rigid security policy of "compartmentalization": each was told only what he needed to know for his separate task. The policy was inevitably violated by the scientists, but it may have been effective in restricting discussions of the broader moral implications of atomic weaponry. Groves took the lead in establishing targeting policies intended to display the bomb to its best effect by placing it in the center of a Japanese city for maximum destruction.

As we have seen, Groves also helped shape Truman's statement announcing the bomb and selected and supervised William Laurence, the bomb's public spokesman. And in conjunction with the Interim Committee, Groves stifled emerging protest from the atomic scientists by means of a Scientific Advisory Panel, which he maneuvered into narrow consideration of a demonstration shot and away from the larger moral issues that were beginning to trouble some of the scientists.

In his dealings with Stimson and Truman, Groves represented the Manhattan Project and thereby spoke for Oppenheimer and the other scientists who worked with such dedication and brilliance to bring the bomb into being. Although psychologically and politically he could hardly have been more different from Groves, Oppenheimer shared with his administrative "boss" a commitment to get the bomb made—and used—as quickly as possible. On several occasions he deflected or suppressed protest statements (or even moral reflection) on the part of fellow scientists, telling them that they were not qualified to make such judgments and that their political and military leaders would do so responsibly. Oppenheimer's attitude undoubtedly reflected his profound psychological involvement with the bomb developed over the course of his extraordinary immersion in the project and his leadership of the scientists. But insufficiently appreciated is the extent to which Oppenheimer—a man whose charismatic talents masked his own need for higher authority—came under Groves's powerful influence.

It was Groves who made the unlikely choice of Oppenheimer to head the Los Alamos laboratory because he thought him "a genius" who "knows about everything." In that choice he ignored Oppenheimer's relative lack of scientific accomplishment and, still more seriously, his political background, which included a number of family members who belonged to the Communist party, and his own activities with various pro-Communist and left-wing organizations. Groves put his own future on the line in overruling the judgments of security officers, declaring Oppenheimer to be "absolutely essential to the project." But Oppenheimer was surely aware of the security investigations that continued throughout the Los Alamos years and knew how dependent he was upon Groves as his protector.

Observers agree that the two men in their common goal—to make the bomb—formed an effective working relationship, even a friendship. But little has been said about the extent to which Groves, while encouraging the full freedom of Oppenheimer's scientific imagination, came otherwise to manipulate and control him. Groves was shrewd in sensing, and skillfully exploiting, Oppenheimer's shaky psychological balance—he had been susceptible to severe anxiety and depression—and in particular his vulnerability to authority. Groves would later condescendingly comment that Oppenheimer was "brilliant," but "like so many of those scientists, he needed someone with a strong character to manage him." (This one-sided relationship was undoubtedly operative in Oppenheimer's pressing the Scientific Advisory Panel to reject the feasibility of a demonstration of the weapon, beating back the advocacy of his prominent colleague, Ernest O. Lawrence.)

While Oppenheimer and his colleagues were the actual bomb scientists, Groves positioned himself to be the scientific spokesman for the weapon, a role he could carry out effectively because of his training in engineering and his scientific literacy. In discussions with Stimson, the president, or other military and political leaders, he was the atomic priest bringing forth the secret mysteries (which they could not have access to even though they knew the "secret" of the overall bomb project), as well as the aggressive military bureaucrat. Groves could, moreover, convey his knowledge in such a way as to discourage not only alternative possibilities for the bomb's use but moral and political questions about what was being decided. He controlled not only the production of the bomb but also much of the discourse concerning it.

Truman thus encountered in Groves a man at the center of the technological and bureaucratic momentum, one who was formidably able to enter into, direct, and accelerate that momentum. The new president was subjected to Groves's fierce determination to plunge ahead with the weapon in order to avoid any chance the war might conclude before the bomb could be used on Japan. The means to an end had become an end in itself. And although the original purpose of the Manhattan Project was to beat the Nazis in the race for the bomb, Groves did his best to speed up, rather than slow down, the work after the surrender of Germany.

One important reason for this "unusual haste" was his fear of "the greatest congressional investigation of all times" that might occur in connection with the enormous amounts of money spent, particularly the four hundred million dollars specifically devoted to work on the plutonium bomb that was eventually dropped on Nagasaki. In the last days of bomb preparation at Los Alamos, Philip Morrison felt that work was accelerated so intensely that certain measures to maintain the safety of scientists and technicians were relaxed. Morrison acknowledged that Groves might have been reflecting pressure from above (in ways that we will see), but he was convinced—and there is much other evidence for this—of his extreme personal motivation in the matter. At issue was what has been called Groves's "abiding interest in showing off the bomb," in creating combat uses of the new weapon.

His demonstrated abilities led General Marshall to turn over to him a good deal of the planning for the weapon's use, much to his surprise and delight. This was one of the key decisions in the process leading to Hiroshima, for now "the nexus was complete," Ian Clark has observed. "The link between making the bomb and using the bomb had been formally established." The man who had the strongest desire to drop the bomb, and the most to gain from it, was now in charge of operational planning.

Among other matters, Groves was given the authority to supervise the selection of possible targets. He ordered that the bomb be used in a manner that would (as he later put it) "most adversely affect the will of the Japanese people to continue the war." At the key meeting of his Target Committee (in Oppenheimer's office at Los Alamos) the sites selected were referred to euphemistically as "targets in a large urban area," not as cities. Groves would later claim that he insisted that the cities be "military in nature," yet in these meetings this was not mentioned among the three "qualifications" for their selection.*

With Marshall's blessing, Groves also drafted the order for dropping the two weapons over Japan (these were issued under the name of a higher-ranking general). And it was Groves, along with an associate, who promoted the idea of dropping the two bombs in rapid order, rather than allowing Japan a few days to surrender after the first blow. To facilitate the bombs' use, Groves gave the field commanders some leeway for the final targeting and timing of the attacks. As he later put it, "I didn't have to have the president press the button on this affair."

Groves had come to experience a particularly strong merging of self

---

* In describing Kyoto, the preferred target, planners failed to mention any military value but did observe that it had a population of one million. They also pointed out, according to the minutes, that since it was an "intellectual center" the people who resided there were "more apt to appreciate the significance" of an atomic bomb. Hiroshima, the number two choice, was surrounded by hills, which would likely "produce a focusing effect which would considerably increase the blast damage." As a smaller city it also had "the advantage of being of such a size . . . that a large fraction of the city may be destroyed." This would not only impress the Japanese—it would enable the Americans to assess accurately the power and effects of the bomb.

and bomb. He was the "Atom-General" in the early stages of a worldview that envisioned "nothing less than an American-administered Pax Atomica," an American-dominated world held together by the bomb. Groves thus transmitted to Truman, at whatever level of consciousness, the psychological sense of omnipotence, individual and national, bestowed by the new weapon.

The Roosevelt Legacy

Hovering over everything Truman did and felt during this early phase was the psychological presence of Franklin D. Roosevelt. Truman was in awe of Roosevelt, spoke of him as a "great leader," but at the same time had reason for deeply ambivalent feelings toward him. Roosevelt had treated Truman in a manner that varied from the cavalier to the contemptuous. Though Truman mostly contained his resentment, it would emerge now and then: as when he complained to Henry Wallace soon after taking office that "they didn't tell me anything about what was going on," or when he declared, "I'm not a superman, like my predecessor." Or when, three years later, he wrote on his calendar: "I don't believe the USA wants any more fakers—Teddy and Franklin are enough." At times he would also mock Roosevelt's upper-class accent.

But Truman meant it when he declared, two days after Roosevelt's death, "There have been few men in all history the equal of the man into whose shoes I am stepping" and added, "I pray God I can measure up to the task." No one was surprised when he had a portrait of Roosevelt hung near his desk and told visitors that "I'm trying to do what he would like." In the statement that "President Truman is following the Roosevelt policy" (a point Henry Wallace was about to put in a speech) Truman inserted the phrase "to the letter."

That sentiment was not only appropriate for the "new boy" replacing a legend but was also consistent with the work of mourning. An important part of the mourning process is the assertion of a continuous tie with the dead person by furthering what he stood for, carrying on his work. But the other side of mourning has to do with separating oneself from the person who died, from death itself, in order to reassert the flow of one's own life. Both aspects of the process are made more difficult by preexisting ambivalences, all the more so when resentments have been suppressed.

Given his conflicted feelings toward Roosevelt and his immediate responsibilities, Truman could hardly carry out the psychological work of mourning. His resulting pain and confusion—along with the death-linked anxiety of a mourner—rendered him vulnerable to humiliation and highly susceptible to the influence of strong-minded advisers. Those feelings, and his sense of unworthiness, could also have intensified his need to hold closely to what he took to be Roosevelt's course, at least at the beginning. In any case, his early avowal that he would not change direction was what Truman needed to feel and just about every other American wanted to hear.

Stimson and Groves, in briefing Truman about the atomic bomb, made clear that the project had been initiated by Roosevelt and undoubtedly conveyed the sense that the great man would have made appropriate use of the weapon to win the war. They knew—but chose not to tell him —that Roosevelt and Churchill had prepared a memo at Hyde Park in September 1944, stating that the weapon "might perhaps, after mature consideration, be used against the Japanese, who should be warned that this bombardment will be repeated until they surrender." The reasons they withheld this ambiguous information are by no means clear. But advisers always bring a president selective information, and Truman's advisers did so throughout this period.

Groves maneuvered to prevent Truman from hearing anything on the order of a full discussion of alternatives, insisting that failure to use the bomb would "cast a lot of reflection on Mr. Roosevelt," raising questions like "Why did you spend all this money and all this effort and then when you got it, why didn't you use it?" During this beginning period in particular, Truman was totally dependent upon his advisers.

Truman's psychological state during the days immediately following Roosevelt's death can best be described as a struggle for survival. He looked "absolutely dazed." "I feel like I have been struck by a bolt of lightning," he said, and "I'm not big enough. I'm not big enough for this job." This was not just a fear of failure but of falling apart—of the self's disintegrating in response to demands as sudden as they were overwhelming. Always a convivial man, Truman could call forth his resilience by drawing upon the strength of others. Hence his tearful plea to reporters on his first day of office: "Boys, if you ever pray, pray for me now. I don't know whether you fellows ever had a load of hay fall on you, but when they told me yesterday what had happened, I felt like the moon, the stars, and all the planets had fallen on me."

Another means of psychological survival was a compensatory assertion of control. In order to overcome an inner feeling of being out of control, he could become inappropriately tough and undiplomatic, as in an incident, eleven days after becoming president, in which he bluntly lectured Soviet foreign minister Molotov on the breaching of agreements. Soon afterward he revealed his deeper uncertainty when he described, to an adviser, having delivered to Molotov "the old one-two to the jaw"—and then, sensing possible disapproval, asked humbly, "Did I do right?"

A related expression of what could be called *hypercontrol* was a pattern of premature decisiveness, as described by Henry Wallace in a diary entry two weeks after Roosevelt's death: "Truman was exceedingly eager to agree with everything I said. He also seemed eager to make decisions of every kind with the greatest promptness. Everything he said was decisive. It almost seemed as though he was eager to decide in advance of thinking." Significant in that passage is not only the price of control ("in advance of thinking") but its relation to dependency ("exceedingly eager to agree with everything I said"). This tendency toward premature decisiveness diminished somewhat as Truman gained confidence but remained a psychological inclination whenever he was under duress.

The day after Truman assumed office, Stimson noted his conscientiousness and willingness to learn but saw him as "necessarily laboring with the terrific handicap of coming into such an office where the threads of information were so multitudinous that only long previous familiarity could allow him to control them." Stimson undoubtedly had bomb-related issues in mind. The alternatives to dropping the bomb could hardly be grasped by Truman at the onset. Indeed, given the nature of the problem, the behavior of his advisers, and his own self-protective tendency to cut off reflection, he was probably never quite able to grasp them—certainly unable in any real sense to "control" them.

Truman and Stimson—Folie à Deux

As Truman, over subsequent days, oriented himself to the presidency, he remained highly dependent upon advisers but became more selective about which advisers he leaned on. As in the case of all leaders, his preferences had to do with immediate needs—political, military, and psychological—and with the flow of larger events. These multifaceted needs in connection with the bomb took him first to his fallen predecessor, to what he could perceive to be Roosevelt's policies and wishes; then to his secretary of war, Henry Stimson; and finally to his "assistant president" and secretary of state, James Byrnes. We shall see that in all three cases, Truman combined respect for a "teacher" with unspoken glimmers of resistance or resentment.

Henry Stimson's background could not have been more different from Truman's. A member of the Eastern elite educated at Yale and Harvard, Stimson's high-level involvements went back five administrations to President Taft. A near legendary figure at seventy-eight, he was widely respected for his intelligence, honesty and decency, and dedication to public service. But he could also be tough-minded and even cynical, manipulative, both haughty and vacillating, and capable of considerable self-deception. And of great significance for events of the time: his physical and mental powers were waning.

Stimson was Truman's connecting figure to the bomb project. One may say that "ownership" of the weapon moved from Oppenheimer (its master builder), to Groves (its military-bureaucratic champion), to Stimson (its highest overseer and presidential representative), and on to Truman.

When Truman assumed office, he and Stimson already had a bomb-related history of a less than harmonious nature. In 1943, as the chairman of a Senate committee investigating waste and corruption in defense industries, Truman had come upon suspicious expenditures for something called the Manhattan Project. When told by Stimson that it was part of "a very important secret development," Truman immediately backed down and promised that "you won't have to say another word to me." But hearing more about waste and inefficiency at the Hanford division, Truman sent an investigator. When the two men talked this time, Truman was persistent and Stimson angry; the secretary wrote in his diary: "Truman is a nuisance and a pretty untrustworthy man. He talks smoothly but acts meanly."

When Truman became president, Stimson became a critical, somewhat patronizing mentor, who nonetheless found signs of progress. On the day of Roosevelt's death, Stimson observed: "The new President on the whole made a pleasant impression, but it was very clear that he knew very little of the task into which he was stepping and he showed some vacillation on minor matters . . . as if he might be lacking in force. I hope not." But a few days later after a Cabinet meeting: "It was a wonderful relief to see the promptness and snappiness with which Truman took up each matter and decided it." And a few weeks later: "The President so far has struck me as a man trying hard to keep his balance."

Even more than other holdovers from the Roosevelt administration, Stimson tended to manipulate the information available to the new president, particularly in relation to the bomb. On the evening of Roosevelt's death, he stayed on after other Cabinet members had left to advise Truman "about a most urgent matter . . . about an immense project . . . looking to the development of a new explosive of almost unbelievable destructive power." Stimson did not see fit to communicate with the president more specifically about the weapon until eleven days later, when he sent a note urging that they speak "as soon as possible on a highly secret matter," adding that he had brought it up when the president first took office "but have not urged it since on account of the pressure you have been under." Truman responded by arranging the meeting with Groves and Stimson the next day, but here we see Stimson taking it upon himself to decide when the president was "ready" to be briefed in detail about this extraordinary matter.

The mentorship on the bomb that Stimson brought Truman had nothing to do with science and everything to do with its use and impact. Like Groves and Oppenheimer, Stimson's professional relationship to the bomb led quickly to a psychological merger with its power. His entailed a kind of distant awe, along with anxious pride at being party to, and in a sense the keeper of, its fearful and yet exquisite mystery. Hence the euphemisms for the bomb mentioned earlier—which included not only "the secret" but "my secret."

Indeed, one senses from Stimson's reactions that these aspects of nuclearism are almost inevitable in anyone who takes on "professional responsibility" for such a weapon. What Stimson conveyed to Truman was the tension within him between his duty, as secretary of war, to shepherd a powerful new weapon in the midst of a desperate war from its conception and technical realization to its use against the enemy—and his realization that this was no mere explosive but a revolutionary device that threatened the human future and raised questions that "went right down to the bottom facts of human nature, morals and government."

Throughout all the maneuverings of American decision-makers, Stimson was adamant about the significance of the bomb in a postwar power struggle with the Soviet Union and the danger of an atomic arms race. He insisted perhaps more than anyone upon the centrality of the bomb in our thinking and actions. One observer, Martin Sherwin, has wondered why a man so capable of looking at the broadest issues associated with the weapon never once advised either Roosevelt or Truman about the moral consequences of its use on a population—offering as a possible reason a suggestion once made by Felix Frankfurter that Stimson tended to set his mind "at one thing like the needle of an old Victrola caught in a single groove."

If so, that groove was one of nuclearism, of a spiritual faith that the ultimate power of the emerging weapon could serve not only death and destruction but also continuing life, could be beneficent in the extreme, used for equally revolutionary forms of human good. Yet even there, his certainties were to give way to ambivalence as he witnessed in James Byrnes a kind of caricature of his own nuclearism.

Stimson's particular version of nuclearism held sway, first in dialogues with Roosevelt and then mentorship to Truman. For instance, in notes on "S1" (a code name for the bomb) made in preparation for a meeting with Roosevelt in August 1944, Stimson included "the necessity of bringing Russian orgn. into the fold of Christian civilization," and "the possible use of S1 to accomplish this." With Truman he was even more straightforward in his famous diary entry of May 15, 1945, declaring that the new weapon would be America's "master card" in diplomatic struggles with the Soviet Union. These far-reaching projections were inseparable from military policy, so that for Stimson, as Sherwin has observed, it is likely that contemplating the anticipated effects upon both Japanese and Soviet leaders "was what turned aside any inclination to question the use of the bomb." In his bureaucratic maneuvering on behalf of these policies, Stimson was no less skillful than Groves, and his prestige and experience enabled him to be even more persuasive in a quieter, less military fashion.

But given his awareness of the weapon's destructive power, he required a formidable psychological mechanism to maintain his own inner division—a strong measure of psychic numbing and other forms of dissociation, probably furthered by his age. Inevitably, he brought these psychological mechanisms to his encounters with Truman—mentorship, that is, in diminished human feelings. Always claiming to be against the bombing of civilians, Stimson's numbing was prodigious as his War Department presided over heavy American participation in saturation bombing of cities first in Europe and then in Japan.

Viewing the Dresden firebombing as "terrible and probably unnecessary," he obtained on March 5 what he took to be a promise from an assistant secretary of war that in Japan there would be "only precision bombing" of military targets, even as the Air Force actually escalated its saturation attacks. (The firebombing of Tokyo, which took 100,000 lives, occurred on March 9.) When he complained about the area bombing to Air Force General Henry H. ("Hap") Arnold, the reply was that the density of industrial areas and housing in Japanese cities made it "practically impossible to destroy the war output of Japan without doing more damage to civilians connected to that output than in Europe." Stimson was always assured that the Air Force would try to keep civilian casualties "down as far as possible." He could then tell Truman on May 16, "I'm anxious to hold our Air Force, so far as possible, to the 'precision' bombing which it has done so well in Europe. I am told that it is possible and adequate." Here he combined with his numbing strong elements of denial (the escalation had already taken place) and illusion.

The quotation marks around *precision* suggest that Stimson might have partly recognized his own illusion—or to put the matter another way, had some sense of it along with an inability and disinclination to take in the fact and consequences of the cruel bombings of civilians. In the same memo to Truman he made clear that he was extending that self-protective psychological constellation to the atomic bomb: "I believe the same rule of sparing the civilian population should be applied as far as possible to the use of any new weapons."

Years later, McGeorge Bundy told us that Stimson strongly disapproved of city bombing, that "he thought he had tried to stop it," so that "one has to say there that a very old man simply wasn't watching what bombing was going on until it hit him in the newspapers." Since Bundy began to work closely with Stimson not long after these events, this was a highly revealing statement concerning the secretary's partial enfeeblement at the time.*

But Harry Truman, with no such enfeeblement, manifested the same pattern of severe psychic numbing and denial, when he wrote in his diary on July 25 at Potsdam:

> The weapon is to be used between now and August 10th. I have told the Sec. of War, Mr. Stimson, to use it so that military objectives and soldiers and sailors are the target and not women and children. . . . he & I are in accord. The target will be a purely military one . . .

Yet Stimson's Interim Committee, as we have seen, had already determined—at the suggestion of James Conant—that "the most desirable target would be a vital war plant. . . . closely surrounded by workers' houses." Of course women and children, as well as male civilian workers, lived in those houses. Stimson himself had, with equal contradiction, declared that the targeting "could not concentrate on a civilian area," but "we should seek to make a profound psychological impression on as many of the inhabitants as possible. . . ."

What we encounter is a shared wartime psychological process so intense that we may call it a numbed *folie à deux,* a mutually reinforcing pattern of extreme dissociation, self-deception, and illusion. In each case, the dissociation (which included numbing and denial) took the form of an inner division that permitted different parts of the mind to "know" and act on separate realities. That led to self-deception, and this protective but increasingly distorting psychological process culminated in true illusion: the conviction that area bombing was *actually* being curtailed, that targets

---

* Stimson's numbing and contradictions are further highlighted by a statement he made some time later to Robert Oppenheimer to the effect that he "found it appalling that there had been no protest over the air strikes we were conducting against Japan which led to such extraordinarily heavy losses of life." He thought "there was something wrong with a country where no one questioned that."

were *actually* purely military ones, and that lives were thereby *actually* being saved.

Those distortions were maintained by Stimson's one real attempt to combat city bombing—his insistence that Kyoto be spared because of its special historical and religious significance. Here he was aggressive in demanding that Groves show him the target list for atomic bombing, rather than simply having it approved by General Marshall; and then resisting Groves's arguments concerning Kyoto's suitability (". . . a population of over a million [and] . . . any city of that size in Japan must be involved in a tremendous amount of war work"). Stimson had visited Kyoto decades before and had been deeply impressed by the city's ancient culture. Even from Potsdam in July when Groves made a final effort to designate Kyoto as the primary target by sending an urgent telegram saying that "all your local military advisers" favored that policy, Stimson wired back angrily: "Aware of no factors to change my decision. On the contrary new factors here tend to confirm it."

The numbing could stop *there;* but the more troubling aspect of the psychological sequence is that this act of saving Kyoto undoubtedly enabled Stimson to feel that he *was* doing something to curtail city bombing in general and thereby helped him maintain his general psychological constellation of numbing, self-deception, and illusion.

Again Truman joined Stimson not only in policy but psychological motivation. In that diary entry about limiting the weapon to "military objectives and soldiers and sailors," Truman also wrote: "Even if the Japs are savages, ruthless, merciless and fanatic, we as the leader of the world for the common welfare cannot drop the terrible bomb on the old capital or the new." He then affirmed his accord with Stimson concerning "a purely military" target. Truman's dissociative processes went even further than Stimson's: the new capital, Tokyo, had already been annihilated by conventional bombing with casualties that turned out to be about as great as the atomic bombing of Hiroshima. But as Bundy has written, there was for Truman "a human content in the word Tokyo that he did not find in Hiroshima"—because "one [was] a great city he had heard about for years, and the other only a place name for an army headquarters." In supporting Stimson's position on Kyoto, Truman was probably able to reinforce his broader dissociative adaptation.

The strange pattern of numbed *folie à deux* was absurdly rendered by Stimson in a June 6 diary entry: "I told him [President Truman] how I was trying to hold the Air Force down to precision bombing but that with the Japanese method of scattering its manufacturing it was difficult to prevent area bombing. I did not want to have the United States get the reputation of outdoing Hitler in atrocities; and second, I was a little fearful that before we could get ready, the Air Force might have Japan so thoroughly bombed out that the new weapon would not have a fair background to show its strength. He laughed and said he understood." The sequence went from double self-deception (about his own efforts at restraint and the Air Force's rationale), to an uneasy need to distinguish American behavior from Hitlerian atrocities, to the numbed wartime cynicism behind the "fear" that no Japanese city would be left standing to display the bomb's power. No wonder Truman laughed.

One suspects that the laugh was not necessarily mirthful, more likely an uncomfortable recognition at some psychological level of the contradiction between claims of decency while annihilating enemy cities, on the one hand—and the dearth of possible targets for the atomic bomb, on the other. Truman's laugh might also have served the psychological function of taking him over a threshold into the cynical logic of preserving cities for a display of atomic devastation (which Truman authorized Stimson to do).

Everything said so far about Stimson's influence on Truman reflected his passionate reliance on the new weapon and his assumption that the bomb should be used against Germany or Japan if the weapon was ready before the end of the war. But by the spring of 1945, Stimson began to waver. He never directly opposed the use of the weapon against Japan, but over the next few months he was increasingly drawn to the conviction (espoused, as we have seen, most vigorously by Joseph Grew, acting secretary of state) that the Japanese were ready to surrender without any great additional loss of life if we were willing to tell them that they could retain their emperor (or a "constitutional monarchy"). This was being suggested in various Japanese diplomatic overtures—to Russian, Swedish, and Swiss officials—though in ways that were generally tentative and confusing in that they reflected deep divisions within the Japanese government and military. But having monitored Japanese diplomatic cables (through breaking their codes) as well as news broadcasts, American officials, by mid-July, "knew that the critical condition for Japan's surrender was the assurance that the throne would be preserved."

Stimson himself not only had regular access to these reports but came to recognize, with other high-ranking American officials, that communicating a willingness to retain the emperor would significantly strengthen the hand of those Japanese officials seeking peace, and would also have enormous later value in maintaining order during an American occupation. For such American officials, the doctrine of unconditional surrender was a strong barrier to peace. It had been proclaimed by Roosevelt at the Casablanca conference in January 1943 in a manner sometimes described as casual, but certainly purposeful (a mixture of propaganda, war aim, and peace term). Through passionate wartime repetition it became a rallying cry and at the same time an unbending policy. Indeed, when Truman delivered his first speech to Congress upon assuming the presidency, his clear declaration that "our demand has been, and it *remains*—Unconditional Surrender" brought the chamber to its feet in resounding applause.

On May 28, Joseph Grew conferred with Truman and told him that "the greatest obstacle to unconditional surrender by the Japanese is their belief that this would entail the destruction or permanent removal of the Emperor and the institution of the Throne," and that preserving the institution would help the Japanese to reject, rather than support, "extreme militarists" responsible for the war. Grew reported that the president expressed interest "because his own thoughts had been following the same line," and the next day Stimson endorsed the statement in principle but asked that its release be delayed because he thought that the atomic bomb, nearing completion, would be "the real feature which would govern the situation." Significantly, Grew also met with resistance from two of the more liberal voices in the State Department, Archibald MacLeish and Dean Acheson, who opposed altering the doctrine of unconditional surrender both because of their democratizing impulses (they wanted the emperor deposed) and their readings of congressional and public opinion.

Stimson, on the other hand, was willing to resist what he called the "war passion and hysteria that had seized the country." He was increasingly influenced not only by Grew but by John McCloy, his close colleague in the War Department and an intimate friend, who became a strong advocate of the Grew position. Increasingly, Stimson found himself caught between his commitment to the bomb and his sensitivity to the mounting evidence for the logic of a war-ending diplomatic approach. His behavior at an important June 18 meeting with Truman and military leaders on immediate war policy demonstrates the severity of his conflict.

The night before, McCloy made a strong appeal to Stimson's "sense of moral statesmanship" in stressing that they would stand on firmer ethical ground if they at least offered to maintain a constitutional monarchy. McCloy had the impression that the two men had reached full agreement and, when Stimson asked McCloy to represent him at the meeting the next day (fearing that his migraine headache would prevent his attendance), "I had Mr. Stimson's authority to develop with the President and the Joint Chiefs of Staff the conclusions we had reached." But Stimson did get to the meeting, and rather than espousing the emperor position, he made vague reference to the existence of a peace faction in Japan.

Yet when Truman offered a last-minute opportunity for McCloy to express himself and the latter turned to his boss for permission, Stimson immediately told him to "say what you feel about it." McCloy did so, insisting that "we ought to have our heads examined if we don't explore some other method by which we can terminate this war than just by another conventional attack and landing." He proposed the immediate overture to the emperor as having the possibility of ending the war without the necessity of Soviet assistance (scheduled for August). He also suggested informing the Japanese "that we had the bomb and that we would drop the bomb," adding further that "our moral position would be better if we gave them specific warning of the bomb." Truman responded positively ("That's exactly what I've been wanting to explore") and told McCloy to speak to James Byrnes about the matter.

In talking specifically about the "atom bomb," McCloy had the distinct impression that, although everyone in the room knew about the project, he had nonetheless broken a taboo. There was a hushed silence, and McCloy sensed that "chills ran up and down the spines" of others present, the entire atmosphere "even in that high circle . . . like mentioning Skull and Bones [a secret fraternity] in good Yale society." That horror at the breaking of the taboo reveals the power and the magic the mysterious weapon held for the very men who were to decide how to use it.

Ending the war without an invasion, and perhaps even before the bomb was ready, now became an explicit option. Stimson in the weeks that followed focused on the need to change the terms of surrender, sensing the urgency of pressing the emperor position. Yet even then his ambivalent unclarity showed. His statements on the matter were never as clearcut as those of Grew or McCloy (or of Admiral Leahy or Ralph Bard, who were still more outspoken in opposing use of the bomb). He cautioned Grew about "timing." He endorsed a clause pertaining to the emperor in a draft of a statement (originating in Grew's office) that was later to become the Potsdam Declaration—but failed to contest elimination of that clause. Then, at the Potsdam conference, Stimson made a series of passionate efforts to influence Truman—and when that failed, Churchill—on the wisdom of the emperor clause. But the efforts were too little and too late.

One observer has spoken of "Stimson's torturous arguments with himself." Indeed one could speak of an inner division so extreme as to constitute a form of *doubling,* of the formation of separate, relatively autonomous selves: one self that of the official in charge of the military and of enhancing the bomb's development and facilitating its use; the other self that of the humane statesman who felt compelled to do what was possible to employ wise diplomacy in place of carnage. The second self gained ascendancy in the last weeks, but never sufficiently to take over from or negate the power of the first.

As for Truman, he first accepted strong mentorship from Stimson's *bomb-promoting self* as a means of coming to a presidential position on the matter; then he also saw the logic of his *humane diplomatic self.* But rather than embrace and act on that logic, Truman turned elsewhere for support and advocacy.

James Byrnes and the Illusion of Control

James Byrnes had none of Stimson's ambivalence or hesitation. A self-confident and highly successful politician who expected others to acquiesce in his wishes, Byrnes came to Truman in a privileged position. Just six years his senior but infinitely more experienced in political life and a leading figure in the Senate, he had served as a kindly "older brother" to Truman in that body and later helped him raise desperately needed funds for his 1940 reelection campaign. The relationship became complicated when Byrnes, the heavy favorite for the vice-presidential nomination in 1944, was rejected by Roosevelt in favor of Truman because of calculated political considerations. Not only was Byrnes deeply resentful of FDR's betrayal but he never quite got over the conviction that it was he, and not Harry Truman, who should have become president. When Truman did become president, he immediately sought out Byrnes to be his secretary of state and "assistant President," both because of his respect for his savvy and judgment and because Byrnes had been considered FDR's "assistant president" during the previous two years (as head of the Office of War Mobilization) and had worked very closely with him on foreign policy.

Truman also thought of Byrnes as the person best qualified to succeed him in the presidency (the secretary of state is next in line after vice president) and was pleased to "balance things up" in relation to the 1944 Democratic Convention. Truman could speak of him as "my able and conniving Secretary of State" then adding, however, "My, but he has a keen mind! And he is an honest man." He was later to change his view about that last observation and undoubtedly had mixed feelings from the beginning. But during the early months of Truman's presidency no one was politically, and few were personally, closer to him than Byrnes. Different as they were, these southern country politicians understood each other.

Concerning the bomb, Byrnes had been at first unusually skeptical about the bomb project, particularly about its cost-effectiveness. When he changed his mind and began to embrace the effort, he did so with the unbounded enthusiasm of a convert. And his conversion embraced international projections, so that as early as April 1945 he told Truman that "the bomb might well put us in a position to dictate our own terms at the end of the war"; and in May he told Leo Szilard that "our possessing and demonstrating the bomb would make Russia more manageable in Europe."

Characteristically, Byrnes took it upon himself to rival Stimson as the president's informant concerning the weapon. Even before the Stimson-Groves briefing of April 24, Truman recalled Byrnes telling him that a new bomb contained "an explosive great enough to destroy the whole world," and soon afterward that "it would be capable of wiping out entire cities and killing people wholesale." More than that, Byrnes wielded consider-

able power on the Interim Committee, as the president's personal representative. He succeeded there in negating suggestions for sharing the secret
of the bomb with the Russians and pressed successfully for recommending
that the bomb be used as soon as it was ready, against an industrial target
surrounded by civilian housing, and without warning.

Byrnes's zeal concerning the bomb stood out even among enthusiastic
colleagues, convinced as he was of the bomb's capacity to benefit us in "all
fields." It could help us not only win the war without Russian participation but also "save China" and even reverse some of the unfortunate
arrangements made at Yalta. Joseph Davies, the American diplomat, observed Byrnes's overall attitudes to have "changed dramatically" because of
the bomb (causing Davies to see the weapon as "full of unknown and
dangerous psychological explosive power"). The very weapon that so
threatened the world with chaos was, for Byrnes, a means of ordering
everything. He "suggested that the New Mexico situation [the bomb] had
given us great power," Davies observed, "and that in the last analysis it
would control." That illusion of control was to be at the heart of all
subsequent American and international nuclearism.

By early July arrangements for the Potsdam conference revealed Truman's
relative reliance on Byrnes and Stimson. It was Byrnes who was invited
to travel to the conference with the president on the cruiser *Augusta*.
Stimson had not been asked to attend the conference at all and had to
request that the president include him (and then travel separately), with
the two men agreeing on a face-saving but highly improbable explanation that only Stimson's frail health had been the cause of his original ex-
clusion.

On shipboard—"between poker games," as some put it—Byrnes is
believed to have carried out his work of eliminating from the planned
Potsdam declaration all references to keeping the emperor. During this
journey, when they were isolated from Truman's other top advisers,
Byrnes undoubtedly impressed upon the president the political problems
that could result from a congressional investigation of the two-billion-
dollar Manhattan Project should the war end without its having produced
results. Everything is multicausal, of course: Byrnes was on the ship with
Truman because the president preferred his company to Stimson's; because
Byrnes and not Stimson was secretary of state and therefore the president's

main negotiator; because Byrnes had become Truman's most intimate adviser on the bomb as on everything else; and because Truman wanted to go in the atomic direction Byrnes was taking him.

Byrnes saw to it that Stimson was excluded from most of the work of the conference and took control over the timing and content of what was to become the Potsdam Declaration. In the end it said nothing of the emperor, nothing about the atomic bomb, and nothing about the entry of Russia into the war—each of which would have pressed the Japanese toward surrender. Instead the Declaration became, as Leon Sigal has observed, "neither a gesture of conciliation nor an ultimatum [but] was reduced to mere propaganda." Truman and Byrnes had their own mutual self-deception: a form of dissociation bound up with the idea that the *bomb could enable one to control events both large and small.*

More than any other adviser, Byrnes went the whole way with the bomb. Even Stimson, ardent nuclearist that he was, recognized that the bomb had diplomatic limitations and raised moral questions. Byrnes, in contrast, formed a totalistic relationship with the weapon; he imposed no such limits and "seems to have given no thought to the moral implications." His message to Truman was that the atomic weapon was all-powerful; with it *we* were all-powerful and could not only immediately obtain our war aims but also control our own and others' destiny.

Yet after two bombs had been used, Truman turned back to Stimson and away from Byrnes. On August 10, the day after the Nagasaki bombing and two days after the Soviet entry into the war, the Japanese, as we have seen, sued for peace with a qualification that the emperor remain. Among the president's immediate advisers, all were inclined to accept that condition in one way or another, except Byrnes, who feared that the American public's reaction to keeping the emperor would be so aggrieved as to lead to "crucifixion of the President." But Truman was now ready to accept Stimson's argument that the emperor would in any case be necessary to arrange the surrender of the "many scattered armies of the Japanese." At the same time he encouraged compromise wording to the effect that the emperor and the Japanese government be subjected to the authority of the American supreme commander, with the long-term future of the emperor system more or less unclear.

Truman and Byrnes later experienced a bitter break over the long-standing question hovering between the two men: Who is the *real* president? In a letter to Dean Acheson a decade later, Truman mused on Potsdam and "what might have been" had Acheson then been his negotiator instead of Byrnes, whom he came to see as a betrayer ("I trusted him implicitly—and he was then conniving to run the presidency over my head!"). Truman was surely saying that Acheson at his side would have made the outcome of myriad diplomatic decisions at Potsdam more favorable. How that retrospective musing might have applied specifically to the atomic-bomb decision is far from certain, but it is not impossible that, in some corner of his mind, Truman wondered whether, without Byrnes, the bomb would have been used.

Other Influences: Grudging Acceptance

Although no figure influenced him as much as Stimson or Byrnes, Truman had additional important advice, mostly from the military. Truman was continuously exposed to rival service advocacies: the Army's focus on an invasion of Japan; the Navy's on blockade and bombardment; and the Army Air Force's on continuous bombing. Significantly, no individual service depended centrally on the bomb. The Air Force itself was not without ambivalence: it was to derive enormous glory from the atomic bombing, but it could also be seen, as General Curtis LeMay put it in 1946, as "the worst thing that ever happened" to that service because it distracted Americans, he believed, from the achievement of conventional bombing, which had already won the war.

The central military figure, certainly for Truman, was General George C. Marshall, the Army chief of staff, a man whom he admired greatly. Marshall was never a strong advocate of the bomb but was not a dedicated opponent of it either. He generally took the Army position that, with or without the bomb or other expressions of air power, an invasion of Japan would be necessary. There is some dispute among historians as to whether Marshall (in a statement made during the June 18, 1945, White House meeting) came to believe that the Soviet entry into the war would make an invasion unnecessary—the dispute itself perhaps a reflection of his own uncertainty.

Marshall's other important act was giving Groves the responsibility for planning the actual use of the new weapons. This was pragmatic, since Groves's knowledge of all phases of the weapon had become abundantly clear to Marshall. Since Groves was strongly committed to making maximum use of the bomb, giving him that additional authority could well have been, at whatever level of Marshall's awareness, an endorsement of that intent. In late May, Marshall advised holding back on modifying the unconditional surrender principle lest it be interpreted by the Japanese as a confession of weakness. But Marshall also, as Bernstein puts it, "struggled to retain the older code of not *intentionally* killing civilians." If the weapon were used, he strongly favored a "straight" military target—such as a large naval base—and some form of advance warning.

Admiral William Leahy, the president's chief military adviser, opposed the bomb, partly because of his commitment to the Navy position. He would later refer to his sense of it as a "barbarous weapon," but Bernstein finds no written evidence of his having said this at the time. He and Admiral King, the Navy chief of staff, always felt that a naval blockade in itself would be sufficient to bring about the Japanese surrender; and General Arnold and General LeMay believed conventional bombing would accomplish this.

In Truman's later claims that his leading military advisers recommended the bomb's use, "he may have mistaken grudging acceptance for affirmation," Leon Sigal observed. Generally speaking, the military, with the notable exception of Groves and his associates, refrained from either endorsing zealously the weapon or forcefully opposing its use. One could hardly expect from the military—even from branches whose goals were at odds with the bomb—anything like a sustained effort to resist use of an available weapon. The absence of any such effort, given the prevailing dynamics, could be interpreted by a president as something close to an authoritative go-ahead.

The one adviser who urged Truman to alter the plan for using the bomb was Ralph Bard, undersecretary of the Navy and member of the Interim Committee. Bard believed that Japan "was licked" and that the Army wanted to drop the bomb so it could "be in on the kill." After speaking with McCloy, and learning that scientists had proposed a demonstration shot, Bard wrote a memo to Stimson on June 27. It called for the U.S. to explicitly warn Japan in advance about the new weapon. Bard was concerned about America's standing as "a great humanitarian nation," but he also believed that the Japanese leaders were looking for an excuse to surrender. It seemed "quite possible" that a warning would provide "the opportunity the Japanese are looking for." He concluded: "The only way to find out is to try it out." But Bard was left with the impression that he was "hammering on locked doors."

CHAPTER 2

TRUMAN HIMSELF:
THE MAN IN THE DECISION

No one is ever completely his own man, least of all an American president. But there are variations and degrees in the autonomy of the presidential self. In the case of Truman and the atomic bomb, his autonomy was considerably less than he would have us believe—and yet perhaps much greater than many observers have acknowledged. The collective psychological flow affecting Truman's decision was formidable—which is what we mean by an atrocity-producing situation—but increasingly thrust into that flow were his own political and military judgments and emotional needs. In that process he became aware of himself as the person with final responsibility.

Truman still confuses us with his mantra of "decision." When he declared, early in his presidency, that "I am here to make decisions, and whether they prove right or wrong, I am going to make them," he was saying something important about his sense of both the presidential self and his own psychological function. "Deciding" would hold things together and take precedence over everything else. That is what Henry Wallace perceived in that shrewd and unkind observation that Truman "seemed . . . eager to decide in advance of thinking." Inevitably and correctly, commentators have identified a compensatory quality in this "air of decisiveness," an underlying uncertainty or need to fend off uncertainty. But Truman was also fending off ambiguity and shadings of any kind in his quest for unencumbered clarity and, above all, for presidential authority.

When Truman, on a dozen later occasions, stated that he alone bore the responsibility for using the atomic bomb, he alone "made the decision," he was asserting a form of personal agency and (however ironically) individual *life-power* of a kind we all seek. In his case, however, that quest for autonomy became entangled with his illusion of *control* shared first with Henry Stimson and then, even more intensely, with James Byrnes. Yet it would be inaccurate to say that Truman had little capacity to influence events. Indeed, he seemed to require an exaggerated claim of autonomy and control in order to carry out the more limited, yet very significant, degree of influence that he was actually able to muster.

There has been controversy over when and whether Truman specifically ordered use of the atomic bombs on Japanese cities—and about the significance of this very ambiguity. Truman usually asserted that he gave the order on July 25, shortly after a Potsdam meeting with the Joint Chiefs, though on one or more occasions he described the final order as being given while at sea returning from Europe, which would make it sometime on or after August 2. (Barton Bernstein has studied the question closely, and concludes that Truman's instructions that the July 25 order would stand unless the Japanese made a satisfactory response to the Potsdam Declaration was probably "an informal but clearly understood arrangement" subsequently "transformed" by Truman and his ghostwriters into a *firm* order.) Given Truman's uncertainty and the much greater variability in his many statements on the number of lives ostensibly saved by the weapon, one is tempted to conclude, with Stewart Udall, that during his "torturous atomic ride during the first four months of his presidency . . . he was never in a position to be decisive about atomic issues . . . ." But one needs to probe further.

Any such large event—and any decision about it—can only be understood as part of a general process. There are always questions about relevant documents and their significance for the decision and for the event. Bernstein reminds us that "various records, and especially a participant's post-facto explanations and recollections, have a complex social role: usually to make that individual seem reasonable, authoritative, and even wise." This was surely the case with Truman's recollections. But Bernstein goes on to caution that these historical materials "can easily, and hungrily, be seized upon by interpreters when the recollected material supports larger frameworks and beliefs."

These ambiguities and contradictions about the bombing order itself, and especially about lives saved, are powerful evidence of Truman's conflict and discomfort concerning his role in the process. But they do not negate the importance of his participation in that process, a process he found so difficult to control or even understand. And finally, some time before the moment we take to be that of his final decision, the process had probably become irreversible.

A Survivor of War

Truman's earlier military experience, a critical moment in his life, had an important bearing on his decision. Coming as it did in the slogging infantry-artillery battles of World War I, it might appear to have little relevance to the revolutionary technological dimensions of atomic warfare. But Truman's extraordinary psychological investment in that war rendered the experience a prism through which he viewed the rest of life. He had been something of a confused, no-longer-young man of thirty with few successes until World War I. Truman discovered himself in the war and emerged as a highly capable officer. The war had been "the most terrific experience of my life." His political career depended largely upon his war service, and even after he became president it was observed that "he never forgets to wear his American Legion button in his lapel."

The centrality of that war experience for his sense of self was expressed in one of the most revealing of all his writings, an autobiographical sketch he wrote on the twenty-seventh anniversary of the Argonne offensive of 1918. He speaks of "a serviceman of my acquaintance" who at 4 A.M. on September 26, 1918, stood behind a battery of artillery, initiating a "forward movement" that "did not stop until November 11, 1918." The "acquaintance" came home and "was banqueted" but before long "the home people forgot the war," endorsed disarmament to the point of helplessness until "in 1932 a great leader came forward and rescued the country from chaos." Then another European war came along, the "great leader" tried to prepare the country, was vilified, but led the country to an awakening as "we were forced into the war." We achieved "the greatest war production program in history . . . manned and fought the greatest Navy in history, created the most powerful and efficient Air Force ever heard of . . ." Ultimately "the great leader . . . passed to his great reward" and "my acquaintance . . . took over." Again there was "elation" among the "home people" followed by "selfishness, greed, jealousy" among all groups. "But my acquaintance tried to meet every situation and has met them up to now. Can he continue to outface the demagogues, the chiselers, the jealousies? The answer is: Time will only tell. The human animal and his emotions change not much from age to age. He must change now or he faces absolute and complete destruction and maybe the insect age or an atmosphereless planet will succeed him."

Truman here defines himself by his World War I combat experience. It is still the "serviceman" who commanded the artillery battery who "took over" and became president. Significantly, the atomic bomb decision as such does not enter the tale but the weapon at the time was much on his mind. Nobility derives from honorable efforts at fighting and winning wars; danger resides in the amoral aftermath. Truman thus saw himself as a war veteran–survivor with a mission to keep alive that nobility and thereby give meaning to the profound encounter with death that had both shaken him to the core and renewed his life energies.

We need to be aware of those war-related survivor emotions when he tells us (on various later occasions) that he viewed the atomic bomb as "just the same as artillery on our side" and "the same as . . . an armored division"; that it was "merely another weapon of war to be used for the purpose of winning the war." In a 1953 interview, he objected to Stimson's emphasis on the bomb's psychological impact on Japan: "As far as I was concerned it was not psychological—it was a military blow to destroy Japan's production potential. . . . to create a military surrender." And he went on to invoke the end of World War I when "if you will remember the Germans were not completely defeated—Germany was never invaded and never touched except by a few air raids . . ." The association, although slightly confused, suggests that the bomb, by decisively ending

World War II, completed the unfinished work of World War I—the kind of sentiment that can often occur in relation to a war-survival experience. Truman added that "I don't believe in speculating on the mental feeling and as far as the bomb is concerned I ordered it for a military reason." Such mental speculation, that is, interferes with the self's claim of absolute clarity and moral necessity.

Rendering the weapon "purely military" required considerable psychic numbing, since, as McGeorge Bundy has accurately observed, there was a side of Truman that knew very well that the bomb was much more than just another military weapon. Our argument here is that the earlier military-psychological model in Truman's mind could enhance his numbing concerning the dimensions of the bomb, could help him to maintain his blinders and later say: "I regarded the bomb as a military weapon and never had any doubt that it should be used."

The Pre-Hiroshima Treadmill

Over time, Truman did manage to assert strong views and feelings about the bomb. During the late 1970s and early '80s the discovery of Truman's Potsdam diary and of letters he wrote at that time to his wife revealed his active involvement in the Hiroshima decision. As one historian put it, the new evidence "does not close the book" on bomb questions but "opens it to a previously unseen page." And with that evidence of energetic influence, another scholar observes, the alternative question arises as to "why Truman often seemed so confused about issues relating to the bomb" and "why Truman and other top policy makers did not act to assert greater control over decisions about the bomb or to overrule their subordinates."

Truman anticipated with dread his meeting at Potsdam with Stalin and Churchill: he was newly in office, had virtually no international experience, did not seem to be comfortable leaving American soil, and Stalin had shown much evidence of intransigence. Not surprisingly, he delayed the conference, but significantly he scheduled it to coincide with the July 15 date of the testing of the new weapon at Trinity. He seemed to wish to draw both political and psychological strength from that weapon, which, according to a later statement by Byrnes, "he had been giving serious thought to . . . for many days," and about which "he was just as reluctant as a man could be to decide . . ." Allowing for retrospective coloring, we can still surmise that, in addition to other issues of Potsdam (notably the Polish question), Truman's anxiety bore some relation to his decision about the bomb. We may say that, amid the powerful flow of bomb-related feeling from Groves, Stimson, and Byrnes, Truman was seeking to find his own stance—not only his own policies but also his own relationship between self and weapon.

Truman's diary entries at Potsdam suggest conflict. On July 16, on returning from a tour of the rubble of Berlin, he mentions past cities destroyed by conquerors, observing that "machines are ahead of morals by some centuries," and that "we are only termites on a planet and maybe"—in what seems to be a definite reference to the atomic bomb—"when we bore too deeply into the planet there'll [be] a reckoning—who knows?" But that awareness of vast technological danger seems to be reversed in Truman's observation two days later that Stalin had his "dynamite" (in the Soviet proposals) but that he, Truman, had "some dynamite too which I'm not exploding now"—a reference to the bomb as a usable weapon.

Then on July 25, the day on which he records his final decision on the weapon's use, he writes: "We have discovered the most terrible bomb in the history of the world. It may be the fire destruction prophesied in the Euphrates Valley Era, after Noah and his famous Ark." The biblical reference suggests his sense of the weapon's revolutionary nature, its totality of destruction. But just two paragraphs later comes the statement: "I have told the Sec. of War, Mr. Stimson, to use it so that military objectives and soldiers and sailors are the target and not women and children"—here holding to the image of an ordinary, controllable weapon. Observing further the good fortune "that Hitler's crowd or Stalin's did not discover this atomic bomb," he then expresses both dread and the nuclearistic claim of the weapon's liberating possibilities: "It seems to be the most terrible thing ever discovered, but it can be made the most useful." Truman knew that the weapon was murderous on an unprecedented scale and that, targeted on a city, it would kill an enormous number of civilians. But he could call forth sufficient numbing to negate that knowledge, to replace it in his mind with a different set of images of the bomb as another weapon of war "just the same as artillery."

One must wonder whether Truman experienced a sense of guilt in using the weapon and feelings of remorse later on. Our conviction is that Truman did indeed experience conflict, that he could never fully dismiss from his awareness an unacceptable recognition of what the bomb did to large numbers of human beings, but that he had ways of avoiding a conscious sense of guilt. He called forth his "decisiveness" to block out remorseful reflection of any kind, in that way suppressing conscious feelings of self-condemnation. But these mechanisms for avoiding guilt undoubtedly took their toll. They left him on a treadmill of constant justification, with ever more need for numbing, illusion, and, as we shall see, confabulation.

Had these same self-protective mechanisms prevented Truman, before Hiroshima, from exploring alternatives to using the weapon? They undoubtedly helped limit such explorations but by no means prevented them entirely. We know that Truman expressed interest in the emperor option, telling both Grew and McCloy that his thoughts went in the same direction. Truman had been briefed by Stimson on Japanese peace overtures and, by early July, knew that the critical condition for Japan's surrender was an assurance that the emperor would be preserved. Truman was extraordinarily sensitive to the *American* political implications of this issue, as was Byrnes, and both were reluctant to make any public commitment to sparing the emperor. Truman was especially worried about potential accusations of "appeasement" and of being associated with "the soft peace boys."

Since Truman at least partly gave way in eventually accepting the emperor as part of the Japanese surrender, the question has been raised as to how committed he was on the whole issue. Stimson had earlier observed that Truman and Byrnes "were not obdurate on it." But whenever it came up Truman seemed to push it aside, as though reluctant to trust in it as a basis for action. In his increasing commitment to the bomb, he may well have resisted taking in the full significance of an emperor clause. Finally, after Hiroshima and Nagasaki, he could give up some of this distancing and permit an ambiguous version of that clause—because now the bomb had been used and surrender was close at hand.

Concerning questions of the Soviets, Truman seemed more sharply focused, but also considerably ambivalent. In his Potsdam diary he celebrates Stalin's promise to "be in Jap war on August 15th" and adds: "fini Japs when that comes about." And he wrote to his wife on July 18 that

"I've gotten what I came for—Stalin goes to war on August 15 with no strings on it. . . . I'll say that we'll end the war a year sooner now, and think of the kids who won't be killed!" As Robert Messer points out, these passages are "devastating" for the official narrative since they make quite clear that "for Truman the end of the war seemed near" and the issue was only "how and on whose terms," so that "he must have realized that if the bombs were not used before that date they might well not be used at all."

From the time of the successful Trinity test, Truman and Byrnes began to focus on how to end the war sufficiently quickly that the Soviets would not gain a foothold in Japan. We can probably take Byrnes at his word when he said frankly many years later that "neither the President nor I was anxious to have them enter the war after we heard of the successful test" and "it was important to bring about an end to the war—and if possible to do that before Russia came into the war." Truman acted on these views.

Truman's pre-Hiroshima treadmill, then, had to do with continuous self-assertion in a situation that was fluid and did not readily lend itself to the peremptory decisiveness he required of himself. He resorted to an aura of decisiveness even as he wavered, so that later he could claim that he had never wavered at all. Putting the matter another way, we can say that Truman experienced considerable hesitation and ambivalence in relation to the weapon but was able to suppress these feelings—and suppress any tendency to reflect—in the service of what he took to be steadfast commitment to bold action.

That tendency toward bold action in the service of renewal is a side of Truman's psychology not much commented upon. The Tennyson poem, "Locksley Hall," which he carried in his wallet from the age of eighteen and was said to have pulled out on the sea trip to Potsdam, described the wonders of airships and air warfare: "Saw the heavens fill with commerce, argosies of magic sails/. . . . heard the heavens fill with shouting, and there rain'd a ghastly dew/from the nations' airy navies grappling in the central blue/. . . . till the war-drum throbb'd no longer, and the battle flags were furl'd/In the Parliament of Man, the Federation of the World." Truman was not the first midwestern farmer to bring a biblically based apocalyptic embrace to the most "heavenly" of technologies, but he alone found himself in a position to act powerfully within that vision of destroying the world to remake it.

Truman could reconcile any such apocalyptic impulse with his presidential duties through a form of patriotism that amounts to fierce American nationalism. "I'm not working for any interest but the Republic of the United States," he wrote in his diary on the way to Potsdam. That cosmic and national focus also helped him to exclude from his consciousness more frightening images of large-scale death and killing in relation to the weapon.

His psychological style, in any case, lent itself to a considerable capacity for numbing and for denial of death. That capacity was dramatically evident in relation to Roosevelt. By the spring of 1944, it was generally apparent that Roosevelt's health was failing, and party insiders, just before the convention that chose Truman as the vice-presidential candidate, "realized that the man nominated to run with Roosevelt would in all probability be the next president . . ." A month or so later, at a private luncheon, Truman was shocked by Roosevelt's condition: "His hands were shaking and he talks with considerable difficulty. . . . physically he's just going to pieces."*

Truman's partial awareness of Roosevelt's nearness to death was reflected in a nightmare he had on a campaign train, soon after having been nominated: Roosevelt was dead and he was president. Truman could suppress that awareness by means of denial—not only his own, but also Roosevelt's. In their conspiracy of silence, Roosevelt did almost nothing to prepare Truman for the presidency, and, even more startling, Truman did virtually nothing to prepare himself for it. As Truman later put it, "I had been afraid for many weeks that something might happen to this great leader, [but] I did not allow myself to think about it after I became Vice President."

To be sure, it was a situation likely to produce some denial in almost anyone. Entering into it, as suggested by Truman's dream, might well have been a glimmer of an unacceptable wish that Roosevelt die, along with a much stronger sense of terror that this might happen. What concerns us

---

* *A major reason for Truman's resistance to the nomination was his fear of what would surely follow—the public disclosure of his wife's father's suicide. He had himself been at the center of a strict policy of family denial, with the subject never brought up and his daughter, Margaret, not even aware of it until told by a family member just before the 1944 campaign. While the family policy had to do with shame specific to suicide, the pattern reveals some of his own capacity for denial in connection with death.*

here is the extent to which Truman's overall capacity for death-connected numbing and denial entered into his atomic-bomb struggles.

These conflicts could produce bodily symptoms. After a Cabinet meeting on August 10, the day on which Truman decided the surrender terms, Henry Wallace told the president how well he looked. But Truman replied by saying that he "had bad headaches every day." When Wallace asked, "Physical or figurative?" Truman replied, "Both." Truman did suffer over his decisions, and also from his need to minimize that suffering in order to be the kind of leader—the kind of person—he thought he should be.

Truman, then, was very much *in* the atomic-bomb decision. Whatever his apparent confusion about some certain issues, he pressed toward the bomb's use. While Truman depended heavily upon advisers, his style of decision making discouraged nuanced reflection on their part in favor of mutual arrival at black-or-white positions. That style was "hardly conducive to probing his advisers for latent disagreement, let alone reaching beyond them for additional information and options," Leon Sigal observed, adding that Truman probably never "fully appreciated exactly what the plans for atomic bombing called for." Or, to put things more generally, he plunged into decisions while inwardly protecting himself from awareness of troubling details and larger consequences.

Truman later claimed that "I made the only decision I ever knew how to make. I did what I thought was right." He no doubt believed that, but such moralism could intensify his belligerent behavior while permitting him to retain a sense of virtue.

The Trinity Power Surge

Trinity, the successful atomic-bomb test at Alamogordo, transformed the emotional world of Truman and his advisers. Now the abstract "thing" had turned into an awesome actuality that engulfed them all. Truman, Stimson, Byrnes, and other American leaders at Potsdam were taken directly into the event by the official report General Thomas Farrell wrote for General Groves, who forwarded it immediately to Potsdam. In it

Farrell sounds less like a military engineer than an awed religious supplicant overwhelmed by a supernatural force:

> No man-made phenomenon of such tremendous power had ever occurred before. . . . Thirty seconds after the explosion came, first, the air blast pressing hard against the people and things, to be followed almost immediately by the strong, sustained, awesome roar which warned of doomsday and made us feel that we puny things were blasphemous to dare tamper with the forces heretofore reserved to The Almighty. Words are inadequate tools for the job of acquainting those not present with the physical, mental, and psychological effects. It had to be witnessed to be realized.

Such feelings can readily become associated with an embrace of the all-powerful entity. That was very much the case with the American leaders at Potsdam, as they were drawn into this unprecedented eruption of power. The report was sent through channels by special courier from Groves to Stimson, who read it out loud, in full, to Truman and Byrnes, over the course of about an hour. Stimson noted that Truman was "immensely pleased" and "said it gave him an entirely new feeling of confidence." Churchill observed that Truman had been "much fortified by" something and, upon reading the report, said that "he now understood how this pepping up had taken place and that he felt the same way."

Eight days later Stimson noted the decision makers' "difference of psychology" since the successful test, from which he himself was not immune—"A great change . . . had [been] produced in my own psychology." Indeed, upon receiving the earlier cable, Stimson himself was observed to be "visibly jubilant" and the ancient diplomat even "cut a gay caper." Among the American delegation in general, few could contain their enthusiasm for the bomb. Truman observed that "Byrnes and my fellows seemed to be walking on air." Significantly, even those who had been skeptical or critical of the bomb, such as Admiral Leahy, joined the general sense that the Soviet Union was no longer needed to terminate the war successfully. Truman himself became more assertive and "bossed" (in Churchill's phrase) the Potsdam meetings.

What was the nature of the psychological change that so struck Stimson? The experience included a surge of power, a new and transcendent blending of self and weapon based no longer on its mysterious potential but on its actual manifestation of a realm of force so vast as to seem more than natural. The reports of Trinity, combining direct personal experience with more detached scientific observation, enabled American leaders far away in Potsdam to share in the kind of conversion reaction undergone by William Laurence and some of the nuclear scientists. Given his authority as president and his personal psychological struggles, Truman was especially susceptible to that kind of conversion to nuclearism—to an embrace of, and lasting dependency on, the bomb's "doomsday" power.

More than that, the self could now be allied with a brilliantly success-ful project, one that promised ultimate solutions to multiple problems, including checking the Soviets. The illusory quality of these expectations was recognized at the time by McCloy, who noted that Truman and Churchill went off to their next round with Stalin "like little boys with a big red apple secreted on their person." McCloy himself feared "the com-mencement of the destruction of modern civilization" and commented further in his diary that, with "the callousness of men and their leaders, the whole thing seems ominous." What was ominous was the rush of power and energy toward use of the bomb experienced by the people making the decisions, most significantly by Truman himself.

There is still another way to look at Trinity that has not been fully appreciated. Prior to the test there had been active, if brief, discussion about the advisability of a *demonstration* of the bomb's destructive power in an uninhabited area. The Scientific Advisory Panel, chaired by Oppen-heimer, could recommend (as we have noted) no feasible demonstration likely to bring an end to the war. In addition to defusing the scientific protest, that focus on a demonstration set up a technical either–or situation: either you demonstrate the bomb in a harmless fashion or you use it to kill many people. Left out of their equation was the very real possibility of achieving a Japanese surrender by allowing them to keep their emperor or waiting for the Soviets to enter the war. These options were never pre-sented to the scientists, and Oppenheimer later testified that he and his colleagues "didn't know beans about the military situation in Japan," only that an invasion was "inevitable."

Yet, with Trinity, a demonstration did indeed take place—not before Japanese or United Nations or Russian leaders but before *American* scien-tists and high-level administrators. The vivid reports on Trinity extended the demonstration up the ladder of decision making so that Stimson, Byrnes, and Truman could feel like virtual witnesses of the extraordinary event. One could say that the demonstrators became victims of their own demonstration—transfixed, enthralled, and subsumed by the very power they had unleashed. So we did demonstrate the bomb after all—but only to ourselves.

And once demonstrated in this fashion, no further demonstration for others was required. The weapon was ready for use, and those in charge of it were ecstatically bound up with that readiness. As McCloy's biographer has observed, from that moment "the fact of the atomic bomb as at last an operational weapon was always uppermost in the minds of American officials. . . . Truman himself was now counting on the bomb, perhaps to end the Pacific war and certainly to ameliorate some of his diplomatic problems with the Soviets." In practical terms, then, for Truman and others, the demonstration resulted in a powerful bomb-centered surge.

The Trinity power surge is all the more tragic when one imagines a quite different reaction that conceivably could have occurred. The bomb tested at Trinity produced two unexpected results: The force of the blast exceeded all expectations (by a factor of four), and the so-called visual effect was beyond imagination. If not for the power surge, these two surprises might have raised troubling questions about going ahead with using the bomb against Japan. Much greater explosive force meant much higher casualties in a target city. On the other hand, the spectacular visual display made a demonstration shot more likely to produce a Japanese surrender.

Oppenheimer himself would later admit that, after witnessing the test, he thought that a demonstration, which he had previously ruled out, might actually work—perhaps a bomb detonated high over Japan at night, lighting up the sky everywhere. But he did not try to reopen this option. Three other prominent scientists immediately suggested that the atomic explosion be used to blind Japanese troops rather than kill noncombatants, but nothing came of their idea. As Oppenheimer later observed, it was too late . . . "the whole mechanism for use had been set in motion."

Theoretically, however, the explicit reports from Trinity sent to Truman and his party in Potsdam could have caused a change in plans. Stimson, for example, noted "far greater destructive power than we expected" from the test. Yet there is no record of any of the men at Potsdam pausing to consider the moral implications of unleashing the "far greater" force over the center of a large city. Instead, that power, which they now controlled, was experienced only as a virtue.

Kai Erikson has raised another vital issue surrounding Trinity: The successful test signaled with virtual certainty that the planned invasion of Japan would never take place. "For what sane power, with the atomic weapon securely in its arsenal," Erikson asks, "would hurl a million or more of its sturdiest young men on a heavily fortified mainland?" After Trinity, Truman could drop the bomb or negotiate: these were the only genuine choices. The risks in waiting to use the bomb were small—no major battles with the Japanese were on the horizon. And if negotiations failed, Truman always had the option of dropping the bomb.

But the Trinity power surge had the opposite psychological effect. It transported Truman and his advisers into the center of the bomb's energy field.

The president's excitement concerning the weapon was reflected by his impatience to tell outsiders about it. On August 3, Truman's first full day at sea on the *Augusta* returning home, he called together the correspondents on board and, making use of a looseleaf notebook, "began telling them about the atomic bomb and its history." He spoke with emotion, "thankful that we had a weapon in our hands which would speed the end of the war," but with some apprehension about "such a monstrous weapon of destruction." What is remarkable about this scene is that it reportedly occurred three days *before* the bombing of Hiroshima. The entire atomic-bomb project was still top secret, including the Trinity test and certainly the plans for bombing two Japanese cities. The reporters, who pledged to keep the information to themselves, found "the secret . . . so big and terrifying that we could not discuss it with each other," one of them later observed. Yet Truman had the need to share his exuberance with others, even with those who would ordinarily be the last people one would choose to share a secret.

Truman apparently did the same thing two days later, with an audience of the *Augusta*'s junior officers at dinner over dessert and coffee. Answering questions, he said that he had made no special deal with the Russians because the United States had developed a new weapon and now did not need them to defeat Japan. He explained further that the weapon was equal to twenty thousand tons of TNT "exploded on a single target at one time," that it had been "developed in total secrecy," and "had been tested, and reports indicated that it could end the war." He added the observation, just before leaving, that it "is the biggest gamble in history," with two billion dollars having been spent on it, and "We will have the final answer on its effectiveness in a very short time."

Significantly, he did not mention these incidents in his memoirs, where he spoke of briefing the journalists and others on the bomb project only *after* Hiroshima. But here was the president revealing America's ultimate secret, and doing so enthusiastically, in some detail, with little concern about who might be listening—and not just once but twice. To be sure, he was on a ship in the middle of the high seas, so he could be confident that the information would be kept from the outside world—but for how long? In the second incident he no doubt took pleasure in informing servicemen that the war would soon be over and they could go home. But what if the Hiroshima and Nagasaki bombs did not work, and what might have happened to his political career if this violation of secrecy were revealed and had significant consequences? One can only assume that he was so excited by the weapon about to be used, his mind so possessed by it, that he could not contain himself, could not refrain from sharing his atomic rush with friendly groups that happened to surround him.

Then on August 6, upon receiving a message from Stimson that Hiroshima had been successfully bombed, Truman grabbed the officer carrying the message and said, "This is the greatest thing in history!" After a confirmatory second message a few minutes later, he called out across the enlisted men's mess to Byrnes and read him the message aloud, adding, "It's time for us to get on home." He was "exuberant," in a manner comparable to the scientists at the moment of the Trinity test. So much so that he tapped on a glass with a utensil to make an announcement to the enlisted men present—much as one might do before making a toast—declaring that "we have just dropped a new bomb on Japan which has more power than twenty thousand tons of TNT. It has been an overwhelming success!" The crew cheered and Truman himself, according to a reporter, "was not actually laughing but there was a broad smile on his face." He then went to the officers' ward to make the same announcement and declared, "We won the gamble." And he said that he had never been happier about any announcement he had ever made.*

One must quickly add that Truman's euphoria was shared not only by Byrnes and other advisers and the crew on the *Augusta,* but also by the American people. But Americans in general had not, at least at this point, allied themselves with the weapon as Truman had. His embrace of its infinite power, and resulting sense of omnipotence, could be termed his ultimate self-deception.

Power and Fear

Why did Truman decide to drop the atomic bombs? We already know that there is no single answer, no single "reason." We know also that he was at first caught up in a flow of feeling surrounding the weapon and that subsequently he came to assert himself by entering actively into that flow and contributing a great deal toward its culminating in the weapon's use. To be sure, the kinds of struggles we have described in him—particularly the numbing and dissociation in connection with the bomb—could have occurred in others thrust into his position. To some degree, such patterns are inherent in dealing with the weapon itself.

But we must come back to the fact that it was he who underwent them, he who made a fateful decision. And there remains the possibility that at least some people in that situation might *not* have made that decision. McCloy was hinting at such a possibility when he said of Truman, "He always gives me the impression of too quick judgment," and viewed him as "less composed" and speaking with "less of an air of thought and experience about him" than either Stalin or Clement Attlee (who replaced Churchill at Potsdam upon his election as prime minister). McCloy was similarly critical of the president's closest advisers, notably Byrnes, as neither "particularly intellectually minded" nor "enlightened," so that in all the Potsdam discussions "there was no clear evidence of an outstanding mind." What McCloy seemed to mean by "an outstanding mind" is one

---

* *Then he went off to attend a comedy revue put on by the crew, "bellylaughing at the entertainment,"* News-week *reported.*

that might have transcended immediate pressures in favor of a wiser policy. We will return to that theme in raising such a question—admittedly only conjecture—about Franklin Roosevelt. But first we need to consider the question of why Truman acted as he did, which in turn tells us much about why the bomb was used.

We have seen that Truman inherited a project with powerful secret momentum, technological and political and bureaucratic, derived from an assumed "race" for the weapon that would "win the war"; and that the product of that project, in turn, was drawn into the lethal momentum of the air war's extension into unhindered city bombing. That combined momentum was intensified by military and intellectual impulses to "try out" this extraordinary device and "see what it would do"—along with a less frequent but occasionally articulated (by people like Conant and Oppenheimer) assumption that dropping the bomb on a city would sufficiently shock world leaders to bring about some form of international control of the weapon. Well under way when Truman entered the scene was what Michael Sherry called the "slow accretion of large fears, thoughtless assumptions, and incremental decisions" that led to Hiroshima and Nagasaki. Collective energies and passions created a high likelihood of use, which is why we can speak of an atrocity-producing situation, but never to the point of eliminating the possibility of actions by individual people, notably Truman, that could have prevented such use.

One way of grasping Truman's complex motivations is to return to the concept of "demonstration." Trinity, as we have seen, was a demonstration for American decision makers. The impulse toward using the weapon on Japanese cities had to do with a further, much more concrete, demonstration of the weapon's effects on structures and people, with at least three significant audiences in mind: the Japanese, the Russians, and the Americans.

The Japanese always remained the primary audience, the ones who would be overwhelmed by the weapon and quickly surrender. The Russians increasingly became an audience with the growing antagonisms between the two countries in 1945 about postwar policies. For an American audience there was a need to justify the two-billion-dollar bomb project. But given the extraordinary daily pressures from all directions—and the way in which we function psychologically—these "audiences" inevitably merged in Truman's mind. The specific importance of any one of them became difficult to gauge, for Truman himself at the time and for all subsequent observers.

For instance, as president and commander in chief, Truman felt impelled throughout to prosecute the war vigorously, win it absolutely, and take any steps that could save American lives. But as he began to realize that the war had been won, and came to see the Russians as dangerous and the American people as restive, he underwent a shift in focus. As a number of observers have noted, that shift was from military to political imagery. He had said of the Russians when anticipating the success of the weapon, "I'll certainly have a hammer on those boys," and, with Byrnes, associated the weapon's use with exerting "control" over the Russians. He also shared with Groves and Byrnes a profound anxiety about the effects on the American public of a congressional investigation of an unproductive Manhattan Project, all the more so as one who had made his name as a demon congressional investigator of defense industries. (When interviewed years later for his ghostwritten memoirs and asked about his *first* thought upon hearing from Groves and Stimson about the atomic program, his reply was: "I hoped that it would be successful, particularly since it cost $2,600,000,000 . . . that was $200,000,000 a pound for the first bomb, an expensive bit of explosive.")

These motivations involving Russian and American audiences could be discussed in-house among the decision-making elite but were morally unacceptable—to Truman himself or as an explanation to the American public—as reasons for dropping the bomb on a civilian population. Dropping the bomb to shock the Japanese audience into surrender was the only *acceptable* motivation, and was certainly real for Truman, but also exaggeratedly seized upon by him. That psychological maneuver, mostly outside of awareness, rendered the Japanese the *only* audience and thereby negated the other two in his own reconstruction of events. He could fuel this Japanese-centered motivation with his long-standing rage at the enemy for its atrocities.

Did Truman ever consider using the emperor option to end the war without using the bomb? He apparently did, at least part of the time and in part of his mind. But the idea of doing that was fearful on several counts. It could be seen (and experienced by him) as an expression of "appeasement" or weakness and a betrayal of those who had made so many sacrifices in war. Also, moral clarity concerning the enemy's evil and our own virtue required that the surrender be "unconditional." Moreover, there was no certainty that overtures toward the emperor would actually bring about a surrender, given the known intra-Japanese conflicts and the persistent influence of military fanaticism. These fears became part of overall anxiety in Truman and others about not using a formidable weapon to further most aggressively our war aims.

Overall, we can say that these various fears of alternatives to the bomb could powerfully evoke Truman's doubts about his own strength, courage, and decisiveness as president and commander in chief. Deeply concerned about living up to the standards of earlier American leaders, Truman could associate use of the bomb with self-worth and American loyalty.

His fears combined, strangely and tragically, with bomb-centered omnipotence. Particularly after Trinity, the bomb could seem to enable one to do *everything*—to solve and transcend all immediate problems, bring about instant victory as well as control of the future, and offer those who used it a deity's dominion and immortality. Truman decided to use the bomb because, like so many others, he was drawn to its ultimate power—and because he feared *not using it*.

Nagasaki

And what about Nagasaki? As noted earlier, there was no presidential directive—or decision by anyone else—specifically related to dropping the second bomb. The atomic weapons in the U.S. arsenal, according to the July 25 order, were to be used "as soon as made ready," and the second bomb was ready within three days of Hiroshima. Nagasaki has been termed a victim of automated atomic warfare, but that is not precisely accurate, for the assembly line (as we will now see) was subject to fits and starts, and Truman could have shut it off at any time.

Criticism of the attack on Nagasaki, which has always exceeded that of Hiroshima, has centered on the issue of why Truman did not reserve for himself the authority to order each atomic attack separately; and in any case, why he did not step in and stop the second mission after the success of the first to allow Japan a few more days to contemplate surrender (especially because the Soviet entry into the war was imminent). The first bomb was apparently sufficient to speed the surrender offer, which emerged from Tokyo on August 10 (and could not have come much quicker). "The rights and wrongs of Hiroshima are debatable," Telford Taylor, the former chief prosecutor at the Nuremberg trials, once observed, "but I have never heard a plausible justification of Nagasaki"—which he labeled a war crime.

A few critics, mainly in Japan, have suggested that the reason the bombs were used in tandem was that the U.S. wanted to try out both the uranium and plutonium bombs. Yet one need not accept that motivation to wonder about the overwhelming, and seemingly thoughtless, impulse to automatically use a second atomic bomb even more powerful than the first.

Evidence concerning why Nagasaki was not spared reveals much about Truman's handling of the entire process of using the bomb. A major factor was the single-minded insistence of Leslie Groves that it would take two bombs, delivered in quick order, to make the necessary impression on Japan. As the British author Ian Clark put it, the quick one-two punch "had never been explicitly endorsed" by Truman or anyone else. After the Hiroshima bombing, Groves pushed for another drop as soon as possible. The second run was originally scheduled for August 11, and if that schedule had been adhered to, it would have come a full day after Japan's initial offer to surrender—meaning the mission likely would have been canceled. But bad weather was forecast, so Groves, anxious to get the bomb in the air, pushed the date up two days, knowing that this would involve rushing preparations.

On August 9, however, there was rain and lightning, a serious problem because operational plans called for "visual bombing." There were so few atomic bombs on line, they could not afford to waste one because of a radar mistake, and the Target Committee had declared that a bomber should return to base without dropping the bomb rather than use radar. Still, Groves "decided that we should take that chance," and so General Thomas Farrell (his representative on Tinian) ordered that the flight proceed.

But where the Hiroshima mission had gone off without a hitch, the Nagasaki run was beset by problems. Before takeoff, a fuel pump in the lead bomber, *Bock's Car,* piloted by Charles Sweeney, had failed, meaning several hundred gallons of fuel could not be used. Still, the B-29 took off. Then a rendezvous with a spotter plane was delayed, and Sweeney encountered dense clouds covering Kokura, the primary target. With fuel running low, and no guarantee of better weather over Nagasaki, operational plans dictated a return to base. But instead, Sweeney pushed on. Now there was no turning back: *Bock's Car* either had to drop the multi-million-dollar bomb on Nagasaki or dump it in the ocean, for there was no way the plane could reach Okinawa on low fuel bearing a heavy load.

Over Nagasaki there were more clouds. Sweeney decided to drop the bomb by radar if necessary, *despite orders to the contrary.* According to bombardier Kermit Beahan, an opening in the clouds appeared at the last moment, he spotted a portion of the city, and hurriedly released the bomb. The weapon exploded over the largest Catholic cathedral in the Far East, missing its target by about two miles. It caused horrendous casualties and devastation, but only about half of what would have occurred had the bomb hit its mark. The most authoritative account would later estimate that of the more than one hundred thousand dead in the city, only about two hundred and fifty were Japanese military personnel—the same number of prisoners of war killed or injured by the blast.

In the case of Nagasaki, the date of the mission was advanced, a defective plane was allowed to take off in bad weather, the mission was not aborted over Kokura, and an atomic bomb was dropped off target instead of in the ocean. The question, of course, remains—Why did all this happen? Surely crucial was Groves's determination to follow the Hiroshima bomb with a knockout blow: his conviction was that "once you get your opponent reeling, you keep him reeling and never let him recover." As Ian Clark recently concluded, Groves "was prepared to sacrifice all of the previously elaborated guidelines in order to implement his own strategy." This sense of absolute urgency was passed down the line from Groves to Farrell to Sweeney and carried the mission through to its grim conclusion.*

Many years later, Groves would explain that Truman or Stimson could

---

* *Groves, upon learning of the Japanese surrender offer, decided that his "one-two" strategy had worked. But now that it had worked, he was pleased to learn that the Nagasaki bomb—which exploded with nearly twice the explosive power of the Hiroshima bomb—had landed so far off target. "I was considerably relieved when I got the bombing report," Groves revealed in his memoirs, "which indicated a smaller number of casualties than we had expected." This is surely one of the saddest commentaries of its time. "If ever a dark view of human nature had a profound source," an English scientist has written, "the destruction of Nagasaki touched that source."*

have stopped the Nagasaki mission with a single word. But until he heard that word, he was running the show. Similarly, Martin Sherwin has commented, "If Washington had maintained closer control over the scheduling of the atomic bomb raids the annihilation of Nagasaki could have been avoided." But neither Truman nor Stimson was overseeing those bombing arrangements. Authority had devolved to military and technical people—that is, to Leslie Groves. After learning of Nagasaki, as we have seen, Truman quickly ordered that no further bombs be dropped without his express permission, to give Japan a reasonable chance to surrender, and to restore his control of the process.

If Roosevelt Had Lived

The question is frequently asked whether Roosevelt might have done things differently. That question is not really answerable, but its asking has significance. Its subtext is: Could a stronger, wiser person have found an alternative to dropping the atomic bomb on a populated city?

The question can be read almost as a plea, whether for a magical reversal of history or for a different outcome next time. It is the kind of wisdom sought as early as May 1945 by Oswald C. Brewster, an obscure engineer working in a branch of the Manhattan Project, in his prophetic letter (which Henry Stimson called "a remarkable document") warning of the danger of bringing the bomb into the world. He pleaded, among other things, that Truman seek "disinterested counsel" from an "unbiased" group of people—as distinguished from those involved in the project and therefore committed to its successful completion. It is a request not likely to have been directed at Roosevelt, for he had been president for so long and assumed such stature that for many he had come to embody something close to omniscience.

The actual evidence on what Roosevelt might have done is meager, yet suggestive. We have mentioned his memo, with Churchill, that when available, the bomb "might perhaps, after mature consideration, be employed against the Japanese." Four days later, Roosevelt had an extensive discussion on the bomb with Vannevar Bush and raised the question as to whether the bomb might only be held as a threat instead of actually being used, a question they decided to postpone until the bomb was closer to completion (this was just September 1944).

Finally, Alexander Sachs, the investment banker who served as intermediary in getting the Einstein-Szilard letter advocating work on an atomic weapon to Roosevelt's attention in 1939, claimed to have had a series of conversations with FDR between then and 1944 in which the president explored various alternatives. Sachs told Henry Wallace that, "the way he [Sachs] had planned it out with Roosevelt was that the first bomb would be dropped with representatives present from all neutral nations, including those neutrals who leaned toward the fascists" and the second "on an island off the coast of Japan, after the Japs had been warned to vacate all their civilian population." Sachs went on to condemn our use of the bomb and to make derogatory comments about Groves ("very ambitious, intelligent, and a fascist"), as well as Bush and Conant (each "a tool of the big corporate interests"). There is some possibility that Sachs exaggerated his own involvement in the bomb issue, as well as Roosevelt's reserve about the weapon. Nonetheless, the overall evidence suggests that Roosevelt did have an early sense of the bomb's danger to the world and that he at least entertained concrete alternatives to using the weapon on a heavily populated city.

Hence, McGeorge Bundy speaks of "tantalizing hints that Franklin Roosevelt was troubled about the basic question of using the weapon against Japan in a way that his successor never was." In talking to us recently about this matter, Bundy said Roosevelt could have acted differently because he really did "have it in his head that you're not sure you want to use this damn thing. . . . and if he had been the senior decision maker, what are the chances the Grew idea would have been heard . . . way up?" Some years ago the historian Samuel Eliot Morison similarly emphasized the likelihood that Roosevelt would have taken Grew's advice "to give public assurance that if Japan surrendered 'unconditionally,' she could keep her Emperor." He stressed that Grew was "an old school mate and personal friend of President Roosevelt's," and that the position he espoused was one the Department of State "had envisaged . . . even at the beginning of the war."

Interestingly, two scientists, prominent in relation to the bomb, also expressed the belief that Roosevelt might not have used it. About a year after Hiroshima and Nagasaki, Albert Einstein declared (as reported by the

United Press) "that President Roosevelt would have forbidden the atomic bombing of Hiroshima." He inferred that Roosevelt would have been less susceptible to "a desire to end war in the Pacific by any means before Russia's participation," which Einstein believed to be the American motivation for using the bomb. Philip Morrison, more recently, told us that "I think if Roosevelt had lived, it's possible that things would have gone differently." In Truman's case, even if he had not wished to use the weapon, "they [presumably Groves, Byrnes, and others] would have talked and talked and talked, brow-beating him until he gave in. He had no authority over them. He was neither eloquent nor tied to them by great bonds of obligation. Obviously he was not a great man the way Roosevelt was." In contrast to Truman, Morrison concluded, "Roosevelt found immediate obedience to anything he said," and, moreover, could well have had "wiser things to say."*

Our discussion of Roosevelt raises the more general question of the possibility of human autonomy and wise restraint in relation to such weapons and to the radically new historical situation created by them. One could say that, because history is forward moving, one's past experience can never fully prepare a leader (or follower) for what will be encountered. Certainly, no one could be ready for the atomic bomb. The question then is, How much could any American president have extended his moral imagination to address the new phenomenon in ways most beneficial to human beings in general?

Truman was knowledgeable about history but suspicious of change and disinclined to moral reflection. Roosevelt, these commentators suggest, was more capable of moral reflection, more imaginative concerning change, more complex and many-sided—all of which could have contributed to his response to such a demanding historical moment. And he did, of course, command much greater presidential authority than Truman. It could be further argued that Roosevelt, having authorized the bomb, was more psychologically able to stop it. Truman, in contrast, inherited that authorization—or responsibility—from Roosevelt and might well have felt

---

* Both Einstein and Morrison saw themselves as contributing to bomb work for a Roosevelt-led country. Moreover, a scenario of FDR's preventing the use of the bomb on a population more or less reverses the actual outcome in a way that could ameliorate their personal guilt. These psychological currents in no way invalidate Einstein's and Morrison's speculations.

unable or disinclined to "violate" that authorization by not using the weapon.

Our view is that, yes, Roosevelt could possibly have taken a different turn—which means that it was at least possible for Truman to do the same. One must add, however, that such an act on the part of either would have required an extraordinary combination of courage, moral vision, and capacity to step back from immediate pressures (on behalf of a commitment to humankind)—a combination sufficiently rare that it should discourage all of us from creating situations in which it is required of any president.

CHAPTER 3

The Afterlife

"Hideously Uncomfortable"

In November 1945, Robert Oppenheimer and Dean Acheson, then undersecretary of state, met with President Harry Truman in the White House. Oppenheimer had sought high audience to convey his mounting agitation about atomic danger and to urge immediate steps toward arrangements with the Soviet Union and others for international control of the weaponry. Apparently feeling that his sense of urgency was not sufficiently shared, Oppenheimer blurted out something on the order of "Mr. President, I have blood on my hands." Truman quietly reassured Oppenheimer that appropriate steps were being taken, and ended the meeting shortly thereafter. Truman made his displeasure clear enough in telling Acheson after the meeting not to "bring that son of a bitch around here again." Truman referred to the incident in writing months later and told the story on a number of occasions, referring to Oppenheimer not by name but as "the crybaby scientist." The president would imitate the scientist's wringing of the hands and explain, "I told him the blood was on my hands—to let me worry about that."

What infuriated the president here—and what was to upset him for the rest of his life—was any reflection that focused upon ethical responsibility for the bomb's mass killing. To cut off such reflection, Truman had to construct a simplified image of a president taking responsibility for his people, a father bloodying his hands to protect his family. In actuality, however, Truman was protecting himself from psychological culpability and pain. In this incident and related defensive maneuvers, Truman did much to create the model for overall American responses to Hiroshima and Nagasaki—responses having to do with insistent numbing and agitated dismissal of moral reflection.

To grasp this response, one must recognize the difficulty—perhaps impossibility—of anyone closely involved with the decision to open himself fully to its grotesque human consequences without being overwhelmed by anxiety and self-condemnation. It was Oppenheimer who remarked, "there is no doubt we were hideously uncomfortable about being associated with such slaughter," but Truman was subject to such uneasiness as well. To overcome it he invoked mechanisms that enabled him to avoid perceptions of "slaughter" in favor of those having to do with war-ending military necessity; and he even reversed the idea of slaughter with the refrain of having "saved lives."

Truman's—and America's—early post-Hiroshima triumphalism was inevitable, given the bomb's association with the victorious end of the war. That is why Truman's "greatest thing in history" statement could be followed by a declaration soon afterward that the news of Hiroshima had been the "happiest" announcement he ever made. That early triumphalism had enormous significance because it created a psychological model, in Truman and others, for associating the bomb with joyous and immortalizing victory.

But as evidence of what happened in Hiroshima became available, Truman experienced alternative feelings having to do with awe, dread, and self-doubt. In Stimson's diary entry of August 8, he tells of showing the president a photograph revealing "the total destruction and . . . the radius of damage," which led Truman to speak of "the terrible responsibility that such destruction placed upon us here and himself." That same day a friendly Democratic committeeman sent a telegram to Truman expressing dismay over his reported jubilation: ". . . no president of the United States could ever be jubilant over any device that could kill innocent human beings. Please make it clear that it is not destruction but the end of destruction that is the cause of jubilation." Truman responded the next day with a note claiming, with almost bizarre falsification, that "the good feeling on my part was over the fact Russia entered the war with Japan and not because we had invented a new engine of destruction."

Then, after the reporting of the Nagasaki bomb on August 9—in response to the telegram from Senator Russell urging him not to let up on "total war"—Truman replied (as we noted earlier) that "I can't bring myself to believe that, because they are beasts, we should ourselves act in the same manner." He said further that "I certainly regret the necessity of wiping out whole populations because of the 'pigheadedness' of the leaders of a nation, and . . . I am not going to do it unless it is absolutely necessary." Two days later, Truman called upon similar imagery in replying to a letter from a church official protesting the Hiroshima decision. "When you have to deal with a beast you have to treat him as a beast," Truman explained. But he also asserted that "nobody is more disturbed over the use of Atomic bombs than I am."

The pressure, from within and without, to acknowledge at least minimally the human effects of the bomb is revealed in revisions of the August 9 speech Truman made to the nation. The original draft referred to Hiroshima as "purely a military base," but "purely" was deleted in the final version. The assertion in the draft that "we did not want in the first attack to destroy the lives of women and children and innocent civilians" was changed to "we wished . . . to avoid, in so far as possible, the killing of civilians" (more killing is acknowledged but worded more abstractly). As Bernstein observed, "Hiroshima and Nagasaki had started to transform official thinking about atomic weapons before altering most popular American thinking. Nuclear war would never again seem so morally comfortable. . . ."

Staying with the Weapon

But that was as far as it went for Truman, and even then he expressed not the slightest suggestion of doubt or regret concerning his decision. Acknowledging the atomic "tragedy" in no way stopped him, or other American policy makers, from continuing to regard the instrument as a weapon to be further developed and tested. Indeed, Truman's avoidance of broader reflection contributed to his reluctance to explore fully the possibilities for international control of the weapon. Here he differed from Conant and Oppenheimer, who grew impatient with Truman's lack of initiative.

The tests at Bikini in July 1946 were to emerge out of bitter Army-Navy rivalry, along with Truman's willingness to turn over weapons policy to the military bureaucracy. Oppenheimer wrote to Truman expressing reservations about the wisdom of the tests and politely asked that he be excused from his designated role as an observer. Truman of course associated this with the blood-on-my-hands incident and, in a memorandum to Acheson, expressed contempt for the " 'crybaby' scientist." He added: "I think he has concocted himself an alibi in this letter." The alibi had mostly to do with avoiding participation in the Bikini tests but also, from Truman's psychological vantage point, with Oppenheimer's general unwillingness to defend unconditionally, and *extend through new actions,* his own role in making and using the weapon. Oppenheimer was, after all, not just *any* crybaby scientist; moral conflicts expressed by such a leading figure (though Oppenheimer was far from consistent in these matters) could threaten Truman's own inner struggle to suppress such doubts.

More than that, Truman gave evidence of a certain amount of nostalgia for the power he wielded when using atomic bombs. Truman wrote many angry or nasty letters and memos that he knew better than to send or implement, but which he nonetheless wished to be identified with as he did not have them destroyed. One such desk note of that period expressed frustration with people who seemed to stand in his way in both domestic and international issues, and included the following: "Get plenty of Atomic Bombs on hand—drop one on Stalin, put the United Nations to work and eventually set up a free world." The memo suggests not only the range of Truman's angry fantasy but his continuing sense of the atomic bomb as a powerful personal ally and a usable weapon. Even when expressed as fantasy, such sentiments required of Truman the kind of numbing and closure that he was already cultivating.

At the same time, Truman could be quite systematic in his efforts to promote acceptance of the atomic bombings. His response to a letter from Roman Bohnen, the actor who portrayed Truman in the original version of the MGM atomic bomb film *The Beginning or the End,* reveals this impulse clearly.

As we will explore later, the movie studio deleted a key scene in the 1947 film after the White House complained that it pictured Truman making his decision to use the bomb in a hasty manner. For the re-take, based on a new script revised by the White House, MGM replaced Bohnen with another actor and instructed him to portray Truman with more of a "military bearing." No doubt upset, Bohnen wrote the president a polite, but slyly barbed, letter. He noted Truman's concerns about the depiction of the Hiroshima decision, adding that he could "well imagine the emotional torture you must have experienced in giving that fateful order, torture not only then, but now—perhaps even more so." People would be talking about the decision for a hundred years, he observed, "and posterity is quite apt to be a little rough" on Truman "for not having ordered that very first atomic bomb to be dropped *outside* of Hiroshima. . . ." His suggestion: Truman should play himself in the film. If he believed in his decision so strongly, why not re-enact it himself?

A few days later, Truman responded warmly, despite Bohnen's thinly veiled sarcasm. He thanked the actor for his suggestion but admitted that he did not have "the talent to be a movie star." Then he took the trouble to defend the decision to use the bomb, which revealed his edginess on this subject. After the weapon was tested, and the Japanese given "ample warning," the bomb was used against two cities "devoted almost exclusively to the manufacture of ammunition and weapons of destruction":

> I have no qualms about it whatever for the simple reason that it was believed the dropping of not more than two of these bombs would bring the war to a close. The Japanese in their conduct of the war had been vicious and cruel savages and I came to the conclusion that if two hundred and fifty thousand young Americans could be saved from slaughter the bomb should be dropped, and it was.

What is most surprising about this episode is that Truman generally ignored critical letters like Bohnen's—or else wrote an angry, unsent response. It is possible that his inner discomfort on the subject prevented him from grasping the irony of Bohnen's remarks.

Repeat Decision

When the time came to make a decision about the hydrogen bomb (in late 1949 and early 1950) Truman had settled into the presidency and was accustomed to wielding its power, as he had not been at the time of the atomic-bomb decision. But he must have been struck by the fact that many of the leading scientists in the atomic-bomb effort (including Oppenheimer, Fermi, and Conant) now took a stand against the development of hydrogen bombs, noting their limitless destruction and calling them "weapons of genocide." They were joined by such prominent nonscientific figures as George Kennan and David Lilienthal. Truman, however, had become increasingly antagonistic toward the Soviet Union and was profoundly affected by the terrifying idea of the enemy potentially possessing of the hydrogen bomb—all the more so as the Soviets had recently detonated an atomic bomb and were known to covet the next generation of weapons as well. Truman was under enormous pressure from most of his political and military advisers (notably Dean Acheson), and from pro-bomb scientists (notably Ernest Lawrence) to go ahead with the project—so much so that there existed what was called a "steamroller" effect.

Observers differ as to whether negotiation with the Soviets to find a way to prevent these draconian devices from being developed could have succeeded. The American physicist Herbert York, himself long involved in weapons making, explored the question and concluded that Truman, with minimal risk, could have at least initiated such an attempt. According to David Holloway's more recent study based on Soviet documents, any such effort would have been doomed to failure. Yet it must be said that even Truman's generally hagiographic biographer, David McCullough, was troubled by the alacrity of the hydrogen-bomb decision. Truman, he pointed out, left nothing in writing about the decision, making it difficult to tell how much he had struggled with it. "It would have been preferable surely—wiser, more prudent—to have given the entire question longer, closer examination . . . ," McCullough observed. McGeorge Bundy called the decision "quick and unexamined." Truman asserted that "there actually was no decision to make on the H-bomb," a close adviser noted at the time. Later, Truman claimed that the "original program inaugurated by President Roosevelt was intended to create the so-called Hydrogen Bomb. There wasn't any reason for all the conversation and foolishness that went on publicly about it, as the machinery had been set in motion to arrive at that conclusion in 1943."

Yet this may well have been the most significant decision ever made in relation to nuclear weapons, as it carried military destructiveness into the realm of the infinite and, in that sense, could be considered more revolutionary even than the atomic bomb. Moreover, careful scientific calculations were available about precisely this aspect of the weaponry, quite unlike the radical uncertainties surrounding the appearance of the atomic bomb. The announcement Truman prepared, with the considerable help of his spokesman, Charles Ross, misleadingly de-emphasized this revolutionary feature, but there was considerable truth nonetheless in the sentence "I have directed the Atomic Energy Commission to *continue* its work on all forms of atomic weapons, including the so-called hydrogen or super-bomb."

After Hiroshima and Nagasaki, Truman maintained a policy of ongoing development and testing of the various facets of the weaponry. Whatever his moments of humane concern, he was reluctant to take any steps that might throw into question America's security and dominant standing in the world. With the hydrogen bomb, then, Truman once more found himself in an atrocity-producing situation; once more he was drawn into the weapon's unique radius of power and at the same time was afraid not to take the next step.

Indeed his earlier decision had great bearing on this one. Having committed himself to the principle of the atomic bomb as a weapon—and just as important, having the need to defend that commitment—he was hard put not to act on that principle again, whatever the revolutionary dimensions of the new device. To stop and reflect not only was alien to his style but also could have raised intolerable questions about the morality of his earlier decision.

"I'd Do It Again."

Because the hydrogen-bomb decision did not result in mass killing, it was the atomic-bomb decision Truman spent his life defending. His responses were always curt, but they hardened over the years as he developed a consistent way of addressing the matter—or, one might say, of avoiding any broad approach to it. "We just had to drop the bomb," he explained.

Although he did everything to maintain psychological distance, the subject would not go away. As more was learned about aftereffects, or new evidence about the Hiroshima decision emerged, Truman was inevitably, and repeatedly, asked to respond. At a press conference in 1947, Truman insisted that "I didn't have any doubt at the time" and had never had any doubt since, pointing to the lives saved. When a reporter mentioned a recent military analysis claiming that dropping the atomic bomb was unnecessary because the war had already been won, the president told a story about how a young student in a history class commented on mistakes in the maneuvers of General Lee and General Meade at Gettysburg, leaving the wise professor to observe that "any schoolboy's afterthought is worth more than all the generals' forethought." Truman became fond of uttering versions of that story to negate all questions about his decision to use the bomb. He would do the same with a more contemporary idiom (used also by Conant) in calling any questioning of the decision the opinion of a "Monday-morning quarterback." Truman's psychological policy was expressed by his comment "I don't believe in speculating on the mental feeling."

A favorite phrase was "I'd do it again" (1956) or "I would not hesitate to drop the A-bomb again" (1965). Or when asked if he would do it again, Truman might turn the question back on the journalist by asking in turn "Would you use artillery in a war?"—and when the answer was in the affirmative, Truman would declare triumphantly, "Well, there's your answer." On one occasion he snapped his fingers to indicate how quickly he had made up his mind to use the bomb. The response, of course, became ritualized but represented nonetheless a continuous assertion of intense defiance. The answer did not always make a clear distinction between using the weapon again in the same circumstances, or in new circumstances where its use might again be deemed necessary. Either way, the claim was that, under certain conditions, he was willing to inflict once more the grotesque suffering on a human population that the weapon caused.*

The Truman metaphor that perhaps became best known had to do with sleep. As early as 1959, he declared, as he did many times subsequently, that "I never lost any sleep over my decision." When asked later about having made such a glib claim, he made a stark distinction: "I lost plenty of sleep—but not over saving Japanese lives. I lost sleep worrying about our boys. . . . and it broke my heart when just one of our soldiers, sailors, or marines died." Much earlier he had summoned Paul Tibbets, the pilot of the *Enola Gay,* to the White House to tell him "Don't you ever lose any sleep over the fact that you planned and carried out that mission. It was my decision. You had no choice." Truman wanted *no one* to lose sleep over the bombings; they were to be understood as life-enhancing and necessary.

The image of sleep had particular importance for Truman. Although he did at times experience insomnia in connection with episodes of anxiety, especially when he was younger, he would later boast to people that he would fall asleep within seconds of his head's touching the pillow, and that this capacity enabled him to wake early and well rested. Quick sleep, then, was bound up with his overall self-confidence and efficacy. In emphasizing that he experienced no loss of this precious commodity in relation to the bomb, he was in one sense speaking literally and in another referring metaphorically to what was for him an ultimate form of moral steadfastness in preserving what was so crucial to preserve.

Truman consistently fended off requests for statements on the atomic age from groups concerned about the weaponry. When asked in 1957 by the editor of the *Bulletin of the Atomic Scientists* for a statement answering certain questions, his response was a refusal that, although terse, included his contentions that the bomb was a weapon of war and saved lives—and then he added:

---

* *Years after the atomic bombings people in Hiroshima were more angered at this kind of statement than by Truman's original decision to drop the bomb. As much as they deplored the weapon and viewed it as criminal, some expressed understanding of how it might be used under the pressure of war; but to speak more or less detachedly of using it again was to dismiss what victims had been subjected to and reject human lessons of the weapon.*

There has been a tremendous amount of conversation and writing on this subject, and undoubtedly there will be much more. Little of it, however, will be based on fact.

Three years later, in response to a similar request from the same journal for a statement for the fifteenth anniversary of its founding, Truman simply scrawled across the page a note to his secretary, "File. Know not very much about it."

His most demanding and (to us) interesting exchange took place in 1958. The Hiroshima City Council had sent him a resolution it had passed, which began politely but then protested "in deep indignation" a statement he had made about having felt "no compunction whatever" about ordering the atomic bombs dropped on Hiroshima and Nagasaki and that "hydrogen bombs would be put to use in [the] future in case of emergency." The resolution called the statement "a gross defilement committed on the people of Hiroshima and their fallen victims."

The former president wrote back thanking the chairman for the "courteous letter" and stated that "I am not in any way offended by the resolution"—a statement belied by the rest of the letter, for Truman went on to render an abrasively pedantic history lesson: The Japanese started the war by bombing Pearl Harbor without provocation, and "thousands of young Americans sailors and civilians [were] . . . murdered by this unwarranted and unheralded attack"; America's ultimatum from Potsdam in 1945 "evoked only a very curt and discourteous reply"; after a successful American demonstration on July 16, 1945, "of the greatest explosive force in the history of the world," it was decided to drop the weapon on two Japanese cities "devoted to war work," resulting in Japan's surrender a few days later; "the sacrifice of Hiroshima and Nagasaki was urgent and necessary for the prospective welfare of both Japan and the Allies"; "the need for such a fateful decision . . . never would have arisen . . . had we not been shot in the back by Japan at Pearl Harbor"; and that "in spite of that shot in the back . . . the United States of America has been willing to help in every way the restoration of Japan as a great and prosperous nation."

Truman reconstructed the series of actual events in a way that rendered history little more than a simple morality tale in which the Japanese bore total responsibility for the atomic bombings and he, as the American leader, performed an act of mercy in ordering them, even if that required a certain amount of sacrifice on the part of victims. Then he instructed his secretary to send the letter airmail. "Be sure enough stamps are on it!" he added.

The Japanese reply, after acknowledging the evil of Pearl Harbor, again protested Truman's justification of the original atomic bombings: "Why didn't you have conscience enough to avoid using such means as to completely destroy humanity and human civilization? Do you consider it a humane act to try to justify the outrageous murder of two hundred thousand civilians of Hiroshima, men and women, young and old, as a countermeasure for the surprise attack?" It went on to ask: "Do you consider your country which, having manufactured the atomic bomb, was aware of its explosive power and could anticipate the formidable destruction, be excused, just because it is a conqueror, for the crime of the first, the most cruel, and the largest-scale man-slaughter that has ever taken place in the history of mankind?" The letter closed with a request for a "frank and thoughtful reply"—a reply that never came, as Truman at that point ended the correspondence.

A few days later, a United Press dispatch recorded that Truman said, "He could not understand why the people of Hiroshima, however terribly they may have been hurt, still won't accept the fact that he had to give the order to drop the first atomic bomb on the Japanese city." That rather strange comment, on one level, asserts the logic of *everyone*—even, perhaps especially, the victims—accepting his justification of the decision. There is also at least the possibility that it contained (along with other actions to be discussed) an inchoate wish on his part for some kind of reconciliation with the people of Hiroshima.

Truman was sufficiently threatened by reflection on the atomic bombings that he would sometimes attack even those who were broadly sympathetic to him. The historian and former State Department official Herbert Feis had been introduced to Truman by Dean Acheson in 1957. After this he published a book in which he said that the Japanese would have surrendered within a few months even without the bomb, but its use was nonetheless justified by saving lives and ending the war as soon as possible. When Feis contacted the president again to obtain more precise details about his order, Truman responded with one of his most vitriolic unsent letters: "You write just like the usual egghead. The facts are before you but you'd like to garble them. The instruction of July 25th, 1945 was final. . . . it ended the Jap war. . . . now if you can think of any other, 'if, as, and when' egghead contemplations, bring them out. . . . it is a great thing that you or any other contemplator 'after the fact' didn't have to make the decision. Our boys would all be dead."

By the late 1950s his touchiness led him to object to remarks made by Thomas Murray, an AEC commissioner, who advocated "the Christian tradition of civilized warfare" and insisted that "total war in the nuclear age must be rejected." In a letter to Murray, Truman ridiculed the idea of civilized warfare, insisting that "it has always been a matter of slaughter of innocents and never civilized."

Mostly, when people criticized his actions or sought to engage in moral dialogue with him, Truman simply refrained from answering. A letter of protest from a lawyer in Seattle named Jack R. Cluck inspired Truman to instruct his secretary: "Just an ignorant 'Cluck' apparently. File it." Or he could send abrupt, insulting replies even to people of some standing. "Your own letter misses the key point. . . . yours is a typical case of misplaced sentiment. . . . some people simply cannot get it through their heads that the bombs were dropped to save a half million lives . . ." were some of the phrases he used in a 1963 letter to a university vice president. He simply wanted everyone to see "the Jap bomb affair"—his name for a file he kept on Hiroshima-related correspondence—the way he saw it.

Mythic Numbers

But there were cracks in Truman's defenses—inconsistencies, confusions, and fabrications. A telling example was Truman's much varied numbers of "lives saved" by use of the bombs, consistent only in their being highly inflated. Barton Bernstein and others have pointed out that the actual pre-Hiroshima estimates of military planners for American lives that would be lost in an invasion varied from 20,000 to 63,000, and that the much-multiplied claims of Truman and others of hundreds of thousands, a million, or more, were "a postwar creation." (Others contributed to this postwar creation: Shortly after the Nagasaki bombing, Churchill said that the atomic bombings had saved well over 1,200,000 Allied lives, a million of them American; Groves found that number "a little high" and estimated slightly under a million.)

During the remainder of Truman's presidency, he usually gave a figure of about a quarter of a million, sometimes 200,000, but after leaving the White House began to raise the number so that the first draft of his memoirs mentioned "half a million [U.S. and Allied] casualties with at least 300,000 dead," while the final draft simplified the matter by increasing the number to "half a million American lives." Truman would sometimes refer to Japanese lives as well: "I knew what I was doing when I stopped the war that would have killed a half million youngsters on both sides. . . ." He claimed in 1953 that, just before Hiroshima, Marshall had given him an estimate of five hundred thousand expected American lives lost. But the records suggest otherwise; that Marshall was in agreement with the military planners' estimate of forty-six thousand—and with his military colleagues when they dismissed as "entirely too high" the suggestion by a "layman" (Herbert Hoover) of possibly a half million dead. Whether Truman got the figure from that (rejected) suggestion is hard to say, but the evidence is that no reputable military figure made any such estimate.*

Truman hammered away at the "lives saved" argument because it placed the atomic bombings in the realm of moral virtue. And the more lives saved, the greater the virtue. (As one of Truman's top aides observed, "The size of the casualty figure is very important.") Even with his inconsistency, Truman probably did come to believe that the bomb had saved something on the order of 500,000 lives, but both the inflation and the inconsistency suggest psychological unsteadiness in the belief and a pressing, not entirely successful, need to quell inner doubts. Those doubts had to do with the numbers he was putting forward and, therefore, with the decision itself, which the inflated numbers were protecting. At a certain point the figure 500,000 became the constant, rounded figure that could take its place in Truman's inner mythology about what he had done and why he had done it. His touchiness and his discrepancies suggest that he was never entirely at ease with that personal myth, but it did help him to

---

* World War II veterans tell of having speculated informally among themselves at the time about invasion casualties of hundreds of thousands or a million men, suggesting that the large figures might have been influenced by an informal oral history of this kind.

maintain a workable psychological equilibrium in relation to the bomb and to the rest of his life.

But in the process Truman contributed crucially to a more encompassing American myth about the bombing—the larger myth sometimes calling forth the figure 500,000, equally often one million, and, in a startling recent incarnation during the debate about the Smithsonian exhibit, *six million,* the last figure undoubtedly influenced by the European holocaust. As with Truman himself, the myth contributes to a broader American sense that in dropping atomic bombs on Hiroshima and Nagasaki, our country was behaving ethically and in the interest of human life. Then the bomb need no longer be psychologically experienced as a brutal killing device but rather as a newly powerful means of preserving lives.

Deep Confusions

Truman's contradictions and confabulations extended into other Hiroshima-related areas as well. For example, he claimed on one occasion (as we observed earlier) that the Japanese "were offered the terms, which they finally accepted, well in advance of the dropping of the bomb. I imagine the bomb caused them to accept the terms." That reconstruction reverses the actuality the Japanese had *not* been offered previously the emperor-sustaining terms they finally accepted; rather, *they* had unofficially suggested, as a basis for surrender before the bomb, essentially the terms we imposed afterward. A confabulation is an untrue belief or reconstruction that can unconsciously alter events in favor of one's own moral claim. It can change what one actually did into something one's conscience can accept—and this confabulation had the specific psychological function of placing blame for the bombings entirely on the Japanese.

In all this we observe Truman's unconscious capacity for retrospective manipulation of events in ways that distorted or even reversed their actualities, and for doing so in a manner that was logically and morally compelling both for himself and many others. But still the confusions broke through. That was notably the case in the letter he wrote to Stimson in 1946 in which he urged his former secretary of war to write the crucial article defencing the use of the bomb. He spoke oddly of having appointed "a Commission [the Interim Committee] consisting of Mr. Byrnes, Vannevar Bush and someone else, whose name I have forgotten"; and stated that the surrender ultimatum "was sent to Japan through either Switzerland or Sweden, I can't remember which . . ." Similarly, when interviewed in 1953, he spoke of "an ultimatum to Japan through Sweden or Switzerland—one or the other, I forget which . . ." One must conclude that the manner in which the war ended remained in important ways psychologically problematic for him.

Truman constantly referred to the atomic bomb as "just another weapon" and insisted that he and his advisers chose as targets cities "devoted entirely to war production." Yet in an interview for his memoirs he said that "the Japs were much more vicious fighters hand-to-hand than the people we had been standing up against [in Europe]. I thought that wiping out complete cities with the bomb would be better." And at a meeting with advisers a few years earlier he was quoted as saying that the atomic bomb was "destructive beyond anything we have ever had. You have got to understand that this isn't a military weapon. It is used to wipe out women and children and unarmed people, and not for military uses. So we have got to treat this differently from rifles and cannon and ordinary things like that." He thus contradicted almost everything else he said about the device by acknowledging its fundamental difference from what we call weapons and its inevitable killing of vast numbers of helpless civilians. It was significant that these latter remarks were made privately or confidentially, while the alternative view of the bomb as an ordinary weapon of war was his more public version and more central to his personal mythology. But even as his personal mythology became ensconced in his mind, it was never completely uncontested there.

Sometimes he would falsify events quite baldly, as in his August 1945 letter asserting that his jubilation following the atomic bombing was related not to it but to the Russian entry into the war. Because Truman *was* jubilant about the bomb and ambivalent about the Soviet declaration of war, one is tempted to view this reversal as a lie. But given Truman's penchant for bomb-related confabulation, it is more likely that he became convinced that a man like himself would not be joyous over massive destruction.

Truman also manifested an odd psychological pattern in relation to Soviet atomic weaponry. Not only did he share Groves's early illusion that it would take the Russians two decades to acquire the weaponry, but he resisted the fact of the Soviet bomb *after it had arrived*. His first response to the Soviet detonation in 1949 was that "German scientists in Russia did it." Soon afterward he apparently expressed doubts about whether the Soviets really had a usable atomic bomb, despite clear evidence they did. (Three years before that, when Oppenheimer told him he did not know when the Soviets might be able to build the weapon, Truman's answer was, "I know. Never.") Truman was probably better able to accept his use of the bomb against Japan in a world kept under control by exclusive American possession of the weaponry—as opposed to that use initiating an atomic arms race and a possible atomic war.

Reconciliation?

Not surprisingly, Truman was wary of meeting with Japanese atomic-bomb victims, but he did receive a contingent of survivors at the Truman Library in 1964. Perhaps at the age of eighty, he encouraged the visit, once assured it would be friendly, out of a suppressed desire (mentioned earlier) for reconciliation.

The public transcript of the meeting is all sweetness and light. Truman: "It's very nice of you to [come] under the circumstances." Dr. Matsumoto: ". . . well, it must have been a very heavy responsibility on your part to lead your country during . . . wartime." But when, at the end, the same Dr. Matsumoto declared, "We certainly hope that anything of this sort [the use of the bomb] will never happen again," Truman responded: "You don't hope it any more than I do. I don't want to see it happen again, 'cause it's absolutely unnecessary and was in the first place." His avowed meaning was surely that dropping the bomb would not have been required had the Japanese not started the war, yet one can only wonder whether Truman was expressing (through a slip of the tongue) a sense that the American use of the weapon in 1945 really was "unnecessary."

It is hard to picture Truman traveling to Hiroshima to meet with survivors there—but in 1962 he said he was willing to do just that. Merle Miller and a television producer then involved with Truman in a series about his presidency proposed that he visit the city and speak in the museum there, preferably to a group of schoolchildren, essentially emphasizing that the bomb must never be used again. Truman apparently reacted with a look of "quick suspicion" but then replied: "I'll go to Japan if that's what you want, but I won't kiss their ass." By expressing his usual defiance, he could permit a softer aspect of himself to emerge in agreeing to a remarkable undertaking. But such feelings were never to be tested, as the entire television project eventually fell through.

Yet he gave an added indication of interest in such a visit in response to a 1966 letter from a member of the Oregon State legislature, in which information about Hiroshima was enclosed. Truman wrote of having read the letter and enclosure "with deep concern," adding that "I had hoped that someday I would visit, to pay my respects, to that part of the world—and the place where it began and should have ended." Again Truman's meaning is uncertain, as it might well have been to himself at the time. Yet for him to use a phrase like "pay my respects" in connection with a possible Hiroshima visit suggests that something in him wished to be relieved of a burden, wished to make his peace with those who had been at the other end of the weapons.*

The Weapons Themselves—
Avoidance and Embrace

But Truman had difficulty making his peace with nuclear weapons in general. While he presided over America's development of hydrogen bombs and managed to avoid their use, he gave evidence of continuing ambivalence and confusion concerning all post-Nagasaki weaponry. At a Cabinet meeting in December 1945, Truman became involved in an odd exchange concerning existing stockpiles, as described by Henry Wallace. When Robert Patterson, the secretary of war, observed that scientists were exerting pressure on senators to determine how many atomic weapons we

---

* There is evidence that Truman never ceased to be preoccupied with his decision. Tom Clark, who had been his attorney general, told of visiting Truman in a Kansas City hospital four or five months before his death. Though told to stay only briefly, Clark remained for about forty-five minutes, during much of which Truman "defended his dropping the bomb."

possessed—but these senators "really did not want to know"—Truman "chimed in to say that he didn't really want to know either."

Wallace was apparently dumbfounded by that and declared ("with the greatest earnestness," as he put it), "Mr. President, you *should* know; also the Secretary of War should know, and the Secretary of the Navy." At that, "the President retreated in some confusion and said he guessed he should know and then covered up by saying, 'I do know in a general way.'"

Wallace concluded that "it was utterly incredible that Patterson and the President should be willing to trust full information and responsibility on this to a man like Groves and his underlings without knowing what was going on themselves." Wallace was describing here a long-standing tendency of Truman to permit military authorities (mostly Groves) to handle important aspects of the weaponry while he (along with the secretaries of war and navy) maintained a certain distance from them—intervening only sporadically where he saw the need to invoke his style of decision making. But psychologically there was more to the exchange. The president who had given the order to use the weapons emerged from that experience with considerable unease in relation to them, and seemed in fact to want to wash his hands of them to the point of not knowing much about them. He seemed almost to forget that he was president, perhaps because he did not want to be once more the president who had used them.

Another incident in November 1950 also revealed confusion and ambivalence about the weaponry, though in it Truman had a different tone. At a press conference during the early stages of the Korean war, when the American position was extremely tenuous, Truman talked of increasing American military strength in a way that included "a substantial amount for the Atomic Energy Commission" (meaning nuclear weapons). When questioned about the conduct of the war, Truman declared that "we will take whatever steps are necessary to meet the military situation, just as we always have." When a reporter asked if that could include the atomic bomb, Truman replied, "That includes every weapon we have." Another reporter then asked whether that meant that there was "active consideration of the use of the atomic bomb" and Truman declared: "There has always been consideration of its use."

Truman went on to say that he didn't want to see it used because it is a terrible weapon "and . . . should not be used on innocent men, women and children who have nothing whatever to do with this military aggression." But when another reporter asked whether what Truman had said meant "that the use of the atomic bomb is under active consideration," he replied, "Always has been. It is one of our weapons." When asked further whether such use required authorization by the United Nations (the official intervening body in Korea), Truman said no and added, "The military commander in the field will have charge of the use of weapons, as he always has."

At a very difficult moment of the Korean war, Truman wished to rally the American people and perhaps threaten the enemy by making clear his willingness to call forth unlimited military power. (There had in fact been some discussion in the military about the possibility of using an atomic bomb if things got still worse.) But in this press conference Truman not only went further than anybody else had in talking about using nuclear weapons but also implied that the decision could be made by a field commander, although the Atomic Energy Act specifically provided that only the president could order their use. There were lurid headlines in America and other parts of the world that we were considering the use of atomic weapons in Korea; administration spokesmen struggled with explanations that could serve to calm things down; and Clement Attlee, the British prime minister, rushed to Washington for the same purpose. David McCullough speaks of that press conference as "devastatingly foolish . . . a fiasco."

It was that, but psychologically speaking it represented Truman's ambivalent confusion about the weapons: they were horrible and killed vast numbers of innocent civilians, something he knew all too well, did not want to know, and did not want to again take part in; but they were also weapons of war, indeed weapons of ultimate power, a point of view he had acted upon and had the need to defend endlessly. Truman made frequent pledges not to use atomic weapons in Korea, but later research revealed that in December 1950 nonassembled bombs were secretly transported to a U.S. aircraft carrier stationed off the peninsula, and U.S. planes made simulated nuclear bombing raids over Pyongyang.

A few years afterward, Truman spoke of his nuclear restraint in refusing MacArthur's desire that the weapon be used extensively to widen the Korean war: "If I had been in that frame of mind I could have knocked out Peiping, Shanghai and Canton and killed seventeen or eighteen million people. But that would have just been murder." He pointedly contrasted such behavior with his authorization of the use of the atomic bombs during World War II: "I instructed them to inform me which cities in Japan were most nearly fully devoted to the war potential for the Japanese army and navy, and those were the cities that were bombed." Truman was at pains to assert this distinction and, even more, to hold on to his own conviction of its validity.

Much uncertainty remains concerning Truman's attitude toward use of the bomb in the Korean war. In one diary entry (which resembles in tone many of his unsent letters) Truman wrote bitterly of Communist propaganda and stalling at the Korean armistice conferences, and about the vast numbers of people killed by the Communists in Korea, Russia, East Germany, and Poland. He denounced Communist regimes for breaking "every agreement," for having "no morals, no honor," and the Koreans and Chinese in particular for their "lies and propaganda." Then came his threat: "Now do you want an end to hostilities in Korea or do you want China and Siberia destroyed? You may have one or the other, whichever you want. These lies of yours at this conference have gone far enough. You either accept our fair and just proposal or you will be completely destroyed." Making allowances for the self-expressive function of this kind of bombastic statement, we nonetheless recognize in it his impulse to make use of the power he could call forth with atomic bombs.

McGeorge Bundy, in his survey of that period, claimed that "Truman never came close to the use of nuclear weapons in Korea . . ." Bundy was convinced that "what Truman had thought about using the bomb to end World War II was not what he thought about using it in later years." Yet Bundy goes on to tell of "one myth about Harry Truman and the bomb that is his own fault," having to do with an "ultimatum" Truman sent Stalin in March 1946 concerning Soviet failure to live up to an agreement to withdraw their forces from Iran. Truman apparently told Senator Henry Jackson that he had called in the Soviet ambassador to inform him that if his troops were not withdrawn in forty-eight hours, the United States would use the atomic bomb. Actually, this seems to be another confabulation on the part of Truman, as no such meeting took place with a Soviet ambassador, and in the diplomatic exchanges that did occur there was nothing remotely like an ultimatum, or reference to the bomb.

Bundy deplores Truman's "faulty recollection" as "doubly unfortunate" in that he invented "an explicitly nuclear threat that never happened" and also obscured a diplomatic intervention that was effective and admirable, "all the more so because it did *not* take the form of atomic diplomacy." The image of a nuclear ultimatum permitted Truman to embrace the weapons as a source of toughness and irresistible power—to avoid actually using them while legitimating such use if necessary. Truman's false memory once more has to do with his intense, and intensely unresolved, emotions and attitudes concerning atomic weapons. Those personal confusions contribute greatly to the differing judgments made by others on his inclinations and policies regarding possible use.

Struggle against Feeling

After ordering the use of two atomic bombs, Truman spent the rest of his life in the throes of *unrealized guilt*. He sometimes seemed to approach more genuine moral reflection. In October 1948, he departed from a prepared text during a campaign speech in Toledo to declare that "for peace, I took it upon myself to make one of the most terrible decisions that any man in the history of the world had to make," identified the decision as that of ordering the dropping of the atomic bomb, and then repeated: "That was the most terrible decision that any man in the history of the world had to make." After defending the care with which he had considered the matter before giving the order, he went on to declare: "I never want to have to do that again, my friends. . . . right then and there I made up my mind that that must never happen again if it could conceivably be avoided."

On another occasion the idea of ultimate judgment and possible damnation for ordering the use of the bomb was actually raised—but only in a highly mocking fashion under the considerable influence of alcohol. Margaret Truman tells of a lively "small stag dinner" that Truman gave for Churchill during a visit just before the president was to leave office, which included high Truman administration officials such as Robert Lovett, Averell Harriman, General Omar Bradley, and Dean Acheson. Amidst the ebullience, Churchill turned to Truman and declared: "Mr. President, I hope you have your answer ready for that hour when you and I stand before St. Peter and he says, 'I understand you two are responsible for putting off those atomic bombs. What have you got to say for yourselves?' "

Margaret Truman went on to say that "this could have been a rather unpleasant subject," but Lovett "came to the rescue" by deflecting the issue back to Churchill by asking whether he was sure that he would "be in the same place as the president for that interrogation." There followed a series of "humorous" comments by the various participants with Churchill eventually put on the dock in a secular trial. He demanded "a jury of my peers," which led the others to see themselves as representing such historical figures as Alexander the Great, Julius Caesar, Socrates, Aristotle, and George Washington. Churchill then wanted to "waive a jury" but was not permitted to do so. "Dad was appointed Judge," Margaret reported. "The case was tried and the Prime Minister was acquitted."

Truman's daughter does not tell us anything of what he said during the lively and lubricated exchange. One may suspect that he seized upon the role of judge and thus avoided that of heavenly or secular defendant. Still, one may apply here the principle of *in vino veritas*, of psychological truth released by alcohol. That truth had to do with at least a consideration of the question of moral guilt, of a final judgment made on those responsible for dropping the two atomic bombs. While Churchill brought the subject up in a way that bracketed himself with the American president, everyone understood that Truman was the one essentially responsible for the decision. And Truman, it is clear, joined gaily in the "trials" and thereby accepted the idea of exploring moral guilt. But the combination of alcohol and mockery was also a way of saying "Look how absurd all this is!"—of negating the validity of any such accusation of guilt. Even then, Truman the judge had to stop short of a guilty verdict, had to declare Churchill—and by clear implication, himself—innocent. Again, imagery of moral judgment was put forward, but in such a way that precluded its being genuinely addressed.

In much psychological work, guilt feelings in adult life are traced to actual or imagined childhood transgressions. Because one did, or strongly wished to do, something one was not supposed to—a sexual act or defiance of a parent—a store of guilt was built up that could readily intrude upon ordinary, even reasonably decent, adult behavior.

But with Truman there was something of a reversal of that model. At the age of sixty-one he made a decision that resulted in the destruction of two cities and hundreds of thousands of deaths. Although he did so in a wartime context from which he could draw justification, he could never fully free himself of the sense that he had, in Martin Buber's phrase, brought about a considerable "injury" to the "human order of being." But from childhood he could call upon a pattern for *avoiding* guilt feelings, of stifling reflection on behalf of "decisiveness." Beyond any individual-psychological traits, the extraordinary dimensions of both the weapons project and the resulting injury to the human order seemed to transcend any judgment—or self-judgment—on a single person.*

Truman's particular pattern of numbing prevented him from achieving an animating relationship to his guilt: from confronting his own actions and transforming his guilt into the anxiety of responsibility. That would have meant bearing witness to the full scope of pressures and motivations (the kind of flow of feeling) that brought about his decision, as well as to the terrible human consequences of the weapon—which would have meant bearing witness to the larger threat to humankind. Whenever he approached such witness, it would be undermined, or completely shut down, by his need for self-justification.

That need would affect anyone ordering massive destruction of this magnitude, rendering genuine witness psychologically difficult in the extreme. A decent man, Truman felt it necessary to suppress his own compassion. His struggle against authentic witness began with the first photo of the Hiroshima destruction he was shown and continued throughout his subsequent exposure to various forms of evidence of what the bomb had done to human beings. Similarly, his declaration that two hundred thousand people killed in the two cities constituted "a price that had to be paid" was an aggressive rejection of witness and of the feelings of guilt that would have accompanied witness.

Yet one suspects that some corner of his mind was affected by those two hundred thousand souls. Nor could he entirely ignore the moral vehemence of writers like Hanson Baldwin, the distinguished military affairs

---

* Similarly, Hiroshima survivors tell of the difficulty they had in determining whom to blame: "the Americans" in general, the pilot, President Truman, their own leaders for starting the war?

analyst and graduate of the United States Naval Academy, in characterizing Americans as "inheritors of the mantle of Genghis Khan" and declaring that "we are now branded with the mark of the beast"—no wonder Truman was so upset upon encountering Baldwin's words that he anointed him one of those "Monday-morning quarterbacks." Again one is struck by the applicability of Oppenheimer's observation about the "hideous discomfort" of "being associated with such slaughter."

In December 1947, at the Washington Gridiron Club's annual occasion for presidential humor and self-mockery, Truman told of appointing a secretary of reaction: "What a load he can take off my mind if he'll put the atom back together so it can't be broken up." There was more gallows humor here than realized, and the atomic "load" never left Truman's mind. He could never fully overcome the discrepancy between the slaughter of civilians and his own moral convictions, but he never permitted himself to touch psychologically that discrepancy. So he remained on his spiritual treadmill, with his compensatory declarations of atomic virtue, his edgy inconsistency about numbers of "lives saved," and his overall contradictions, confusions, and confabulations.*

During his last years, his defensiveness hardly abated. But as a Christian and a human being facing death, he seemed, quite outside his own awareness, to wish for a measure of reconciliation with those victimized by the weapon. It was not a matter of sin and redemption—he could not approach that model—but rather an easing of his burden before death and of the "final judgment" to be made on him, whether by God or history. That wish, as already suggested, could well have been behind his mention on two occasions of a willingness or desire to visit Hiroshima, however aggressively or vaguely that willingness was expressed. Consistent with such an assumption would be the quotation from *Hamlet* that Truman is said to have underlined in his library: ". . . let me speak to the yet unknowing world/how these things came about: So shall you hear/of carnal, bloody, and unnatural acts, of accidental judgments, casual slaughters,

---

* *Truman never explicitly expressed regret about using the bomb—except perhaps on one occasion. Former White House photographer Joe O'Donnell recently told us that in 1950 he accompanied Truman on his famous trip to Wake Island to meet with General MacArthur. Truman took a stroll along the beach with a couple of newsmen, and O'Donnell (who as a Marine photographer had been sent into Hiroshima and Nagasaki in 1945) dared to ask if he had any "second thoughts" about the decision to drop the bomb. According to O'Donnell, Truman quickly replied, "Hell yes!" and then added, somewhat cryptically, "I've had a lot of misgivings about it, and I inherited a lot more, too."*

. . . ," ending with the lines: "But let the same be presently perform'd,/ even while men's minds are wild; lest more mischance,/On plots and errors, happen."

But the most reliable evidence of an inclination toward witness came in Truman's farewell speech upon leaving the presidency. There he spoke of "the stakes in our search for peace" as being "immeasurably higher than they have ever been before," of the danger that war would "dig the grave not only of our Stalinist opponents, but of our own society," of our "new era of destructive power" in which "the war of the future would be one in which man could extinguish millions of lives at one blow, demolish the great cities of the world, wipe out the cultural achievements of the past— and destroy the very structure of a civilization that has been slowly and painfully built up through hundreds of generations," concluding that "such a war is not a possible policy for rational men."

Although the rest of the talk was by no means free of cold-war rhetoric, Truman was clearly reaching for a form of witness concerning the nuclear weapons with which he had formed a unique and irreversibly tragic relationship. The speech had some parallels with Eisenhower's later warning, upon his leaving the presidency, against the dangers of the "military-industrial complex" and its relation to weaponry and possible nuclear war. This phenomenon, the "retirement syndrome," enables an official, upon leaving office, to express the doubts one has so fiercely suppressed in connection with one's nuclearism, and then speak with the special authority of one who has truly "been there." But in Truman's case, those words came very late, their power limited by his long and continuous struggle against feelings that could be associated in any way with self-condemnation for the atomic bombings.

CHAPTER 4

LIVING HIS OWN HISTORY

In the American Grain

To grasp more about Truman's behavior at an unprecedented historical moment, one must locate him in his own history. One must say something about the psychological patterns, individual and collective, that formed his sense of self over his first sixty-one years. Nothing in his prior life can serve as the "cause" of his atomic-bomb decision, or of his insistent defense of it But he brought an overall psychological constellation to the shockingly new external forces confronting him as president. And that constellation of self entered importantly into the flow of feeling culminating in the atomic bombings, and also greatly affected his subsequent life-long stance toward what he had done.

Truman's background, as many have noted, is connected with the American frontier, but it was a frontier that had disappeared. His maternal grandfather, Solomon Young, was a quintessential frontier hero whom Truman frequently cited as an inspiration for his own commitment to clear and simple principles. But in Harry's childhood, Young was an "old man," compelling but not very likable, and his appreciation for him came mainly on reflection after the grandfather's death. Frontier influences on Truman, then, were real but nostalgic, already partly mythical, and could therefore be seized upon with compensatory zeal. His mother grew up on a comfortable farm, attended a two-year Baptist college, played the piano, and loved books. His father was an extremely hardworking farmer and businessman with only periodic success, small and pugnacious (it took very little for him to start a fistfight), who was fond of reading to his son from Plutarch's *Lives*.

While parental identifications contributed to young Harry's interest in books, he startled everyone around him in rural Missouri with his omnivorous reading. That reading took many directions—the Bible at an early age and many times over, but especially history and biography. Early heroes were drawn from a four-volume set, *Great Men and Famous Women,* given him by his mother for his tenth birthday, and included Hannibal, Theodore Roosevelt, Andrew Jackson, and Robert E. Lee; the last was his mother's hero (hers had been a southern, slave-holding family), and he once said that he studied the careers of "great men" in order to be worthy of her. From this background he eventually emerged politically as beholden to certain American "fathers"—presidents who represented combinations of frontier spirit, American glory, egalitarian populism, and broader idealism. (Ulysses S. Grant in particular, but also Theodore and Franklin Roosevelt, and another hero, General John J. Pershing from World War I, were associated with principles of "unconditional surrender.") With his ordinary-man pride and suspicion of the American elite, however, came strong regional prejudices against such groups as blacks, Jews, Catholics, and, to some extent, all foreigners—prejudices strong in the young Truman, for the most part admirably overcome, but that may have never entirely left him.

Truman has been described as a nineteenth-century man, either removed from or antagonistic to many of the artistic and intellectual developments of the twentieth century, always suspicious of the century's shifts, multiplicities, and relativities, always longing for the simple verities of the imagined past. Yet he was also in tune in a number of ways with the twentieth century: from a love of railroads he developed enormous affection for automobile journeys and for the American road. He told John Hersey, "I like being on the road"—that penchant contributing to Truman's first great Washington success as the chairman of an itinerant Senate committee investigating corruption in American defense production, and to his considerable success as a political campaigner in the style of the time. And his inclination toward movement was accompanied by wide-ranging curiosity and knowledge, as well as considerable flexibility in adapting to a number of environments radically different from that in which he was brought up.

Truman's relationship to the nineteenth and twentieth centuries takes on particular importance because of his own obsession with history. His lifelong passion for reading history, together with his near-photographic memory of what he read, gave him extraordinary knowledge of historical details, especially but not exclusively American—knowledge that would often startle and impress both associates and other statesmen. But as one observer shrewdly commented: "His reading of history was often uncritical and idiosyncratic . . . [and] too often he substituted history for philosophy, which is just as dangerous as substituting philosophy for history." Indeed, Truman had a highly static view of history: people did not change, and truth in the past was still truth for us now. As he put it, "The only thing new in the world is the history you don't know." Truman once listed only classics when asked about the ten most important books to read, and his interrogator asked if he would like to add anything "to prepare a man specifically for life in the atomic age." His response was: "Nothing but the lives of great men! There's nothing new in human nature; only our names for things change. Read the lives of Roman emperors from Claudius to Constantine if you want some inside dope on the 20th century. . . ."

That static view of history readily combined with frontier nostalgia; the result for Truman could be a narrow form of American patriotism, whatever his knowledge of national experience. For much of his life Truman attempted to maintain a mythologized past: "In those days what was right was right and what was wrong was wrong, and you didn't have to talk about it." The potentially chauvinistic side of his nationalism was fed by America's emergence toward the end of World War II and afterward as the world's dominant military and industrial power along with its compelling claim to national virtue in having contributed so much to defeating fascist evil. Truman had that American sense of our fundamental goodness being so strong that actions on our part that seemed cruel or aggrandizing should not be understood to be such.

This kind of American nationalism could lend itself all too readily to a simplistic reading of events—for example, the assumption made by Truman and many other American leaders that the invasion of South Korea by northern forces in 1950 was orchestrated from Moscow. He also shared some of the American anxiety and agitation over socialism and communism in initiating a repressive loyalty program for government workers; his need to take the issue away from the Republicans was only part of his motivation. Truman was confusing because he carried within him, on the one hand, genuine Jeffersonian principles of individual freedom and opposition to exploitation from above, principles that extended into an embrace of the values of the New Deal; and on the other, a narrow and suspicious American chauvinism that could cause him to initiate such a loyalty program and, less than a decade later, led him to tell a Cornell University audience that Communists were engineering the student sit-downs at segregated lunch counters in the south. When later challenged to offer proof, he admitted that he had none, "But I know that usually when trouble hits the country the Kremlin is behind it."

The Quest for Vitality

Also important is Truman's evolving sense of vitality, of both maleness and general capability or efficacy. Here the matter of Truman's unusual eye malformation (of "flat eyeballs" or hypermetropia) greatly impaired his sight until, at about the age of six, his near-blindness was noted and he was provided with thick-lensed eyeglasses. While his world of vision was dramatically widened, he was told to avoid physical sports that might result in his breaking his glasses and "I was afraid my eyes would get knocked out if there was too much of a rough and tumble play."

He was already a somewhat delicate child whose mother would say he was "intended for a girl" and grew up surrounded by doting women. Now, in rural Missouri, wearing glasses of that kind made him an oddball. "To tell the truth, I was kind of a sissy," is the way he later put it, meaning that he ran from fights and avoided strenuous sports and games. Instead, he read voraciously and attained a certain standing as a boy who knew things and had a talent for settling disputes in ways other than fistfights. His best friends were two female cousins, who remained close throughout his life, and who read Shakespeare aloud with him, nicknaming him Horatio after Hamlet's staunch friend. Also contributing to his sense of physical deficiency was a severe, near-fatal bout with diphtheria at the age of ten, resulting in symptoms of paralysis that affected his speech as well as his limbs, so that he had to drop out of school for several months and be wheeled about in a baby carriage.

With the encouragement of his parents, both of whom loved to sing hymns, Truman studied the piano seriously for years with the best teachers available, attended concerts whenever he could, and on one occasion expressed his devotion to classical music with the image that "some of the old masters must have been in communication with a fairy goddess of some sort . . ." While he never lost his love of music or his ability to play the piano, he stopped his lessons at the age of thirteen when "I got the notion that to do this made a boy of that age a sissy." Friends would later say that it took "courage" in rural Missouri for Truman to have studied the piano as long as he did, but one gets the sense that in early adolescence he felt the need to cast off as much as he could of the more tender "female" side of himself in favor of a "tougher" masculinity.

He could bring to this effort a long-standing attraction to great military generals he encountered in his reading, beginning with Hannibal. He was fourteen when the Spanish–American war broke out and he took the lead in forming the Independence Junior Militia, a rifle company with .22 caliber weapons. The twelve or so boys combined their sense of being young soldiers ready for the call with a bit of adventure in occasionally shooting a neighbor's chicken and cooking it in the woods. Throughout all this, however, he was known as a very good and sensitive boy who cultivated the approval of his teachers and everyone else. But over time he would continue to suppress much of his tenderness, or limit it mostly to intimate relationships, in favor of often exaggerated forms of public male assertion.

Attracted to the military, Truman for a time held a dream of attending West Point and even did some preparation for it until becoming convinced that his eyes would disqualify him. The death of his father in 1914 left him bereft and confused but also perhaps freer to act when Woodrow Wilson called for a declaration of war in April 1917. Truman experienced a surge of excitement, compared himself to "Galahad after the Grail," rejoined the

National Guard and was elected a First Lieutenant (according to the custom of the time) by the men, and was enormously proud of his uniform which he wore day and night, intent on not being seen as a "slacker." As with generations of Americans and others, war was perceived as a test of manhood. While inwardly worried "that he might somehow fail to measure up as an officer and be disqualified and disgraced," Truman might have surprised himself with the success he had in handling men and conducting himself in combat. The nonviolent "sissy" had managed ritual violence quite well, had further honed the male self he craved. This personal affirmation undoubtedly helped him cope with the extraordinary carnage of the war. He could experience a surge of vitality derived from not only masculine pride but a newly achieved sense of efficacy in the world.

With that combination in place, Truman could embark on his political career. He made use of associations formed in the military (particularly a friendship with a member of the powerful Pendergast family that ran Democratic politics in Missouri) and of his new standing as something of a local war hero. Before this happened he was to undergo a major financial failure (his famous haberdashery shop), so that a political career became a desperate refuge for a man now married and thirty-eight; he jumped at the chance to be a local candidate because "I've got to eat."

But in politics he found a metier for which he had developed the psychological equipment: public expressions of bravado and toughness, great energy and administrative ability, a blend of austere moral focus (avoiding the rampant forms of corruption around him) with a malleability derived from his more compliant and softer side. So inclined was he to please almost everyone that later in his career he became known as "go-along, get-along Harry." At one point he even initiated membership in the Ku Klux Klan in order to obtain its support in an election but backed away from the organization upon finding out more about it. Over all, Truman's sense of self could find in politics forms of vigorous life-power while continuing to hold back much, but not quite all, of his more tender inclinations. That is why politics seemed to come naturally for Truman. "There," his close cousin said, "he struck his gait."

All this required, however, a never-ending struggle for inner balance and outer affirmation. Hence his "dogged determination," as one observer puts it, "to shoulder the burdens of responsibility and to achieve goals that he often felt were beyond his personal capabilities." He was bedeviled by the image of being just a "little man" who could not be expected to act significantly on the world, and he needed to see himself as acting quickly, boldly, and above all, decisively. Although anchored in family and region, he felt a need to buttress constantly his sense of a coherent self, remaining always vulnerable to a fear of unmanageable complexity, ineffectiveness, and even (as we shall see) of falling apart.

The struggle could take him in strange directions. Despite his own broad forays, through his reading, into vast realms of human experience, he could become fiercely opposed to intellectual exploration—and intellectuals in general—as threats to the simple clarity he craved. He needed to fight off complexity as a way of maintaining his sense of strength and coherence. Psychologically speaking, he often felt himself at war: "I want peace and I'm willing to fight for it" is a characteristic statement. That battle to hold on to self rendered him enormously susceptible to slights and insults, whether to himself or to close family members in whom his tenderness was invested. He required violent images, many of them quite available from his background, for imagining the annihilation of those who threatened him, and thereby buttressing the self and restoring its vitality. His enraged unsent letters were means of testing his violence while keeping it under control. On one well-known occasion he actually mailed such a letter, threatening to cause bodily harm to the music critic who derided his daughter's singing. The attack on his most treasured family member, along with considerable duress from other sources, had so upset his psychological balance that he felt the need to send the violent image to its specific target.

To keep the self functional a man like Truman needs power surges. He received just that when he gave his first presidential speech to Congress and mentioned his commitment to unconditional surrender. At that moment, he could blend with the maximum principle of overall American power and feel both the principle and his own strength profoundly affirmed by the extraordinary enthusiasm of the audience. Trinity was an even greater power surge, as we have seen, to the point of enormously intensifying the flow of feeling culminating in the use of the bomb. With that kind of experience, one sweeps away death and becomes part of an omnipotent and immortal force.

But such moments were rare. More frequently Truman inwardly

doubted his power and, upon Roosevelt's death, it took months for him to feel the connection between his own limited self and the American presidency. His frequent expressions of self-doubt, together with his unprepossessing appearance, greatly troubled some of his advisers. At one point General Marshall even specifically warned him that he must, as commander in chief, be careful not to appear weak.

Truman had considerable resilience in maintaining this balance and could at times carry out difficult tasks with great energy and confidence. He did this by maintaining a sense of control over his environment through hard work bordering on obsessiveness (keeping a "clear desk" while reading endless documents) and maintaining a supportive human environment. The latter was extremely important to him, to the point of requiring the kind of people around him with whom he felt comfortable and affirmed in his self-worth. These "cronies" were frequently derided because their main talent seemed to be joining Truman in poker playing, drinking, and exchanging yarns, but his need for them was profound. Part of the need had to do with the enormous cultural gap between rural Missouri, on the one hand, and Washington and the rest of the world on the other. More than that, these friendships could shore up a sense of strength and head off feelings of isolation and deep vulnerability. (His relationships with his wife and daughter served a similar function but, being more profound, they were also more complex and prone to various forms of conflict; and the two women were often living in a different city.) In addition, the cronies, whatever their limitations, were more associated with policies and decisions in the public realm, where Truman especially required nurturing reassurance.

It did not always work. While much of the time dapper, bright eyed, and brisk, Truman was frequently covering over a masked depression. As we have noted, he was not the kind of man who could readily acknowledge depressive feelings or even sustain sadness. Rather, he would experience various physical symptoms or else would temporarily flee from a situation in which he felt overwhelmed. At various times in his life he suffered from extremely severe headaches, often with dizziness and insomnia; from stomach and gallbladder symptoms; and from a sense of extreme stress and fatigue, on one occasion with collapse and fear of a heart attack. On a number of occasions he checked himself into a hospital, convinced that he was physically ill, and would be told that he was suffering only from undue stress and fatigue—or, as his personal doctor put it once, "a nervous disorder." At other times he would not seek medical help but would take off on a trip, often combining it with a professional purpose but occasionally just getting away from all pressures and checking himself into a hotel making sure that no one but his family knew where he was.

Truman was also apparently upset by the moral compromises of politics and subject, according to a biographer, to "mornings of dark despair," along with feelings of guilt over specific actions he felt impelled to take. Additional guilt could well have derived from his inability at times to carry through his own aspirations. His rage at alleged enemies could also serve to ward off depression: anger can be much more comfortable than anxiety, self-condemnation, or deep sadness. Depressive feelings are hardly unusual; they are among the most basic human emotions and tend to be associated with all kinds of psychological difficulty. What was striking about Truman, however, was his constant need to fend off feelings of sadness, guilt, and loss in favor of compensatory expressions of assertion and control. To defend against the fear of disintegration that occurs in depression, he would deny, assert, and *boldly decide.*

That kind of premature boldness occurred in another of Truman's crucial decisions, his military intervention in Korea. There are different political views concerning the wisdom of the American intervention, but there is no doubt that, as Robert Donovan wrote, "Truman moved with such celerity it seemed as if he could not wait to make decisions and act."

Margaret Truman describes how her father "made it clear, from the moment he heard the news [of the North's invasion of the South on June 24, 1950], that he feared this was the opening of World War III," a perspective that was widespread in Washington at the time. As early as the next day it was clear to Margaret, from what her father told her, that "we are going to fight." And on arriving in Washington on the evening of the twenty-fifth Truman declared in his limousine, "By God, I'm going to let them have it." Truman saw himself as preventing another Munich and as preserving the UN, and no one in his advisory group seemed to doubt that what was happening in Korea was being directed from Moscow. He quickly mobilized an American military response via the United Nations, with Acheson's help.

"It would be said of Harry Truman," David McCullough wrote, "that without consulting Congress or the American people, he had rushed to judgment; that 'as Hermann Goering, when he heard the word culture, reached for his gun, Harry Truman when he heard the word problem, reached for a decision.' " McCullough went on to point out that "the last thing Truman wanted was a war in Korea, or anywhere," which was undoubtedly true. And it is also true that, in eventually firing MacArthur —though here he showed considerable hesitation and ambivalence—Truman was actually taking steps to avoid what really could have turned into World War III.

But there is no doubt that his exaggerated boldness and "celerity" in decision making contributed to the American plunge into what General Omar Bradley was later to call "frankly, a great military disaster" and "the wrong war, in the wrong place, at the wrong time, with the wrong enemy." Also characteristic was Truman's way of putting his quick decision behind him. At the completion of a crucial meeting, he ordered a drink for everyone and commented: "I have hoped and prayed that I would never have to make a decision like the one I have just made today. Now, with this drink, that's out of my mind." Having mobilized his assertive action, he could not afford to dwell on its consequences; he had the need to dismiss it from awareness in order to prepare himself for the next round of his struggle with assertion and efficacy.

In making decisions he cleared away ambiguity, doubt, conflict; in making bold decisions, he could feel vital and strong overcoming anxiety and heading off feelings of depression. But these decisions were made within a historical context, deeply affected by existing political and military currents. What Truman's psychological style required was to prematurely block out potential alternatives to those decisions. It also caused him to defend them, sometimes with extremity and distortion, for the rest of his life.

The Hiroshima Temptation

No one is more overburdened than a modern American president. As historians have pointed out, he must be both chief executive and king. He is also entangled in the enormous bureaucracies that have grown up in all three branches of government. As we have seen, Truman's fear of *not* using the bombs had significant origins in the technological and organizational momentum of the various American political, military, and scientific bureaucracies. Such bureaucratic blurring makes it difficult to assess any president's responsibility for events. If anything, Truman wished to project an aura of *complete* responsibility: "Let *me* worry about that!" Whatever his bravado, there was truth in his insistence that ultimate responsibility must be assumed by the president and commander in chief, however great the bureaucratic blurring or momentum.

Nuclear weapons, as we have seen, can radically transform both bureaucratic momentum and the president's psychological relationship to life and death. There can result an atrocity-producing situation of revolutionary proportions, which can all too readily be created, re-created, and acted upon. Such an atrocity-producing situation can do more than sweep up nuclear decision-makers: it can lure them, with the promise of omnipotence, to their own assertive embrace of the weapons, as was the case with Truman. Once all that has happened, the model is ever available: "By using nuclear weapons in combat, the Truman administration established the principle that though genocidal they were legitimate."

Nor can one who has taken that plunge ever escape the struggle for justification. In his twenty years of postpresidential defense of his use of the bombs Truman spoke both with the authority of the former chief executive who made the decision, and with the ritual magic of the president-king. That is why it was he who was always singled out to comment on new evidence about the weapon or the decision to use it. He was surely more influential than any other person in establishing the overall American response. His numbing, denial, distortion, and confabulation were seized upon or absorbed by all of us until we have made them our own, but not without struggle, and not without glimmers of more authentic response, as we will see next.

PART III

MEMORY AND WITNESS—
STRUGGLES WITH HISTORY

Introduction:
On Historical Memory

What we call historical memory is a creature of time and place. Emotional and political needs of the present intersect with past events. For memory, like perception, can never be simply factual. All our memories are reconstructions. Someone is doing the remembering and brings his or her personal history to the reconstructed event. The same is true of group memory, where collective struggles for meaning influence whether and how a particular event is remembered.

Historical memory begins with the witness of survivors. Those who have lived through events tell their stories, which are then recast by others in creating an intelligible narrative. A group or nation's understanding of particular moments in its history may come to differ from survivors' original accounts but remains significantly affected by them—for survivors are the primary witnesses, even if we depend upon secondary witnesses (such as historians, journalists, and political leaders) to elaborate further.

Survivors bring to historical memory their own quest for meaning, seeking significance in what might otherwise be painful (and psychologically unabsorbable). When they have survived mass killing, either as perpetrators or victims, the meaning they find is itself death-haunted, and part of an unending struggle for ethical coherence. Bearing witness to that experience—telling their version of events or explaining their actions—is at the heart of that struggle. A group's need to "own" its experience can extend to a claim of ownership of that entire segment of history. Concerning Hiroshima, those claims bring different groups of Americans into fierce contention.

In a very real sense, all of us are survivors of Hiroshima. This especially is true (as it was with Truman) of those who helped create or use the atomic bomb—administrators, scientists, bomber pilots—and veterans of the Pacific war who feel the weapon saved their lives. Very few Americans experienced the direct effects of the bomb, but many others arrived in Hiroshima and Nagasaki afterward and confronted some of the results of the atomic attack. These included U.S. soldiers who occupied the two cities; military personnel and civilians who evaluated the effects of the weapon; and later arrivals, including tourists, peace activists, and writers and scholars (like the authors of this book).

Many of these visitors took in something of what had happened in Hiroshima and experienced certain survivor-like emotions. They became survivors by proxy and embarked on their own form of witness. The same can be true for those affected by images or published accounts of Hiroshima. Even Americans with minimal exposure to Hiroshima are periodically exposed to words or photographs depicting the horror.

Americans were perpetrators of Hiroshima rather than victims. Hence the survivor struggle has been less that of the victim ("Why did I survive while others died?") than of the agent ("Why did we perform an act in which so many people, and in such a grotesque way, died?"). Even victims can struggle with feelings of guilt, but perpetrators of such an event are likely to expend enormous energy in fending off self-doubt. One can do that either by investing the event with virtue (the claim of saving lives) or by seeking to divest oneself of the perpetrator's role and take on that of the victim.

This latter tendency is enhanced by the fact that Hiroshima took place at the end of a war we waged against tyranny—on behalf of victims in Europe and Asia. By asserting our virtue in using the weapons, or proclaiming our own victimization (at Pearl Harbor and Bataan, for example), Americans can avoid or minimize what took place at Hiroshima.

All these emotions, then, reverberate among Americans as they contemplate, or avoid, Hiroshima. The groups we discuss—U.S. presidents, bomb pioneers, veterans, scientists, antinuclear activists, journalists, and historians—have been crucial in developing what Michael Kammen calls America's "public memory" of Hiroshima. But all of us actively share in "mind-manipulating the past in order to mold the present," as Kammen puts it, for public memory is contested memory.

The struggles of Americans described in subsequent chapters deserve our sympathetic understanding. Problems often arise, however, when individuals attempt to extend their rendering of events into ownership of ever-larger portions of that history—in the process ignoring or neglecting painful truths. "The past," as Kammen points out, "may be mobilized to serve partisan purposes." That form of public memory, feeding on nationalism and patriotism, amounts to "a civil religion resting upon a hollow sense of history." Such a tendency shaped the bitter Smithsonian controversy, as we describe later in this section. By exploring these varied expressions of survival and witness over the past fifty years, we can begin to extricate ourselves from the burdens of "mind-manipulating the past" and enhance our moral and political imagination.

CHAPTER 1

AMERICAN PRESIDENTS AND THE
LESSONS OF FIRST USE

American presidents significantly shape public memory. Those who followed Truman inherited from him an affiliation with the Hiroshima narrative, an association enhanced by the fact that until Bill Clinton took office every American president since Eisenhower had served during World War II, several in the Pacific.

Their specific attitudes about Hiroshima tend to be hidden. Most have avoided commenting on the use of the bomb against Japan, although several presidents invoked the spirit of the Manhattan Project in proposing crash programs of their own. Biographies and memoirs contain few clues about their personal feelings concerning Hiroshima. One thing is certain: no president while in office has publicly questioned dropping the bomb. Indeed, such questioning came close to a taboo, especially within the White House itself. In failing to raise questions about Hiroshima, each of these survivors of World War II strongly reinforced the official narrative.

Harry Truman's legacy to later presidents was powerful, but not always clear. Like him, they tended to have a contradictory view about weapons of mass destruction. At one time or another several of them threatened to use the bomb as a military weapon. Many of them presided over massive nuclear buildups. Yet each also made statements to the effect that nuclear weapons could destroy human civilization and should not be used. There is considerable dispute as to how close we have ever come, under various presidents, to actual use. But because none of them, in the end, used the weapons, we do well to ponder the source of restraint.

We make no specific claims about the role of Hiroshima in this regard, but knowing what happened to Hiroshima and Nagasaki, however indirectly, may have been a factor in this retreat from the nuclear brink. It would seem that, for American presidents, historical memory of Hiroshima cuts both ways. On the one hand, it conveys the idea of nuclear weapons as usable, fortifying the official U.S. first-use policy from which no president has deviated. On the other hand, recalling the effects of the bomb contributes to a sense that the weapons are *not* usable. Those antithetical historical legacies have probably coexisted in the mind of every president since World War II. Hiroshima's legitimation of first-use constantly hovers over and threatens to overwhelm the image of restraint also derived from Hiroshima.

Only one American president has shown any significant tendency to stray from the official version of Hiroshima. That allegiance to the narrative has had profound consequences—in maintaining a climate of first-use advocacy and in strongly discouraging any questioning of Hiroshima by others.

Eisenhower and "That Awful Thing"

The one president who disputed the Hiroshima decision did so both before, and after, serving in the White House. General Dwight D. Eisenhower first made his views public in his 1948 memoir *Crusade in Europe*. Eisenhower revealed that in July 1945, upon learning that an atomic bomb was about to be used against Japan, he told Stimson he hoped "such a thing" would not happen because "I disliked seeing the United States take the lead in introducing into war something as horrible and destructive as this new weapon."

Eisenhower was one of the most admired men in America. His critically acclaimed book became a best-seller. Yet in the wake of Henry

Stimson's article, this revelation—America's most respected general arguing against the military use of the bomb—passed almost without notice.
Eisenhower's muted doubts were largely disregarded in cold-war America
"because Stimson and his cohorts had succeeded, magnificently, in quell-
ing suspicions about the A-bomb decision," Barton Bernstein later commented.

Fifteen years after his mild criticism in *Crusade in Europe,* Eisenhower
spoke bluntly in a second memoir, *Mandate for Change.* There he described
the same meeting with Stimson at Potsdam:

> During his [Stimson's] recitation of the relevant facts, I had been
> conscious of a feeling of depression and so I voiced to him my
> grave misgivings, first on the basis of my belief that Japan was
> already defeated and that dropping the bomb was completely un-
> necessary, and secondly because I thought that our country should
> avoid shocking world opinion by the use of a weapon whose
> employment was, I thought, no longer mandatory as a measure to
> save American lives. It was my belief that Japan was, at the very
> moment, seeking to surrender with a minimum of loss of "face."
> The Secretary was deeply perturbed by my attitude, almost angrily
> refuting the reasons I gave for my quick conclusions.

Eisenhower's anecdote was again generally ignored by reviewers—
although it did catch the attention of Leslie Groves, who personally investigated whether his former commander in chief was telling the truth. In a
later interview, Eisenhower reiterated that Japan was close to surrender at
the time of the atomic bombing, adding, "It wasn't necessary to hit them
with that awful thing." A book by General Omar Bradley endorsed Ike's
version and recalled a similar Eisenhower-Truman discussion at Potsdam;
and historian Stephen Ambrose confirmed both meetings.

Barton Bernstein has raised questions about whether Eisenhower actually spoke to either Stimson or Truman about the bomb before Hiroshima.
Whether or not Eisenhower objected to the use of the bomb in advance,
the fact remains that he firmly, and quite publicly, criticized its use afterward, and only a handful of others—Leahy, McCloy, Grew—did that.
Bernstein also wonders about Eisenhower's motives in condemning the
atomic attack. Ike might have wanted to advance his reputation as a "moral

military man" who "deplored the horror of war." Or he might have been attempting to salve a guilty conscience for *not* having raised objections to the bomb at Potsdam. Nevertheless, what remains significant is that Eisenhower vigorously criticized the use of the bomb and no other president ever has.

How did Eisenhower's attitude about Hiroshima affect his behavior during his eight years in office? It certainly did not stop him from overseeing an enormous nuclear buildup. Eisenhower, wrote James Reston of the *New York Times,* "couldn't quite make up his mind about the atom bomb." He "talked carelessly but acted cautiously." The enigmatic Eisenhower was quick to threaten to use the bomb but loath to use it: in Korea, in Vietnam, at Quemoy and Matsu. This reflected what might be called a *double sense* of Hiroshima.

Some of Eisenhower's top advisers, such as John Foster Dulles, shared Ike's ambivalence. Reston spoke with Dulles often during this period and later captured the blinding contradictions of the entire nuclear era in one remarkable sentence:

> I got the impression that Dulles regarded the atom bombing of Hiroshima and Nagasaki as an unnecessary slaughter of helpless civilians, but later he felt that perhaps that terrible event was a restraining influence on the Soviet leaders, and he boasted about his willingness to go to the brink of war in order to intimidate the Communists.

Many American leaders, indeed, had been willing to go *past* the brink to end the Korean war. Representative Lloyd Bentsen of Texas, for example, advocated threatening to use the bomb against "principal North Korean cities" if the enemy did not withdraw from the south.

Others sought to use the bomb without warning. One of them was Representative Albert Gore of Tennessee (father of the future vice president). Complaining that Korea had become "a meat grinder of American manhood," he had advised President Truman in a personal letter: "Something cataclysmic, it seems to me, is called for. We have it. Please consider using it." One of Gore's proposals was to use the bomb to "dehumanize a belt across the Korean Peninsula" to create a deadly neutral zone. Any Communist soldiers who entered the area would face "certain death or slow deformity." This would be "morally justifiable under the circumstances."

But Eisenhower, perhaps affected by Hiroshima, never came close to using the bomb. He made the crucial decision to establish a formal first-use policy as the major deterrent to Soviet aggression and approved a policy directive which held that the U.S. "will consider nuclear weapons to be as available for use as other munitions" in the event of war. He directed a massive nuclear program and the rapid nuclearization of America's conventional forces. But he also took steps to avoid a nuclear showdown. Describing the aftermath of an atomic attack, he went beyond platitudes: "Surely no sane member of the human race could discover victory in such desolation. Could anyone wish his name to be coupled by history with such human degradation and destruction?" Perhaps he wished to avoid Truman's fate.

Eisenhower specifically referred to Hiroshima when an adviser raised the possibility of giving the French "a few" atomic bombs to use against the Vietnamese at Dien Bien Phu. "You boys must be crazy," Eisenhower said. "We can't use those awful things against Asians for the second time in less than ten years. My God."

Hiroshima in the White House

John F. Kennedy did not have the kind of brush with Hiroshima that Eisenhower may have had at Potsdam. On August 6, 1945, he was flying home from Europe, a naval officer nursing an injury. But like Eisenhower (and most other presidents), Kennedy was willing to practice nuclear brinksmanship while acting cautiously behind the scenes. The most dramatic example of this, of course, was the Cuban missile crisis. Kennedy helped precipitate it by stationing U.S. missiles in Turkey, and then defused the threat by acting with relative patience and restraint.

It is hard to say how Hiroshima played on the minds of Kennedy and other decision-makers during this crisis. Tapes of their discussions released in 1994 reveal that they recognized the consequences of nuclear war all too well, and that this significantly guided their behavior. According to one inside account of the crisis, what "disturbed" Kennedy "the most" was the possible death of innocent children "who had no role, who had no say, who knew nothing even of the confrontation, but whose lives would be snuffed out like everyone else's." The connection to Hiroshima is clear.

McGeorge Bundy, an important Kennedy adviser during the crisis, told us that at the White House nobody talks about Hiroshima but "everybody knows about Hiroshima." There is no doubt that "the fact that you have used it [the atomic bomb] weighs on the side of the people who say it's a weapon" and therefore can be used again. Yet, he explained, Hiroshima is remembered not only as "a model" but as "a warning." It is this latter aspect of Hiroshima the decision makers in the Cuban missile crisis called forth.

It is impossible to know for certain what any American president ultimately would have done if one of our many nuclear threats had not worked; if a bluff had been called. A first-use policy announces what the U.S. intends to do under certain circumstances but does not compel it to do anything. If Khrushchev, for example, had refused to remove Soviet missiles from Cuba in 1962—would Kennedy have launched a pre-emptive attack? Robert McNamara disclosed not long ago that he "recommended, without qualification," to Presidents Kennedy and Johnson that they never initiate, under any circumstances, the use of nuclear weapons, and he believes they accepted this advice. If this is true, first-use *was* all bluff during the Kennedy-Johnson era. Perhaps every secretary of defense makes a similar plea, perhaps every president accepts it. No one knows about that —or about the kinds of psychological forces that could cause a president to use the weapons, whatever the recommendation.

We do know that Lyndon Johnson never came close to using the bomb in Vietnam, even though he must have been sorely tempted, considering his tortured involvement in our difficulties there. Johnson had wavered in his attitude about the use of the bomb. In 1946, "closer to the shock of Hiroshima," as writer Ronnie Dugger put it, LBJ advocated outlawing the bomb and pursuing world government, or else, he warned, "civilization is going to be wiped out." Then, in the early 1950s, as a confirmed anti-Communist, Johnson raised the threat of using the bomb in Korea or against the Russians. He proclaimed that following the next case of aggression by *any* Communist regime the U.S. should strike at the Soviet Union, unleashing "all of the power at our command."

Johnson chose not to initiate nuclear warfare but, like Kennedy, his restraint did not extend to modernizing and stockpiling nuclear weapons, which continued, endlessly. The arms buildup persisted throughout the 1960s, and beyond. Until the end of the cold war, in fact, every president, while holding to restraint in first-use, endorsed the technological imperative that had produced both the atomic and the hydrogen bombs.

Lyndon Johnson rarely referred to Hiroshima. On one dramatic occasion he consciously tried to avoid it, but Hiroshima came to the White House, anyway.

The year was 1965. Johnson invited a wide range of painters, sculptors, and writers to the White House for a one-day festival of the arts. Five authors and poets were asked to read from their works. The poet Robert Lowell, protesting the Vietnam war, declined the invitation, explaining that the U.S. "may even be drifting on our way to the last nuclear ruin." But a decision by one of the other writers, who opposed the war but elected to attend the festival, caused just as much anguish at the White House. John Hersey, invited as a novelist, announced that he would read instead from *Hiroshima,* and he planned to update his account with statistics on the destructive power of existing nuclear weapons.

After discussing the matter with her husband, an enraged Lady Bird Johnson summoned the festival organizer, historian Eric Goldman (then a consultant to LBJ), to the White House. She recited one of the passages Hersey intended to read, which described Truman's announcement of the Hiroshima bombing. "The president is very close to President Truman," she explained icily. "He can't have people coming to the White House and talking about President Truman's brandishing atomic bombs." Then, coming to the point, she complained that her husband was being criticized "as a bloody warmonger. He can't have writers coming here and denouncing him, in his own house, as a man who wants to use nuclear bombs." Goldman explained that Hersey did not believe that Johnson *wanted* to use nuclear weapons, only that in the nuclear era any war was extremely dangerous. She replied: "The President and I do not want this man to come here and read this." Twice more he objected and twice more she responded with the same words.

Goldman refused to tell Hersey what to do, and the invitation stood. President Johnson, meanwhile, ordered a media blackout of the festival. He also requested FBI background checks on some of the guests.

When Hersey appeared behind the podium at the White House, Lady Bird Johnson was right there in the third row. Hersey prefaced his reading from *Hiroshima* with the following statement: "We cannot for a moment forget the truly terminal dangers, in these times, of miscalculations, of arrogance, of accident, of reliance not on moral strength but on mere military power. Wars have a way of getting out of hand." Occasionally he lifted his eyes from his text and looked at Lady Bird for emphasis. When Hersey finished, he was greeted by vigorous applause. "The First Lady, who clapped for all other readings, sat motionless," Goldman later reported. And when the president heard about Hersey's reading (and some other activities he viewed as hostile) he cut short his appearance at his own festival.

Nixon in Hiroshima

Only two American presidents have visited Hiroshima, and they did it either before or after being elected to office.

The first was Richard Nixon. Whatever other faults he may have had, Nixon often went where others feared to tread. During a tour of Japan in 1964, four years before he was elected president, Nixon spoke at a gathering of the nation's leaders in Hiroshima. Like many other dignitaries—but no other prominent American political figure that we know of—Nixon laid a wreath at the memorial cenotaph and offered a silent prayer. Hiroshima, he told reporters, "has made the world promise to strive for peace." Years later he recalled the official function in Hiroshima he attended afterward where he witnessed the "traumatic effect" of the bomb:

> The Japanese are excellent hosts. They drink pretty good, as we say. All through my speech there was clapping and laughing, and then I mentioned the bombing, something to the effect that it should never happen again—and the light went out of their eyes. All the smiles went. Like that. Hiroshima was simply too horrible to think about.

But what impression did Hiroshima—the bombing and the aftermath —have on Nixon? He talked about this at some length in a revealing interview with *Time*'s Roger Rosenblatt in 1985. Analyzing the decision to use the bomb forty years after Hiroshima, he admitted there was "no simple answer." Nixon explained that he had once spoken to General MacArthur about it: "He thought it a tragedy that the Bomb was ever exploded. MacArthur believed that the same restrictions ought to apply to atomic weapons as to conventional weapons, that the military objective should always be limited damage to noncombatants." Nixon agreed that in World War II "the whole concept of targeting civilian populations was morally wrong."

But then Nixon put this "in context." Could the U.S. have won the war without firebombing German and Japanese cities? And, he added, most experts held that the atomic attacks had saved lives: "perhaps a million American casualties" (and the same number on the Japanese side). The atomic bombs cost two hundred thousand civilian lives, "and that's terrible," Nixon observed. "But it may have saved ten times that number."

This was the same Nixon who said of MacArthur: "The nuclear thing turned him off, which I think speaks well of him." Yet the "nuclear thing," as Nixon made clear, did not turn *him* off. In the *Time* interview he criticized those who downplayed the role of atomic diplomacy, and he suggested that nuclear threats had played the decisive role in ending the Korean war and resolving other superpower crises. He spoke almost proudly about the numerous times he "considered using nuclear weapons": when the Soviets threatened to intervene in the Egypt-Israeli war in 1973; when a Soviet-Chinese border dispute flared; during what he called the "Indo-Pak war" in 1971. In this final instance, the U.S. sent a large naval force equipped with nuclear weapons to the Bay of Bengal. Nixon told *Time*, "There was *no question* what we would have done."*

McGeorge Bundy disputes Nixon's credibility in some of these statements, calling him a "mythmaker." But there is no doubt about Nixon's hardheaded attitude toward the bomb (despite his visit to Hiroshima). In one of his memoirs he derided America's "obsession with the evils of nuclear weapons" as "self-flagellating irrationality."

At the close of the *Time* interview, Nixon asserted that the world was

---

* *There is some dispute about whether Nixon overtly threatened to use nuclear weapons against North Vietnam. In his memoirs, H. R. Haldeman recorded a conversation when Nixon set forth the infamous "Madman Theory": someone could "just slip the word" to the North Vietnamese that Nixon was so obsessed with Communism he "might do anything to stop the war . . . and he has his hand on the nuclear button. . . ."*

a safer place in 1985 than it had been in 1945. Asked if Hiroshima, then, was good for the world, Nixon answered "yes."

Of all recent U.S. presidents, Jimmy Carter seems least likely to be associated with nuclear threats. Indeed, he proposed ridding the world of nuclear weapons. Yet he also called for a new generation of first-strike nuclear weapons—and "made one of the few explicit threats of nuclear first-use issued by an American president," according to Morton Halperin. In January 1980, in the midst of the Iran hostage crisis, Carter announced that the U.S. would use "any means necessary" to halt a Soviet military move into the Persian Gulf. In his memoirs, Carter confirmed that he meant it as a nuclear threat, and that the Soviets got the message.

Significantly, this episode marked the first time in which the use of the atomic bomb against Japan was explicitly invoked to lend credence to a nuclear threat. In a television interview, an assistant secretary of state observed that "the Soviets know that this terrible weapon has been dropped on human beings twice in history and it was an American president who dropped it both times. Therefore, they have to take this into consideration in their calculus."

During the late 1980s, on one of his many trips to Japan after leaving office, Jimmy Carter stopped in Hiroshima and visited the Peace Museum, but he did not take part in any ceremony, nor comment on his visit afterward.

Ronald Reagan, who accelerated Carter's nuclear buildup, also made few public references to Hiroshima. In 1980 he told reporter Robert Scheer that the bomb "ended a great war—and probably saved, well, it's been estimated 2 million casualties, in what would have eventually been the invasion of Japan." On the fortieth anniversary of Hiroshima, Reagan said Americans must never forget what happened there. "Yet we must remain mindful," he added, "that our maintenance of a strong nuclear deterrent has for four decades ensured the security of the United States and the freedom of our allies in Asia and Europe."

Looking to the future, however, Reagan frequently asserted that the biblical Armageddon might be at hand, and would be nuclear in nature. On one occasion he confided that a passage in the Bible, portraying an invading army from Asia destroyed by God, specifically foretold Hiroshima. It described a plague during which "the eyes are burned from the head and the hair falls from the body and so forth," he explained.

The link between Reagan's belief in Revelation and his nuclear policies is confusing but probably strong. This belief, and its relation to Hiroshima, does not explain any one of his nuclear proposals but rather the extremity of nearly all of them. Reagan promoted a massive nuclear buildup, announced plans to build the neutron bomb, and advocated a space-based defense system—but when he met privately with Mikhail Gorbachev in Reykjavik he spontaneously proposed eliminating nuclear weapons from the face of the earth (the meeting led to the first round of meaningful arms cuts). We might say that here Reagan acted in part on his Hiroshima imagery, causing him, at least in that moment, to attempt to prevent the nuclear Armageddon he foresaw. It is significant that Reagan chose to deliver his most important statement on this subject—"A nuclear war can never be won and must never be fought"—during a visit to Japan.

Under George Bush, Hiroshima for a second time was invoked to bolster a nuclear threat.

In the early weeks of our conflict with Iraq in 1990 nuclear weapons were at the center of the dispute. One of the stated reasons for standing up to Saddam Hussein (besides his invasion of Kuwait) was that Iraq was purportedly building the bomb. Nuclear fear, therefore, was used to justify a conventional intervention. Then, as our military assault on Iraq neared, several American spokesmen let it be known that if Hussein resorted to chemical warfare against Israel or the U.S., he could expect nuclear retaliation.

In a television interview, Defense Secretary Richard Cheney stated that the U.S. was not prepared to use nuclear weapons "at this point"—but he emphatically agreed with another guest, George Will, that Harry Truman had acted morally and "made the right decision when he used the bomb on Hiroshima." The historical allusion, as James Hershberg has pointed out, "sent a crystal-clear message to Hussein." Iraq apparently did not use chemical weapons in the war, while the U.S. relied on a deadly new generation of conventional weapons—which produced massive casualties.

On another occasion, however, Hiroshima served a different purpose.

When the fiftieth anniversary of the attack on Pearl Harbor arrived in late 1991, George Bush was an effective spokesman for reconciliation, for he had been victimized by the Japanese in the war: shot down in the Pacific. But then a controversy erupted linking Pearl Harbor to Hiroshima. Top Japanese officials had expressed "remorse" over the December 7, 1941, attack and the country's parliament debated a resolution finally to offer the U.S. a formal apology.

This led to a good deal of public talk in both Japan and America about whether the U.S. would respond with some sort of statement of regret about Hiroshima. When a television reporter asked Bush about this, he replied: "Not from this President. I was fighting over there. . . . Can I empathize with a family whose child was victimized by these attacks? Absolutely. But I can also empathize with my roommate's mother, my roommate having been killed in action."*

In his adamant refusal, Bush was expressing not only the enduring influence of the Hiroshima narrative but also the powerful emotions of a World War II survivor who had lost friends in the fighting. Saying "war is hell," he declared Truman's decision to use the bomb correct, for it saved "millions" of American lives. The remarks set off a furor in Japan, ending any chance of an apology for Pearl Harbor.

A CBS News/*New York Times* poll taken at this time found that only 16 percent of Americans favored apologizing for dropping the bomb. Among the age group that included most of Bush's fellow World War II veterans, that figure was only 8 percent. Yet Bush might have rallied considerable support had he seized the moment and proposed meeting a Japanese apology with one of our own. The same poll indicated that the percentage of Americans who favored apologizing for Hiroshima if Japan apologized for Pearl Harbor rose to 50 percent. This surprising finding suggests that Hiroshima indeed rests uneasily on the American conscience, and that one day a president will have to address it.

* On April 7, 1995, President Clinton declared that the U.S. did not owe Japan an apology for using the atom bombs and that Truman had made the right decision "based on the facts he had before him."

CHAPTER 2

DEFENDING THE BOMB: PIONEERS, PILOTS AND CREWMEN, VETERANS

Historical memory is affected by any personal relationship with the Hiroshima bomb. Leading figures in its development, and the pilots and crewmen specifically responsible for delivering the weapon, had unique psychological and moral investments in the atomic bomb. A quite different but equally compelling relationship was that of veterans who experienced the bomb as ending the war and saving their lives. Individuals expressed different attitudes about nuclear weapons, but few expressed serious doubts about the Hiroshima decision. In their reconstruction of events, they sought to emphasize the value of the weapon in terms of their own connection with the Hiroshima drama.

Bomb Pioneers: Oppenheimer and Conant

— Robert Oppenheimer and James Conant, central figures in creating the atomic bomb, were men of extraordinary intellectual reach and broad human concerns. That their reconstructions of Hiroshima were so complex is no surprise.

ROBERT OPPENHEIMER:
"I NEVER REGRETTED . . . HAVING DONE MY PART OF THE JOB."

For Oppenheimer, Hiroshima was an appalling event for which he felt considerable responsibility. That was evident in his "blood-on-my-hands" statement and in the desperate urgency of his plea to Truman for international control. In 1964 when he made that statement, "There is no doubt we were hideously uncomfortable about being associated with such slaughter," he was referring as much to himself as to any of his fellow atomic scientists. During that interview, he was even critical of "how we used it": "I do not have the feeling . . . that it was done right. . . . Our government should have acted with more foresight and clarity in telling the world and Japan what the bomb meant. The [Potsdam] ultimatum to Japan was full of pious platitudes."

Yet in what amounted to another side of Hiroshima reconstruction, he refused to speak self-critically, during perhaps hundreds of interviews, about his part in producing the bombs that destroyed the two cities, or even to express regret. To Lansing Lamont he declared, "About the making of the bomb and Trinity, I have no remorse." This should not be taken at face value, but it was consistent with the pride he took in the extraordinary accomplishment of producing the weapon. In that effort, Oppenheimer was a brilliant and compassionate leader, deeply appreciated, even loved, by most of the other scientists. For a man who made no discovery in physics commensurate with his intellectual gifts, it could be argued that Los Alamos was the most realized moment of his life.

Despite his misgivings about "how we used it," Oppenheimer expressed collegial respect for the decision makers: "I understand why it happened and appreciate with what nobility those men with whom I'd worked so closely made their decision. . . . It wasn't a pretty world. After the Tokyo fire raids, what possible moral reason could we have had for *not* using the atomic bomb? It's always easy to enjoy another man's bad conscience." He knew that he himself was virtually a decision maker and implies (at whatever level of awareness) that his own "bad conscience" is also too easily "enjoyed" by critics.

Oppenheimer's statements were confusing because they combined overt rejection of moral guilt with strong suggestions of self-condemnation or guilt *feelings*. This confusion was present in his famous statement that the physicists had "known sin," which was by no means a simple confession of wrongdoing. A number of observers have pointed out that, rather than expressing personal guilt, he was telling his fellow scientists that they had been engaged in a necessary project that had resulted in grotesque killing and suffering; and that this gave them (as he added) "a knowledge" —an experience—"which they cannot lose." Underneath whatever he meant to convey, however, he was undoubtedly struggling with his own survivor emotions—with death guilt and death anxiety he could not entirely avoid. These emotions had to do not only with creating a murderous weapon but, just as importantly, with having embraced that weapon as a beneficent force.

During the postwar years prior to being declared a security risk, Oppenheimer lived out both sides of his Hiroshima reconstruction: an intense commitment to international control of the weapons and, at the same time, an equally intense involvement in further atomic-weapons development. When later he opposed the hydrogen bomb, even if ambivalently and by no means entirely, we can suspect that his retained imagery of Hiroshima destruction may have helped tip the personal psychological balance—all the more so because this time it was not "his" bomb that was at issue. When he was immersed in nuclearism, he was a national hero; when he painfully extricated himself from that condition, he was crucified at a famous security hearing as a dangerous apostate of the civil religion surrounding nuclear weapons.

Among the leaders in making and using the atomic bomb, only Oppenheimer would visit Japan, traveling to Tokyo in 1960 to attend a conference, against the advice of friends. On arriving in Tokyo, however, and facing the inevitable questions about Hiroshima, he replied: "I do not regret that I had something to do with the technical success of the atomic bomb." Then he added: "It isn't that I don't feel bad, it is that I don't feel worse tonight than I did last night." By saying these things in Japan, Oppenheimer was probably expressing an impulse toward reconciliation while, at the same time, asserting the moral position to which he clung.

When W. L. Laurence (the original bomb spokesman) asked him in 1965, shortly before his death, if he had any misgivings about building the

Hiroshima bomb, his answer revealed a hardening of his defenses: "I never regretted, and do not regret now, having done my part of the job . . . I also think that it was a damn good thing that the bomb was developed, that it was recognized as something important and new, and that it would have an effect on the course of history." In his last years, Oppenheimer's face— so tormented as to resemble a death mask—reflected his life tragedy, perhaps most of all his particular struggle with Hiroshima-haunted historical memory.

JAMES CONANT: "DISTASTE . . . FOR THE WHOLE ROTTEN BUSINESS"

James Conant's response to Hiroshima resembled that of his good friend and ally Robert Oppenheimer. There are parallels between Oppenheimer's emergence following World War II and Conant's rise after World War I: each man had honed his gifts on work with grotesque new weaponry, in the process of becoming legendary intellectual figures of their time. Not surprisingly, the two men were similar in their advocacies. They came to share a devotion first to making and then using the weapon—and then seeking means of controlling it.

Trinity and Hiroshima took their toll on Conant. When he returned to Harvard soon afterward, it was with a relief that probably had to do with removing himself from an enterprise he had experienced as both heroic and tinged with evil. His description of Trinity tells us a great deal: "My first impression remains the most vivid, a cosmic phenomenon like an eclipse," he recalled the day after the event. "The whole sky suddenly full of white light like the end of the world. Perhaps my impression was only premature on a time scale of years!" This was the image of global destruction survivors in Hiroshima and Nagasaki were to experience, a form of existential terror associated with the end of everything. It never left Conant. It was surely central to his Hiroshima construct and greatly affected everything he subsequently thought and did in relation to restraining the weaponry.

When not defending the official narrative (as with the Stimson article), Conant's other side, his commitment to international control of the bomb, emerged. A more indirect consequence of Trinity and Hiroshima was a remarkable episode expressing a near grandiose sense of personal responsibility to the future. Conant asked a Harvard librarian to prepare a report on books and other printed material that would constitute a record of our civilization—to be microfilmed in ten copies and buried in different places around the country. Conant explained that the atomic bomb might cause our present civilization to "come to an end," and we should try to avoid what happened when Rome fell and almost all written records were lost. Eventually following the librarian's advice to abandon the enterprise, Conant probably became somewhat ashamed of it, as he never mentioned it in public or in his memoirs.

Many of Conant's other bomb-related advocacies were subject to shifts and contradictions—until the debate about the hydrogen bomb, in which his opposition was both strong and sustained. As with Oppenheimer, this opposition enabled him to resolve his personal dilemma about the weapons and assert Trinity/Hiroshima wisdom.

As Truman's decision on the hydrogen bomb neared, Conant firmly expressed his opinion that this new, genocidal weapon would "louse up the world still more." Scientific speculation that the fusion bomb might cause a chain reaction that would wipe out life on the planet may have reawakened Conant's apocalyptic image at Trinity. Also like Oppenheimer, Conant believed that existing atomic devices were adequate for all military purposes, and he advocated further development of smaller, tactical nuclear weapons. While Oppenheimer rendered the most eloquent critique, it was Conant who was more passionate—during one discussion becoming so upset that he was described as "looking almost translucent, so grey." Conant recalled early discussions about the atomic bomb, making him feel he was "seeing the same film, and a punk one, for the second time." And he was described as displaying "an immense distaste for . . . the whole rotten business."

Was Conant here expressing a sense of guilt in relation to his overall nuclear weapons involvement? We may assume that he was, at least to a degree. While embracing a policy of nuclearism, decision makers numb themselves to the grotesque human effects of the weaponry and thereby suppress potential feelings of guilt concerning their advocacy. With the advent of a new generation of weaponry, with which they had no previous involvement, they can undergo a form of nuclear backsliding in which those human images become conscious, and they experience stirrings of guilt in relation to them. Opposition to the new weaponry can then permit them to ward off such guilt, to transform it into the anxiety of responsibility. This is what probably happened in Conant's case. Hence his comment, during an internal debate in 1952, that "the atomic bomb is a bad weapon from the United States point of view."

After his unsuccessful opposition to the hydrogen bomb, he more or less lost interest in nuclear weapons, rejecting various appointments he was offered in relation to them. His sense of despair was expressed in an interview in 1952, when he declared that he no longer had "any connection with the atomic bomb" and that "I have no sense of accomplishment."

Consistent throughout his shifting policy advocacies—and lending passion and sometimes belligerence to all of them—was his intense American nationalism. Conant could look back and describe himself as "one of the first Cold War warriors." Wishing to press for even more rapid military preparations than the Truman administration was already making, he helped form and lead the Committee on the Present Danger.

In later years, Conant expressed misgivings about mass killings of civilians during World War II, about his own initial support of the Vietnam War, about the atomic bombing of Nagasaki, and ultimately, in his fashion, about his own overall role in connection with atomic weapons. These were misgivings about the course of his life. He expressed himself as "heavy with grief" at the "highly unpleasant revolution" in science that had so improved "the killing power of weapons." When he declared, "I do not like the atomic age or any of its consequences," one may assume that he was expressing a certain dislike for himself, given the inseparability of his adult life and the emergence of the atomic age. The psychological equation is given further credence by a self-denigrating statement he made in the early 1950s: "Since 1933 I can't claim to have advanced the barriers of science one millimeter."

Conant was a near-great man, a person with extraordinary gifts who never quite achieved the breakthrough that might have been equated with greatness. Like Oppenheimer, he could be said to have known too much. He spread himself across virtually all areas of knowledge, as opposed to the more limited but personally concentrated knowledge of those who fully realize their talent or genius. More able to manage than to inspire, he achieved much but was repeatedly frustrated by that which could not be adequately managed, and burdened by his own moral compromises.

The effectiveness of Conant's atomic–bomb work depended upon his capacity to focus on immediate tasks or decisions while numbing himself to virtually all else—in this case to the human effects of the weapons. The stirrings of guilt within him, despite his denial, required constant psychological vigilance of a kind he could hardly be aware of. From 1945, he constantly fended off Hiroshima-connected guilt feelings and sought to convert them into constructive advocacies. His granddaughter undoubtedly came closest when she described him as "haunted" by the bomb, "always mulling it over" and studying recent accounts to determine how they treated his role, becoming ever "more fretful" as he grew older. Being so haunted, we may say, was to Conant's credit as was his doubt about the "verdict of history."

But at the time when he did his work on the Hiroshima bomb and helped shape (through the Stimson article) its official narrative, all such emotional conflict was warded off, postponed. Conant's gifts were poured directly into the atomic bomb and into the American response. He was unique in what he brought to bear—advanced scientific and technological knowledge combined with intellectual brilliance and persuasiveness, as well as elaborate bureaucratic and political skills. In his assertive energies and talents, he represented a generation called forth by history to help save the West from tyranny. Those same energies and talents were to find tragic expression in nuclear weapons and, although later mobilized on behalf of nuclear restraint, were never to work free of their connections to the atomic bomb, and Hiroshima.

Pilots and Crewmen

The pilots and crewmen who carried out the Hiroshima and Nagasaki missions in many ways resemble the bomb pioneers. They, too, were an elite group immersed in a highly secret project—in their case, a year of special training for an enterprise they knew to be of enormous significance for the war. Although in no sense creators of the weaponry, they were its first conveyers. Like others in the military, they saw themselves as warriors in a long and bloody battle against tyranny. But these airmen were unique in being the people who actually carried the revolutionary device to its target and dropped it directly over large civilian populations.

Insofar as any group involved with the bomb could be identified as the ones who "did it," this was that group. The high altitude from which they dropped the bomb, and the elaborate technical procedures they had been trained to carry out, distanced them from any visual or other contact with their victims, and they struggled to maintain that distance over much of their subsequent lives. Their form of survival and Hiroshima reconstruction required three specific tendencies: maintaining a particularly strong mode of psychic numbing; asserting their professionalism; and re-creating a sense of military virtue in a war against evil adversaries.

These highly protective patterns enabled the pilots and crewmen to construct a version of Hiroshima history that stresses American achievement and humanity and radically deemphasizes the suffering of Japanese atomic-bomb victims.

Paul Tibbets, the pilot of the *Enola Gay,* exemplifies these patterns. His prominence in the media, along with the deaths of other atomic-bomb spokesmen (Truman, Stimson, Groves, and Oppenheimer), has rendered his Hiroshima commentaries especially influential.

When one of us asked him to express his personal feelings about dropping the bomb, he declared: "I've got a standard answer on that," which he readily provided: "I felt nothing about it. . . . This wasn't anything personal as far as I'm concerned, so I had no personal part in it. . . . It wasn't my decision to make morally, one way or another. . . . I did what I was told; it was a success as far as I was concerned; and that's where I've left it . . . I can assure you that I can sleep just as peacefully at night as anybody can sleep."

This last remark echoes Truman's claim, and indeed the men share similar modes of behavior. He once characterized himself as the kind of person "that if a thing gets to be bothering him, he has the faculty of shoving it in the back of his mind." An incident early in World War II, however, revealed another source of Tibbets's extreme version of numbing. When interviewed by an American reporter just before flying his first combat mission in Europe in 1942, he admitted feeling "sick with thoughts of the civilians who might suffer from the bombs dropped by his machine." And during the actual mission, as he watched the bombs fall, his reaction (as he later confided) was, "My God, women and children are getting killed!" After returning to his base he learned that the bombs had missed their target, and he realized that he had been so "intent on what was going to happen on the ground" that he didn't do "my job right." Tibbets found it necessary to overcome his vulnerability to feelings of compassion.

Henceforth, Tibbets relied heavily on his professionalism (a strong requirement for the Hiroshima mission). He compared his situation to that of physicians he had observed when he was a pre-medical student: Doctors who become emotionally involved with the plight of their patients often become ineffective and eventually have to quit, and Tibbets vowed that this kind of self-destructive empathy would never happen to him. "In a time of war," he would later explain, "a person can't afford to be governed by emotion." This attitude carried over to postwar reflections on Hiroshima, perhaps all the more so because Tibbets had volunteered to command the 509th Bombing Group and could have assigned another pilot to drop the Hiroshima bomb.

Indeed, he has gone to some lengths to assert his technical focus. He toured Nagasaki right after the war with a group of scientists and bought gifts and souvenirs, acting like an American tourist, as he put it. Later he remarked that Hiroshima and Nagasaki had served as "good virgin targets" ideal for "bomb damage studies." In 1976, he reenacted the Hiroshima mission at an air show in Texas, with a smoke bomb set off to simulate a mushroom cloud, and made plans for a repeat performance the following year until pressure from the State Department (there had been a storm of Japanese protest) caused its cancellation. We may consider this an assertive display of feeling nothing lest he feel too much.

But explaining himself as the Hiroshima pilot over so many years took its toll. He came to shun publicity, often traveling under an assumed name. He once complained, "You can only beat a horse so much and then he's dead." His recasting of this familiar saying revealed, however unintentionally, something of the psychological cost of maintaining his version of Hiroshima. Although his numbing was certainly effective, blending with a repetitious narrative, the process required considerable emotional energy to ward off ever-threatening feelings of guilt.

CONFUSION AND CONFLICT

But among some of the atomic-bomb pilots and crew there was more overt conflict and a wider range of expressed emotions, including pain and regret. Whatever the psychological confusion, however, these men continued to endorse the use of the bomb.

For instance, Jacob Beser, the radar expert who participated in both atomic missions, during a 1985 visit to Hiroshima declared defiantly to Japanese reporters: "I have no guilt, I have no remorse, I remember Pearl Harbor, I remember the Bataan Death March. . . ." But when interviewed privately by a fellow American in the Hiroshima Peace Park, he spoke quite differently. He characterized himself as, like all soldiers, "just another hired killer." Stating that "no taking of a human life is easy," he recognized the degree to which air crews were emotionally insulated: "I don't think I could have been an infantryman and looked over the sights of a gun at the man I was going to kill. Aerial warfare is very impersonal. I was 32,000 feet over this city and of course I never saw it—I was busy working." He referred to Hiroshima as "the place where we opened a new era of man's inhumanity to his fellow man," and the city reminded the world "that we must never do it again." But he added, irritably, "To hell with all this 'I'm sorry'—it's crazy! It doesn't mean anything!"—telling us that, although he was quite willing to oppose future Hiroshimas, he was tired of coping with his own emotions, especially involving potential regret or remorse.

Others revealed various forms of discomfort, with intimations of guilt. Charles Sweeney, who piloted the plane that dropped the Nagasaki bomb, donated earnings from a lecture tour to an orphanage in Hiroshima. One of his crewmen said that he wished he had "stayed in the tank outfit," which offered "a nice, clean way to kill people . . . I mean then they can fight back." Another, who had become an obstetrician, said he was happy to bring lives into the world after helping to snuff so many out.

Kermit Beahan, the bombardier on the Nagasaki mission, told how he and his crewmen found it necessary to push images of people "down there" out of their minds because "that would probably drive some people crazy . . . if you think of the women and children." Instead, he tried to think about the many letters he received from American servicemen saying that he saved their lives: "Those are the things that I choose to remember and dwell on rather than the agony that I know must have occurred to the survivors of the two cities." Beahan extended his observations to atomic-bomb pilots in general: "So many of my comrades just arbitrarily and automatically say they don't feel a damn bit of regret or guilt. I know them. I think deep within themselves [and here he included Paul Tibbets], they do."

PUBLIC CONTRITION?

Robert Lewis, co-pilot of the *Enola Gay,* rendered his survivor struggles with Hiroshima in a particularly dramatic, sometimes public, fashion. Lewis kept a log on the Hiroshima mission—as suggested by W. L. Laurence—which included the much-quoted words "My God! What have we done?" Less known is an equally significant passage: "If I live a hundred years, I'll never quite get those few minutes out of my mind." Lewis told a later interviewer, "There was a job to be done. Whether it was good or evil, I don't know."

He also participated in one of the strangest public renditions of Hiroshima, which took place on the May 11, 1955, episode of the popular television show *This Is Your Life.* The program featured the Reverend Kiyoshi Tanimoto, one of the central figures in John Hersey's *Hiroshima,* as well as several of the "Hiroshima maidens," young women who had been scarred by the bomb who had been brought to this country (in a program organized by Norman Cousins) to undergo surgery in New York. Upon arriving at the studio, Lewis learned that he would receive only expenses to appear on the show (he had understood there would be a fee) and reportedly decided to have a few drinks before the program began. Then, while waiting to go on, he peered into the room where two maidens were sitting and anxiously asked another guest: "And there are a hundred thousand more who look like *that?"*

On the program he recalled the words from his log, "My God, what have we done?"; after clasping Tanimoto's hand, he described, almost tearfully, the Hiroshima mission; and later in the show, when the host explained how viewers could contribute money to the maidens project, Lewis stepped forward with the first fifty-dollar check, which he identified as a contribution from the crew of the *Enola Gay.* Lewis was warmly applauded, but as soon as the show ended the network switchboard was flooded with calls, mostly from veterans, who were outraged over his emotional behavior (the Pentagon called him in for a rebuke as well).

His appearance on the television program probably reflected a desire of some kind for public contrition and reconciliation, but the television format and his own drinking combined to blur and confuse the experience.

The fact that Lewis apparently needed the alcohol to get through it did not render his emotions false. But it could suggest that, unconsciously, he felt able to make his confession only when it didn't really "count," at least for him, because he had been drinking.

Lewis may have found a more authentic outlet for his struggles in his avocation as an amateur sculptor. He recreated in stone a billowing mushroom cloud but had difficulty deciding whether to call it *God's Wind* or *The Devil's Wind*. Finally, he settled on a compromise: *God's Wind?*

These contradictory feelings on the part of atomic-bomb pilots and crewmen suggest that, despite the vast technological distancing, the extreme human consequences of such an act can be brought to bear on the individual mind. But that same mind would generally absorb its conflicts and contradictions sufficiently to justify the act. And that expression of "no regrets" could also serve as reassurance (though not without some uneasiness) for many other Americans.

THE EATHERLY EXCEPTION

The only one among the atomic-bomb pilots to express feelings of guilt, clearly and publicly, was Claude Eatherly, who became a cause célèbre in the U.S. and around the world in the late 1950s. Eatherly had flown the weather plane that found the skies over Hiroshima sufficiently clear on the morning of August 6, 1945, for the atomic-bomb mission to proceed.

A skillful and reliable pilot, Eatherly had engaged in a certain amount of heavy drinking and gambling, and he resented not being chosen to drop one of the atomic bombs (as well as the lack of recognition for piloting the weather plane). Later, he served as an airborne monitor at the 1946 Bikini tests, possibly receiving a harmful dose of radiation from flying through an atomic cloud. He was told by doctors that this could be the cause of his wife's two miscarriages and would recall this as the beginning of his compassion for Hiroshima survivors.

Shortly after the Bikini tests, when his mother was dying, he remembered being struck by the phrase "Thou shalt not kill," which he encountered in an open Bible, and "Then and there, for the first time, I realized what I had done." He described experiencing, soon afterward, a recurring nightmare in which he was piloting his plane above Hiroshima and then found himself on the ground in the city among the fires, with children running in and out of the flames. He wanted to rescue them but would weaken and find something holding him back. There followed, after his discharge from the Air Force, a long, confused sequence including job difficulties, marital problems, suicidal tendencies, criminal behavior (including forged checks and armed robberies), psychiatric hospitalization (with diagnoses from severe neurosis to character disorder to schizophrenia), insulin shock treatment, and an increasing tendency to articulate his Hiroshima-related sense of guilt as the source of his misbehavior and need for punishment.

With the help of two extensive dialogues—one with a sympathetic psychiatrist and another with the European philosopher Gunther Anders —Eatherly deepened this self-understanding. In letters he exchanged with Anders, later collected in a book entitled *Burning Conscience,* Eatherly wrote movingly about his pain and his compassion for Hiroshima survivors. Anders, an early and forceful critic of Hiroshima and nuclear weapons, did much to reinforce an oversimplified cause-and-effect explanation of Hiroshima guilt leading to criminal behavior.

Before long, Eatherly's story became myth. He was often misidentified, in both the U.S. and foreign press, as "the Hiroshima pilot" who dropped the bomb. The European press, always more critical of the atomic bombings than the American media, turned Eatherly into a folk hero, an American Dreyfus. Some alleged that he had been sent to mental hospitals to silence him. Hollywood planned a film on his life (it was never produced). Bertrand Russell, at the age of ninety, wrote about Eatherly; so did Edmund Wilson and Dorothy Day.

Inevitably, an anti-Eatherly backlash appeared. William Bradford Huie wrote a highly intemperate denunciation in a book that pointed out inaccuracies in what Anders and others had written, stressed Eatherly's unstable behavior before Hiroshima, and portrayed him as a fraud. Finally, Ronnie Dugger, a fellow Texan, took a more sensitive and compassionate approach, citing evidence that, whatever the complexities involved, Eatherly's sense of guilt was genuine: "The sources of his troubles were various, but his active role in the world-deforming genesis of the atomic age was among them." In his book *Dark Star,* Dugger saw Eatherly as a "nuclear penitent"—as in Camus' terms, both executioner and victim. Dugger went on to stress Eatherly's coming to symbolize "the guilt of the man who obeys an order to help cause mass death." What is important for

Hiroshima history, Dugger tells us, is that Eatherly was able to say "No, wait. I helped do it. I'm responsible."

Eatherly broke down for many reasons, including long-standing personal problems, but Hiroshima and Bikini surely played a part. What his detractors were too quick to dismiss was Eatherly's survivor struggle to articulate and come to terms with bomb-related feelings of guilt and to reconstruct a moral version of Hiroshima history. Yet if Eatherly was the symbolic nuclear penitent Dugger saw him to be, he was indeed a frail reed on which to place America's moral concerns.

Three decades later, many Americans continue to believe that the Hiroshima pilots, and others involved in dropping the bombs, all went mad, committed suicide, or went to jail. Referring to these reports, Paul Tibbets once said: "I've been a drunkard. I've been insane. I've been a recluse in a monastery. I've been in prison." The rumors are remarkable, because Eatherly was virtually the only Hiroshima flyer who broke down. It suggests that many Americans truly want to believe that if you helped drop a nuclear bomb you were likely to go crazy. Perhaps Americans wish to feel remorse about the atomic bombings—to create a more responsible Hiroshima narrative—but are unable to do that directly, and so we adopt the image of mentally disturbed pilots as our surrogates.

The Veterans

American servicemen, especially those stationed in the Pacific, were understandably jubilant in 1945 at the news of Hiroshima. Many had survived extensive bloody combat, and Hiroshima seemed to signal that they would now survive the war.

Whatever they learned subsequently about the horrors of the atomic bomb, American veterans mainly associated it with joyous survival. When others questioned the bomb's use, veterans would feel their own lives were not being valued. And since the bomb was the price for their lives, they have felt a psychological need to emphasize what the bomb purchased (ever-larger figures of lives saved) and to justify the payment (the Japanese started the war, and there was no alternative to using the bomb). They could then justify, and continue to feel, their original bomb-related jubilation. Whenever the justification was threatened—when the bomb was described as unnecessary and a danger to the human future—their own comfort in survival could also be threatened by inner questions.

More than that, servicemen were well aware, and justifiably proud, of the enormity of the cause for which they fought. In connection with the recent Smithsonian controversy, a number of veterans have said, in effect: "If we hadn't fought for this country, there would be no possibility of historians debating Hiroshima or anything else." (They are quite right, even if one must add that they were fighting for, among other things, the right of historians and other Americans to freely explore all versions of truth.)

The emotions of soldiers reverberate through society. That was certainly the case with the joyous response to Hiroshima. Americans connected the atomic bombings with the survival of our country and its fighting forces. Indeed the veterans' narrative of Hiroshima became the basis for our official narrative, and for the American public's embrace of that narrative.

From the very beginning the veterans' views have dominated public discourse. Just days after the atomic attack, newspapers and magazines were filled with accounts of their elation. The sentence that best summed up the feelings of soldiers, their families, and many other Americans (as quoted in a number of sources), was "Thank God for the atomic bomb"—a sentiment that goes beyond joy and even suggests divine intervention. After interviewing many veterans, the author of a recent book about Okinawa observed: "Certain that only 'the beautiful bomb' saved them, they would feel pity, contempt or anger—which turned to resignation over the years —for noncombatants who would later brand its use unnecessary and immoral."

Those who fought in the Pacific had witnessed death all around them and often had the sense that next time their turn would come. "The veterans in the outfit felt we had already run out of luck anyway," recalled marine E. B. Sledge in his moving memoir of the Pacific war. "We viewed the invasion [of Japan] with complete resignation that we would be killed —either on the beach or inland." In his book *WWII*, the novelist James Jones portrayed the early preparations for an invasion and wondered what it must have been like for a tough old survivor of Guadalcanal or the Philippines "to stand on some beach and watch this huge war machine beginning to stir and move all around him and know that he very likely had survived this far only to fall dead on the dirt of Japan's home islands. . . ."

Norman Mailer recalls being so elated by the news of Hiroshima that he was "stunned and euphoric" for three days, impervious to anything about the atomic bomb other than its "miraculous" offering of life for him and others who were convinced that they would die in the invasion. Those feelings were confirmed for Mailer and his buddies when they landed on southern Honshu in the early occupation and saw what they took to be gun emplacements in protective mountain areas. Later an opponent of war and nuclearism, Mailer felt at that time that "You couldn't say anything bad about the atomic bomb."

Referring to the prospect of fighting a mobilized Japanese population on its homeland, another veteran asked: "Who the hell could have shot those women and kids? I guess we'd have had to." Little wonder, then, that marines in E. B. Sledge's company greeted the news of the end of the war "with quiet disbelief coupled with an indescribable sense of relief. We thought the Japanese would never surrender. Many refused to believe it."

> Sitting in stunned silence, we remembered our dead. So many dead. So many maimed. So many bright futures consigned to the ashes of the past. So many dreams lost in the madness that had engulfed us.

These views and memories have not changed over the years, and when they write or talk about the atomic bombings veterans consistently raise the same major points:

- An invasion of Japan would have been even bloodier than Okinawa.

- Only the use of the atomic bomb prevented the invasion and saved the soldiers' lives.

- Only those who served in the war—not historians or journalists—can truly appreciate what it meant to survive that brutal conflict.

- It's a pity that so many had to die in Hiroshima and Nagasaki, but the Japanese started it, with Pearl Harbor, and then lost all claims for mercy by their treatment of American POWs.

- It doesn't matter whether the casualty estimate for the American invasion was twenty-five thousand or one million—not one more American should have been killed if we had the means to end the war as quickly as possible.

- Any commemoration of the Hiroshima mission must reflect credit on all veterans and not impugn the motives of the servicemen or the decision makers involved in the mission.

It is the invasion the atomic bomb prevented that gives the veterans' story, and the entire official narrative, such power and legitimacy. It is the invasion scenario that draws so many veterans who "survived" it into the Hiroshima narrative in a personal way, for it involves not just those already in the Pacific who would have been part of the first landing party in November 1945 but potentially everyone else in uniform—in Europe or back in the States—as well as every American male of draft age not yet called to service. They all might have been involved in the assault on Japan if the war lasted well into 1946.

Take the number of men in all those categories in 1945, then add the number of their children and grandchildren, and the number of potential lives saved reaches into the tens of millions. Then one can begin to understand the motivation and the emotional power of testimonials to the bomb over the years.

Shortly after the war ended in 1945, an editorial cartoon in a Tennessee newspaper showed an American soldier striding ashore in Japan with a corpse labeled *Avoided Costs* sprawled on the sand beside him. A mushroom cloud loomed in the distance. On his back the soldier bore the legend *Bloodless Invasion*. The caption for the drawing read, "But for the Grace of God—." Ever since, the media has emphasized the invasion scenario and dramatized it at every turn. One highlight of the fortieth-anniversary coverage in 1985 was a *Nightline* docudrama that depicted the hypothetical invasion in all its horror. That program, like most other accounts of the atomic bombings, stated flatly that the bomb did not merely contribute to, but was solely responsible for, ending the war.

This view is understandable but, in a way, self-diminishing for the veterans, because it shifts the credit for defeating the Japanese from the military personnel in the Pacific to a small group of bomb makers in New Mexico and decision makers in Washington. To fully justify the use of the bomb is to reject the notion that Japan was already on its knees, devastated and surrounded, and ready to surrender, thanks to the U.S. soldiers, pilots, and seamen who had defeated the enemy, at great cost, in one battle after another across the Pacific. Veterans accept, even promote, the bomb as necessary to end the war when they could, with justification, claim that *they* had already completed the job.

Indeed, most of the top military leaders at the close of the war felt the bomb was not required to end the conflict. General Hap Arnold disclosed in his memoirs that "It always appeared to us that, atomic bomb or no atomic bomb, the Japanese were already on the verge of collapse." General LeMay found the atomic bombing "anticlimactic" because "the verdict was already rendered." Just weeks after Hiroshima, President Truman publicly declared that the bomb "did not win the war," and General Groves privately confided that "surrender was an ultimate certainty in any case of course. . . ." As much as Truman and Groves surely wished to portray the bomb as the decisive weapon, each felt compelled to state that the American serviceman had actually produced the victory. To do otherwise in 1945, with the bloodshed on Iwo Jima and Okinawa still fresh in mind, would have insulted America's fighting men.

The most revealing statement on this matter, although forgotten today, came from Secretary of State Byrnes on August 29, 1945. The *New York Times* reported it on the front page under the headline: "Japan Beaten Before Atom Bomb, Byrnes Says, Citing Peace Bids." Byrnes had been angered by Japanese spokesmen who claimed that the atomic bomb was primarily responsible for forcing surrender. He must have sensed, accurately as we now know, that the Japanese leaders were seeking to build acceptance among their citizenry for the surrender, as well as to picture their nation as the loser in an essentially unfair fight—defeated by a cosmic force, not by the American military.

Byrnes wasn't going to let them get away with it. He declared that the bomb had merely "facilitated the surrender," and he cited, according to the newspaper report, "what he called Russian proof that the Japanese knew that they were beaten before the first atomic bomb was dropped on Hiroshima." (This was a reference to Japan's attempted peace initiative through Moscow.) Then, according to the article, Byrnes "made it clear that he believed that the men who had fought the war up to that point in the Pacific and Asia deserved full credit for victory." Here was the man who probably had as much to do with the bomb's being used as anyone, granting "full credit" to the servicemen, not the weapon, for winning the war. Yet, as years passed, the veterans, in endorsing the evolving view of the bomb as essential—the bomb as savior—would unwittingly shift much of that credit from themselves to civilian decision makers like Byrnes.

Paul Fussell and the Price of Experience

Certainly the most provocative and oft-quoted statement by a survivor of the Pacific war is Paul Fussell's 1981 magazine article "Hiroshima: A Soldier's View," later published in a volume called *Thank God for the Atom Bomb and Other Essays*. (The book jacket featured a drawing of a falling bomb with a smiling face on it.) In August 1945, Fussell was a twenty-one-year-old infantry soldier stationed in Germany awaiting shipment to the Philippines to prepare for his role in the invasion of Honshu. He and his comrades cried tears of joy upon hearing of the bomb, for they had expected that in another six months they would be rushing up the beaches near Tokyo "assault-firing while being machine-gunned, mortared, and shelled. . . ."

Fussell is a compelling, and respected, commentator on the subject. He has written acclaimed books on World Wars I and II that view the motivations and behavior of all sides in those conflicts stripped of sentimentality. Indeed, in his atomic-bomb essay, he observed that U.S. troops in the Pacific had engaged in "much sadism and cruelty, undeniably racist," sometimes using surrendering Japanese soldiers for target practice. Fussell harbored no illusions about the nobility of the Hiroshima mission, calling it a "ghastly affair" and admitting that one of the reasons the U.S. used the bomb was to "irrationally Remember Pearl Harbor with a vengeance." The purpose of the atomic assault, he wrote, in typically bracing fashion, "was political and military, sadistic and humanitarian, horrible and welcome."

Yet he went on to belittle intellectuals and historians who question the Hiroshima decision, establishing as his overriding thesis—and here his opinion reflected the average veteran's—"the importance of experience, sheer, vulgar experience, in influencing, if not determining, one's views about that use of the atomic bomb." Only those who served in the ground forces, "where coarse self-interest is the rule," have anything relevant to say about Hiroshima. In a "collision between experience and theory," only experience counts. (Fussell noted pointedly that Truman was "the only President in my lifetime who ever had experience in a small unit of ground troops whose mission it was to kill people.") From this vantage point, he mocked revisionist scholars who were infants, or not even born, when the bomb fell.

Faced with the testimony of certain veterans of the Pacific who questioned the use of the bomb, Fussell carried his thesis a step further by invoking the principle that "the farther from the scene of the horror, the easier to talk." Only those who served on the front lines in the Pacific (or who, like Fussell, were slated for the planned invasion of Japan) had any credibility. Referring to one prominent critic of the decision to use the bomb, Fussell wrote: "I don't demand that he experience having his ass shot off. I merely note that he didn't."

The *New Republic* essay provoked an avalanche of positive mail from veterans, but Michael Walzer, author of *Just and Unjust Wars,* responded with an impassioned critique. Fussell had written from the perspective of the ordinary soldier, Walzer observed, and "That standpoint is human, all too human: let anyone die but me! There are no humanitarians in the foxholes." This is perfectly understandable, he added, but with Fussell, it seems, "There are no limits at all; anything goes, so long as it helps to bring the boys home." It was Walzer's view that combat should be a struggle between combatants. "There is a code," he declared. "Hiroshima was a violation of that code. . . . If Harry Truman's first responsibility was to American soldiers, he was not without responsibility elsewhere; no man is."

Fussell responded by re-stating his arguments (and noted that Walzer was only ten years old in 1945). Years later, asked to comment on the Smithsonian's controversial *Enola Gay* exhibit, Fussell affirmed that he was "delighted' that the bomb had been dropped, for "It saved my life, and the lives of many others . . . The war was godawful, but it had to end some way, and I'd rather have some Japanese women and children burnt up than have myself killed on the beach at Kyushu."

This, of course, was nothing more than the natural ethic of the soldier, carried perhaps to an extreme. What is problematic about Fussell's thinking is not his insistence on the value of personal history in the Pacific but the certainty with which he rejects all other historical considerations—all other perspectives on Hiroshima—including evidence of what was happening elsewhere at the same time. After all, the decision to use the bomb was not made in the Pacific, but in Washington and at Potsdam. Fussell's argument, his entire historical reconstruction, depends upon a principle of inevitability: "And the invasion was going to take place: there's no question about that," he wrote. With that insistence, he cannot consider any possibility that the bomb may not have been the necessary ingredient for the war to end and his life preserved.

Further, Fussell urges us not to "misimagine the circumstances" of the Hiroshima bomb because of the obvious "stupidity" and "mismanagement" of the nuclear arms race that followed. But as British writer Ian Clark has pointed out in his comment on the Fussell essay, "This is to miss the point completely."

> It is palpably the "mis-imaginings" of the Hiroshima experience (of which Fussell's is a splendidly eloquent example) that have contributed directly to the ensuing "stupidity" (if such it be) about which Fussell himself laments. Fussell's warning that we should not read the history of the nuclear age backward sits uncomfortably given the more frequent tendency to misread that history forward from 1945 to the present: it is this latter tendency that has been such a dominant (if often unspoken) influence upon the strategic culture of our age.

Fussell and many other veterans, quite understandably, remain in thrall to the emotions surrounding their own survival. Their survivor mission has come to include justifying the means by which they believe their lives were spared. In that way, veterans often consider the atomic bombings apart from all subsequent events. In doing so, as Clark observes, they fail to recognize, quite tragically, "the intimate connection between the justifia-bility of what was done then and the legitimacy of what has followed since."

It is not uncommon for people to hold on to powerful emotions experienced at the moment of survival—in isolation from everything else. But when the "everything else" includes the use of atomic weapons, the effect on historical memory—and on national consciousness—can be dis-torting and dangerous in ways we have seen. One needs to recognize the genuine sacrifice of World War II veterans and at the same time distinguish that sacrifice from the specific horror and threat to the human future embodied in two of our military acts late in that war.

CHAPTER 3

A Different Witness:
Scientists and Activists

The forms of witness we have described so far each follow the outline of the official narrative. But other expressions of witness were always possible, in fact inevitable. Two groups of Americans—atomic scientists and antinuclear activists—have warned the public about the danger Hiroshima brought into the world. They bear witness to the atomic bombings not only as horrific events but also as indicators of a new potential for destroying the world.

Scientists involved in making the Hiroshima bomb have varied significantly in their responses, but from them came a cadre of what we call prophetic survivors. They articulated the apocalyptic potential of the technology that the scientists themselves had created. For decades after, antinuclear activists would return to the authoritative testimony of the troubled, enlightened scientists. In that testimony, Hiroshima was no longer a symbol of victory, and had significance beyond human suffering: it became a profound source of knowledge in both a technological and spiritual sense.

The New Knowledge of the Scientists

None of the other Manhattan Project scientists had as much responsibility as Oppenheimer and Conant, but they too became intensely aware that their dedicated, often brilliant, work culminated in the devastation of two cities. Whatever their form of witness, they could never free themselves from what they had created. When the results from Hiroshima came in, only they possessed special knowledge of the dark force they had brought into the world. They had (in Oppenheimer's phrase) "known sin" both in what they had done and what they had learned. Although many made constructive use of their special knowledge, very few would clearly condemn their own role in making the bomb—or its use against Japan—lest they be burdened with overwhelming feelings of guilt.

Some strongly defended the use of the bomb and tended to maintain intense commitment to weapons work. A smaller group spoke out against the Hiroshima decision and abandoned the bomb program immediately after the war (in one case, even before the summer of 1945). Perhaps the largest group struggled painfully with the Hiroshima decision, neither able to fully condemn nor accept it, but expressed their special knowledge in fervently testifying to nuclear danger. The witness of these last two groups could be said to be prophetic, informed by their own descent into the netherworld of the bomb.

Among those who endorsed the bombings was physicist Harold Agnew, who accompanied the first atomic mission and declared many years later that the Japanese at Hiroshima and Nagasaki "bloody well deserved" what they got. Luis Alvarez, who also flew over Hiroshima on August 6, said he "could muster very little sympathy" for colleagues who felt "responsible for killing civilians." He expressed feeling "great pride" in helping create the bomb and said he had "difficulty understanding why so many people see nuclear weapons as mankind's greatest threat. Not one of them has been used since World War II. . . ." In these cases, and many others, the pride of scientific achievement extended into sustained enthusiasm for the weaponry in a survivor pattern that blocks out concerns about past victims or future dangers, and stifles self-condemnation.

After Hiroshima, Edward Teller became a zealous, some might say fanatical, advocate of the hydrogen bomb, and the most extreme of nuclearistic true believers. He later claimed that the atomic bombings were "unnecessary," and that he told Oppenheimer this before Hiroshima. Several prominent historians have questioned this account, pointing to a letter he wrote around the time of the Hiroshima decision which seem to suggest grudging approval. Whatever his initial attitude, his later advocacies were consistent with the *meaning* he took from Hiroshima. In his 1962 book, *Legacy of Hiroshima,* he observed: "Hiroshima has haunted many scientists and has distorted the judgment of quite a few United States policymakers. The idea has become fixed in the minds of our people that atomic weapons are instruments of indiscriminate destruction." Pointing to Hiroshima's rapid recovery, he asserted that the lethality of nuclear weapons was exaggerated, "a dangerous myth."

This suggests that Teller, however concerned about the loss of life at Hiroshima, was also worried about the extent to which negative images concerning the atomic bomb could affect support for his own obsession, the hydrogen bomb. His nuclearism has sometimes led to fantasy and illusion. Nearly fifty years after Hiroshima, for example, Teller told Christopher Hitchens of the *Nation* that his "chief regret" about the nuclear era was "the propagation of unreasoning and unverified fears concerning the danger of radiation." Hitchens noted that not once but several times Teller stated that "a little radiation can be good for you."

One of the few Los Alamos scientists who considered Hiroshima indefensible from the very beginning was Robert Wilson. He was the young scientist who became physically sick after learning that the bomb had been dropped over the center of a city, prompting Oppenheimer's famous remark, "The reaction has begun." Wilson could never forgive himself for not having left the project earlier. "I would like to think now," he said in the early 1980s, "that at the time of the German defeat I would have stopped and taken stock . . . and walked away from Los Alamos. In terms of everything I believed in before, after and during the war, I cannot understand why I did not take that act. On the other hand it was simply not in the air. . . . Our lives were directed to do one thing, it was as if we were programmed to do that, and we as automatons were doing it." It took Trinity to really jar him, providing him for the first time "a real, an existential, understanding of what we had been making." Wilson was overwhelmed with horror after Hiroshima, and "I still am," he said more than thirty-five years after the fact.

For some, feelings of guilt came later. Nearly forty years after Hiroshima, Seth Neddermeyer (the "father of implosion") confessed that he felt "overwhelmed" by guilt whenever he thought about the atomic bombings. "This is what bugs me more than anything else—I don't remember having any strong feelings about [the bombings] at the time," he explained to a writer, almost in tears. "I guess I just got caught up in the mindless hysteria."

Only one scientist, the British physicist Joseph Rotblat, left the bomb project when it became apparent that Germany would soon surrender and the race for the bomb (which was always one-sided) was over. What prompted his departure, however, was the "disagreeable shock" of hearing first-hand from General Groves (as Rotblat revealed in a little-noted 1985 article) that "the real purpose in making the bomb was to subdue the Soviets." Later he called his entire involvement with the bomb a "traumatic experience . . . Our concepts of morality seem to get thrown overboard once military action starts." Afterward, he refused to work on weapons, choosing instead, he explained, "an aspect of nuclear physics which would definitely be beneficial to humanity: the applications to medicine."

Scientists who tried desperately to prevent the use of the bomb before Hiroshima, such as Leo Szilard and Eugene Rabinowitch, nonetheless felt guilty afterward. Szilard condemned himself not only for working on the bomb but for failing to halt its use. In his parable, "My Trial As a War Criminal," he brought himself to justice (an impulse that recalls the mock trial involving Truman and Churchill). Szilard defended himself, in the fable, by declaring that he had circulated an anti-bomb petition among scientists. But the prosecution pointed out that this had no effect because he foolishly went through the proper channels—where the petition could be quashed—instead of obeying his own impulse to act more radically. And so at the end of the story, Szilard declared himself as guilty as the next scientist.

Eugene Rabinowitch actually considered taking a step Szilard perhaps only fantasized about. During the summer of 1945, haunted by the unstoppable momentum of the decision to use the bomb against Japan, Rabinowitch and some of his colleagues "walked the streets of Chicago," he later wrote, "vividly imagining the sky suddenly lit by a giant fireball, the steel skeletons of skyscrapers bending into grotesque shapes and their masonry raining into the streets below, until a great cloud of dust rose and settled over the crumbling city." This was so unsettling that Rabinowitch, who had already signed Szilard's petition and co-drafted the Franck Report (which also challenged use of the bomb against Japan), considered drastic action. Of all the top scientists who worked on the bomb, only Rabinowitch seriously considered leaking to the news media the plan to drop the bomb on a Japanese city—a shocking breach of security—and spent several sleepless nights pondering it.

But, like Leo Szilard, he failed to make the next, difficult move—and like Szilard he would regret this failure for the rest of his life. "Twenty-five years later, I feel I would have been right if I had done so," he revealed in an extraordinary 1971 letter to the *New York Times*. (The letter was inspired by Daniel Ellsberg's release of the Pentagon Papers during the Vietnam War.) On another occasion, Rabinowitch explained that if he had alerted the public they would have at least known *in advance* of "a crime" that was to be carried out in their name. He harbored no illusions that the American people would have tried to prevent the atomic bombings; more likely, the vast majority would have "enthusiastically favored" it. Still, he affirmed, "they should have been given the opportunity to accept the responsibility for mass murder on an unprecedented scale—of which they now stand guilty before history without having known anything about it beforehand."

After Hiroshima, each of these scientist-survivors attempted to bear witness to the atomic bombings by campaigning for arms control and a nuclear test ban, to keep the weapon from ever being used again. Rothblat helped organize the scientists' movement in England, Wilson directed the Federation of American Scientists, Rabinowitch edited the *Bulletin of the Atomic Scientists,* and Szilard founded the Council for a Livable World. They had found their survivor meaning in an animating relationship to guilt, a capacity to confront the source of that guilt in a manner that could lead to positive action. In that way self-condemnation can be transformed into the anxiety of social responsibility. But the process can be incomplete and erratic, with painful feelings of guilt still finding periodic expression.

• • •

A third group of scientists has responded forcefully and often eloquently to the lessons of Hiroshima—even while refusing to condemn their work on the bomb project. Among them, most notably, are Hans Bethe and Philip Morrison. Each has contributed significantly to the control of nuclear weapons since Hiroshima.

Bethe, the wise and humane physicist, has described his three immediate reactions to Hiroshima as "fulfillment," "What have we done?" and "It should not be done again"—and then spent a lifetime attempting to prevent a repeat. Bethe was an early advocate of a no-first-use pledge, declaring that "no nation has the right to use such a bomb, no matter how righteous its cause." Still, he felt connected to Los Alamos and the challenge of perfecting the weapons. He "hated" the idea of a hydrogen bomb, denounced Truman's decision to build it, and hoped it wouldn't work, yet eventually joined the project.

"You may well ask," he said later, no doubt referring to himself, "why people with a kind heart and humanist feelings would go and work on weapons of mass destruction." The answer is not simple and has to do with Bethe's sense of the feasibility of making the weapon, the Soviets' capacity to make it, and his own long-standing identification with the weapons. But underneath all that, one suspects, was a need to find value and even nobility in his earlier work on the atomic bomb. Such survivor meaning can be enhanced by supporting nuclear power as a potentially life-enhancing product of the bomb work—a moral counterweight to the mass killings in Japan—and Bethe has been one of the most intense proponents of that technology. His Hiroshima survivor mission has been contradictory and yet consistently active on behalf of restraint.

Philip Morrison has established a similar pattern. Perhaps more than any other scientist, he has acted as a witness to Hiroshima, despite—or perhaps because of—his conflicting feelings over the use of the bomb. One observes in Morrison's life a trajectory from the atomic-bomb project to undoing its influences, with everything he undertakes more or less driven by that earlier experience, and admirably so.

Involved with the Manhattan Project from an early stage, Morrison followed the Hiroshima and Nagasaki bombs from Los Alamos to Trinity to Tinian, and was one of the few scientists (as we have seen) to observe their effects in Japan. He felt the impulse to witness even then, volunteering for the Hiroshima scientific survey in September 1945 so he could "follow the whole thing." Ever since, when asked about the weapon being used again, he invokes Hiroshima, because he fears that the people who would make such a decision would not be "very close to what was actually happening. When you go there," he says of his own mission to Hiroshima, *"you saw what it was like."*

For him, Hiroshima was "a crime and sin" not because it was the last event of World War II but as "the first event of a future that's intolerable." Much worse than the bomb's use against Japan was "it's being a token of what lies in the future. That was the danger." Rather than dwelling on the decision to use the bomb, Morrison has always focused on the future— one reason for his accomplishments as an advocate of nuclear restraint. "We can't undo the past but we can undo the future," he told us. To "put Hiroshima behind us," the United States must sign treaties that would stop nuclear testing forever and severely reduce nuclear stockpiles. "Fifty years of Hiroshima," he observes, "is enough."

Scientists were perhaps the most active and varied American witnesses of the Hiroshima experience. One segment did much to support the official narrative and propel the arms race; others became dedicated antinuclear crusaders. A problem has been the frequent occurrence of important elements of each of these survivor missions in the same individual. Even so, the scientists provided the most significant early challenge to the official narrative, and a basis for much of the questioning that followed.

Activists: A Bridge to Hiroshima

Many Americans who oppose nuclear weapons seek wisdom or inspiration in opening themselves to Hiroshima. They attempt to learn from Hiroshima survivors—through direct contact, writings, or visual images—what happened there, how the weapons kill people, and what they do to those who survive. In the process of becoming witnesses, activists find themselves sharing the survivor emotions of victims of the atomic bombing.

From the first stirrings of an American disarmament movement, activists recognized the grim significance of Hiroshima and Nagasaki to their cause. Over the years, many traveled to the two cities and, transformed by the experience, returned home to deliver speeches, write books, or make films. Others arranged to bring survivors of the atomic bombings to America to offer their personal testimony at forums and peace rallies. Some who had no direct contact with the survivors nevertheless attempted to expose Americans to what happened in August 1945 by appropriating images (such as shadows of vaporized victims left on sidewalks) from Hiroshima and Nagasaki.

Each act of witness was, consciously or not, an attempt to break through the official suppression and personal numbing that surround the atomic bombings. Hiroshima became for them a symbol, a warning, a rhetorical device—even a kind of sacred text. Hiroshima held out important truths for the atomic age: the totality of destruction, the bomb's unending lethal influence, its capacity to exterminate the species. The two cities conveyed a sense of nuclear actuality. The bombs were really used there. Americans could read, view and, if they allowed themselves, contemplate what happened to the victims. In the process, they might feel awe, dread, or anger, emotions appropriate in imagining the possible effects of a future nuclear war. What could be called the Hiroshima connection was a bridge of memory between what human beings have already done and what they should do to prevent a recurrence.

The first acts of witness, after the bombs fell, came from a small number of Americans who called on their country to help rebuild Hiroshima and undo some of the damage it had done. This plea did not just arise from pacifists and liberals but, as we have seen, from some religious leaders, as well as conservative editor David Lawrence. Officials in Hiroshima occasionally put forth this suggestion themselves. A few Americans, especially Quakers, contributed money, material, or their own labor. This showed American concern, but the effort was limited. There was no dramatic project to rally around, and memories of the Pacific war were still vivid. Most who took part in these programs claimed they were motivated not by guilt but a desire for reconciliation, yet surely the two were intertwined.

American activists held vigils every August 6, but on the whole they did not dwell on American culpability. Hiroshima was invoked primarily as a warning of what awaited the entire world if it did not control the atom. The decision to use the bomb was rarely attacked, mainly because of expediency. One activist observed, "People don't like to have their noses rubbed in their mistakes." Pacifist leader A. J. Muste was once rebuked by a church official for denouncing the decision to use the bomb, claiming it would "divide our forces." Avoiding the Hiroshima decision was often justified by activists for the same reason, though their own numbing and discomfort, which they shared with other Americans, also undoubtedly played a part. The peace movement, which had practically disappeared during World War II, was still quite small, and public condemnations of the atomic attacks were so rare that when the Fellowship of Reconciliation circulated a statement calling for "confession and repentance" signed by forty activists, including Lewis Mumford and A. J. Muste, it made national news.

In the mid-1950s, however, some activists found a way to remind Americans of the human effects of the Hiroshima decision without risking political capital. Except for that brief period that followed John Hersey's article, this remains perhaps the only instance when the personal costs of Hiroshima and Nagasaki came vividly to life for mainstream America—and the survivors' experience was at its core.

The Hiroshima Maidens

The episode evolved out of a visit to Hiroshima in 1949 by Norman Cousins, who would bear witness to the atomic bombings in numerous and varied ways for the rest of his life. Cousins looked beyond the new buildings in the city and saw a vast number of ill-treated orphans. He initiated a Moral Adoption program to provide funds to feed, educate, and shelter several hundred children. He, too, emphasized reconciliation, not atonement. Guilt "was real enough," he admitted, but that was "not the whole answer and we knew it."

The adoption program faded quickly as fears about a new bomb, the H-bomb, overcame misgivings about the effects of the first. Then, in 1954, fallout from a U.S. test in the Pacific contaminated a Japanese fishing vessel, the *Lucky Dragon*. One man died, sparking worldwide condemnation and a brief re-examination of the plight of other Japanese bomb victims. According to reports, at least five thousand *hibakusha** were receiving inadequate medical help.

Among them was a large group of young women badly disfigured by the bombings. Rev. Kiyoshi Tanimoto, one of the central characters in Hersey's *Hiroshima,* was determined to send the girls to the U.S. for plastic surgery. He approached Eleanor Roosevelt during her visit to Hiroshima in 1953, but she turned the idea aside. Tanimoto finally found a patron in Norman Cousins, who set out to raise funds to sponsor the trip and convinced the chief plastic surgeon at Mt. Sinai Hospital in New York to head the medical team. The Air Force agreed to fly the group of twenty-five girls, now known as the Hiroshima Maidens, to America. The State Department promised not to stand in the way of the mission, providing it was not billed as an act of atonement or restitution.

But as the departure neared, "We got a little nervous," Assistant Secretary of State Walter Robertson later admitted. "My main concern was that this project might lend fuel to the public opinion in favor of outlawing the atomic bomb." He feared that the Maidens might be "put on exhibition throughout the country to point up the horrors of nuclear warfare." The day before the Maidens were set to leave Japan, an American consul in Hiroshima tried to scuttle the trip. He cabled the State Department that the project was not in keeping with "our worldwide efforts to de-emphasize the destructive effects of nuclear weapons." Senior officials at the State Department ordered the flight canceled—minutes after the plane carrying the Maidens had left for America.

When they arrived in New York, the Maidens received a warm reception. The project, usually hailed as a "mercy mission," received its widest exposure from the television program *This Is Your Life,* which also featured the controversial appearance of *Enola Gay* co-pilot Robert Lewis. Twenty thousand viewers contributed $55,000 to the Maidens project. Cousins was overwhelmed by requests from the press and television for interviews.

Now State Department officials were doubly concerned. They stopped an effort by a group in Mobile, Alabama, to begin a Nagasaki Maidens project. (An internal memo warned of "a rush of 'Hiroshima Girls' projects in major American cities.") For a while, "It almost seemed that this had become one of the biggest international issues facing the

---

* *Hibakusha is a coined word whose literal meaning is "explosion-affected person(s)" and is used specifically for survivors of the atomic bomb.*

governmert," a State Department official marveled later. A State Department official urged Cousins to make every effort to keep the project from "stirring up propaganda against nuclear weapons."

Actualy, Cousins needed no encouragement. Friends asked him to let the Maidens speak widely on the immorality of atomic weapons, but he was determined not to "exploit" them in that manner. He was more interested in "the power of the example." If Americans realized that it would take over a year of surgery even to begin to correct damage inflicted in a fracticn of a second, they might finally begin to understand the true nature of the bomb. "My hope," Cousins explained, "was that Hiroshima might become something of a classroom in which the world's statesmen might be students."

Yet, at the same time, the gracious demeanor of the Maidens suggested that *hibakusha* did not blame anyone for their misfortune and considered the atomic bombings unavoidable. One of the Maidens, visiting Pearl Harbor, asserted that the Hiroshima victims "should have repentance rather than hatred." Like the rebuilding of Hiroshima, this was reassuring to Americans, if highly misleading. Certainly, it did not represent the feelings of most *hibakusha* and other Japanese.

By the following year, officials' fears that the Maidens' visit would unleash antinuclear activism had subsided. But one historian has observed that "the 'curing' of the Maidens symbolized the healing of wartime hatreds and projected an image of American compassion, benevolence, and generosity toward a former foe." This allowed Americans "to demonstrate personal sympathy and to experience vicarious gratification without having to repent the atomic bombings."

Years passed, and American activists continued to bring *hibakusha* to this country from Japan and Korea to take part in speaking tours, but only rarely did their words reach a mainstream audience.* Encountering the survivors often proved to be a moving experience for those who met or heard them, but the visitors from Japan mainly preached to the converted. Some Americans admitted discomfort. One sympathizer, reviewing a documentary about *hibakusha* (based on *Death in Life*), observed: "We are

---

* An estimated 30,000 Koreans, most of whom had been conscripted to work in Japan during the war, were killed in the atomic bombings.

embarrased, annoyed, angered by survivors . . . bearing witness, prisoners of their escape," who "persist in uttering the unutterable."

Yet the stories of the *hibakusha* sometimes broke through. An American publisher presented drawings and paintings by the survivors. Another
reprinted two volumes of *Barefoot Gen,* cartoon books by Keiji Nakazawa,
a survivor of Hiroshima. Art Spiegelman, who had just started work on his
cartoon masterpiece, *Maus*—which brilliantly depicts the struggles of survivors of the Nazi Holocaust—encountered *Barefoot Gen* and found that it
"burned its way" into his brain, unquestionably influencing his own work.
"Its conviction and honesty allow you to believe in the unbelievable and
impossible things that did, indeed, happen in Hiroshima," Spiegelman
commented. "It is the inexorable act of the witness." Nakazawa's act of
witness, then, was joined by the American publisher and then by
Spiegelman, who not only wrote about *Barefoot Gen* but absorbed it into
his own work.

American Hibakusha

As it turned out, activists did not have to look as far as Japan to find
hibakusha. More than a thousand survivors were living in America, mainly
on the West Coast. Some of them had emigrated from Japan after the
atomic bombings. The majority, however, were American citizens trapped
in Hiroshima, attending school or visiting relatives, when war broke out.
They were Americans victimized by their own country's bomb. Several
hundred Japanese-Americans died in the bombings. Many who survived
lost family members in the attack.

The existence of these American *hibakusha* was not recognized until
the 1970s, after a group of them formed the Committee of Atomic Bomb
Survivors in the U.S. The American survivors are more deprived than the
350,000 *hibakusha* in Japan, who receive free medical care from their government. The American *hibakusha* receive no such benefits, even though
they confront the same delayed effects of radiation as their Japanese coun-
terparts, and it was their own country that dropped the bomb.

For twenty years, bills have been introduced in Congress to provide
medical assistance, but none has come close to passing. In 1988, Congress

passed a landmark bill providing compensation for American servicemen who may have been harmed in nuclear tests. Two years later, it passed another law providing benefits for civilians—the "downwinders"—who lived in the path of fallout from the same tests. But still the American survivors from Hiroshima were ignored. An attorney who lobbied for the *hibakusha* explains that legislators commonly cite the political risk of providing benefits to people who "were part of an enemy nation at the time of the bombing."

Starting in the late 1970s, antinuclear groups began inviting American survivors to speak at meetings and rallies. There is, of course, something particularly poignant, and shattering, about the ironies these survivors embody, and can speak to. This is equally true of another group of Americans who also could be considered atomic bomb survivors: the thousands of U.S. soldiers sent into Hiroshima and Nagasaki shortly after the attacks.

The first of these American troops arrived in Nagasaki in September 1945 and in Hiroshima a month later. Because the U.S. military, in its hastily conducted and incomplete surveys, had found what it considered only negligible levels of residual radiation, soldiers were not urged to take precautions. The soldiers bunked down in buildings close to the hypocenter, even slept on the ground and engaged in cleanup operations, including the disposal of bodies, without protective gear. "We walked into Nagasaki unprepared . . . Really, we were ignorant about what the hell the bomb was," one soldier recalled. The occupying force, mainly in Nagasaki, grew to more than twenty thousand. Some stayed for months.

When they returned to the U.S., many of them suffered from strange rashes and sores; years later some were afflicted with disease or cancers (such as multiple myeloma) associated with radiation exposure. Little could be proven beyond a doubt, and for years their compensation claims were denied. What they endured, according to a 1982 account of their experience, "closely resembles the ordeals of a wide range of American radiation victims, consistently ignored and denied at every turn by the very institutions responsible for causing their problems." Eventually, however, Congress conceded that they may have been harmed by the bomb, making them eligible for compensation under the same measure that covered the other 250,000 "atomic soldiers."

Few of these survivors, who tend to be politically conservative, have spoken out against the use of the bomb, or America's reliance on nuclear weapons ever since. Yet they are still important witnesses of Hiroshima. Their experience dramatizes the dangers of lingering radiation from nuclear weapons and draws attention to the same pattern of secrecy, arrogance, and inattention many other Americans exposed to radiation have encountered. Describing his experience in Nagasaki, one of the veterans recalled: "In the back of our minds, every one of us wondered: What is this atomic bomb? *You had to be there to realize what it did.*" After describing the horrors he witnessed, he added: "We did not drop those two [bombs] on military installations. We dropped them on women and children. . . . I think that is something this country is going to have to live with for eternity."

Other American soldiers who occupied Hiroshima and Nagasaki in 1945, although not afflicted by disease, were affected in powerful and enduring ways by their experience. Mark Hatfield, a young naval officer and later a U.S. senator, would explain that the "shock to my conscience registered permanently within me." It is likely that this experience had some connection to his emergence, first, as a leading foe of the Vietnam War; and later a strong advocate of nuclear disarmament. He also sponsored the first exhibit of photos from Hiroshima and Nagasaki at the U.S. Capitol.

The biologist Jacob Bronowski revealed in 1964 that his classic study *Science and Human Values* was "born" at the moment he arrived in Nagasaki in November 1945. That moment, he wrote, "is present to me as I write, as vividly as when I lived it." It was "a universal moment; what I met was, almost as abruptly, the experience of mankind. . . . Nothing happened in 1945 except that we changed the scale of our indifference to man; and conscience, in revenge, for an instant became immediate to us." Bronowski called it, memorably, "civilization face to face with its own implications."

The Camera as Witness

Like the American *hibakusha* and the soldiers, a third group of survivor/ witnesses emerged only around 1980, inspired to speak out both by events (Three Mile Island and the beginnings of the nuclear-freeze movement) and a belated but powerful sense of mission. In this group were American physicians, photographers, filmmakers, and other specialists sent to Hiroshima and Nagasaki, usually by the military, during 1945 and 1946, to study or document the bomb's effects. In most cases, they remained silent about, or even repressed, their experiences for decades until sparked by a memory, or by a chance encounter, to speak out.

The story of one individual is particularly haunting, for his experience captures the conflict between suppression and witnessing that has surrounded Hiroshima from the start. Herbert Sussan was an Army filmmaker who served, under Daniel McGovern, with the U.S. Strategic Bombing Survey unit that shot the only color footage in Hiroshima and Nagasaki after the atomic bombings. These thirty hours of film represent the most powerful visual indictment of weapons of mass destruction ever compiled. As we described earlier, the footage was classified top secret by Pentagon officials who, according to McGovern, did not want Americans to see graphic evidence of the bomb's effects on human beings.

Sussan had taken on the burden of witness from almost the moment he arrived in Nagasaki. "I felt," he later said, "that if we didn't get a picture of what had happened—this holocaust—nobody would ever know." He felt uneasy asking bomb victims to display their burns for the camera, but he hoped "it would prove to the world that this weapon should not exist." In Tokyo he met with John Hersey, who was about to make his first trip to Hiroshima, and suggested a few individuals he should interview.

His experience in Japan haunted Sussan when he returned to New York City. He imagined town houses in ruins and keloid scars on the faces of passersby. He found among average Americans "very little understanding of what nuclear weapons were or what had happened in those two cities, other than the one picture of the mushroom cloud that people had seen." As one of the Americans who did know what the bomb could do, he embarked on his survivor mission: to get the footage shown on national television. He would spend the next forty years on this mission. "I wanted to find the footage," he later explained, "so that the American people could see, firsthand, what the effects of the bombs were. And if they saw the effects, I felt there would be a groundswell against ever using nuclear weapons of any type again, and the arms race would end. It would be the greatest argument for peace the world would ever see. I was very idealistic and very naive, it turns out."

After the war, Sussan worked at CBS as a pioneering network television director (he would win an Emmy and many other awards). He wrote President Truman in 1950, informing him that the "times fairly scream out for release of this motion picture material." The White House replied that because of "the scientific nature of the footage" it would have little "public appeal or information value." (The government also turned down a proposal from Warner Brothers to make a feature film out of the footage.) Thirteen years later, Sussan produced a film documentary about Truman, and at lunch with the former president raised the subject again, but was later informed that the film was still classified.

Over many years, Sussan approached other influential figures, including newsmen Edward R. Murrow and Chet Huntley, Robert F. Kennedy, and top military officials. They either expressed little interest in the project or informed Sussan that the footage was still classified. "Herb was frustrated that he couldn't get his hands on the material," Daniel McGovern later explained, "but I had been told that under no circumstances would it be released. The AEC had the power of god over everybody, and they did not want that film out."

Then, in 1978, Sussan visited a photography exhibit at the United Nations featuring photographs from Hiroshima and Nagasaki. He mentioned to the Japanese curator that he had shot color footage in the two cities in 1946. The curator was shocked—no one had ever seen color footage from that period—and when he investigated he found that the footage was now at the National Archives, and declassified. This inspired a mass movement in Japan to collect money to purchase the footage. With that raw material, the Japanese made several documentaries; and in the 1980s the footage started appearing in American films, including *The Day After* and the award-winning *Dark Circle*. "I think our government didn't want Americans to see what we had actually done in Japan—and didn't want them to think about *themselves* being in that picture," observed Chris Beaver, co-director of *Dark Circle*. "It's one thing to know about that and another thing to see it."

Sussan had waited thirty-seven years for this moment, but by now he had grown ill. Diagnosed with a form of lymphoma his doctors linked to radiation exposure (and which has increased incidence in *hibakusha),* Sussan considered himself another victim of the bomb's concealed effects. "I want my children and their children to live full lives," he said. "Nuclear war represents the end of everything." When he died in 1985, at the age of sixty-four, he at least had the satisfaction of knowing that the footage he shot, and then drew attention to, had finally become one of the primary source documents of the nuclear age.

The Movement and Hiroshima

Since the late 1940s, there have been only two periods of intense antibomb activity in America: the test-ban movement of the late 1950s and early 1960s; and the antinuclear movement of the early 1980s. The voices of the atomic scientists contributed significantly to each of them. Another group of professionals who played a prominent role were the activist doctors. Although not themselves survivors, the physicians took on a survivor mission as the impetus for their antinuclear activities.

During the campaign against nuclear testing, medical researchers joined the chemist Dr. Linus Pauling in providing evidence about the dangers of radioactive fallout (such as Strontium-90) in the air, in food, and in milk. Dr. Benjamin Spock became co-chairman of SANE, which was founded in 1957. Four years later Physicians for Social Responsibility (PSR) declared in its statement of purpose: "The physician . . . must begin to explore a new area of preventive medicine, the prevention of thermonuclear war." PSR also raised questions about the effectiveness, and the psychological message, of the government's civil-defense plans.

During the early days of the 1980s nuclear-freeze campaign, physicians were at the forefront of raising public awareness. They conducted hundreds of "bombing runs": lectures and slides that gave the audience a full idea of what the aftermath of a nuclear attack on their own city might look like. These accounts were riveting, and the public (in a period of superpower confrontation) was ready for them. The doctors often opened their presentations with Hiroshima and Nagasaki, describing deaths, injuries, delayed radiation effects, and psychological suffering, as well as the severe shortage of medical help for the survivors. The next nuclear attack would be much worse, they argued: *No* healers would be around to treat survivors because they would all be dead.

Hiroshima was therefore invaluable as a human base line—along with

Nagasaki, the only firm evidence of what the weapons really do to people —and as an indication of medical helplessness. In the process, Hiroshima shaped the antinuclear views of two generations of activist doctors, who in turn strongly influenced the media and the public. The physicians' movement spread to more countries. When their umbrella organization, the International Physicians for the Prevention of Nuclear War, won the Nobel Peace Prize in 1985, the award was accepted by the co-presidents— from the U.S. and the Soviet Union. The doctors had become symbols as well as active agents for combating the nuclear arms race.

In their crusades against nuclear weapons, few of the physicians explicitly denounced the decision to use the bomb against Japan. Neither did many of the activists in the nuclear-freeze campaign, long-established SANE, or the myriad of other groups that formed during the 1980s. They invited *hibakusha* to America, staged rallies every August 6 in hundreds of cities, and conducted civil disobedience near the Nevada test site on Hiroshima Day and Nagasaki Day. "No more Hiroshimas!" became a rallying cry. This was something on which most Americans could agree. But why did few of these organizations mount a sustained challenge to the use of the bomb in 1945?

There is no single reason. Faced with an ever-expanding nuclear arms race, the activists concentrated on curbing the development, and preventing the use, of the new weaponry. In addition, movement leaders were often uncertain about their own attitudes toward the Hiroshima decision and the new evidence about it that was emerging. Their personal witness was to what happened in Hiroshima—not to the Hiroshima decision.

The disarmament movement, in any case, achieved important victories, with periods of intense activity separated by years of inaction. Disarmament activists raised a public clamor that led to the U.S.-Soviet agreement in 1962 banning nuclear testing in the atmosphere. The activists, however, failed to stop all testing, their ultimate goal, and the arms race accelerated as the era of multiple-warhead missiles arrived. The antinuclear movement of the early 1980s helped discredit the notion of a "winnable" nuclear war emerging from the Reagan administration, and strongly contributed to establishing a political climate that finally ended the arms race (other factors, including turmoil in the Soviet bloc, also played a significant role).

It is hard to tell whether confronting the Hiroshima decision would have made the antinuclear movement more effective in halting the arms race earlier Probably not, since Americans, according to surveys, supported the use of the bomb by a wide margin. Condemning the atomic attacks would have been unpopular—but Truman's decision would never become less popular unless openly challenged. And by rarely confronting the Hiroshima decision, the activists weakened their moral position. The principle of opposing *any* potential use of nuclear weapons lost some clarity. Yet, at the same time, disarmament activists, more than any other group of Americans, took in Hiroshima, drew lessons from it, and brought those truths to the public.

CHAPTER 4

The Media, the Historians, and the
Illusion of Consensus

Scholars, editors and journalists, and creative artists act as mediators of the Hiroshima narrative. But they do more than simply circulate information and images within the culture, for they have the freedom to express views of their own. Because so few Americans are familiar with the history of the atomic bombings, the mediators' influence can be vast (as demonstrated by the Stimson and Hersey articles).

Historians were the first to challenge the official version of Hiroshima, starting in the mid-1960s, and the debate among scholars remains vigorous today. The media, on the other hand, rarely question the prevailing wisdom. Creative artists—especially filmmakers, painters, and fiction writers —have often explored the nuclear threat but have disregarded the specific subject of Hiroshima almost entirely. (We examine cultural responses to Hiroshima later, in the appendix.) The overall response, therefore, reflects what Michael Kammen has called the American inclination to minimize memories, and causes, of conflict, "and achieve at least the illusion of consensus."

The Media

Since the late 1940s, media coverage of Hiroshima has followed a consistent pattern. For special commemorations—the major anniversary years—the decision to use the bomb, and its effects, receives considerable attention. In "off" years, Hiroshima is rarely mentioned, except around August 6, and sometimes not even then. Reporting on Hiroshima, for the most part, has been rather undistinguished, marked by an almost total absence of investigative journalism. News coverage, in fact, has been almost totally reactive. Revelations about the decision to use the bomb, and its human effects, have come almost entirely from historians and independent researchers. With the exception of writers like Norman Cousins, Daniel Lang, and Jonathan Schell, journalists mainly have been content to report the findings of others, as published in scholarly journals or books. News analysis has been just about nil.

Access to evidence was always a problem. Years after the atomic bombings, nearly all the documents that might shed light on the Hiroshima decision—from the White House and the War Department, from Los Alamos and the Manhattan Project—were still classified. This included minutes of important meetings, intercepted Japanese cables proposing terms of surrender (pre-Hiroshima), and projections of American casualties in an invasion of Japan. Michael Amrine wrote a book called *The Great Decision* in 1959 but admitted it was far from complete. "There are official records that should be opened now," he complained. "Some contain no official secrets. . . . It is time for these records to be opened, but, so far, the doors have remained shut to journalists, historians . . . even to famous American officials who lived through these events. A nation, like a man, cannot fully understand its future if it does not understand some of the secrets of the past."*

Whenever new information about Hiroshima did emerge during the 1950s and 1960s, reporters went to Harry Truman for a comment, and the

---

* History was so tightly controlled that the government even kept classified until 1960 the unofficial names for the bombs dropped on Hiroshima and Nagasaki: Fat Man and Little Boy. Christian Herter, the secretary of state, lamented "the public release of the unfortunate wartime code names of the bombs, which those who underwent atomic attack in particular, and others as well, could consider as evidence that the United States regarded lightly those awesome weapons."

story inevitably ended there. Even now, fresh evidence often receives little consideration. Media coverage of the Smithsonian controversy was remarkably shallow, factually distorted, and one-sided. Little has changed since 1948 when Herbert Marks, general counsel of the Atomic Energy Commission, observed that the press covered the agency "rarely with more penetrating comment or follow-up than that which accompanies the society news."

At first, few reporters traveled to Hiroshima to witness the aftereffects of the bombing. Occupation authorities, as we have seen, discouraged or prohibited it. As years passed, restrictions were lifted, but reports from Hiroshima—usually during the key "anniversary" years—focused on reconstruction and renewal, not scars and recrimination. This was certainly the easier story, and the more hopeful one; but it was also tragically misleading. As Mary McCarthy pointed out, the lesson of Hiroshima was not how many survived but how many died—but the dead could not talk to reporters.

As years passed, the media provided sympathetic, often moving, profiles of individual *hibakusha*. Television and print journalists have followed the admirable example of John Hersey—but they have done little more, failing to deeply explore unresolved issues, such as the decision to use the bomb. Often, in the same accounts that depict the *hibakusha* with great compassion, reporters provide balance by affirming that dropping the bomb on these unlucky souls was necessary to end the war. Even so, many Americans who strongly support the Hiroshima decision complain about the media coverage, using words like *handwringers* and *liberal sob sisters* to describe journalists who write profiles of survivors. Even after decades have passed, some apparently feel that expressing sympathy for the victims raises questions too uncomfortable to consider.

In examining Hiroshima and the media, one must distinguish between news coverage and commentary. News stories about Hiroshima, although few in number, sometimes do include facts or quotes that challenge the official narrative. On the other hand, newspaper editorials, opinion columns, and television specials tend to reassert the narrative. They seldom challenge the decision to use the bomb. That the bomb, and the bomb alone, ended the war and saved countless American lives remains an article of faith. The message is: We had to use the bomb—it may not have been desirable but it was necessary. Commentators almost always adopt a grave tone in discussing Hiroshima. They mention the enormity of the destruction, the tragedy of a nuclear arms race, and the importance of avoiding another Hiroshima (or worse). Yet they invariably, if reluctantly, throw their editorial weight behind Truman's decision.

It must never happen again, they often hasten to add. Usually missing is the question: Did it have to happen at all?

Television coverage, in combining journalism, images, and commentary, can be both fair-minded and one-sided at the same time. An important example was Fred Freed's NBC *White Paper* documentary in 1965, entitled "The Decision to Drop the Bomb." Narrated by Chet Huntley, it remains the most thorough examination of the subject to appear on network television. The producers presented several sides of the story, and like much coverage of Hiroshima, the NBC special was fairly evenhanded when it stuck to actual facts. But then came the "editorial" portion and, as usual, this was an entirely different story. Huntley closed the program by reciting the final sentences of the famous Stimson essay—lamenting the slaughter in Hiroshima but calling it America's "least abhorrent choice." After many minutes of conflicting testimony, the official narrative had gained the upper hand again

Until 1970, visual images of Hiroshima on television were restricted to shots of rubble. That year, Eric Barnouw completed his landmark documentary, *Hiroshima/Nagasaki, August 1945*, which made use of film shot by Japanese cameramen in 1945, then seized by the American military. This was grainy, black-and-white footage, but few Americans had seen anything like it before. It included scenes (as we described earlier) of Japanese doctors treating victims suffering from horrendous burns and radiation disease.

Barnouw was shocked by the absence of interest from television networks, including public TV. NBC declared that it might air part of the film if it could find a "news hook." Barnouw later commented: "We dared not speculate what kind of event this might call for." A *Boston Globe* editorial condemned the networks for ignoring the Barnouw movie, which it called "the most important documentary film" of the century, adding that every American should see it. This provoked National Education Television (the forerunner of PBS) to schedule a broadcast of the film on August 3, 1970, marking the twenty-fifth anniversary of Hiroshima, and it produced one of the network's largest audiences ever. Apparently only one station excised what Barnouw called the "human-effects" footage.

Barnouw was pleased but also haunted by his experience. He felt that if the Japanese footage "hadn't been suppressed, and if the public had seen it and Congress had seen it in the 1950s, it would have been a lot harder to appropriate money to build more bombs."*

There were other reactions, of course. Jack Gould in his *New York Times* review criticized the film for not providing the context for the use of the bomb, which might well have saved "more lives than would have been involved in an invasion of Japan"; and for not discussing "whether nuclear warfare is a deterrent to global extinction." The Barnouw film, in any case, was a kind of aberration. For many years afterward, television images of Hiroshima once again emphasized rubble and excluded human effects.

The fortieth anniversary of Hiroshima and Nagasaki in 1985 arrived at a high nuclear moment. Hundreds of disarmament and arms-control groups were challenging President Reagan's nuclear buildup. Hiroshima as a historical event was receding, but the Bomb loomed larger than ever. The media responded with what some called an "orgy" of coverage. There were prime-time television specials and live remotes from Hiroshima's Peace Park. *Time* and *Newsweek* produced special issues on the Atomic Age. Newspapers carried numerous articles, columns, and editorials. But nothing really had changed.

Time and *Newsweek* each paid respects, in words and pictures, to the *hibakusha*. But scholarly arguments against the use of the bomb received little notice, and when the authors of these special reports spoke in their own voice they seemed to endorse the official narrative. The other major magazine spread was a *Life* magazine feature, "The Great Invasion the A-Bomb Canceled." It set American lives saved by the bomb at "up to a million."

Nearly every magazine and newspaper columnist defended the Hiro-

---

* *A 1972 study of how the film affected a large group of viewers in Missouri found that it substantially raised their anxiety level about nuclear weapons, decreased their desire to survive a nuclear war, and made them want the U.S. to use greater restraint in possibly using such weapons.*

shima decision. The Stimson article—thirty-eight years after it appeared—remained a popular source. William F. Buckley in the *National Review* set the lives saved at two million. In the *New Republic,* Henry Fairlie complained that for weeks the press had "wallowed" in Hiroshima, making far "too much of a bad thing." He lamented the "breast-beating" and "mea culpas." Fairlie seemed outraged that survivors of the bombing received so much recognition. Interviews with *hibakusha,* he confessed, "did not make me think or feel anything deep." Instead, they made him "restless," for there was "nothing atrocious in the motives" for the bombing and, considering the context, "nothing particularly atrocious" about its consequences. What worried him most was that questioning the use of the bomb fed "an underlying anti-Americanism that can only paralyze the exercise of American power."

George Will, the syndicated columnist, agreed with Fairlie. After estimating the number of American lives saved at one million, Will advised that the dropping of the bomb was "a deed profoundly Machiavellian and moral." This seemed like an odd pairing, but Will explained:

> . . . Machiavelli's bad reputation is the unjust price he paid for being an unsentimental moralist in a world addicted to moral evasions. He said that a material and mental capacity for violence underlies a great nation's power. The moral imperative is to economize violence by distinguishing between legitimate and illegitimate uses. Legitimate uses are to reduce violence and preserve or promote good objectives.

Nowhere in any of these explanations of the atomic bombing was there any mention of Nagasaki. It was as if the second bomb, always harder to justify, never existed.

On television the story was much the same: elegies for the victims and justification for the act that terrorized them. One of the low points was a *Today* show segment that contrived a brief meeting between a *hibakusha* and two of the *Enola Gay* crew members. The Hiroshima mission, one of the airmen said, was "just another flight." Then the next guest, Pat Boone, came on.

Another widely watched program was a special edition of *Nightline* entitled "What If . . . We Hadn't Dropped the Bomb?" This clever docudrama depicted how Roone Arledge's ABC news operation might have covered an invasion of Japan in 1945—complete with Sam Donaldson at the Truman White House. "What happened over Japan forty years ago today was a human tragedy which cost tens of thousands of lives," Ted Koppel said in introducing the show. "But what was planned to take place in the war between Japan and the United States would almost certainly have been an even greater tragedy, costing hundreds of thousands of lives."

One could chuckle over Sam Donaldson's deadpan report that "the president doesn't trust Marshal Stalin anymore. Just look at the record." But the program had a sobering effect, literally putting flesh on the bones of the unavoidable "lives saved" argument. *Nightline* showed American soldiers cut down by Japanese gunfire while a reporter cried, "I have never witnessed such horrible scenes of death. . . ."

As usual, media interest in the atomic bombings nearly disappeared after 1985. It seemed like a subject destined to remain obscure until 1995: the fiftieth anniversary year. But the controversy over the *Enola Gay* exhibit at the Smithsonian Institution in 1994 created an early surge of interest, and perhaps the media's most narrow coverage ever. But that is another story.

Historians

Historians have approached the Hiroshima decision with a far more critical eye than the media. Yet to judge by media commentary and most public-opinion polls—and, again, by the Smithsonian controversy—their impact has been relatively limited. A lively debate over facts and analysis surrounding Hiroshima has raged for years in academic circles, but only there has such an open discussion occurred.

And that debate did not begin until the mid-1960s, so the Hiroshima narrative, as re-established by the Stimson article, had twenty years to accumulate credibility. Why did historians wait so long to challenge the official version? Few were inclined to do so, and those with a critical eye faced the usual problem of having to wait for personal papers and diaries to be donated to libraries, and for official records to be declassified (in the latter case, a very long wait indeed). One scholar lamented that the subject of the Hiroshima decision appeared to be "closed." But then that scholar, Gar Alperovitz, produced a book in 1965 called *Atomic Diplomacy*.

Only one previous book that vigorously attacked the Stimson version had received much attention: *Fear, War, and the Bomb* by P. M. S. Blackett, the noted British physicist. Adopting a view expressed earlier by Norman Cousins, Blackett asserted that dropping the atomic bomb "was not so much the last military act of the Second World War, as the first major operation of the cold diplomatic war with Russia now in progress." Blackett's book was widely attacked—the usual fate for challenges to the Hiroshima narrative. Many reviewers cited the author's leftist politics. I. I. Rabi labeled the book "propaganda" and dismissed "the wailing over Hiroshima." Blackett's thesis remained dormant until Alperovitz revived it in the mid-1960s.

In *Atomic Diplomacy,* Alperovitz boldly declared that he believed "the atomic bomb was not needed to end the war or to save lives—and that this was understood by American leaders at the time." Why *did* the U.S. drop the bomb? Alperovitz tentatively concluded that the major reason was "to make Russia more manageable" (a phrase attributed to James Byrnes). Political, not military, considerations played the larger role in the decision. Truman and his advisers saw the bomb as a diplomatic lever that could stall Soviet aggression in Eastern Europe and the Far East. Furthermore, the bomb guided American behavior at Potsdam. Alperovitz even made the claim—considered dubious at the time, but accepted later—that Truman had postponed the Potsdam conference until the bomb could be tested at Trinity.

Alperovitz had consulted newly available material, principally the papers and diaries of Henry Stimson. He quoted Stimson referring to the bomb, pre-Hiroshima, as a "master card" of diplomacy. (Stimson did not say anything like that in his *Harper's* article.) Yet response from fellow scholars was mainly hostile. As Alperovitz later reflected, "many people were, not surprisingly, disturbed by the idea that other than purely military factors were involved." One historian described Alperovitz's findings as "implausible, exaggerated, or unsupported by the evidence." Another alleged that he had willfully distorted excerpts and quotes and charged that it was "disconcerting . . . that such a work could have come to be consid-

ered a contribution to the historical literature on the period." Several
writers, mainly in liberal journals such as the *New York Review of Books* and
the *New Republic,* praised the book, but the *New York Times Book Review*
assigned its review to Senator Clinton Anderson, a member of Truman's
cabinet in 1945. Anderson found Alperovitz "unobjective" and his thesis
wholly "inaccurate." To accept Alperovitz meant admitting that Truman,
Stimson, and Byrnes had all been less than candid in their memoirs, and
Anderson stated that this could not possibly be true. He concluded the
review with a lengthy quote from the Stimson article.

Another reviewer, the normally temperate Michael Amrine, also
recommended reading Stimson as an "antidote" to Alperovitz, whom
he depicted as "a cold-blooded cousin of Herman Kahn and Dr.
Strangelove." Suggesting that Truman and Stimson had ulterior motives in
using the bomb "is more than thinking about the unthinkable," Amrine
concluded. "It is believing the unbelievable."

Yet despite such criticism, younger historians were taking Alperovitz seriously (although by no means uncritically). Doubts about the official narrative had finally emerged mainly because of the availability of new historical
evidence, but the Vietnam War also played a part. Ronald Steel, in reviewing *Atomic Diplomacy,* attributed the growing suspicions about the Hiroshima narrative to the fact that "we are no longer so callous about the
slaughter of the innocent, whether at Hiroshima or in the villages of Vietnam." New generations of Americans, Steel added, "see the dropping of
the bomb on Japan as a decision which weighs heavily on all of us who are
its descendants."

Alperovitz's influence was felt immediately, and several years later important new books on the subject began to appear. Martin J. Sherwin's *A
World Destroyed* rejected Alperovitz's claim that the bomb was used *mainly*
for political purposes, but he agreed that the desire to use the bomb "as a
potential instrument of military and diplomatic policy" did play an important part. Sherwin also charged that Truman and his advisers did not seriously explore alternatives to using the bomb.

Then, in 1978, important new evidence (mentioned earlier) appeared.
Scholars discovered a large sheaf of handwritten notes misfiled at the Truman Library, including journal-like entries penned by the president during
the summer of 1945 (which became known as his "Potsdam diary"). An

archivist also discovered letters from Truman to his wife from this same period. Together they provided the best evidence yet of what was really on the president's mind during the final weeks before Hiroshima.

The picture that emerged was often ambiguous (as we have already explored in Part II), but revealing. Two conflicts the new material did settle: there was no longer any question that Truman recognized the diplomatic value of the bomb ("I have an ace in the hole") and was aware the enemy was exploring avenues of surrender (he referred to a "telegram from Jap Emperor asking for peace"). And Truman's private assertion that the Soviet declaration of war could provoke a surrender ("Fini Japs when that comes about") meant that he recognized that the atomic bombing was not necessary to end the war, although he surely felt it would shorten the conflict. That was something critics of Truman's decision had long alleged but never proven.

By the time of the fortieth anniversary of the atomic bombings in 1985, the official narrative was under siege. J. Samuel Walker, historian for the Nuclear Regulatory Commission, concluded that the younger scholars had, indeed, "shaped the debate over the bomb and how historians approached it . . . The major issue was no longer whether the bomb was necessary to end the war as soon as possible. Rather the central questions had become: What factors were paramount in the decision to use the bomb and why was its use more attractive to policy makers than other alternatives?"

In academic journals, scholarly books, and popular histories, writers raised significant questions about the wisdom, necessity, or morality of dropping the bomb (although these doubts were not often reflected in the media).* The eminent historian Gaddis Smith now affirmed that the decision to use the bomb was "centrally connected to Truman's confrontational approach to the Soviet Union." Martin Sherwin cited a "considerable body" of new evidence that suggested the bomb may have cost, rather than saved, Americans lives. That is, if the U.S. had not been so deter-

---

* The debate has been confused by the often-pejorative application of revisionist to those historians who question the official version of Hiroshima. In its original meaning, the term could be applied to anyone challenging the accepted view of historical events. But here it becomes associated (particularly in the media but also in political debates) with "changing history" in a way that makes America look bad. It may even take on some of the opprobrium of "Holocaust revisionism" (which falsely denies Nazi mass murder) in a way that reverses the actual intent of scholars who raise questions about Hiroshima.

mined to complete, test, and finally use the bomb, it might have arranged the Japanese surrender weeks earlier, preventing much bloodshed on Okinawa.

Barton Bernstein analyzed a recently declassified paper written by a Joint Chiefs of Staff advisory group in June 1945. It estimated the number of American lives likely to be lost in an all-out invasion of Japan as ranging from twenty-five to forty-six thousand—grim enough but a fraction of the number asserted by Truman, Stimson, and others. General Marshall studied this document and informed Stimson that he agreed with it. A later report by another Joint Chiefs advisory board predicted that the dreaded assault on the Tokyo plain would actually be "relatively inexpensive" in terms of casualties. Bernstein entitled his article "A Postwar Myth: 500,000 U.S. Lives Saved."

Critics of the Hiroshima decision have influenced at least one of the men who helped shape the official narrative. McGeorge Bundy in 1988 produced a thoughtful history of nuclear policy called *Danger and Survival*. Bundy admitted that Stimson in his 1947 article overstated the extent to which Truman and his advisers considered alternatives to using the bomb. "One must regret," Bundy wrote, that "more extended deliberation" over the use of the bomb had not occurred. He also suggested that a "three-part" strategy of warning the Japanese explicitly about the use of the bomb and the Soviets' plan to enter the war, and offering to retain the emperor, might have brought about immediate surrender.

This is not to say that critics of the atomic bombing have triumphed. A consensus among scholars has formed around the idea that political concerns (i.e., intimidating the Soviets) played at least *some* role in the Hiroshima decision. Walker identified another area of general agreement: "The bomb was not needed to avoid an invasion of Japan and to end the war within a relatively short time." But the key phrase in that statement is *within a relatively short time*. There is still nothing approaching consensus on the question of whether the U.S. was justified in using the bomb to end the war in the fastest way possible.

The mainstream holds fast to the view that only the use of the bomb could have brought the war to a conclusion quickly. And the mainstream still holds sway, to judge by major histories of World War II (such as John

Keegan's *The Second World War* and William L. O'Neill's *Democracy at War).* Books that challenge the official narrative proliferate but most struggle to find readers.

The most acclaimed and widely read recent account of the Hiroshima decision appeared in David McCullough's *Truman.* The biography not only won major awards, it also became a best-seller; and judging by the many times it has been cited by political figures and reporters, it is clear that it has become not only a standard reference work on Truman, but on Hiroshima as well. McCullough reveres his subject, declaring in interviews that Truman was "exactly the kind of president that the founding fathers had in mind" and that "God was good to us when he gave us Harry Truman." In *Truman,* McCullough firmly defended the use of the bomb, ignoring most of the revisionist literature, and editing documents in a way that seems overly protective of his subject.*

A number of reviewers who admired the book nevertheless pointed out that its treatment of Hiroshima was inadequate. Ronald Steel, a critic of the book (calling it a "Valentine" to Truman), wrote that "the question is not whether the revisionists or the traditionalists are right. A biographer is not obliged to settle that old dispute. But he should do more than skim over the surface of the argument." And C. Vann Woodward, perhaps the dean of American historians, told an interviewer that "McCullough should be faulted for not citing the revisionists."

Moreover, McCullough recently admitted that he misquoted a key document in support of his claim that Truman or his advisers were told, *before* Hiroshima, that using the bomb would save 500,000 to one million lives. That document, he acknowledged later, actually suggests that such figures were "entirely too high." Yet his original assertion had already appeared in more than a million copies of the book and was frequently cited during the Smithsonian controversy. *Truman,* even after three decades of "revisionism," remains perhaps the most influential expression of the Hiroshima narrative to appear since the Stimson article. Yet even *Truman* could not overcome the increasing doubts among scholars concerning the official story of Hiroshima—critical perspectives that inevitably led to the conflict at the Smithsonian.

---

* *For example, he quotes the first sentence of Truman's August 6 announcement but omits its reference to Hiroshima as a Japanese "Army base."*

CHAPTER 5

COMMEMORATING HIROSHIMA:
THE SMITHSONIAN CONTROVERSY

How, then, would America as a nation bear witness to Hiroshima on the fiftieth anniversary? We would expect pain and controversy, and that arrived even before 1995, in the dispute that erupted over the *Enola Gay* display at the National Air and Space Museum. How would America exhibit what may be the most tragic, contested, and foreboding single act in our entire history? Confronting Hiroshima at a moment that required commemoration—a kind of collective witness—would require questioning the official story that has prevailed for nearly half a century.

Fiftieth anniversaries "intensify argument over any form of remembrance," observes Edward Linenthal, an expert on war memorials, and adviser to the *Enola Gay* exhibit. "Fiftieths are the last time when you have massive groups of veterans or survivors who are able to put their imprint on the event." The bitterness and anger that quickly surrounded the *Enola Gay* exhibit tell us that the Hiroshima raw nerve is as sensitive as ever.

In the course of the Smithsonian dispute, many of the themes that have persisted since the dropping of the bomb reappeared, dramatically. Most of the groups that have been in conflict over Hiroshima (including journalists and scholars, veterans and peace activists) were at odds once again. And so it went, as it had often gone before. One historian called it "an intellectual bloodletting." But the struggle over the exhibit—over history and meaning—nevertheless had enormous value. From this controversy emerged the first national debate over Hiroshima in almost fifty years.

The Smithsonian Institution is America's national museum and repository of memory. Easily its most popular attraction is the National Air and Space Museum, which houses, among other objects, Lindbergh's plane, John Glenn's space capsule, the Apollo 11 command module that went to the moon—and replicas of the Fat Man and Little Boy bombs. About eight million people tour the Air and Space Museum every year. Occasionally more than 100,000 arrive on a single day. It is the most visited museum in the world.

In the late 1940s, the Smithsonian took charge of the *Enola Gay,* the fabled B-29 that carried the atomic bomb over Hiroshima. Years passed, but the plane was never put on display, and its condition deteriorated. Military groups demanded that the Smithsonian restore the plane and exhibit it proudly. They felt it was a disgrace that the *Enola Gay* had been kept in storage for so long, pointing out that *Bock's Car,* the plane that dropped the bomb on Nagasaki, had been displayed for years at the U.S. Air Force Museum in Dayton, Ohio, generating little controversy. The *Enola Gay* was transported in pieces to a warehouse in Maryland, and in the mid-1980s restoration began with the aim of putting it on permanent display, perhaps at Dulles Airport.

With the fiftieth anniversary of Hiroshima approaching, the Smithsonian announced that a commemorative exhibit would open in May of 1995. The centerpiece would be the gleamingly restored fuselage of the *Enola Gay:* fifty-eight feet of metal with no wings attached (due to space limitations). Resting in its belly would be a replica of the atomic bomb. But the Smithsonian would not simply celebrate the hardware, as it so often had done. Martin Harwit, director of the Air and Space Museum, was determined to explore the full story of the atomic bombings.

In his six years at the museum, Harwit had led it in a new direction, rejecting the notion that history is the winner's version of what happened, as Howard Zinn once put it. An exhibit on strategic bombing, which included screenings of the films *Dr. Strangelove* and *On the Beach,* drew protests from military groups. Veterans also criticized an exhibit on air power in World War I for "focusing graphically on death and destruction on the ground" (as one critic put it). This reaction was not surprising. Images of mass killing from the air are not embedded in the collective memory of Americans, for this is a country that has never been strafed, rocketed, napalmed, or firebombed. In fact, it has never been bombed at all—except at Pearl Harbor.

The museum decided to surround the *Enola Gay* with four extensive displays, exploring the final months of the Pacific war, the decision to drop the bomb, the devastation of two Japanese cities, and the postwar legacy of a nuclear arms race. Tom Crouch, head of the museum's aeronautics division, had mounted dozens of shows, including a controversial exhibit on the Japanese-American internment camps, but expected this to be "the toughest exhibit I've ever been involved in." No matter what the museum did, criticism would abound. As Crouch put it, "It's one of those issues on which I think there's very little middle ground."

Even before plans were set, World War II veterans were writing letters of protest, based on rumors that the exhibit would offer apologies to Japan. This may have been sparked by reports that curators in Hiroshima and Nagasaki had agreed to send artifacts to the museum.

Harwit assured the veterans that the exhibit would neither glorify nor apologize for the bombings, but it was clear the official Hiroshima narrative would be on trial. An early planning document promised a "nuanced picture of the decision-making" that went beyond the "dogmatic belief in the official explanation that dropping the bomb prevented a bloody invasion." Another internal report asserted that the primary goal was to encourage visitors to undertake "a thoughtful and balanced re-examination" of the events of August 1945. A full and frank discussion of the decision to use the bomb would be presented. Those who toured the exhibit "will thus leave, we hope, thinking and debating these most crucial historical events of the twentieth century."

Internal memos show that even in the early stages the exhibit caused consternation—within the Smithsonian. While praising the planning document, Robert Adams, the head of the Smithsonian, suggested shifting the focus away from *the bomb* and more toward *the end of the war*. An exhibit that makes the bomb "the central subject," he wrote, "greatly—and I think unacceptably—increases the risk to SI [Smithsonian Institution]." Already Adams was worried about what "critics concerned about the atom bomb as the subject of an exhibit" would say. He referred to a letter he had received from Barber Conable, a former Republican congressman —now a Smithsonian regent—who had emphasized the horrors of the invasion of Japan in which he had been slated to take part.

Tom Crouch, the project manager, responded with a memo to director Harwit, arguing that it was a mistake to think that by slightly shifting the focus of the exhibit—which, after all, had the *Enola Gay* at its center— "we can delude visitors into thinking that it is not really about the atomic bomb, or produce an exhibition with which Mr. Conable will ever be comfortable. . . . Do you want to do an exhibition intended to make veterans feel good, or do you want an exhibition that will lead our visitors to think about the consequences of the atomic bombing of Japan? Frankly, I don't think we can do both."

The Veterans Object

Even before curators completed their first script, they were bombarded with protests from veterans. Someone within the museum hostile to the aims of the exhibit had leaked copies of internal memos to veterans' groups, which revealed their plan to re-examine the Hiroshima decision and the effects of the bomb. For veterans the proposed show triggered emotions about "the importance of the commemorative voice," observed Edward Linenthal. "They see their numbers dwindling, and they want their imprint and their narrative of events left behind."

Indeed, from this perspective, there is reason for concern. A recent Gallup poll suggested that 53 percent of Americans over the age of sixty-five approved of the use of the bomb against Japan, but just 32 percent of those under thirty felt that way. The same survey found that in that under-thirty sample, only one in five could identify Truman as the president who ordered the bomb dropped on Hiroshima; half did not even venture a guess.

A tentative script for the exhibit emerged in January 1994. As promised, it examined a wide range of issues related to the Hiroshima decision.

"To this day," it declared right at the start, "controversy has raged about whether dropping this weapon on Japan was necessary to end the war quickly," and it explored the debate in an evenhanded way. Contrary to later criticism, it did not champion the "revisionist" view; it merely treated it with respect. Actually, the Truman decision was a rather small part of an exhibit dominated by the *Enola Gay* and preparations for its mission—and a depiction of Hiroshima ground zero that included artifacts and graphic photographs few Americans have ever been exposed to.

The script contained several weak passages, but then it was only a first draft. Curators, in any case, received broad support from their advisory board. Barton Bernstein judged the script "fair, balanced, and historically informed," while Richard Hallion, the Air Force historian, found it "impressive . . . comprehensive . . . and obviously based upon a great deal of sound research." Ironically (considering the tenor of the debate that followed) the only strong protest came from what might be called the revisionist camp. Martin Sherwin objected to displaying the *Enola Gay*, calling an exhibit centered on the plane inherently "celebratory," even "obscene." A similar viewpoint was expressed in a letter to the museum from a man in Japan. He suggested exhibiting the plane not at Air and Space but in the Holocaust Museum.

Museum officials met with leaders of military groups and incorporated some of their suggestions into the script. The review process continued quietly. But then the Air Force Association, which claims 180,000 members, turned up the pressure. Museum officials had given the group, founded by General Jimmy Doolittle in 1946, a copy of the script for comment. But instead of responding to the curators, the group went public with a special report by John T. Correll, editor of *Air Force* magazine. The association also publicized a campaign by a group of former B-29 fliers who had collected 8,000 signatures on a petition asking the Smithsonian to either display the *Enola Gay* "proudly and patriotically" or turn it over to a museum that would do so.

Correll accused the museum of "politically correct curating," a charge the media would later borrow. The script, he wrote, focused far too much on the Japanese civilians who died at Hiroshima and Nagasaki rather than the Japanese militarists who started the war. Asked by a reporter if veterans suspected that the Air and Space Museum was an "unpatriotic institution,"

Correll replied: "The blunt answer is, yes." An Air Force Association spokesman charged that the museum was using the *Enola Gay* as a "front" for an exhibit that "intended to defame" strategic bombing during World War II. It made Japan look like the victim and the U.S. the perpetrator of a "war crime."

In his review of the script, Correll favored statistical analysis; even a body count. He identified plans to use forty-nine photos of Japanese casualties and only three photos of American casualties. But was this inappropriate for an exhibit about the atomic bombings? Correll seemed agitated that slightly more than half of the photos of dead Japanese showed women and children, and he specifically objected to displaying a schoolgirl's charred lunchbox. Yet he overlooked the overwhelming physical and emotional presence of the *Enola Gay,* which would likely offset whatever photographic imbalance existed.

Correll admitted that the script treated the airmen who dropped the two bombs "extensively and with respect." But in a follow-up report, he complained there was too much emphasis on "historical controversies," such as: Was an invasion inevitable without the bomb? "A recurring undertone in the plans and scripts for this exhibit has been suspicion about why the United States used the atomic bomb," Correll wrote. "Museum officials have seemed reluctant to accept the explanation that it was a military action, taken to end the war and save lives." Finally, he observed that the script was drafted by four people, none of them veterans—and Michael Neufeld, the curator, was Canadian.

The Air Force Association analysis drew wide attention. Senator Nancy Kassebaum wrote to the Smithsonian secretary, suggesting that he cancel the show and transfer the *Enola Gay* to a museum in her state of Kansas. An American Legion committee condemned the museum for allegedly depicting the U.S. airmen as war criminals—even though a segment on Paul Tibbets's landing on Tinian after dropping the bomb was titled "Return of a Hero."

After weeks of silence, Tibbets released a statement calling for the *Enola Gay* to be displayed without commentary of any kind. Paul Fussell agreed, informing a reporter that museum officials in America treated everyone "like babies." At the Imperial War Museum in London, he pointed out, they display German V-2 rockets "which killed a great many people. And they're just hanging from the roof, with a little tiny label down below saying, 'This is a V-2.'"*

Most of the news articles pictured the Smithsonian conflict in the kind of either/or terms favored by the veterans. A story in the *Washington Post* typified this approach. It explained that the dispute was over how the atomic bombings would be remembered: "as an event that ended great suffering or as one that caused it." This was misleading, for the Hiroshima attack contributed to ending the suffering *and* caused more of it. The question at the heart of the Smithsonian script, but rarely recognized by the veterans and the press, was: Might there have been a way to end the war without mass slaughter on *either* side?

Crouch and Neufeld, the curators, privately admitted that they had underestimated the emotions swirling around the subject of Hiroshima. Still, they complained that critics were misinterpreting many aspects of the exhibit and encouraging wild exaggerations in the media—such as the charge that the script pictured the Americans as the aggressors in the war. "I think what fundamentally bothers people about this show," Tom Crouch said, "is that it attempts to tell the fullest story possible. In other words, it doesn't end when the bomb leaves the bomb bay. It says, look, if you really want to draw your own conclusions, you have to know the whole story—and that's something that begins with the decision to build the bomb, and ends with what happens on the ground." On another occasion, Crouch observed, "There's real discomfort about looking at destruction on the ground. . . . I hear critics saying, 'Don't tell part of the story.'" He also said: "These issues are really close to where people live. They define the different ways that people look at the world."

In their many meetings, curators and veterans also battled over casualty estimates for the planned invasion of Japan. The museum emphasized the figure (based on recently declassified documents) of 30,000 to 50,000, while the veterans endorsed the official figure of 500,000 to a million. Publicly, the veterans claimed the casualty debate was beside the point. As one of their leaders observed, "The use of the weapon against a brutal and

---

* *The analogy to the* Enola Gay *was imperfect, however, because the British were the victims of the V-2, not its creators.*

ruthless aggressor to save 30,000 American lives was as morally justifiable as to use it to save a half a million." Still, they privately pressed for the higher figure, perhaps wishing to leave no doubt that possible lives saved outnumbered known lives lost.

The veterans also pressed for the removal of the last section of the exhibit, on the bomb's legacy. It was as if they felt it was unfair to tarnish the Hiroshima mission with a litany of the hazards—from nuclear proliferation to nuclear waste—that followed.

To provide what he called "balance," Martin Harwit promised to enlarge the exhibit's opening section on Japanese atrocities and the war in the Pacific. He also deleted a brief passage in the script about America waging a "war of vengeance" (because of Pearl Harbor) that the veterans had found offensive. But he dismissed as "absolute nonsense" the charge by Richard Hallion, the Air Force historian, that the museum was "still pushing the thesis that the atomic bomb shouldn't have been dropped." Back in February, Hallion had described the original script as "an impressive job" that only required "a bit of tweaking." But now, in the wake of the Air Force Association protest, he was calling it "a poor script, lacking balance and context."

Despite ordering revisions, director Harwit held his ground on the overall tone and content of the exhibit. Some of the veterans, he observed, "don't want to hear what Truman was thinking. They resent it, perhaps because they would like to think that Truman wanted only to save their lives, and they resent the idea that part of the reason for dropping the bomb might have been to impress Josef Stalin."

Harwit brought an interesting perspective to this debate. A native Czech, he had arrived in the U.S. in 1946 at age fifteen, having escaped the death camps in which many of his relatives perished. Harwit drew on this experience in explaining that he didn't need to be reminded about the justness of the American cause in World War II. In the mid-1950s as a U.S. Army physicist he had observed nuclear tests in the Pacific. This experience "inevitably," he said, influenced his thoughts about the *Enola Gay* display. "I think anybody who has ever seen a hydrogen bomb go off at fairly close range," he said, "knows that you don't ever want to see that used on people." Later, in planning the *Enola Gay* exhibit, Harwit visited Hiroshima and Nagasaki twice.

In the summer of 1994, as media interest in the controversy increased,

Harwit wrote a pair of perceptive articles explaining his position. In the *Washington Post* he identified two "divergent but widely held views" defining the controversy. One had existed since 1945 and appealed to our national self-image. "The other point of view, slower in coming to the fore, is more analytical, critical in its acceptance of facts and concerned with historical context. It is complex and, in the eyes of some, discomfiting." The veterans who criticized the show wanted the museum "to tell their story the way they have always told and retold it." He concluded:

> We have found no way to exhibit the Enola Gay and satisfy everyone. But a comprehensive and thoughtful discussion can help us learn from history. And that is what we aim to offer our visitors.

Harwit appeared haunted by the possibility of failing in this mission. In an article for the Smithsonian's *Air & Space* magazine, he warned that "fifty years may not be enough time to prepare the nation to confront such a history. How we resolve this fundamental issue will determine what we choose to remember about World War II in this exhibit and in our collective memory as a nation." If we "remember selectively" we may repeat the mistakes of our past. Some of the "long-cherished" beliefs of the veterans, he wrote, "have been contradicted by documentary evidence," yet the exhibit would include "both the widely held views and the facts supported by documents." He concluded on a somber note:

> With passions running so high, the worrisome question is whether we will succeed in providing a historically accurate account of the atomic bombings and the end of the war. If we cannot mount a thoroughly documented exhibition, then we have little hope of learning from these epochal events. And if we are unable to draw wisdom from the war's conclusion, we will have marked its anniversary with a deplorable failure.

Outside Pressure:
Congress and the Media

But now Martin Harwit found it increasingly hard to hold the line. Tension at Air and Space mounted due to a hostile media and a meddling Congress.

On August 10, twenty-four members of Congress sent a letter of protest to the Smithsonian secretary, charging that the script was "narrow" and "biased." The Senate, meanwhile, unanimously passed a resolution by Nancy Kassebaum declaring that the exhibit was "revisionist, unbalanced and offensive" and reminding the museum of its "obligation to portray history in the proper context of the time."

Members of Congress called Martin Harwit to Capitol Hill for questioning. Rep. Tom Lewis of Florida issued a blistering press release charging that the exhibit offered "an apology to Japan" and amounted to "a radical anti-nuclear demonstration." More significantly, he threatened to attempt to cut off taxpayers' funds for the exhibit. "I will not allow their money to be spent revising history," he said. Although the Smithsonian is governed by an independent board of regents, about eighty-five percent of its operating budget comes from Congress—and conservatives had already complained about "political correctness" in a number of recent exhibits.

As chilling as any of the political pressure, according to some Air and Space officials, was an editorial in the *Washington Post* on August 14, taking Harwit and the curators to task. "When even a so-called liberal newspaper came out against us it symbolized that we had no friends in this town," an Air and Space official privately explained. "From that point on, the director [Harwit] caved in because of orders from above—and the censoring and cutting up of the exhibit began."*

Media treatment of the controversy followed patterns we have seen before. Reporters rarely took the trouble to examine one of the widely available scripts to determine if the veterans' complaints were valid. Instead, they accepted at face value the Air Force Association's interpretation —including such false assertions that the script did not mention Japanese

* *Museum officials we contacted were not willing to speak for attribution, fearing they might lose their jobs if they did. We also interviewed American Legion and Air Force Association spokesmen, other veterans, and members of the exhibit's advisory board.*

brutality. They frequently quoted passages in the script that had been deleted months before. Articles in *Time* and *Newsweek* were clearly slanted against the exhibit. Hugh Sidey, the veteran *Time* reporter, displayed dubious taste in observing that American veterans were "feeling nuked" by the Smithsonian. A *Newsweek* article chided the museum for challenging the "inescapable" logic of the decision to use the bomb.

A front-page article in the *Washington Post* reduced the controversy to a generational conflict between patriotic veterans of World War II and "anti-government, anti-war" protesters of the Vietnam era who have an "antagonistic view of this nation and its past." To bolster his account, the reporter pointed out that Tom Crouch had gone to college "during the Vietnam War," while Michael Neufeld spent his undergraduate years in Calgary "when Americans were fleeing to Canada" to escape the draft. He presented no evidence that the curators actually protested the war, let alone that they were "anti-government." The two men were defined generationally, rather than as the authors of scholarly books (Neufeld's acclaimed study of the V-2, *The Rocket and the Reich,* was about to be published).

Editorials were almost uniformly hostile to the Smithsonian. The *Wall Street Journal* said that the museum had "rewritten history as never before," adding that it was clearly in the hands of "academics unable to view American history as anything other than a woeful catalog of crimes and aggressions against the helpless peoples of the earth." Obviously appealing to Congress, the *Journal* demanded to know "what is going on at the taxpayer-funded Smithsonian—and for how long it is going to be allowed to continue." *USA Today* erroneously charged that the exhibit would carry no explanation of "why President Truman sent the *Enola Gay* to Japan in the first place." One of its commentators established a new high for American lives saved—six million—and claimed that this was "the consensus view." Syndicated columnist Charles Krauthammer called the display "an embarrassing amalgam of revisionist hand-wringing and guilt." The *New York Times* deplored congressional "tampering" but reprinted a cartoon that reduced the controversy to a trivial question of "political correctness." (The drawing pictured the *Enola Gay* bearing the label *Built by oppressed female workers and piloted by the white male establishment*. The irony, of course, is that challenging the Hiroshima narrative has never been a "politically correct" position.)

All four panelists on the ABC television program *This Week with David Brinkley* denounced the Smithsonian. Cokie Roberts offered the opinion that "to rewrite history makes no sense." George Will declared that dropping the bomb saved millions of casualties and was a "moral act." Truman never lost a minute's sleep over the decision, Will recalled, "and that is exactly right." The curators "obviously hate this country," he added, and "shouldn't be working there."

Such was the public discourse inspired by the Smithsonian dispute. One museum official complained that "the media reflects the public, and the public doesn't want to hear the full story." More than forty-nine years had passed since Hiroshima, and if media treatment had changed at all, it had changed for the worse. In 1945, after all, no prominent figure publicly challenged the patriotism of David Lawrence, Norman Cousins, and the handful of other critics who raised questions about the decision to drop the bomb.

A new script, responding to the latest criticism, appeared in late August, and it contained many significant changes. The opening section had been expanded yet again and retitled "The War in the Pacific, An American Perspective." Japan's preparations for an invasion, including the arming of women with bamboo spears and ordering children to work in weapons plants, would now be vividly depicted. So would Japanese atrocities, such as the beheading of a POW. The "ground zero" display, however, was shrinking. Removed were more than a dozen powerful photographs of badly injured or dead Japanese victims of the bombing, as well as many artifacts related to damage in temples and churches and schools. Also deleted was Truman's remark "This is the greatest thing in history!"

But the crucial revision—because it set the tone for the entire show—was the deletion of the opening statement that the Hiroshima decision had sparked "controversy" over the years. Indeed, there was no longer any mention of public or scholarly debate over the use of the bomb. The exploration of Truman's decision was severely curtailed and veered closer to the official narrative. A wall panel examining the important question "Was an Invasion Inevitable Without the Bomb?" would now carry the legend *Hindsight*—as if that question had never been raised *before* Hiroshima.

Yet military leaders, editorialists, and conservatives in Congress demanded further changes. A *Washington Post* columnist labeled the exhibit, even in its heavily revised form, "anti-American propaganda" reflecting a vision "somewhere between self-delusion and insanity. . . ." On *Nightline,* Charles Sweeney, who piloted the plane that dropped the Nagasaki bomb, called the exhibit "certainly un-American," adding that "it might be close to treason."

As the protests grew louder, the White House remained silent. Vice President Gore, a member of the Smithsonian's board of regents, was said to be monitoring the crisis closely. President Clinton did not respond directly, but Secretary of Veterans Affairs Jesse Brown wrote Martin Harwit. "How can one allow hindsight 50 years later," he asked, "to question the righteousness of a decision to quickly end this unspeakable chapter in world history?" To make judgments about the use of the bomb, he advised, would dishonor all those who served their nation in the Pacific.

This linkage was at the heart of the Smithsonian dispute. Battling Japanese soldiers on the Pacific islands and dropping a revolutionary new weapon on Japanese civilians were distinctly separate acts. None of the brave servicemen had anything to do with deciding to drop the bomb, yet they felt their honor was inextricably bound up with it. One vet told us that what he most feared was that children and other visitors would "walk out of that exhibit with the feeling that the American servicepeople . . . were warmongers, bloodthirsty, or they were acting out of vengeance."

Historical Cleansing

In September, after months of attempting to maintain the original shape of his exhibit, Martin Harwit gave up the fight. His own staffers were now bitterly opposed to further changes (as well as many of the revisions already made). Some of them called for the cancellation of the entire exhibit. The new secretary of the Smithsonian, Michael Heyman, considered this option but rejected it. Canceling a show in response to political pressure would set a bad precedent, he argued. Some of those working on the show felt that to "warp an entire show" (as one put it) in response to political pressure set a far worse precedent. Soon outsiders as well as insiders would be charging Harwit with "caving in" to the veterans, the media, and Congress.

The American Legion played a key role in the reversal. From the start, the nation's largest veterans group had deferred to the Air Force Association in this dispute. But now, leaders of the Legion, which boasts 3.1 million members (about half of them World War II veterans), planned to introduce a resolution strongly condemning the exhibit at their national convention.

This was the last thing the Smithsonian needed, and so Martin Harwit took bold action: He attended the Legion convention, a slide show of the proposed exhibit in hand. What provoked the meeting, according to a museum official involved with the exhibit, was that Heyman had determined that the only "political solution" for the Smithsonian was to get the Legion to "broker a compromise that would get Congress off our backs, prevent budget cuts, and call off a congressional investigation." In a conference room at the convention, Harwit took questions from a hostile audience, convincing many of his sincerity. A prominent news commentator described this as "a sort of surrender ceremony" for Harwit. The *Los Angeles Times* noted that he had simply "figured out which way the political winds were blowing."

Two weeks later, museum officials and Legion "negotiators," as they called themselves, conducted a pair of marathon bargaining sessions. A line-by-line review of the script resulted not merely in a revision but a major overhaul—"panic cuts and panic censorship," one outraged Air and Space official told us. Martin Harwit informed reporters that the museum had decided to "simplify" the script so that it could not be "misunderstood or misinterpreted. It can only have one message, and it has to be very clearly stated," he said.

The contrast with earlier scripts was striking. Every key quote by an official or military figure (Eisenhower, Leahy, Bard, and McCloy) questioning the Hiroshima decision was deleted. It was as if not one leading American had raised a serious question about Hiroshima in nearly fifty years. (Also cut was a reference to criticism of the Nagasaki mission.) The ground zero display had been reduced by half. Only *one* photograph of dead victims of the atomic bombings remained—contrasted with a dozen photos of rubble, six images of the mushroom cloud, and four pictures of shadows imprinted on walls. The exhibit now included just one photograph of a victim suffering from radiation disease, but two pictures of Americans associated with the medical commission that studied the victims.

One minor change revealed how politicized the script had become: a reference to the "anti-Communist hysteria" of the 1950s was changed to "anti-Communist climate."

The new story line was, as Harwit promised, utterly straightforward: Japan, although "weakened," was nowhere near collapse in the summer of 1945, and it was "quite possible" that the war could have gone on until late 1946. America's *only* choice was invade or drop the bomb. Japan's peace feelers were frivolous; negotiation was out of the question; and the Soviet entry could not have caused a surrender. All of America's top officials and military leaders believed an invasion, therefore, was inevitable, without the bomb. Truman ordered use of the bomb simply to save lives and prevent "an Okinawa from one end of Japan to the other," and no other factor affected his thinking. He believed Hiroshima was a "purely military" target. Indeed, there were virtually no civilians as such left in Japan. Preparations for an invasion had made all of the country a "war zone" and all of its citizens, including women and schoolchildren, "would be involved" in the battle. But as a result of the bomb, and only the bomb, the war would end in "unconditional surrender."

The script now accepted the official estimate of expected American casualties in an invasion of Japan: 260,000 to one million. And it proposed ending the exhibit with the Japanese surrender. There would be little or no mention of the arms race and other postwar nuclear issues. The final script was nothing more or less than the 1947 Stimson article with visual aids—and no updating.

Martin Harwit declared that the Legion should be pleased with these changes and predicted that the newly designed exhibit would find "wide acceptance among visitors." (Only weeks earlier he had expressed the hope that the exhibit would provoke re-examination, not acceptance.) Spokesmen for veterans groups said, off the record, that they were grateful, but shocked, that the Smithsonian had granted them so much power. Michael Heyman expressed appreciation to the Legion for spending so much time helping to improve the fairness and accuracy of the script, so that now it would be "an exhibition in which all Americans can take pride." But on *Nightline,* in a less-guarded moment, he explained: "I'm finding that it's difficult to have a moral debate in the context of the Smithsonian."

The latest round of changes in the exhibit finally provoked a backlash from historians—and not just the so-called revisionists. A member of the exhibit's eight-member advisory board resigned, and several others protested. One adviser, Edward Linenthal, charged that the wholesale changes constituted "a very dangerous precedent for the way we do public history." Powerful groups, aided by members of Congress "who now apparently fancy themselves historians and curators as well as public servants, can through pressure, through innuendo, change the nature of how we present history."

Another adviser, Martin Sherwin, helped draft a strongly worded letter to Heyman, calling the latest script "patriotically correct." The letter, signed by dozens of prominent scholars, charged that the exhibit had been "reduced to mere propaganda," an affront to the soldiers who gave their lives for freedom. It represented "a transparent attempt at historical cleansing," and it was "unconscionable" that an exhibit in this public institution no longer presented a "balanced range" of views and contained assertions of fact "which have long been challenged by careful historical scholarship." The executive board of the Organization of American Historians passed a resolution deploring the removal of documents and other revisions in the exhibit because of pressure from Congress and related factors. Officials in Hiroshima reconsidered their decision to send artifacts to the Smithsonian.

Disarmament activists, who had been quiet until then, denounced the latest script, noting that the same week Air and Space officials met with the American Legion for twenty-two hours they only spent ninety minutes with a peace delegation. (During this session, Harwit cited threats to cut federal funding to the museum as one of the pressures he faced.) Activists appeared most concerned about the elimination of the exhibit's "legacy" section. The script no longer mentioned that radiation from the building or testing of nuclear weapons had caused severe health hazards. It did not refer to the economic cost of producing and maintaining nuclear weapons in the fifty years after Hiroshima, nor that the U.S. still had 20,000 nuclear warheads in its arsenal.

In November, eight scholars and writers (including the authors of this book) met with Martin Harwit and the curators for more than two hours at the museum. Included in the group were two members of the exhibit's original advisory board. After listening silently to a round of criticism and pleas for accuracy and balance, Harwit appeared uncomfortable but conceded nothing. He compared the exhibit to a textbook that has to provide readers with a "basic story" because they can "only absorb a certain amount in one gulp." The first script, he said, was more of a scholarly work, with "provisos and caveats." Now it had been simplified to reflect the "dominant" view of the subject—that is, the official narrative—and all that had been lost was "excessive repetition" and "excessive gruesomeness."

As with any textbook, he said, "an editor may tell you it's too long and can be cut." Several scholars asked why all the cuts were of material that raised questions about the use of the bomb. (In August, Harwit himself had warned, "We cannot afford to remember selectively.") Why, for example, had the quote by Eisenhower criticizing the use of the bomb been deleted? Harwit explained that Eisenhower, when he spoke to Stimson, had merely offered a personal opinion, not military advice—and that "disclaimer" disqualified the quote from the show. Harwit said this so unconvincingly that it was almost painful to watch and to hear. Referring to the script, Harwit exclaimed, "The devil is in the details," and on this question, if no other, there was general agreement.

Harwit closed the meeting by ruling out any but minor changes. Just three months earlier, he had observed that fifty years "may not be enough time to prepare the nation" to confront the atomic bombings. Now it was clear that he was correct. After the meeting, Michael Neufeld and Tom Crouch refused to answer scholars' questions but acted abashed, even apologetic; Harwit, who had to maintain the official line, seemed haunted, almost broken, by what had occurred. They appeared to be three decent men caught in a bureaucratic and ethical vise.

An Air and Space official later confided to one of us: "The exhibit you want is politically impossible." It was clear that this was also the exhibit *he* wanted. "The fundamental lesson we learned is how little debate on this subject the political majority will allow," he added. "Attacking 'political correctness' is a kind of neo-McCarthyism. It's growing impossible for museums to do exhibits that raise questions without being pilloried in the press. And the public is not yet ready to deal with history as a debatable subject. They feel there is only one true history—a set of memorized or unquestionable 'facts,' not a set of arguments."

As 1995 began, the *Enola Gay* exhibit appeared back on track for its May opening. But then it was thrown off course once again, this time for good. The scholars' group (of which we were a part) came to play a contributing role.

In early January, Martin Harwit informed an American Legion leader that the museum planned to revise, once again, its estimate of likely U.S. casualties in the planned invasion of Japan. During the scholars' meeting with Harwit in November, Barton Bernstein had insisted that no official, pre-Hiroshima casualty estimate exceeded 63,000—a figure based on his re-reading of Admiral Leahy's diary. (David McCullough, whom the veterans used as a source on this issue, had just admitted that he mistakenly cited much higher figures in *Truman.*) Harwit, after doing some checking, accepted the Bernstein number and notified the American Legion of the change.

It was a startling faux pas. According to one of his colleagues, Harwit by this time had "deluded himself into believing that this was still a historical project and not a political one. He had forgotten he had made a political deal and that he was trapped."

Immediately, the veterans revolted, claiming that Harwit was tinkering with the Legion-edited script. "We were told this guy [Bernstein] was out of the loop," Legion commander William Detweiler complained. "We're told these people [the advisory board] are no longer involved, and then they show up again." The Legion sent a letter of protest to the White House and key members of Congress. This came as a conservative mood was sweeping Washington with the coming to power of a new Republican majority.

Within days, House Republicans announced hearings, and eighty members of Congress called for Harwit's dismissal. They also promised to "look at future funding of the institution," as one representative put it. Bob Dole, the Senate majority leader, charged that the Smithsonian was "now catering to the revisionists and the politically correct." Ted Stevens, another powerful Senator, and a veteran of World War II, announced, "I think I'm here because of the *Enola Gay.*"

Detweiler met with an aide to Newt Gingrich, the new House

Speaker. Gingrich then called for cancellation of the exhibit, charging that the Smithsonian had become "a plaything for left-wing ideologies." He appointed to the Smithsonian's board of regents, which would meet within days, two conservative critics of the exhibit. They intended, he said, to root out the "political correctness" that had been "distorting" displays at the institution and communicate that the vast majority of Americans believe this approach is wrong.

Media coverage, as before, was sympathetic to the veterans and loose with the facts. George Will and Charles Krauthammer repeated charges that the exhibit was anti-American. Most reporters, still failing to check the actual script, continued to accept assertions that it was pro-Japanese or portrayed Americans as "racist." The *Washington Post* claimed that museum officials had no one to blame but themselves for allowing scripts that were "anti-nuclear and anti-American" in tone. The *New York Times* was virtually alone in highlighting the danger of history "being hijacked by a band of Congressmen and veterans outraged that the exhibit does not tell just their side of the story."

As the regents' meeting approached, Gingrich telephoned Michael Heyman and, according to press reports, discussed a plan to cancel the planned exhibit. It seemed inevitable that the regents would go along with this: besides threats of budgetary cuts by Congress, private fund-raising was suffering due to the controversy.

What surprised some of the scholars and museum officials, however, was that the veterans, who clearly had won the war over the script, were about to sacrifice the fruits of victory—an exhibit that strongly justified the use of the bomb—in a skirmish over the casualty count. This once again revealed the significance of the lives lost/lives saved equation.

But there was more to it than that. For one thing, the Legion leadership was at odds with its membership. Rank-and-file veterans, inflamed by the false or misleading reports in the media about the script, pressed for cancellation, not compromise. According to a Legion spokesman, members were making "indignant calls" to headquarters right to the end, complaining about "statements in the script we had eliminated long ago." Some Legion leaders were looking for an excuse to bow out of their deal with the museum, and now Harwit, unintentionally, had handed it to them.

Another hidden factor was that the veterans, despite strenuous efforts, had not succeeded in completely neutralizing the "ground zero" display. They had banished virtually all questioning of the official narrative—but the ghosts of the atomic bombings simply would not go away. The Legion, as part of its agreement with Harwit, had accepted that the victims must stay in the show, at least in a limited way. But some of the veterans wished them gone.

There was a solution to all these problems, which the veterans, their congressional allies, and finally the Smithsonian's board could all embrace: get rid of the casualty debate, the victims, and all other potentially troubling questions and *keep the plane*. This was what Paul Tibbets, Paul Fussell, and many other veterans had always wanted. The atomic mission would gain glory not so much by what was left in the display as what was absent: what happened after the bomb left the bomb bay.

On January 30, the regents accepted Heyman's call for a drastic scaling back of the exhibit to just the plane, a plaque identifying it, and a video of crew members recounting their experience. The *Enola Gay* and the crew would "speak for themselves," Heyman explained. There was no indication, and certainly no promise, that casualties on the ground would even be mentioned. "They better not let Barton Bernstein draft the copy for the plaque," a Legion spokesman quipped.

At a press conference, Heyman ascribed the decision not to political pressure but a belated recognition that the museum had made a "basic error." In this special anniversary year, veterans and their families expected a tribute to their valor and sacrifice. "They were not looking for analysis and, frankly," he added, "we did not give enough thought to the intense feelings such an analysis would evoke." The "fundamental flaw" in the exhibit was in coupling "a historical treatment of the use of atomic weapons" with a "commemoration of the end of the war." If not its flaw, it was certainly the exhibit's problem: the two commemorations are historically inseparable but psychologically incompatible, at least at this moment.

A White House press spokesman revealed that Vice President Gore had expressed President Clinton's support for the cancellation to Michael Heyman the previous week. "The president and the vice president," he explained, "are very sensitive to the concerns expressed by veterans' groups and others about the exhibit itself." Clinton and Gore believed "firmly that academic freedom has its place" but "nonetheless felt that some of the concerns expressed by veterans' groups and others had merit."

The *Washington Times* praised Heyman's "recognition of the new political order in Washington." CBS News observed that the Smithsonian had "admitted defeat and sued for peace." An Air and Space official involved with the exhibit told one of us he was "not sorry it was killed—it was just six months too late." He seemed relieved to be freed from what he termed "a fatal bargain." So, in the end, this was an exhibit the demands of conscience required but nobody wanted.

Legion commander Detweiler hailed this victory over those "driven by a fervent ideology." He offered a disturbing comparison, calling the fight over the exhibit a metaphor for "the very war it purported to record, and its outcome a metaphor for the war's climactic last act. The winners, just as they were fifty years ago, are the American people." He seemed to imply that the Smithsonian dispute was another battle between the U.S. military and a hated enemy—this time, their fellow countrymen. The outcome, like the Pacific war, was determined by the use of phenomenal firepower (in this case, political pressure). The war over the exhibit had ended with little left standing. The enemy had surrendered, unconditionally. And the Japanese victims, and questions about the decision to use the atomic bomb, were nowhere in sight.

Even that wasn't the end of it, however. In March, Heyman revealed that the simple plaque he had promised had dramatically changed in character. He would write the text himself, he assured a congressional committee, and it would do more than merely identify the *Enola Gay*—it would attempt to justify the atomic bombing. "I essentially am just going to report the facts," he explained. "Something along the lines of, 'This clearly led to the conclusion of the war immediately and resulted in saving untold numbers of lives by avoiding the necessity of invasion.' " Asked whether the text would mention casualties caused by the bomb, Heyman said he was undecided. "Remember, this is a restrained show," he added. "I'm trying to keep it restrained."

To commemorate is to combine memory and ceremony, to remind or be mindful—to witness again. In that sense, America was clearly far from being ready to commemorate Hiroshima in 1995. The Smithsonian's failure of will was a national one, a product of the tenacity of the official narrative, which emerged with Truman's announcement on August 6, 1945, and has held sway ever since.

Although the Smithsonian affair was clearly a disturbing step backward, the struggle over the Hiroshima narrative continues. The Smithsonian debacle may well have been a way of reaching rock bottom prior to an opening out. For it brought national attention to the Hiroshima debate for the first time and inspired both peace activists and historians to take their case to the public. The Smithsonian's "historical cleansing" did not solve anything, it only postponed an inevitable coming to terms with Hiroshima. With its broadening of interest in the atomic bombings, the controversy, along with the entire commemorative year, served as a stimulus for a radical expansion of Hiroshima consciousness, even for the kind of knowledge that has the possibility of wisdom.

PART IV

HIROSHIMA'S LEGACY—MORAL,
PSYCHOLOGICAL, POLITICAL

INTRODUCTION

A half century of Hiroshima distortions was bound to have its effects on the American psyche and American society. Here we enter a very important, but largely unexamined, dimension of Hiroshima: the lasting psychological, ethical, and political impact on those who used the first nuclear weapons, and continued to develop them.

The cumulative influence of Hiroshima turns out to be much greater than most Americans suspect. Indeed, one may speak of the bomb's contamination not only of Japanese victims and survivors, but of the American mind as well. But that very contamination—the aberrations in American life induced by Hiroshima—if confronted, can become a source of renewal.

CHAPTER 1

OUR OWN NUCLEAR ENTRAPMENT

Since Hiroshima, we have been captives of nuclear weapons. We rely on them and we flaunt them, but psychologically and politically they have imprisoned us. In exploding atomic bombs over Hiroshima and Nagasaki we frightened no one more than ourselves. Ever since, we have struggled to overcome our own terror and re-establish lost "security" by means of embracing the objects of that terror and attaching ourselves to their ultimate power, their omnipotence. At the same time our insistent need to justify the atomic bombings has required us to view nuclear devices as potentially usable weapons.

We have created a vicious circle of atomic-bomb use and justification of that use, fearful vulnerability, further atomic and nuclear buildup, imagined or threatened use of the weaponry (from whatever source), more vulnerability and buildup—so that now, tens of thousands of nuclear warheads exist on the earth. To be sure, the first Soviet atomic explosion in 1949 suggested real danger from an adversary. But our essentially hermetic psychological relationship with the weaponry preceded the Soviet bomb, continued throughout the cold war, and is with us still, despite the end of the superpower conflict.

Our entrapment stems from both our "successful" use of the weapon and from the permanent state of fear that use engendered. Thus, a year after Hiroshima and Nagasaki, General Thomas Farrell, Groves's deputy at Los Alamos, could declare that, in an unsafe world, "we must arm to the teeth with the winning weapon." Seeking security, our leaders fashioned a world of total insecurity, as Lewis Mumford observed.

From the beginning, awesome attraction swallowed up fear, as in the response of American leaders to Trinity. The attraction, as we know, is one of merging with a source of power rivaling that of any deity.* There is the further sense that the nuclear deity, in conferring its omnipotence, protects one from death and thereby offers an imagined version of immortality. This embrace of death-conquering power is the essence of the psychology of nuclearism. Such nuclear thralldom requires that each advance in weaponry also be embraced: out of fear (lest the adversary acquire it first), and out of worship.

Significantly, there was a delay in the early 1950s in completing development of the hydrogen bomb, which two knowledgeable magazine writers attributed largely to "a national, psychological reaction to Hiroshima and Nagasaki," the general feeling that "the atomic bomb seemed big enough in all conscience . . ." They looked critically upon this attitude, calling it "a sort of blind spot to other types of weapons." The president's advisers, in an urgent reply, assured Americans that the administration *had* done everything to pursue nuclear weapons development as rapidly as possible. In other words, the Hiroshima-initiated nuclear imperative could not only overcome any psychological resistance to more advanced weaponry but also required reassurances that policies would not be determined by any such resistance.

Hans Bethe recently said to one of us, "Atomic bomb yes, hydrogen bomb no." He was making a distinction between his sense of justification regarding the first and regret regarding the second, in more or less summing up a long relationship with nuclear weapons. Certainly the world in general would be much safer and much less polluted by nuclear waste if the

---

* *This has been more a male than a female tendency, as Carol Cohn and others have noted. In fact, a gender gap in regard to nuclearism has long existed, reflected in various polls that found significantly less support among women than men for using the bomb (in Korea and Vietnam, for example) and more support for a test ban and a nuclear freeze. The March 1995 poll we cited earlier, which suggests that a majority of Americans may now question the Hiroshima decision, uncovered what the Gallup organization called one of the largest gender gaps ever: 61 percent of the men, but only 29 percent of the women, said they would have ordered the bomb to be dropped in 1945.*

revolutionary step to the hydrogen bomb had not been taken. But the difficulty in Bethe's distinction was the extent to which the two weapons were part of the same process, the mindset surrounding the first driving the decision for the second. A similar process affected virtually all American presidents over the years of the post-Hiroshima cold war, each feeling compelled to continue the buildup of genocidal weaponry. The most striking example is that of Jimmy Carter who, in his inaugural address, spoke of ridding the world of nuclear danger but ended his presidential tenure with aggressive first-use policies and weaponry carried further than ever before.

Nuclear weapons thus take their place as the dominant technology of a permanent, self-propelling American megamachine that seems almost independent of human control. In fact, human will is always present, in the form of enthralled endorsement, thereby creating something close to an atrocity-producing situation of ultimate consequence.

This weapons dynamic inevitably extends to non-nuclear devices. Since Hiroshima, they have been known as "conventional" weapons, which suggests ordinariness and relative mildness. Compared to the Hiroshima standard, that is, all other weapons become benign. Their use could even come to be seen as "humane" because nuclear weapons would have been avoided. That kind of psychology undoubtedly influenced the widespread use of highly advanced and lethal napalm in Vietnam and carpet bombing in Iraq. To be sure, pre-Hiroshima saturation bombings set the stage for all this. But Hiroshima and Nagasaki, in turn, radically altered our relationship to any such killing of civilians from the air, rendering it suddenly more acceptable. Almost anything was permissible if used to "save American lives."

Hiroshima has also contributed to what could be called a malignant edge of nuclearism: an impulse to carry through the extraordinary power surge to the end, the literal end in this case, by setting the weapons off. No one can tell us the exact extent of this *Götterdämmerung* impulse toward global murder/suicide. It is articulated by some groups of religious fundamentalists who envision the nuclear event as a purification and a prelude to spiritual rebirth. But there can be secular equivalents, among certain "nuclear fundamentalists" who unconsciously seek the death-defeating apocalypse that they have so long envisioned. Leslie Fiedler (writing in 1964) put the matter more boldly: ". . . for most of the younger writers today, the only war that *counts* is World War III, the war that does not happen, may indeed never happen, but which remains all the same the war for which they long, as all generations long for the *Götterdämmerung* they most fear." Although infused by Fiedler's own apocalyptic rhetoric, the sentence tells us something about the imaginative world initiated by Hiroshima. A more accurate way to put things might be that, while in the past each male generation has longed for a wartime moment of heroic valor, Hiroshima can blur and alter that longing in the direction of *Götterdämmerung*. Those longings become bound up with an attraction of what Frances Ferguson calls the "nuclear sublime"—with the awesome and compelling image of total destruction and absolute nothingness.

The more general Hiroshima influence has been that of nuclear stockpiling so that "the winning weapon" can be called upon again at any time. At one level this has meant a kind of routinizing of the nuclear system and a domestication of the weapons for the purpose of "protection." But a system generates a continuous sense of crisis, of anxiety about dangers both real and fantasized, in a dynamic of threat and counterthreat bound up with ever more bizarre scenarios of the murder of hundreds of millions of human beings.

For ordinary Americans, post-Hiroshima nuclear arrangements have been less than reassuring and frequently highly confusing. Polls show that the public has generally supported nuclear weapons developments and even first use of the weapons.*

Despite America's nuclear buildup over those years and decades, most people felt themselves increasingly less safe and even tended to expect a large-scale nuclear war. Both adults and children frequently doubted that they would be permitted to live out their full lives. Interviews conducted at the Center on Violence and Human Survival in New York City during the late 1980s revealed profound anxiety in anticipation of nuclear chaos. One man imagined a postbomb scene in which he and others were "run-

---

* *According to Gallup surveys, a majority supported using the atomic bomb in Korea in 1951 after China entered the conflict; in Vietnam in 1954 when the French were surrounded; and against China in 1955 during the first Quemoy-Matsu crisis. By a two-to-one margin they rejected using the bomb in Vietnam in 1967 (perhaps because a large percentage did not feel the war "morally justified"), but when the question was phrased differently to ask if they would support use if the military explicitly advised it, the response was nearly evenly split. During the 1980s, with antinuclear sentiment rising, polls showed overwhelming support for a no-first-use pledge—but a later survey found a near-majority backing use of the bomb against Iraq in 1991.*

ning about wildly, flames, terror, a kind of general madness, hunger, a general picture of devastation." A woman told of everything being reduced to "just . . . dust . . . a void," with all death "stripped of human dignity." Some referred to specific Hiroshima images conveyed in various media as a source of nuclear fear. Others were affected by the 1983 television film, *The Day After,* which made use of film from Hiroshima.

Ordinary people, that is, experience their own post-Hiroshima entrapment—mixtures of nuclearism and nuclear terror, of weapons advocacy and fearful anticipation of death and extinction. These feelings could frequently be suppressed, only to reassert themselves when one is reminded of nuclear danger, or unexpectedly in dreams. And even at the end of the cold war, when our interviews showed something of a switch from nuclear to environmental fear, those post-Hiroshima anxieties by no means disappeared.

Hiroshima marks a powerful psychological turning point in our attitude toward our own science and technology. It is true that as early as 1818 Mary Wollstonecraft Shelley warned us of the danger that we might destroy ourselves with our technology. Moreover, in her novel, *Frankenstein: Or the Modern Prometheus,* the monster pleads to his creator, the student-scientist Victor Frankenstein, for understanding and responsibility toward his laboratory product: "I am thy creature." And a century later, H. G. Wells expressed a similar view on the importance of responsibility toward our own technology in his 1914 novel, *The World Set Free,* in which he was the first to speak of "atomic bombs" that could destroy humankind. With Hiroshima, those disturbing prophecies had come to near realization: we had destroyed whole cities with a single small instrument, and that instrument had been a product of a brilliant new development in science. How could we then trust in the beneficence of any scientific work or technology? We hardly gave up on science and technology in general, but we were left with an uneasy ambivalence about our relationship to both.

CHAPTER 2

MORAL INVERSION

From the time of Hiroshima, Americans have assigned themselves the task of finding virtue in the first use of the most murderous device ever created. We have felt the need to avoid at any cost a sense of moral culpability for this act. These efforts have taken us to the far reaches of moral argument, to the extent of creating something close to an Orwellian reversal. And there has indeed been a cost, one much greater than we wish to recognize.

Harry Truman provided in his own life a model for post-Hiroshima national behavior—one of edgy, often confabulatory insistence upon finding virtue in using that device on those two Japanese cities. But collectively we have gone further than Truman in our struggles with not just feelings of guilt but with a larger view of ourselves as a decent people. We encounter continuous doubt about any possible virtue in the atomic bombings—among people elsewhere and, however unspoken, in our own minds as well.

Immediately after hearing about Hiroshima, Albert Camus expressed his concern about the weapon and the "enthusiastic commentaries" on it in American, English, and French newspapers. He added that "it is permissible to think that there is some indecency in celebrating in this manner a discovery, which, first of all, places itself at the disposal of the most awful destructive rage which—over the centuries—humankind has ever displayed" and which adds to a "tormented world . . . a new agony, one that has every chance of being final." In cautioning against celebration, Camus issued a clear, early warning against the kind of moral inversion he anticipated.

For Americans, however, the bomb suddenly manifested itself as the decisive or "winning" weapon in the bloody Pacific war, and celebration was inevitable. It was *our* awesome scientific and technological achievement—something to celebrate in itself, and then celebrate further as a way of avoiding the more painful question of moral consequences. Strongly contributing to this response was the immediate claim that the bomb ended the war quickly and thereby saved lives. By thus rendering the weapon a *preserver* rather than a *destroyer* of life, celebratory emotions have been sustained to this moment. But the upward trend of the number of American lives saved suggests that doubt and general unease have entered into atomic bomb celebration over the years.

In the charged equilibrium between celebration and moral doubt, radiation effects loom large. They are so troubling because they symbolize the bomb's radical discontinuity with previous weapons, its special character as a destroyer of human beings not only at its moment of impact but in its lifelong and transgenerational deadly potential.* In that way, the truths about radiation undermine our effort at justification perhaps more than any other aspect of the weapon.

A devastating reflection of our moral confusions about radiation, and about the bomb, was our official attitude toward studying and treating survivors. American decision makers eventually had to recognize the reality of radiation effects and the importance of studying Hiroshima and Nagasaki survivors as "the first true residents of the atomic age," as Susan Lindee described them. But the official American group performing the research—the Atomic Bomb Casualty Commission—steadfastly refused to offer treatment to the survivors studied, even when they seemed to experience radiation-linked illnesses. Survivors' bitterness was related to their

---

* Disturbing evidence continues to emerge. A Japanese study that examined 2,500 survivors in Nagasaki recently found that nearly one-fifth had developed thyroid diseases, including tumors. This demonstrates "for the first time a significant increase in autoimmune disease among atomic bomb survivors," according to a 1994 article in the Journal of the American Medical Association, and suggests that formation of tumors "is present even more than forty years after" exposure to the bomb.

perception of radiation as "the bomb's unique form of terror" and was often expressed in accusations of being made into "guinea pigs." They felt they were being seen as mere objects of research rather than as suffering human beings, and those feelings were accentuated by the sense that the dropping of the bomb was itself an experiment meant to determine what the weapon would do to people living in a city.

The reason Americans rejected the idea of treatment was expressed by one adviser on the matter who explained that "to do so would have given confirmation to the anti-American propagandists [who] . . . insist that such treatment should be an act of atonement for having used the weapons in the first place." From the standpoint of this argument, as Lindee observed in her recent book on the commission, "whoever provided medical care to the survivors would be accepting moral and historical responsibility for what had happened to them." Hence the American insistence that the Japanese government be the ones to make treatment available. Our official narrative precluded anything suggesting atonement. Rather the bomb itself had to be "redeemed": As "a frightening manifestation of technological evil . . . it needed to be reformed, transformed, managed, or turned into the vehicle of a promising future," Lindee argued. "It was necessary, somehow, to redeem the bomb." In other words, to avoid historical and moral responsibility, we acted immorally and claimed virtue. We sank deeper, that is, into moral inversion.

But what has been called Hiroshima's "ripples of destruction" inevitably made their way into American consciousness. We could not escape some sense of radical evil, of having crossed a terrible boundary into an unprecedented realm of mass killing. We had done something that seemed to endanger the whole world. Such feelings of self-accusation were rendered especially painful by our sense of ourselves as a people of special goodness, indeed as people living always in God's grace. However illusory, this national self-image automatically raised questions of good and evil: "If we have struggled to bring about a Kingdom of Heaven on earth, we have been willing to borrow our tools from the Kingdom of Hell," as one observer put it. Our very claim to virtue can thus contribute to a sense of spiritual fall, all the more so in perceiving the inability of our religious and political leaders to help us look at the dark moral questions. This kind of collective "fall" creates forms of disillusionment that can in turn result in scapegoating, apathy, cynicism, or combinations of all three.

These troubled psychological processes have been further enhanced by a series of international judgments on Hiroshima's moral transgression, including legal ones. At the Nuremberg trials of Nazi war criminals, defense lawyers brought up Hiroshima and Nagasaki in raising the question of "victors' justice" that has haunted that tribunal, despite its overall significance. At the Tokyo war crimes trial of 1948, Justice Radhabinod Pal of India issued a dissenting opinion in which he invoked the "inhuman blasts" leveled on Hiroshima and Nagasaki and criticized a judicial process in which "any crime remains available only against the vanquished in a lost war." In a later Japanese district court judgment, the Shimoda case, five Hiroshima survivors obtained a judgment that the atomic attack violated international law.

There were influential American writers who made similar judgments, as we have seen. Edmund Wilson mocked the Hiroshima maidens project: "We have tried to make up for our atomic bombs by treating and petting the Japanese women whom we disfigured and incapacitated." He went on to assert that if Americans understood the true effects of atomic weapons they would not "approve of our country being the first to introduce such an indiscriminate method of wholesale destruction of civilian life," and spoke further of "a wave of horror and revulsion sweeping over the rest of the world." He then referred to our extensive development not only of nuclear weapons but of germ warfare and declared: "We cannot imagine the figure that is presented to the rest of the world by the United States . . . which first used the atomic bomb and which is promising plague and annihilation if anybody treads on the tail of its coat . . ." And the writer Ann Druyan, referring specifically to Hiroshima, imbues it with Nazi-like imagery: "Our knowledge, our genius, and enormous amounts of our wealth were deployed to invent weapons that could transform whole cities into crematoria, whole continents into gas chambers. We pored over the photographs of the immolated and irradiated victims of the thirteen-kiloton Hiroshima bomb and at the very same time that we were lamenting their suffering, we were building those bombs bigger and bigger . . ."

But the moral inversion could always be reasserted. After all, Hiroshima and Nagasaki were just two cities—the bomb by no means destroyed everything—and those two cities have been fully rebuilt and now stand proudly before us. Accepting Hiroshima meant accepting nuclear weapons as a fact of national and international life, as a psychological and political given. Bernard Brodie, the pioneer among "defense intellectuals," first warned that the chief purpose of military policy must now be to avert war, but he then went on to say that we should appraise the atomic bomb "as an instrument of war—and hence of international politics—rather than as a visitation of a wrathful deity." He was setting the tone for a post-Hiroshima normalization of the weaponry, a tone of moral detachment and visionary scenarios of potential nuclear holocaust.

Brodie eventually had second thoughts, but the tradition culminated in Herman Kahn's wild claims to "rationality" in these scenarios. According to Kahn, if a president asks his advisers, "How can I go to war—almost all American cities will be destroyed?" the answer should be, "That's not entirely fatal; we've built some spares." Colin Gray offered a still-bolder critique of previous strategists for their "Armageddon syndrome," their disinclination to take up nuances of survival. Similarly, for Edward Teller, the "legacy of Hiroshima" is nothing else than continuous nuclear buildup, to exorcise "the ghost of Hiroshima" that makes people anxious about fallout, and insist instead that "we cannot and must not try to limit the use of weapons."

Many whose early reaction to Hiroshima was to warn of the danger of the weapons and plead for international control abandoned that stance in favor of support for our weapons buildup on behalf of national security. A dramatic example is that of Cord Meyer, as a young man the first president of the United World Federalists, but later, a highly successful CIA official ("I had ceased to enjoy my role as Cassandra"). He entitled his personal story *Facing Reality*. Similarly, Thomas K. Finletter took a leading role in advocating world government after Hiroshima, before becoming secretary of the Air Force in the Truman administration in 1950. In such shifts, moral passion is either muted or transformed in the face of temptation to join the dominant American impulse to build upon Hiroshima for national strength, particularly nuclear strength.

Ultimately, the legitimation of Hiroshima had to lead to a broader philosophical position defending the existence and possible further use of the weapons—precisely put forward during the 1980s in Joseph Nye's *Nuclear Ethics*. Nye explained that he had visited Hiroshima and sought to answer questions involving the "real human horror such weapons can produce." But neither in this nor in an earlier book written with others, *Living with Nuclear Weapons,* does Nye deal with the "ethics" of these two cases of exploding the weapons on a human population. The earlier book, in fact, featured in a special box Winston Churchill's statement on the bomb "lay[ing] healing hands upon . . . tortured peoples" and being "a miracle of deliverance."

In *Nuclear Ethics* Nye acknowledges that "deterrence depends upon some prospect of use," then continues blandly, "and use involves some risk that just war limits [refraining from killing large numbers of noncombatants] will not be observed." Moreover there are situations where "it might make sense to initiate [nuclear] war," as when one is "absolutely convinced" that the adversary is about to initiate a nuclear attack. Nye mobilizes an array of philosophical and logical explorations on behalf of defending the will to use the weapon if necessary. He insists that simply because a policy entails a "tiny probability" of human extinction, that does not mean it is wrong to pursue it or "that our generation has no right to take risks." And he rejects a focus on "obligation . . . to future generations" by the claim that this could "establish a dictatorship for future generations over the present one." An equally inverted argument has him insisting that "if someone argued that nuclear weapons are evil because they demonstrate 'scientific hubris,' one could ask whether that fuzzy term does not also condemn kidney transplants and much else in modern medicine"—as though the charge had nothing to do with whether the particular scientific result sustained or destroyed human life. Nye writes in quiet tones, insisting that the weapons should be limited in purpose to self-defense, and that measures be taken to reduce the risk of use. But his apparent caution, along with his insistently "rational" argument—indeed the respectability of this entire approach on the part of a leading Harvard professor and State Department official—lends authority to a more or less formal expression of the moral inversion initiated by Hiroshima.

The same can be said of the earlier book, *Living with Nuclear Weapons,* which was written by the "Harvard Nuclear Study Group" (six people, five of whom were world-renowned Harvard professors, and introduced by Derrick Bok, then president of the university). The tone of the book was similar to *Nuclear Ethics,* its general advocacy that of "balance"—not too many weapons too aggressively flaunted, not too few weapons or too much disarmament. There must also be a balance between "the degree of control required to insure that weapons are not used accidentally and the degree of 'usability' required to insure that the weapons can be used if needed." One senses in these two works a direct continuity from Hiroshima in both a "reasoned" moral acceptance of the weaponry and the advocacy of that legitimation by many among the American intellectual elite.

No wonder, then, that America has consistently opposed adopting a no-first-use policy, as well as international efforts to outlaw or eliminate nuclear weapons entirely. No wonder American presidents, as we have seen, have threatened to use the bomb on numerous occasions. One can speak of a "Hiroshima syndrome" that prevents us from taking a truly moral stand on the weaponry, lest our 1945 actions in Hiroshima and Nagasaki become retrospectively unethical and unlawful—in the eyes of the world and, still more troubling, our own eyes as well. To do that we must retain what Ralph Lapp has called the "great void" in which "Hiroshima . . . has been taken out of the American conscience, eviscerated, extirpated."

Yes, but not quite. What has happened is that we have, as a people, insisted upon the ethical justification of our use of revolutionary new weapons that killed hundreds of thousands of people, and in that way created a counterfeit universe in which weaponry many times more destructive than those early bombs is also honored and legitimated as serving moral purposes. This counterfeit universe, moreover, like the weapons themselves, seeps into various corners of our minds and the broader society, for if we invert our moral imagination in connection with the most dangerous of all matters, does that not set a powerfully distorted standard for addressing all other moral issues?

CHAPTER 3

DESECRATION

The extremity of the bomb's power caused feelings in Americans similar to those of General Thomas Farrell when, at the Trinity test, he referred to the "awesome roar which warned of doomsday and made us feel that we puny things were blasphemous to dare tamper with the forces heretofore reserved to The Almighty." We had entered areas that belong to God or nature. We had disturbed the order of the universe, an order we generally consider (whether speaking in religious or secular terms) to be beyond our tampering, to be sacred. And in that sense it had reverberations of profound desecration.

Hiroshima had not only exceeded all previous limits in destruction but had, in effect, declared that *there were no limits* to destruction. Modern war —World War I and the saturation bombings in Europe and Japan preceding Hiroshima—had long violated the limit of targeting only combatants. But Hiroshima's suggestion of *totality of destruction*—of unbounded annihilation—was of a radically different order. Attempting to end war without committing manpower to the battlefield, we were willing to use nuclear weapons in Hiroshima and Nagasaki "at whatever expense to enemy forces, civilians, infrastructure, or, indeed, the global environment,"

Michael Howard recently wrote. Dwight McDonald observed that "invoking the Forces of the Universe to back up the Potsdam ultimatum is rather like getting in God to tidy up the living room."

Farrell's reference to "doomsday," echoed since by many secular and religious commentators, suggests that the desecration could be fatal to our species. That is why the revolutionary weapon exploded over Hiroshima represented a "potentially terminal revolution."* Americans and all others had to struggle with an image of a radical scientific and technological breakthrough and of that same achievement ending everything. The first image is acceptable, even exciting; the second is virtually unabsorbable. How does one psychologically take in what Edith Wyschogrod calls "the irreversible null point" which could "empty . . . the immense cosmic spaces forever of that 'thinking reed' who alone . . . comprehends them." And if that terminal point were to be reached, it would not be through the vengeance of God or nature but by our own hand, with the technology we ourselves created, and to no purpose. The desecration was, then, fiercely unacceptable: in threatening a human end; in the absence of any convincing reason for or meaning to such an outcome; and in we, ourselves, having been responsible for the act.

The nature of the atomic bomb's desecration and transgression is further illuminated by the Frankenstein myth, though not in the way that myth is usually understood. Most commentators view Frankenstein's creation of a monster whose destructiveness cannot be controlled as a morality tale concerning our relation to technology we ourselves create. There is nothing wrong with that use of Mary Shelley's fable, but it neglects the psychological underpinning of the myth, which renders it so compelling and powerful. Frankenstein, an ambitious Swiss medical student, did not invent technology as we know it; he created a creature that resembled a human being, a humanoid. The young scientist's self-assigned mission was to conquer disease and dying, to "render man invulnerable to any but a violent death." He sought nothing less than the key to immortality and was drawn to past practioners of medicine and alchemy, "when the masters of the science sought immortality and power." That task required him to answer the ultimate question: "Whence did the principle of life proceed?" As he found his answer and "became myself capable of bestowing

* *Described by Lifton in 1979 in* The Broken Connection.

animation upon lifeless matter," he experienced a surge of joy ("a light so brilliant and wonderous") and of omnipotence: "I became dizzy with the immensity of the prospect . . . surprised that among so many men of genius who had directed their inquiries toward the same science, that I alone should be reserved to discover so astonishing a secret."

Later, with retrospective self-condemnation, he was to speak of his "profane fingers" and his "workshop of filthy creation," and to warn of the danger and misery awaiting the man "who aspires to become greater than his nature will allow." Frankenstein, upon first viewing the monster with "breathless horror and disgust," became immediately aware of his dreadful error and experienced bouts of sickness and madness in his obsession with his creation. The monster, in turn, became enraged over being rejected by his creator and by humankind, murdering each of the people Frankenstein most loved.

The Frankenstein myth suggests the kind of hubris that the atomic bomb instilled in those who decided to make it and use it: the assumption of godly prerogatives. Like Frankenstein, these Americans experienced omnipotence—in their case the surge of power experienced from the first bomb explosion at Trinity. Paradoxically, the most life-destroying of weapons can evoke a sense of overcoming death, at least that of oneself and one's group—of acquiring immortalizing power. And like Victor Frankenstein, many scientists and political leaders were horrified at first beholding (through pictures) what their creation had done to fellow human beings in Japan.

But while the Frankenstein myth held to more or less human dimensions—indeed the monster is more sympathetic and "human" than his creator—nuclear weapons were never more than technological objects of indiscriminate killing, anonymous, and potentially absolute. The humanoid monster was, despite its protests, immediately rejected by its creator and became an embittered outcast; but the completely nonhuman, technoid bomb was immediately (after Trinity) embraced and rendered almost human. (The Hiroshima and Nagasaki bombs were called "Little Boy" and "Fat Man," respectively, and were delivered by the *Enola Gay,* Paul Tibbets's plane named after his own mother.) Frankenstein's monster was potentially good but rendered murderous by the pain of rejection; the bomb, as a thing, has no morality, and can only be used for killing, yet is treated as though it were good and decent and even salvational. Frankenstein eventually renounced his immortalizing ambition, refused to construct a mate for the monster, and devoted his life to tracking it down until both met their deaths, by which time the monster had become more and more human. The bomb's creators never fully reject it—it remains dangerous in the extreme precisely because it is *not* sufficiently rejected—and continue to humanize it over "generations" of nuclear weaponry. And in some of the bomb makers there is the Frankenstein-like flaw of loving science too much. "This group love of science . . . we were trying out . . . which didn't work" (as a novelist, writing from the standpoint of a scientist, puts it)—and until like Frankenstein they reach the terrible point where "scientific work only threatens us now."

There is still another important psychological parallel. A number of astute observers, most recently Harold Bloom, have noted that, in Mary Shelley's novel, the monster and his creator are "the antithetical halves of a single being," a frequent phenomenon in romantic literature. One could refine that observation further in bracketing Frankenstein the near-mad creator and his creation *together* as the double of the loving, considerate, and gentle side of Frankenstein the student. The same could be said of those who brought about Hiroshima: the bomb and each man's would-be omnipotent side together became a double of the restrained, nonviolent, and caring human being. This process of doubling enables ordinary people to adapt to potentially murderous environments and projects.

Otto Rank recognized this phenomenon in German romantic literature and described it as often a division between the mortal and immortal self—very much the case in both Frankenstein and those bound up with the Hiroshima bombing. Doubling has been present not only in such extreme cases as the Nazi doctors but also in people involved with the making and projected use of thermonuclear weapons. Doubling is significant in connection with Hiroshima because it suggests a painful but necessary truth: The most decent and loving person could be capable, under certain circumstances, of forming a relatively autonomous second self drawn to and joining in with the immortalizing appeal of nuclear desecration and transgression. We recall Hans Bethe's haunting remark: "You may well ask why people with a kind heart and humanist feelings would go and work on weapons of mass destruction."

With Hiroshima, the poet Campbell McGrath tells us, "America's Century begins in fire and ends,/like any respectable act of creation, in something/resembling ash, Alamogordo to Ragnarok, Genesis/to Naga-saki, the black rain wherein we are forever united/with those whose bodies we jellied to magma . . ." And Rodney Jones: "Praise/Our electrons humming down cables from the split atom./. . . praise our many knowl-edges that came from accidents./From our six fingers come your corrugat-ing fins./From our eyes come the balls of your reticulate feet./From our brains your batteries. From our livers/Your encyclotropic perfumes. And if it is genesis/You would study, imagine us. We lived here./We made our choice between the virus and the germ." The desecration is absolute, all-pervasive.

CHAPTER 4

NATIONAL SELF-BETRAYAL

The atomic transgression enveloped America and Americans. By the mid-1990s, our country found itself in the midst of what *Newsweek* called a "nuclear-waste crisis" which one official saw as "the single largest environmental and health risk in the nation." This vast and lethal "pulsating landscape of atomic waste dumps" stems directly from the manufacture of bombs to use on Hiroshima and Nagasaki, followed by America's cold-war nuclear weapons buildup. From the beginning American bomb-makers, in the rush to produce their product, were erratic and careless in the handling, storing, and disposal of the radiatioactive waste they were bringing into the world. Over the years matters became worse as secrecy and deception—inherited from the Manhattan Project—came to dominate official attitudes. By late 1989 the Rocky Flats plant in Colorado, where plutonium was purified to weapons-grade quality, had to be closed down and raided by the FBI for "environmental crimes," so that today Rocky Flats, according to one expert, "is a *de facto* plutonium dump."

Radioactive plutonium is not the only waste problem, but it is the most lethal. Plutonium was developed by the Manhattan Project for the sole purpose of making bombs and was produced by the bombardment of uranium with neutrons. So poisonous that the tiniest amounts can kill, there is no more deadly substance known to humankind. Kai Erikson has pointed out that the most dangerous of these wastes have half-lives of 100,000 years or more, "and they pose a hazard for a good deal longer than that." For perspective one may ponder that Stonehenge goes back only 4,500 years, the earliest pyramids 5,000 years.

The plant at Hanford, Washington, that produced the plutonium for the Nagasaki bomb—and then for the atomic trigger-mechanism of subsequent hydrogen bombs—has been described as "the single most polluted place in the Western world." Although Hanford has served primarily as a plutonium-manufacturing facility, the radioactive wastes are so varied, extensive, and badly controlled that no one knows exactly what kind of witches' brew is in them. According to a knowledgeable engineer who worked at Hanford for many years, the radioactive wastes released there over the years come close to Chernobyl proportions, and 60 percent of that whole amount was released during 1944 and 1945, the period when the Nagasaki bomb was being constructed.

The Hanford area was chosen for the site of an atomic-bomb facility largely because it was so sparsely populated, but overnight it became a thriving boomtown area with workers in the tens of thousands and posters everywhere enthusiastically announcing "There's a job for you at Hanford." At all levels, people were imbued with the special significance of the project for the war effort and performed their work with pride. There was a sense of urgency, a "can-do spirit," along with constant pressure from General Groves for early delivery of what was called "the product." Macho attitudes on the part of supervisors and workers led to circumventing precautions against contamination. People were reluctant to object lest they be seen as "not on the team." The attitude extended to engineers in their arrangements for handling materials. One spoke of "using sand filters to get rid of radiation—we had to make things up as we went along." This nuclear macho was known as becoming "Hanfordized," and as one commentator put it, "Hanfordization was the dark side of the can-do spirit that made Hanford work during World War II." The attitude continued even after safety rules became more standardized: one engineer, when asked why he did not have the required calculations to support a design for pipes and materials, replied: "We don't have time for that shit."

In recent years it has become painfully clear that the surrounding population has paid the price in the form of high incidence of various forms of cancer, thyroid disease, and infant mortality. Because official statements constantly spoke of safety and denied danger, residents felt deceived. One woman who experienced miscarriages and hair loss declared, "I find it impossible to contain my anger at the government's abuse of my trust." Here she articulates an exact psychological definition of a sense of betrayal—a perception of being harmed by a person or entity one had depended upon for support, nurturing, or protection. The anger and bitterness toward those considered responsible for the betrayal—plant officials, the military, the government—gives rise to more general feelings of alienation and distrust.

That has been the sequence with many living near nuclear facilities. "Our government wouldn't let us work there if it was harmful," is the way one woman remembered feeling. But when her husband was near death from bone cancer, she angrily asked, "How can they do that to their own people? They figure they're all dispensable, why not use them . . ." And indeed, the Atomic Energy Commission had mounted an extensive public-relations campaign that Stewart Udall has called "the most long-lived program of public deception in U.S. history." One prominent pamphlet had a cowboy mounted comfortably on his horse against a landscape surrounded by a mushroom cloud, with the comment: "FALLOUT DOES NOT CONSTITUTE A SERIOUS HAZARD TO ANY LIVING THING OUTSIDE THE TEST SITE."

When evidence mounted that radiation did indeed constitute a serious hazard, the AEC countered not with an admission of mistakes or with added safety measures but with denial backed by further public-relations techniques and manipulated calculations that bordered on complete fraud —all of which led to still-greater bitterness when discovered. To make things even worse, the radioactive waste at Hanford seems to be intractable; efforts at cleanup have failed and appear doomed always to fail. After the government had spent 7.5 billion dollars over a five-year period beginning in 1989, an official from the Environmental Protection Agency could declare: "There hasn't been any real cleanup. We don't have any place to put it."

Victims of radioactivity often connected their plight with American weapons policies. "Go ahead and tell the world," one of them near Hanford said, "America has created nuclear weapons. At the same time, it's also created thousands of victims." More than that, they experienced compassion for Japanese victims: "Forty-four years after the end of the war, I can finally understand what the survivors of Hiroshima and Nagasaki must be going through."

They were to resemble Hiroshima and Nagasaki survivors in another, still more psychologically devastating way. We have mentioned Hiroshima survivors' angry resentment at being made into "guinea pigs" who were studied but not treated. That sense has to do with feelings of being manipulated, attacked, or annihilated at the hands of all-powerful forces who have reduced a person either to a laboratory animal or a nonhuman object.

A considerable number of Americans, again including those living near Hanford, experienced the same feelings in connection with another shocking policy. There has been, over the past decades, a gradual revelation that an elaborate series of radiation experiments was conducted on Americans, mostly by the Atomic Energy Commission—the predecessor of the Department of Energy and successor to the Manhattan Project—but also by the Department of Defense, the National Aeronautics and Space Administration, the Department of Veterans' Affairs, the Central Intelligence Agency, and probably the Department of Health and Human Services (or its predecessor) as well. The experiments were conducted not only in laboratories directly associated with nuclear-weapons development but also at major American universities and medical centers. They were done, for the most part, without anything resembling adequate arrangements for informed consent.

The full extent of the experiments—now officially said to be "in the thousands"—is still not known (as of this writing in early 1995), but what has been learned suggests a pattern of planned experimental abuse that is unique in American history. Congressman Edward Markey entitled the report of his subcommittee's 1986 hearing on the subject "American Nuclear Guinea Pigs: Three Decades of Radiation Experiments on U.S. Citizens." And Energy Secretary Hazel O'Leary, in her dramatic official admission of wrongdoing in 1993, declared: "The only thing I could think of was Nazi Germany."

There were, broadly speaking, two forms of experiments: nuclear "medical" manipulations on individual people; and exposure of large numbers of people, either by means of intentional radiation releases or by placing military personnel at or near ground zero of bomb tests.

The medical experiments began as part of the Manhattan Project, as we observed in part 1, and its need to learn more about what plutonium (a word that was itself "classified"—that is, not mentionable—over the course of World War II), uranium, and other radioactive substances do to the organs of the human body. From 1945 through 1947, bomb-grade plutonium injections were given to thirty-one patients at Strong Memorial Hospital in Rochester, New York, the Manhattan District Hospital at Oak Ridge, Tennessee, and medical centers at the University of Chicago and the University of California, San Francisco. All such experiments were shrouded in secrecy and, when deemed necessary, in lies. Documents that emerged in January 1995 showed that contrary to official claims, not all the patients were terminally ill. Some were young adults and one was an eighteen-year-old youth. The experiments were intended to show what type or amount of exposure would cause damage to normal, healthy people in a nuclear war. The son of one woman included in the plutonium-injection experiment recently observed with some bitterness: "I was over there fighting the Germans who were conducting these horrific medical experiments. At the same time, my own country was conducting them on my mother." In the late 1940s, about eight hundred pregnant women were given radioactive iron so that the effects of that material on fetal development could be observed.

At prisons in the states of Oregon and Washington, inmates' testicles were exposed to X rays in order to determine their effects on sperm production and the amount of radiation necessary to bring about at least temporary sterility. Precisely the same experiment, though in more brutal form, was performed by Nazi doctors in Auschwitz. Indeed, American doctors involved in the work at the time did not fail to note the similarity with Nazi practice. One leading experimenter, Dr. Joseph G. Hamilton, spoke of such investigations as having "a little of the Buchenwald touch" —his concern being only with the way they might *appear,* as he remained very active in the work.

In the early 1950s, residents of a Massachusetts state school for boys and men considered mentally retarded were given a radioactive calcium tracer in their milk. The experiment only came to light through the efforts of a former librarian whose father had died of leukemia after having flown through the mushroom clouds during a Bikini bomb test. As a second-generation survivor, she was appalled by an Atomic Energy Commission document about the project she uncovered and she later explained, "I knew that the AEC was not interested in helping people who were retarded. . . . I saw the experiments against the whole backdrop of lies—the silence of the government, the silence of the professional." One of the school's graduates, testifying at a Senate hearing held at the school, provided what one observer called a "redemptive moment" when he insistently confronted a doctor who was defending the experiments with the question, ". . . if you had a son here, would you have allowed this to happen, knowing what you know about radiation?" That same graduate again spoke poignantly in denouncing the experiments as "morally wrong," insisting that "these kids were put there to be helped, not abused. . . . not to have their bodies guinea-pigged on."

In the beginning the AEC lied, issuing a statement in 1950, for example, that it "has never sponsored a medical research project where human beings are used for experimental purposes." More than that, in at least one documented case, it sought to reverse—that is, falsify—an autopsy finding of a radiation death of a Hanford worker. An anonymous telegram sent from the AEC office in Richland, Washington, to an AEC administrator in Washington, D.C., cited a widow's claim for a pension on the basis of "special hazard injuries" (the code name for radiation effects). A first autopsy (in the Hanford area) gave the cause of death as rupture of the aortic artery and attributed burn-like skin marks to "a nonspecific dermatitis." But a second autopsy done in Chicago, where the body was taken for burial, "stated positively that . . . death was due to excess body radiation." The telegram went on to urge that a doctor at the Industrial Medical Division of the General Electric plant (where the dead man had worked) "go to Chicago as soon as possible prepared to set before said autopsy surgeon [who had made the diagnosis of radiation effects] the facts with respect to [the dead man's] work and exposure records. The purpose of such trip would be to see whether the surgeon's conclusions can be altered." The telegram further proposed that an AEC medical consultant from Chicago also be present. The people involved should then "study all available facts and express conclusions . . . in accordance with procedures developed some years ago," following which there would be a "conference" on the matter, at which additional AEC consultants and representatives would be present.

What is clear here is that no claim for a radiation death was to be approved, and a series of high-powered, pseudo-medical arrangements had been instituted for pressuring honest doctors (in this case a pathologist) to falsify their findings. Atomic-bomb distortions had come full circle.

They came full circle in another way as well: the harmful and sometimes lethal exposure of American servicemen and civilians to radiation effects of our own bomb tests. Here, too, patterns were established in the early pre- and post-Hiroshima period, as revealed especially in the experience of Stafford Warren, the leading medical authority on radiation at the time and Groves's personal adviser on radiation matters. At Trinity, as we observed earlier, radiological safety was secondary to wartime urgency. As Warren's deputy put it, "The idea was to explode this damn thing," and overly liberal standards of permissible radiation without evacuation were set "for the reason that we didn't want to reveal the fact that there was an atomic explosion." The outcome was a matter of chance, depending upon the direction the wind carried the radioactive cloud ("If it went east, I was sunk," Warren later recalled).

Put in charge of combating radiation dangers at the 1946 Bikini tests, Warren provided a program for monitoring radiation hazards and protecting personnel. He insisted upon more elaborate arrangements than many in his accompanying Medico-Legal Board (there partly to prevent later legal problems) thought necessary. But there was an immense amount of radiation released in Test Baker, the second test, which "turned out to be literally a hundred times larger than the original conception," as Warren later put it. Within days, medical personnel had identified sixty-seven sailors with radiation overdoses. Warren then demonstrated heroic determination in convincing disbelieving naval officers that their ships were highly irradiated and could not be reclaimed, perhaps averting a larger radiation disaster.

Part of the problem was that a "staggering" amount of radiation was released, overwhelming all of the preparations. Also, the clear warnings that had been given, by Warren and others, were essentially ignored. Despite "thousands of pages of detailed plans," a recent book on the Bikini tests comments, "the U.S. Navy managed to expose tens of thousands of men and more than 200 ships to radioactive contamination more than

2,000 miles from decent port facilities without ever having attempted experimentally to irradiate a ship or parts of one to determine how—or whether—a ship could be decontaminated." Not only did military officers scoff at invisible dangers, but there was considerable disagreement among scientists themselves. Many of the Los Alamos physicists were critical of Warren's caution—one report of that laboratory spoke of "hysteria"—and ostensibly knowledgeable doctors could also disagree. When told that Groves was "very much afraid of claims by men who participated in the Bikini tests," Joseph Hamilton (later to make the Buchenwald remark) dismissed the matter and said that such suits would be without validity and instituted only by "cranks."

Warren himself seemed to change his views over the years, so that in 1966 he wrote that "at the end of Operation Crossroads it could be said that no one had been injured by the 'peculiar hazards' inherent in it." Warren understandably wished to feel that his emergency measures had ultimately protected all personnel, but there has been considerable evidence of delayed radiation effects in servicemen who had been at the Bikini tests. In that statement, moreover, Warren seemed to be reverting to the position taken by his own Medico-Legal Advisory Board in declaring that, among the 40,000 people engaged in the operations, claims of radiation effects made later on would be invalid because the diseases encountered "appear spontaneously in the human race without previous exposure to man-made radiations." His skeptical point of view was a version of the tendency toward denial so common among American scientists (again, going back to Hiroshima) and so protective of their own country's potential culpability—and so in contrast to the wisdom and courage he had shown at the moment of greatest danger immediately following the tests.

Much of the problem centered on plutonium, discovered only in 1941 and in 1946 still much unknown in relation to its behavior in the body. It was understood to be extremely lethal, and the slowness of its elimination from the body was also beginning to be appreciated. But although Geiger counters measured beta and gamma activity, they could not measure the plutonium in alpha particles.

One particularly poignant aspect of the Warren saga occurred when, desperate for volunteers to serve as radiation monitors, he "practically browbeat" his own eighteen-year-old son into joining the mission. Although this may not have brought harm to the boy, there were some monitors who felt they had been significantly exposed to radiation despite their elaborate protective clothing. One wonders how much Warren was influenced by such things as scientific certainty, need to demonstrate faith in safety precautions, paucity of volunteer monitors, general denial of radiation effects, and specific numbing toward the possibility of causing radiation effects in his son. One wonders also whether he had second thoughts later on.

The more general point is that, as possessors and users of the weapon at Hiroshima and Nagasaki, our need to deny its most grotesque feature has been so powerful that we have extended this denial to situations that endanger our own people. When a particular group takes on responsibility for the weapon, all those who work with it, including scientists and doctors, become susceptible to that suprapersonal denial. And even as more is learned about the lethal substances, particularly plutonium, patterns of denial continue, along with disagreements among scientists and among responsible officials concerning radiation dangers.

Hence the exposure of hundreds of thousands of military personnel to atomic explosions, notably at the Nevada test site between 1950 and 1962. Soldiers would be separated from their original units, sent on special assignment to the test site, and there given a battery of psychological tests prior to their witnessing the atomic explosion at varying distances from the epicenter. They were then often marched to ground zero, without protective clothing and only sometimes with radiation badges, and after returning to their base were often given another battery of psychological tests. The military sought to learn from them how men would react under nuclear combat conditions, but the men were placed under strict secrecy, and it was not until the late seventies and early eighties that their experiences became known. The veterans were often denied access to their own health records. It is estimated that between 250,000 and 300,000 servicemen were exposed to radiation. Again the returns are hardly in, but there is no doubt about the considerable harm done to our own men and women more or less sacrificed to our impulse to harness the deity.

The same ethically distorted impulse was carried still further in the form of several hundred intentional releases of radioactive material over populated parts of this country. A notable case was the notorious "Green Run" carried out at Hanford in 1949. There radioactive material taken from nuclear fuel was deliberately released into the atmosphere in order to

simulate a Soviet atomic-bomb explosion. The word *Green* referred to
"green fuel," fuel that had been cooled for a much shorter time than usual
because that was the kind of fuel used by the Soviets, who had exploded
their first atomic bomb earlier that year. A woman recalled, when Green
Run became known, that she had started to lose her hair about three
weeks after that release while studying at a college about fifty miles southeast of Hanford. Whatever the extent of harm she experienced from Green
Run, or from the more routine radiation releases from Hanford's bomb
work over the years, we can understand her insistence that "the government has a lot to answer for."

In 1982 researchers estimated that "men, women, and children . . .
contaminated by ionizing radiation from nuclear bomb tests . . . together with those who have been exposed through nuclear accidents, nuclear waste, and industrial or scientific work . . . comprises a population
of over one million radiation survivors in the United States alone." With
the more recent information about unsafe conditions, experiments, intentional releases, and secret nuclear tests, the number is undoubtedly very
much greater.

The government, our government, does have a lot to answer for.
Trinity and Hiroshima led to a totalistic embrace of the atomic bomb that
rendered it the central object of our society, around which everything else
revolved. The nurturing of this deified object, as our source of security
and ultimate power over death, became the central task of our society.
This was the "higher purpose" to which questions such as individual
health or well-being had to be subsumed. More than that, our bomb
entrapment required us to violate existing ethical practices in actions aimed
at harming our people and consistently lying to them about that harm, all
in the name of protecting them. We reached the point of such intense
nuclearism that failure to engage in such experimentation could have
seemed remiss, "imprudent" (a favorite word of the time), lax, or irre-
sponsible.

That has been the terrible logic of our national self-betrayal. In a
country created out of concern for individual rights, we have betrayed our
own history, our national entity, and ourselves.

CHAPTER 5

Apocalyptic Concealment

In the beginning were the secrets. The facilities where the bomb's components were built, the men and women who worked on it, the entire enterprise and its desired product—all existed outside the known, visible world in a mysterious realm separate from that world. The word *secret* means "kept from knowledge or observation" and is derived from words meaning "to separate" or "divide off." To be privy to the secret, to be part of the secret megamachine, was to share in a privileged mystery, much in the manner of a childhood secret. Secrets take on great significance for small children and can be associated with a sense of specialness and life-power; but also with confusing and fearful aspects of sex; with one's own destructive, sometimes murderous feelings toward those one is supposed to love; and, most fearful of all, with the idea of death and dying. The atomic-bomb secret could encompass all these psychological dimensions, any of which might become associated with feelings of guilt. Still, until the bomb was actually exploded, the secret was a matter of arcane mystery.

In respect to Hiroshima and Nagasaki, it became more a matter of *concealment*. Secrecy and concealment are used almost interchangeably, but the latter suggests more active steps to suppress actual knowledge and is related in its derivation to the idea of covering, hiding, and (as a concealed place) "the underworld." From this standpoint, we can say that the bomb sequence has been from *the secret* to that which is *actively concealed,* and finally, to *falsification.* It was that sequence, for example, that permitted the nuclear "medical" experiments on Americans and the intentional releases of radiation affecting American populations.*

But the source of concealment and falsification, as we have seen throughout this book, can be traced back to Hiroshima—or even before. It actually started with the decision to build a weapon of mass destruction and hide the nature of that device from most of the 125,000 people who built it. "Only a handful, of course, knew what they were creating," Dwight Macdonald observed shortly after Hiroshima. "It hardly needs to be stressed that there is something askew with a society in which vast numbers of citizens can be organized to create a horror like The Bomb without even knowing they are doing it."

Unfortunately, the concealment not only escalated but settled into American institutional practice and individual American psyches. Forces could oppose the concealment, however, as Susan Griffin makes clear:

Those who worked in the factories at Oak Ridge were not told that they were making a fissionable material to be used in atomic weapons. Almost none of the military men assigned to this project knew its purpose. But wherever a secret is kept it will make its way, like an object lighter than water and meant to float, to the surface. A Navy ensign posted to Oak Ridge suffers a mental breakdown. Is he the repository for the unspoken fears of others? He begins to rave about a terrible weapon that will soon bring about the end of the world. Because his ravings are close to the truth, the Navy builds a special wing of the hospital at Oak Ridge for him, staffed with psychiatrists, physicians, orderlies, and janitors, each chosen especially for this work, judged trustworthy and able to keep secrets. The ensign is given continual sedation. Whenever he begins to speak, he receives another injection. His family is told that he is on a long mission at sea.

---

* *"We were shrouded and clouded in an atmosphere of secrecy," Energy Secretary O'Leary would later comment. "And I would take it a step further—I would call it repression." She estimated that her department's millions of pages of classified documents would tower to a height of thirty-two "Washington monuments."*

Concealment also succeeded all too well in distancing Americans from what happened at the other end of our weapons. Much of our book could be understood as a description of an extraordinarily effective American cover-up. That cover-up, moreover, has been apocalyptic in at least two ways: the grotesque human dimensions of what is being suppressed and the relationship of that cover-up to our continuous embrace of still more destructive devices.

The phenomenon of McCarthyism in the 1950s occurred precisely when atomic-bomb terrors, now associated with the Soviet Union, spread throughout American culture. During congressional witch hunts, Americans were accused of "concealing" their Communist activities and of "secret" ties to America's enemies. These accusations were fed by actual efforts on the part of three scientist-spies (Klaus Fuchs, Allen Nunn May, and Bruno Pontecorvo) to convey bomb secrets to the Soviet Union. But underneath McCarthyite accusations was the uneasy American concealment of what we had done in Hiroshima and Nagasaki, and the equally uneasy secret of our, and the Soviet Union's, preparations for annihilating dozens of other cities and millions of human beings. To be sure, nuclear dangers were talked about, as were some aspects of Hiroshima and Nagasaki. But our apocalyptic concealment applied every energy toward muting and deflecting these matters, rendering them distant, unreal, even unimportant.

McCarthyites, like religious and political fundamentalists today, picked up on these apocalyptic currents and made them into their own version of ancient dualistic Christian and pre-Christian visions of the battle between the children of light and the children of darkness. Diplomats could be accused of "losing China" and "giving away the secret of the bomb," entertainers or government employees could be called "subversive," but what was really at stake was the potential loss of the human species.

The ultimate subversion, however, was the attempt to overturn the apocalyptic concealment and reveal fully what had been hidden. As Morton Halperin points out, "All of our Presidents in the atomic age have resisted . . . debate and sought to control the process by which information on national security matters is released to the public." The purpose was always to retain the military prerogative—without restraint or public redress. Most revealing was a top-secret National Security Council document in 1948 urging the Truman administration to discourage public dis-

cussion of the circumstances under which the U.S. might use atomic
weapons, on the grounds that any debate might focus on morality rather
than security. This could give an enemy the impression that Americans
lacked the will to use the bomb after Hiroshima. Four years later, Truman
and Eisenhower planned a joint statement on the destructiveness of the
hydrogen bomb and the perils of an arms race—but the idea was abandoned for fear that this might incite panic.

This process—and the so-called national security state itself—began
with Hiroshima, with a small group of relatively isolated leaders making
draconian decisions and concealing from the public, then and afterward,
the necessity, nature, and consequences of those decisions.

What has been lost sight of is the role Hiroshima concealment has played
in encouraging subsequent American cover-ups. One need only recall
Vietnam (concealment of unauthorized bombing and human effects),
Watergate (concealment of a string of Constitutional violations), and Iran-
Contra (concealment of illegal government paramilitary activities). Surely
Hiroshima was the mother of all cover-ups, creating tonalities, distortions,
manipulative procedures, and patterns of concealment that have been applied to all of American life that followed. Secrecy has been linked with
national security—and vice versa—ever since.

There is an even more direct linkage between Hiroshima and subsequent cover-ups, which has to do with confusions concerning nuclear
weapons-centered "credibility." A willingness to use the weapons has always been emphasized as necessary to the principle of credibility that
underlies the policy of deterrence. But as Jonathan Schell has pointed out,
all presidents, since Nagasaki, have known in their hearts that the weapons
were close to unusable and therefore frequently found themselves paralyzed and, more than that, frustrated and confused by what could be called
a false reliance on unworkable power. The Vietnam War, from this standpoint, was an effort to maintain American "credibility" by means other
than nuclear weapons. The same was true of the systematic deceptions,
self-deceptions, and concealments associated with that war. And for both
Lyndon Johnson and Richard Nixon and their advisers, the bomb always
loomed in the background as a *possible* weapon that, at the same time, was
fundamentally unusable. These dilemmas are not acknowledged, because
to admit them would be to diminish credibility in the eyes of potential

enemies, and to confuse the American public and undermine its confidence in its leadership.

Bomb-centered credibility contradictions could also have played a significant part in the Watergate scandal. Of course, Nixon's personal tendencies toward revenge and paranoia gave rise to his administration's underworld of law breaking—its break-ins, dirty tricks, buggings, and systematic lying. But struggles with executive impotence, expressed mournfully in his image of America as a "pitiful, helpless giant," surely accentuated such tendencies. They also had a lot to do with the elaborate efforts at cover-up, along with the less acknowledged, unconscious tendencies toward getting caught (for example, the arrangements for recording and preserving recordings that gave rise to the "Watergate tapes"). As Jonathan Schell sees it, that interplay of Vietnam and nuclear contradictions "drove two Presidents into states of something like madness and led to the near-ruin of our political system." That near-madness, we would add, had to do with a combination of impotence and fearful nuclearistic omnipotence—the capacity and periodic inclination to unleash the weaponry that would kill everyone and the pained immobilization in holding oneself back even in the face of American defeat and decline. The more excruciating that set of conflicts, the more the leader in question would feel the need to cover over—at all costs keep from the American people—the entire process. Significantly, our president most associated with "cover-up," Richard Nixon, is also the one who spoke most favorably of making nuclear threats.

In a sense, no American president has recovered from either the grotesque annihilation of Hiroshima or from the power surge of Trinity. Still less has any president been able to manage psychologically or morally the combination of those two incompatible sentiments, or to avoid the elaborate concealment—the deceptive cover-up—of precisely that searing contradiction.

One could well say that Hiroshima initiated an overarching American pattern of atomic cover-up.*

Oppenheimer's own sequence is instructive here. At first he was at the

---

* *The brief discussion over the decision to build the hydrogen bomb was conducted in secret, although in 1949 America was not at war. McGeorge Bundy would call this "a secret debate with only a few participants, no sermons pro and con—no public discussion at all."*

very center of the ultimate secret. In 1945 he wrote: "For the last four years I have had only classified thoughts." The very isolation he presided over in maintaining the secret contributed both to the intensity of the scientists' work and to their corrupting early nuclearism: for example, Oppenheimer's idea that using the bomb would "shake mankind free from parochialism and war," or, as Sissela Bok puts it, his conviction that "the bomb was to save mankind from itself." At the same time, Oppenheimer always advocated greater openness and sharing of ideas *within* the bomb-making community. He retained that duality after Hiroshima, remaining an insider contributing to further weapons development, while also strongly advocating international sharing of atomic knowledge or "secrets."

We have observed the dramatic change in his status from a national hero to a "subversive" or "security risk" who opposed the "super" or hydrogen bomb, for then he truly subverted the dreadful secret underneath the official narrative having to do with our unhealthy embrace of the weaponry. "What does worry me," he wrote, "is that this [weapon] appears to have caught the imagination, both of the Congressional and of military people, as the answer to the problem posed by the Russian advance. . . . that we become committed to it as the way to save the country and the peace appears to me full of danger." Oppenheimer was actually ambivalent toward the hydrogen bomb, but what he subverted in such a statement was precisely what nuclearists, from Truman onward, sought always to conceal: that they had surrendered to and at the same time identified with the weapon's promise of godlike power.

Nor did ordinary Americans escape from these confusions. That was made clear in a study by Michael Carey of the experience of members of his own generation participating in air raid—or "duck and cover"—drills throughout American schools in the 1950s. They remembered being fearful, often terrified, but they also recalled a powerful demand from authorities that they overcome, suppress, numb themselves to precisely any such fears—to conceal these emotions from themselves. Many did exactly that over a period of years. For some, frightening dreams began at the time of the drills and could continue, though there could also be (less frequently) more pleasurable fantasies of sex play in the shelters. A third stage, possibly beginning in late adolescence or early adulthood, could include a broad continuum from powerful bomb fears to periodic anxieties with associations back to the air-raid drills.

And there were lasting effects. These included equating individual death with collective annihilation (a pattern we will discuss in more detail later). There was also a sense that life itself is unmanageable, or at least likely to be suddenly and absolutely interrupted. And, perhaps most important for us here, there was a feeling, even at the time, of the absurdity of the entire enterprise—of authorities advising that all one had to do to survive was to duck under a desk (in the right fashion) or cover one's head with a piece of paper. It is not too much to say that the entire generation —indeed the entire country—was left with a feeling that the world had gone mad in producing and potentially using these weapons, and that certainly authority had gone mad in its arrangements for dealing with them. Even those who defended nuclear-weapons policies had some sense of that absurdity and craziness. All this was reflected in nuclear humor and satire—from Tom Lehrer's songs to *Dr. Strangelove*.

The drills, and American measures for civil defense in general, tended to have effects quite opposite to those intended. People sensed that these measures were pathetically inadequate for coping with the bomb's power to annihilate, which Hiroshima had revealed. The drills have taken their place, along with various other civil-defense instructions, in the cultural mythology of bomb absurdities. Nothing has been as effective in exposing systematically concealed nuclear truths. Here, as in so many ways, secrecy, concealment, and falsification have not been completely sustainable but have led to confused combinations of ignorance, insight, and cynicism toward authorities—along with a sense of the world as deeply absurd and dangerous.

All this was part of what might be called *nuclear alienation*. Starting with Hiroshima, officials advised Americans to leave all problems surrounding the bomb to political, scientific, and military leaders—the nuclear priesthood. Americans were not supposed to think critically or engage in the debate over the gravest issue of our age. Over time, we became accustomed to bowing out of that discussion, and then others involving other major issues. We got used to putting the gravest problems, military and social, completely in the hands of experts and political leaders who claimed to have them under control—only to recognize in painful moments that they didn't have them in hand at all. Surrendering our right to know more about Hiroshima and then nuclear weapons in general contributed to our gradual alienation from the entire political process.

As we have seen, the message of the official narrative was control: controlling the story of Hiroshima, controlling nuclear weapons, controlling history. But the official narrative also increased ordinary Americans' sense of being out of control of their own destiny, of being out of control of the large forces that determined their future.

No wonder, then, that the American people have come to feel deceived by the bomb and its caretakers—not necessarily in a clear-cut, unambiguous way, but varyingly, in some cases periodically, and often angrily. We sense that ominous truths have been concealed from us, starting with Hiroshima. One reason we remain confused is that part of each of us psychologically colludes in the concealment. But our resentment at what has been concealed and falsified does not necessarily limit itself to nuclear-weapons matters but can spread, vaguely and bitterly, into just about any aspect of social and national experience. We have to ask ourselves, then, how much of our rising mistrust for politicians and officials of all kinds, for our government and just about all who govern us—how much this angry cynicism so evident in our public life in recent years is an outcome of the Hiroshima and post-Hiroshima nuclear deceptions and concealments. To what extent do we feel ourselves a people who have been unforgivably deceived in that most fundamental of human areas having to do with how, when, and by whose hand—or lethal technology—we are to die?

CHAPTER 6

AMERICAN NUMBING

Psychic numbing can be defined as a diminished capacity or inclination to feel. When interviewed in the early 1960s, Hiroshima survivors remembered witnessing, at the time of the bomb, terrible scenes of death and suffering—nothing less than a sea of death around them—but found, very quickly, that they simply ceased to feel. They spoke of "a paralysis of the mind," of becoming "insensitive to human death," of being "temporarily without feeling." This was the acute expression of psychic numbing in the form of "psychic closing-off."* It was a useful defense mechanism, preventing the mind from being overwhelmed and perhaps destroyed by the dreadful and unmanageable images confronting it. Numbing in that sense could be seen as a form of psychic deadening (or temporary death) in the service of the mind's long-term survival. But the pattern of psychic numbing could linger in some and give way to withdrawal, depression, or despair.

Those observations raised questions about psychic numbing on the part of those who created the weapon, made the decision to use it, or

* *Described by Lifton in 1967 in* Death in Life.

carried out the atomic bombing. We have seen evidence of precisely that
in all these groups, but the matter extends even further. Arriving in Hiroshima in 1962, seventeen years after this tragically significant event, one of
us found that no one had really studied it. To be sure, there had been
research on its physical impact and radiation aftereffects, but not on its
broadly human consequences. It would seem that a field of numbing had
enveloped the entire Hiroshima experience, as indeed is still the case.
Here, one may recognize two basic sources of that field of numbing: the
extraordinary horror and fear it can evoke in whoever studies or confronts
it; and the sense on the part of a would-be researcher that one must
abandon prior assumptions and approaches—and that full understanding of
the event will be beyond one's grasp.

While the tendency toward numbing in relation to Hiroshima is universal, it is bound to be greatest in Americans, where numbing serves the
additional purpose of warding off potential feelings of guilt. As in the very
different case of German attitudes toward Auschwitz, we have not wished
to permit Hiroshima to enter our psyches in ways that could affect our
feelings. And we are greatly aided in our nonfeeling by the distancing
technology of the Hiroshima attack.

Hence we construct what Edith Wyschogrod calls a *"cordon sanitaire"*
around Hiroshima—a barrier designed to prevent the spread of a threatening disease, the "illness" we block off in this case being what we did in
Hiroshima. That *cordon sanitaire* was transmitted, as official policy, throughout American society. One was supposed to be numbed to Hiroshima. It
became politically correct (before the expression existed) in the deepest
sense to remain numbed toward Hiroshima—politically suspect if one was
troubled or inclined to make a fuss about it. In that way, as a people, we
developed a *habit* of numbing toward Hiroshima, a sustained tendency
toward, one way or another, avoiding feeling in connection with what
happened there.

Thus Scott Russell Sanders describes how, when playing boyhood
games of missile launching, "I knew what sort of bombs had exploded in
Japan," and even understood some of the physics involved in the weapons,
"but I grasped these awesome facts in the same numb way I grasped the
definition of infinity." One can say that Americans have generally possessed a vague, unfelt, half knowledge of Hiroshima—usually of a kind that
interfered with a more general capacity for grasping nuclear-weapons

truths. But that does not mean we are free of fear. One can be most haunted by that which one fails to confront, by that which hovers uncomfortably on the periphery of the psyche. Sally Belfrage, for instance, tells how there was "a solution that's the same for me as for all other kids: Don't think about it. Too grisly. Whatever you do, do not consider this bomb or the way it turned the Japanese into their own shadows." But after hearing about the bomb at the age of eight, "I've assumed ever since that I wouldn't grow up."

Poll results show that the fears, and the numbing, were not limited to the young. Roughly half of all Americans (at least until the late 1980s) expected in their lifetime a nuclear war in which they (along with their family) would likely die. Yet very few—as few as one in ten—expressed any interest in precautionary measures including civil defense.

Over time, the boundaries of numbing can be blurred. Starting with the bomb, the numbing can extend to nuclear threat in general and to other areas. To be sure, one can speak of "selective inattention," as Helen Swick Perry did in 1954, applying a concept of Harry Stack Sullivan to our avoidance of Hiroshima. Paraphrasing Sullivan, she referred to "the universal tendency to selectively inattend that which makes us anxious so that it is very convenient not to attend to what we are actually aware of."

Sullivan is describing a phenomenon very similar to what we are calling psychic numbing. But it may be more accurate to say that the numbing (or "inattention") is in part selective—one avoids Hiroshima more than one does other matters—but also becomes somewhat amorphous: *the numbing does not stop with Hiroshima.* By closing ourselves off from the human costs of our devastating weapon, we are more able to do the same in relation to other experiences of collective suffering—for example, the 1990s genocides in Bosnia and Rwanda. The habit of numbing, that is, becomes a *modus vivendi,* a way of coping with large human disasters, even if we do not bear primary responsibility for them. William Styron recently referred to this as our "quivering edge of tolerance" for "fratricidal horrors and ethnic atrocities."

The tendency can even extend to everyday forms of human interaction. As a character in an Alice Walker novel puts it: "The trouble with numbness . . . is that it spreads to all your organs, mainly the heart. Pretty soon after I don't hear the white folks crying for help. I don't hear the black." As the numbing spreads, we can become increasingly insensitive to violence and suffering around us, to killing in general, but also to poverty and homelessness. And we can come to require—and seek—ever larger doses of violence in order to enhance our capacity to feel. Thus, Don DeLillo describes a family in front of its television set, "watching houses slide into the ocean, whole villages crackle and ignite in a mass of advancing lava," and "Every disaster made us wish for more, for something bigger, grander, more sweeping."

There is no reason to assume that fine lines are drawn in regard to our capacity for empathy and compassion. If we can speak of an age of numbing, especially for Americans, it begins with Hiroshima.

CHAPTER 7

FUTURELESSNESS AND CULTURAL DISARRAY

Hiroshima signified the pointless apocalypse—the sudden realization that we could extinguish ourselves as a species, with our own technology, by our own hand, and to no purpose. This imagery of extinction was prefigured by the new weapon, even though in 1945 it was not yet capable of destroying everything. From the time of Hiroshima, there has been the sense that there is no avoiding doom. "It has already left. It is on its way. . . ./You will be anywhere in the world/and it will find you," is the way the poet Sharon Doubiago put it. And Michael Daley asks "Is it the death of zero we are planning?/. . . . How can we hold the idea?/. . . how can we not?"

That is the crux of our psychological struggle: The idea of doom and futurelessness can be both all-pervasive and unimaginable, both unavoidable and impossible to absorb. There is a generational difference, as Jeff Nuttall suggests. Those beyond adolescence at the time of the bomb, habituated to a sense of continuing human existence, were "incapable of conceiving of life *without* a future," while those who came to awareness after the bomb "were incapable of conceiving of life *with* a future." For them, "Dad was a liar. . . . He lied about the bomb and he lied about the future." That was the kind of point Harry Stack Sullivan was making when he declared, in 1946, "The bomb that fell on Hiroshima punctuated history."

That punctuation seems to be permanent. While overt fear of nuclear war has diminished somewhat since the end of the cold war, it has by no means disappeared. Our own interviews suggest a merging of nuclear fear with other apocalyptic threats, such as environmental destruction and global warming. However altered in its expression, futurelessness initiated by Hiroshima remains.

The first group to respond to Hiroshima as a literary generation was the Beat movement, beginning in the early 1950s. Although generally described as rebels against American middle-class values, which they surely were, the Beats drew much of their primal energies from their horror of the atomic bomb's message of doom. Perhaps the quintessential Beat lines are Allen Ginsberg's "America when will we end the human war?/Go fuck yourself with your atomic bomb." Ginsberg's famous early lines that open his poem "Howl" are direct reflections of that sentiment: "I saw the best minds of my generation destroyed by madness, starving hysterical naked."

The by-now mythic *Port Huron Statement* of Students for a Democratic Society—the defining manifesto of a movement—emerged in 1962, its second sentence reading: "Our work is guided by the sense that we may be the last generation in the experiment with living." And at about that time Norman Mailer was providing his own definition of the hipster or "American existentialist" as "the man who knows that if our collective condition is to live with instant death by atomic war, a relatively quick death by the State as *l'universe concentrationnaire* or with a slow death by conformity with every creative and rebellious instinct stifled . . . why then the only life-giving answer is to accept the terms of death, to live with death as immediate danger, to divorce oneself from society, to exist without roots, to set out on that uncharted journey into the rebellious imperatives of the self."

Without attempting to trace that cast of mind through the nuclear age, we can say that the world's, and especially America's, creative imagination was forever altered by Hiroshima—as much by its larger threat of doom as by its own, immediate horrors. The same is true of the experiential and political rebellions of the late sixties and early seventies, triggered by the Vietnam War but more fundamentally fueled by the terror of futurelessness. That was the message of George Wald's famous speech in 1970 in which he identified the source of students' anger as their sense that "they have no future." This Hiroshima-initiated sentiment extends right into the present. In 1994 Allen Ginsberg again expressed it in such lines as: "Can't imagine how these young people make a life, make a living./How can they stand it, going out in the world with only 10 dollars and a hydrogen bomb?"

To understand the full trauma of Hiroshima to Americans, we must consider general psychological principles concerning the continuity of human life, along with a particular American vulnerability to threats to that continuity.

There is a universal psychological need for larger human connectedness or what we call the symbolization of immortality. Expressions of symbolic immortality can be understood in terms of at least five modes: The *biological mode* (the sense of living on in one's children and their children); the *creative mode* (in one's works or lasting personal influences); the *theological* or religious mode (some form of "spiritual survival"); the *natural mode* (some aspect of "eternal nature" as symbolized in virtually all cultures); or the mode of *transcendence* (a psychic state so intense that within it time and death disappear). Each of these modes of immortality has been significantly affected by Hiroshima—all the more so because of our own culpability in initiating the threat.

First, concerning the *biological mode,* Hiroshima quickly raised doubts about anyone's living on into the future, about posterity in general. Sally Belfrage's Hiroshima-connected assumption that "I wouldn't grow up" was widespread—along with a more general assumption (expressed in the Port Huron Statement) that even if one were permitted to live out one's life, that would not be true of the next generation. Hiroshima, that is, immediately cast doubt upon our capacity to maintain the Great Chain of Being.

Americans have always been edgy about questions of human continuity. In the absence of a traditional culture, with our history dominated by movement and change—by a shifting frontier and continuous immigration—our strength has been in our many-sidedness and mutability. That is why the "protean self" (named after Proteus, the Greek sea god who was a notorious shape-shifter) has been so prominent among us. But by the same token, we have hungered for some form of collective belonging that *feels* biological and can be experienced as more or less eternal—hence our fierce, often desperate emphasis upon American nationalism, upon definitions of Americanism, with the intensity of our quest a function of its elusiveness. Our obsession with "national security" since Hiroshima reflects our anxiety about the continuity of the larger American group, the American nation.

And the process extends backward as well. We have always sought to compensate for the brevity and flux of American history with particularly intense glorification of our past and our "Founding Fathers." The new threat of futurelessness aggravates still further unhealthy forms of nostalgia and the construction of family and societal golden ages that have little to do with the rude struggles of our forebears. No wonder that we are so susceptible to calls to return to "old values," for "American renewal," calls that, however empty, can appeal to our hunger to be part of the endless life of a national community—when, for the first time its very existence has been rendered uncertain.

The *creative mode*—all that we make and do—was also thrown into question by Hiroshima. We suddenly felt uncertain about the lasting possibilities of all we give and receive in connection with love and nurture, of what we work at, produce, teach, or learn. We immerse ourselves in these experiences with a sense that their reverberations are continuous, part of an endless stream of human interaction. When all such interaction is threatened, there are profound consequences, even if we are uncertain about how to measure them.

Johnny Rotten, the notorious punk-rock singer, showed no such uncertainty in declaring "When there's no future there can't be sin." In the mid-seventies he and his band, the Sex Pistols, distilled and amplified a genuine post-Hiroshima sentiment in their lyrics of "No Future," in which they repetitiously shout, "No future for you . . . no future for me!" That cry is not solely about Hiroshima or subsequent bombs. Every kind of economic and social duress undoubtedly enters into it. But Hiroshima surely contributed to a more jaundiced sense of the world's offerings, of what one could expect from others, of ways in which one's own transgressions might be increasingly permissible. Of course people went on working, loving, learning, and teaching. But they did so with greater anxiety about what it all meant, about how long any of it could last. This is the "curse" William Faulkner spoke of in his Nobel Prize acceptance speech of 1950: "There are no longer problems of the spirit. There is only the question: When will I be blown up?"

There has also been a tendency to connect ordinary losses with ultimate ones. A teacher has revealed that as a boy of about seven, he was sent off to a summer camp, which he hated, and then returned home to find his father dead, at which time he also happened to see pictures of Hiroshima and of the death camps. From that time on, all these events merged into one large perception of pain and loss. Although his experience of blending extreme threat with personal loss is particularly dramatic, the tendency is undoubtedly widespread. When one loses a parent or is simply dislodged from a comfortable setting, the loss and the dislocation occur in a larger context of possible world destruction. Every kind of juxtaposition of levels of loss becomes possible, along with every kind of confusion. And just as, after Hiroshima, every antagonism between nations takes on the potential for destroying the entire world, so does every personal trauma potentially take on that end-of-the-world association. Every small act of violence, then, has some connection with, if not sanction from, the violence of Hiroshima and Nagasaki. That is why Norman Mailer could claim that the fate of twentieth-century man was "to live with death as immediate danger, to divorce oneself from society, to exist without roots, to set out on that uncharted journey into the rebellious imperatives of the self."

While that experimentation could be integrative and even revitalizing, the image of Hiroshima cast a lethal shadow over it. As Carolyn Forché writes, "The way back is lost, the one obsession./The worst is over./The worst is yet to come." And *"If Hiroshima in the morning, after the bomb has fallen, is like a dream, one must ask whose dream it is."*

Concerning the *theological mode,* Hiroshima created an immediate religious crisis (whether or not acknowledged). Religious symbolism became both more sought after and more inadequate. The moral dilemma was that of a promise of spiritual continuity beyond individual death in an imagined world in which virtually no human beings are alive.

Hiroshima survivors themselves experienced this dilemma. They remembered such feelings as "There is no God, no Buddha." And although they frequently reverted to religious (mostly Buddhist) ideas for consolation and understanding, they tended to find traditional religious words and images insufficient for their ordeal. What they could make best use of from religious experience was the principle of *akirame,* or resignation, a principle strongly influenced by Buddhism and suggesting not just passivity but carrying on somehow in the face of extreme adversity. But they tended to be impatient with efforts to subsume that ordeal to conventional religious reassurances or religious platitudes of any kind.

One American theologian declared in 1946, "The bomb that fell on Hiroshima cut history in two like a knife," a statement resembling Harry Stack Sullivan's image of Hiroshima "punctuating" history. But about four decades later a survey of post-Hiroshima theology found that the atomic bombings had been surprisingly ignored by most theologians. A few years after Hiroshima, *Christian Century* decried the fact that the churches had reached "a tacit understanding among themselves to blanket in silence" the question of the morality of nuclear warfare. There have of course been periodic condemnations of Hiroshima and of subsequent nuclear buildup from various religious sources, but generally as ethical rather than theological statements. Mainstream American religious leaders, moreover, have more often accepted the Hiroshima bombing than condemned it.*

But at least one theologian wants us to see Hiroshima as "an eschatological symbol of our age, a symbol of the enormity of human evil and its potential for final self-destruction." Eschatology deals with "last things" or ultimate death-related matters—in American and European theology, usually with Christian apocalyptic images of the end of human history. Hiroshima is surely eschatological in that sense, but highly confusing in at least two ways: First, it was a specifically human act—one group of people used a revolutionary device on another group of people. And second, the enormity of the destructive technology blurs the crucial distinction between individual death and the death of everything (as we shall soon discuss). Our point here is that religious arrangements for coping with death—for promising something eternal in the face of death—have been thrown out of kilter. Such *ultimate futurelessness* constitutes an equally ultimate spiritual threat to the world's major religions.

---

* *One important exception was the 1983 pastoral letter on nuclear weapons in which U.S. Catholic bishops declared that "we must shape the climate of opinion which will make it possible for our country to express profound sorrow over the atomic bombing in 1945. Without that sorrow, there is no possibility of finding a way to repudiate future use of nuclear weapons."*

Religious fundamentalists (notably Christian, but others as well) seize upon the situation by constructing a literalized tie between religious end-of-the-world imagery and post-Hiroshima nuclear threat. In that way they do precisely what other religious thinking cannot do: provide an immortality system that includes nuclear holocaust as a *vehicle* for the end of human history and the beginning of a new spiritual era.

There is a connection, then, between nuclear threat and the world-wide epidemic of fundamentalism. Fundamentalism in general, including its political forms stems from the loss, or fear of loss, of fundamentals—of principles and capacities basic to creed, community, and collective life. Hiroshima, suddenly and radically, fueled that fear—fear that *everything* could be lost.

This religious nuclear-age story is far from over. It may be that spiritual response to Hiroshima is just now beginning. But it can extend and deepen only by recognizing the "knife cut" in history that Hiroshima represents.

The significance and the vulnerability of the *natural mode* of immortality are revealed in the most terrifying rumor that swept Hiroshima soon after the bomb was dropped. The rumor (as we have seen) was that trees, grass, and flowers would never again grow there; that the city would be unable to sustain vegetation of any kind—that nature was drying up altogether and life had been extinguished at its source. The rumor suggested an ultimate desolation, a state that not only encompassed human death but went beyond it.

A little later, as people in Hiroshima struggled to find ways to live, they would quote an old Chinese and Japanese proverb: "The state may collapse, but the mountains and rivers remain." That proverb was a gentle assertion of the natural mode of immortality that, however precarious, still held.

In the late 1960s and early '70s, young people in considerable numbers formed rural communes, attempting to grow their own food and live as independently as possible from the rest of society. Noting this phenomenon, Lewis Mumford commented that these young people were acting as though the bomb had already been dropped. It is quite possible, of course, that unconsciously such young people were preparing for an American Hiroshima. But whether or not that was true, the bomb's assault on the entire natural environment of Hiroshima and Nagasaki suggested the extent to which we could, with our new technology, destroy our habitat. That awareness, of course, has been painfully confirmed in the recognition of industrial pollutions, and nuclear waste, and the far-reaching consequences of ozone depletion and global warming. But Hiroshima itself had much to do with the emergence, during the 1960s and in spurts after that, of the American and European environmental movements. Leaders of those movements have utilized the power of images of atomic destruction for awakening environmental concerns. And when a leading antiwar scientist spoke critically of America's conduct in the Gulf War of 1990–91, his association was to Hiroshima's attack on the environment: "It is not an exaggeration to compare the environmental and human destruction unleashed in Iraq and Kuwait to the atomic bombing of Hiroshima." Keeping in mind that kind of sequence, he went on to say, "Our planet has now become a laboratory for atmospheric scientists." Nuclear and environmental end-of-the-world imagery were also joined in the concept of a "nuclear winter."

Hiroshima made clear that what is ultimately destroyed by our new weaponry is not so much a particular human population as the overall human habitat, the earth. Even in the absence of further use of the weapons, our awareness of that possibility has shaken our confidence in the "eternal" quality of "eternal nature."

The experience of *transcendence,* the fifth mode, is in many ways the one most complexly affected by Hiroshima. It differs from the other modes in being an intense psychic state rather than a particular direction of larger continuity. Everyday forms of transcendence are available to us in such experiences as sexual union, dancing, athletics, the contemplation of beauty, painting, and also in childbirth and what is called the near-death experience.

Hiroshima radically confounds all aspects of this mode. First, Hiroshima itself was a product of the experience of transcendence—or high state—accompanying the Trinity test, the "power surge" of the decision makers and their psychological merger with the all-powerful device. That early experience of nuclearism, epitomized by William Laurence, was to extend to and dominate subsequent American attitudes toward nuclear weapons.

At the same time, Hiroshima raised painful doubts about the other four modes of immortality, thereby creating a new hunger for high states as an immediate, alternative means of experiencing something on the order of the eternal. A claimed source of the word *beat* (for "beat generation" or "beat movement") is "beatific," meaning exalted or blessed, and implying transcendence: A "beatific vision," for example, involves "a sight of the glories of heaven." But the other meaning of the word *beat,* as used for the same literary generation, is worn-out, fatigued, overcome. The movement's mind-set surely embraced both meanings, the first a post-Hiroshima effort at reasserting a sense of the eternal in the face of the terror and obscenity of the atomic threat (we recall the various quotations from Allen Ginsberg). The "beatniks" often used drugs to achieve their high states, as did their successors, the hippies, and various subsequent groups of experiential radicals. It would seem that Hiroshima upped the ante of such states: many sensed the weapons' own transcendent power and appeal and plunged all the more strongly, sometimes desperately, into alternative expressions of what was sometimes viewed as escapism but could also be perceived as assertions of life-power and of unending human possibility.

Hiroshima, that is, contributed greatly to the fierce hunger for transcendence that has since gripped our society. That hunger can be indiscriminate in its methods and objects. It can lead to various forms of realization, to fragmentation associated with violence or personal breakdown, or to the deification of the weaponry we have observed in connection with nuclearism. Indeed, nuclearism can become sufficiently perverse to reach the point of seeking an experience of transcendence via a final nuclear apocalypse—which is something on the order of the sexual perversion in which orgasm is sought at the point of death via strangulation by hanging. Campbell McGrath, in his poem "Nagasaki, Uncle Walt, The Eschatology of America's Century," brilliantly captures the many-sided dangers inherent in atomic-bomb-related transcendence:

> I couldn't begin to count the versions of Armageddon
> cast up like driftwood on the shallow bar of my youth. . . .
> No screenplay apocalypse, no scenario for world holocaust
> could fail to provide me with suitable amusement. . . .
> Isn't this another possible ending, a slambang finale

for the movie our search for existential meaning has become?
The gathering-together-of-the-folk-on-the-beach, a millennial
    hootenanny of ludic glee. . . .
the wild blue yonder, the sweet bye-and-bye,
heaven and hell rolled into one brazenly illumed limbo,
the collective Purgatorio of America's Century . . .
the numinous, the sacred—an eternal Las Vegas of the soul. . . .

CHAPTER 8

LATE-TWENTIETH-CENTURY DEATH
—AND RENEWAL

After Hiroshima, it has been difficult to separate individual death from a vast, collective "death event." We still struggle with a foreground of impending personal death but do so against an intrusive background, of vague but menacing impersonal annihilation. And the world consists increasingly of people who have come to consciousness after Hiroshima and have therefore known only that state. The writer Scott Russell Sanders, for example, born in October 1945, tells us: "My birth sign was the mushroom cloud."

By the 1960s, Americans were living a nuclear "double life": aware that any moment each of us and everything around us could be suddenly annihilated, yet at the same time proceeding with our everyday, nitty-gritty lives and conducting "business as usual." But to understand how that inner division came about we need to go back to Hiroshima itself. In receiving the message of the revolutionary destruction of that city, Americans and others throughout the world found that, once and for all, their relationship to death, and therefore to life, had changed. As early as 1946, the psychoanalyst Edward Glover declared that Hiroshima and Nagasaki had rendered actual the most extreme fantasies of world destruction encountered in the insane or in the nightmares of ordinary people. In that way, "the capacity so painfully acquired by normal men to distinguish between sleep, delusion, hallucination and the objective reality of waking life has for the first time in human history been seriously weakened." And later Norman Mailer was to write of being "doomed to die as a cipher in some vast statistical operation"; and with "death being causeless, life was causeless as well . . ."

Both observations suggest that, after Hiroshima, the individual self is threatened with being overwhelmed by, or dissolved into, the larger absurd death event. Our own observation is that the self has been pressed toward an inner division that resembles "doubling"—the formation of two conjoined but relatively autonomous selves, each constructed around a way of anticipating death. We all go through life with both a *measured self* and an *apocalyptic self*. The measured self deals with everyday living, seeks a certain balance between life and death, seeks the culmination of a meaningful life in a "good death." Whatever the historical confusions and threats, the measured self seeks to make its way through the life cycle and to contribute to the work of the world. But breaking out of that mode is the "apocalyptic self," the self preoccupied with the nuclear end, haunted by images of mass killing and dying, and haunted by death in general. The agenda of the apocalyptic self, however addressed, is that of the death event.

The apocalyptic self can readily enter into a fundamentalist scenario, in which a vision of the end of the world is seen as a prelude to new spiritual achievement (such as the Second Coming of Jesus)—so that even nuclear threat can be subsumed to an immortality system. But the apocalyptic self can be quite secular, can, for example, be associated with imagining the nuclear end (Hiroshima is invaluable here) as a means of combating it—the kind of psychological process seized upon by antinuclear movements.

The apocalyptic self has grave dangers. It may press toward totalistic behavior—toward destroying or killing—in order to head off a perceived death event. Expressions of the apocalyptic self invite extremes of ethnic passion and even genocide. The designated victims (as in Bosnia or Rwanda) may have nothing directly to do with Hiroshima or nuclear weapons, but energies of unlimited destruction that were set loose have much to do with psychological patterns of post-Hiroshima apocalypticism.

Yet an element of the apocalyptic self is both necessary and inevitable if one is to imagine our world with any degree of authenticity—to connect the self with the technological apocalypse we human beings may perpetrate. No one, after Hiroshima, is ever completely free from terrifying images of a death that is absurd and unacceptable. Nor is anyone—and this includes the most extreme of fundamentalists—free from a need for a measured self to deal with ordinary life experience and with some anticipation of one's individual death.

It would seem that each of us maintains both a measured and an apocalyptic self, and that we switch back and forth between them according to need and inclination. All of us, in highly varied ways, seek some balance between the two selves, a balance that enables us to cope with both everyday life and a shadow of total death.

Death in the late twentieth century, then, is no less confused than life. Individual death is still very much an issue, even when the apocalyptic self seems to predominate. Christian fundamentalists, for example, remain highly concerned about being "raptured up" and thereby escaping death as individual people. But fundamentalist movements—ethnic, nationalistic, or religious—tend increasingly to provide the immortality systems so hungered for in our age. The great task of this millennial transition is to find modes of larger human continuity—symbolic immortality—that, instead of invoking literalized apocalyptic fantasy, emphasize genuine possibilities for enhancing human life.

RENEWAL

Indeed it may be our very troubled relationship to death—our inveterate concern with its meaning for us—that can call forth our resilience. We can respond to our death anxiety by thrashing about uselessly or even destructively, but we are also capable of re-creating elements of self for coping with our age.

The Freudian revolution emerged from late-nineteenth- and early-twentieth-century confusions and contradictions, largely sexual but also concerned with the broader area of living and dying in the face of extraordinary historical change. Erik Erikson's work on identity extended that revolution and spoke to the radical historical dislocations prior to and in connection with World War II, dislocations that again had to do with how and where one lived and died. Hiroshima forced us to look much further into absurd death in connection with imagery of extinction—with the death event—and into ways of being that might serve us in our benighted but by no means doomed era.

For example, when a Christian theologian calls for a nonfundamentalist "retrieval of the apocalyptic tradition," he is asking for an expression of apocalyptic imagination appropriate to our plight. That kind of imagination can help us to reconstruct our distinctions between individual death and a larger death event. We can do that in our post-Hiroshima world only by confronting both.

For individual death, one requires new versions of ancient wisdom, in recognizing that the matter cannot be avoided. As Chris Offut puts it, "No one surfed the river Styx." And concerning the larger death event, we need to explore what our own growing awareness of the mortality of the planet is. Deepening that recognition could contribute to powerful constructive energies. Western philosophy has long realized that we must imagine our own death in order to live more fully. After Hiroshima, however, our further task is to imagine the end of the world in order to take steps to maintain human existence.

We can then break with the atrocity-producing situation created by the nuclear megamachine even prior to Hiroshima. We can return to human agency in controlling our lethal technology. And we can "disenthrall ourselves" from the nuclear deity and from the Hiroshima narrative that has so long shielded and promoted that deity. We can come to recognize the extent to which that Hiroshima narrative has blunted our senses and subverted our moral imagination. For achieving that disenthrallment, nothing is more powerful than images of the actual Hiroshima experience, of what the bomb did there to fellow human beings.

The effort must extend indefinitely into the future. But if we keep Hiroshima before us, it can be rediscovered by each generation in ways that contribute to nuclear disenthrallment. In the process, we can experience— as Harold Bloom said of our contemplation of Frankenstein's monster— "added consciousness" and "a heightened realization of the self."

Relevant here are present-day capacities for the "protean self" and the "species self." The first represents a reconstruction of that which has been shattered, a putting together of odd elements of self in ways appropriate to contemporary threats and possibilities. The second, the species self, draws upon an oddly hopeful aspect of post-Hiroshima destructive technology. Because all human beings on the earth could be wiped out more or less simultaneously, we are forced to recognize our *shared fate* as fellow members of a single species in trouble. While retaining important parts of existing identity elements (family, religious, occupational, national), these can be subsumed to a sense of being part of humankind.

In these pages, we have explored what Hiroshima means—and has done—to America. After fifty years, Hiroshima still has enormous salience for us. Since the end of the Cold War, our awareness of nuclear threat has diminished, but the weapons continue to endanger us in myriad ways, and the Hiroshima raw nerve remains.

Recent events have produced new worries about proliferation. Just as fear of a "Korean bomb" began to subside came a report that Iran may be able to build the weapon within five years. The odds that terrorists may obtain a bomb have dramatically increased, largely because of the breakup of the Soviet Union and subsequent loss of control over nuclear materials. In America, deteriorating conditions at aging nuclear-weapons facilities, such as Hanford and Oak Ridge, have not only exacerbated the nuclear-waste crisis but also raised fears about possible leakage of plutonium, the release of radioactive contaminants into the atmosphere, or an accidental chain reaction leading to an explosion.

Nuclear arsenals, meanwhile, remain very much in place. Although the U.S. and Russia have agreed to scrap thousands of outmoded warheads, each will retain nine thousand of the newest and most accurate variety even after the next round of arms cuts. Russia remains disturbingly unstable, and in America there are constant calls for spending more on what one high Pentagon official has called "future nuclear weapons missions." With the end of the superpower confrontation, the Hiroshima model for use may be more relevant than ever, for now a nation with the bomb may be more tempted to use it against an enemy without one.

Ian Clark has observed that "anyone who would seek to deny the legitimacy of nuclear weapons must first of all burst open the moral cocoon in which they have been nurtured since Hiroshima and Nagasaki." Confronting the Hiroshima decision would be an important step in properly stigmatizing the weapons. When we admit that the weapons cannot be used, then we can discuss whether they can be eliminated, or reduced to a minimal number, perhaps fewer than one hundred, that would no longer threaten global destruction. This is an idea that is in the air, as the support of a number of respected military leaders suggests. Far fewer nuclear weapons in the world would reduce environmental degradation, limit proliferation, and curb the chances that terrorists might assemble a weapon.

The responsibility, and the blame, is by no means all ours. Soviet leaders in particular have much to answer for in this area, as in many others. But as George Kennan once observed, we must remember that it was we Americans "who first produced and tested" the bomb, "we who were the first to raise its destructiveness to a new level with the hydrogen bomb . . . and we alone, so help us God, who have used the weapon in anger against others, and against tens of thousands of helpless noncombatants at that." He added:

> I know that reasons were offered for some of these things. I know that others might have taken this sort of lead had we not done so. But let us not, in the face of this record, so lose ourselves in self-righteousness and hypocrisy as to forget the measure of our own complicity in creating the situation we face today.

Confronting Hiroshima can be a powerful source of renewal. It can enable us to emerge from nuclear entrapment and rediscover our imaginative capacities on behalf of human good. We can overcome our moral inversion and cease to justify weapons or actions of mass killing. We can condemn and then step back from acts of desecration and recognize what Camus called a "philosophy of limits." In that way we can also take steps to cease betraying ourselves, cease harming and deceiving our own people. We can also free our society from its apocalyptic concealment, and in the process enlarge our vision. We can break out of our long-standing numbing in the vitalizing endeavor of learning, or relearning, to feel. And we can divest ourselves of a debilitating sense of futurelessness and once more feel bonded to past and future generations.

We return to Hiroshima, then, to confront our own dark truths—but also to awaken in ourselves our many-sided moral and psychological alternatives for living and dying, and for enhancing the human project.

CODA

Our book is about America but it emanates from Hiroshima. So we must revisit that city as we reach the book's end. In the memory of Hiroshima survivors reside special truths that exist nowhere else. Their narrative is one of actuality, of consequences.

Hijiyama Hill overlooks the city. It has a haunted feeling, for many of the victims of the atomic bombing escaped to this hill on August 6, 1945, only to die of their injuries. A survivor, a history professor, later told one of us about climbing Hijiyama on that day and looking back at the city. "I saw that Hiroshima had disappeared," he said. "I was shocked by the sight. . . . What I felt then and still feel now I just can't explain with words. . . . But Hiroshima didn't exist—that was mainly what I saw—Hiroshima just didn't exist."

Today, one observes from Hijiyama a thriving, rebuilt city. Yet, from that vantage point, it is still easy to imagine the old Hiroshima, for the topography has not changed. Six branches of the Ota River still snake through the city, and hills surround Hiroshima on nearly every side. These are the hills that provided the "focusing effect" that turned the force of the first atomic blast back on the city.

Looking down from Hijiyama one finds Hiroshima in the bottom of a natural bowl formed by the hills. A visitor cannot fail to envision a weapon of mass destruction exploding in a bright flash high overhead. That image of a flash over the very center of a city is hard to erase, as one imagines it enveloping the entire area and all its people.

Another Hiroshima truth can be found in the Peace Park. It is not one of the more prominent symbols, such as the A-bomb Dome (the crumbling remains of a building mostly destroyed in 1945). Rather, it rests under a plain mound of earth, covered with grass, about ten feet high and fifty feet across.

Inside this hollow mound, a visitor encounters an eerie collection of porcelain canisters sitting on a series of shelves. There are about one thousand cans in all, and each holds the ashes of a victim of the atomic bombing, whose name is written on the side. They have been here for decades now, unclaimed by family members. (In many cases, all the victim's relatives were killed by the bomb.) Most of the cans will remain here forever, now that so many years have passed.

But they are not alone under the mound. Behind two curtains, several dozen plain pine boxes are stacked, rather unceremoniously, from floor to ceiling. They are said to contain the ashes of seventy thousand unidentified victims of the atomic bomb. Many of them were cremated on makeshift altars throughout the city. The ashes were brought to a temple that once stood on this site, and then stored here. The pine crates are marked with the names of the sites where the human dust and bits of bones were found —outside a factory or school, perhaps, or a military camp. But beyond that the ashes are anonymous. Under a mound, behind two curtains, inside a few pine boxes: This is what became of one-quarter of the city of Hiroshima on August 6, 1945.

Americans are strongly aware of 1995 as a year commemorating the fiftieth anniversary of significant events connected with World War II: the liberation of the Nazi death camps, the atomic bombings of Hiroshima and Nagasaki, and the Japanese surrender ending that country's brutal aggression. Our plea is for all to draw upon these commemorations to confront violent and destructive behavior of every kind.

We write this book during difficult days for Americans, a time when many wish to ignore searing human problems of violence, poverty, and general hopelessness, in favor of shallow reassurances and patriotic slogans. We offer this volume as a different kind of patriotic contribution, as an appeal to our own better angels, for the renewal of what is most compassionate and open and honorable in the American spirit.

APPENDIX

CULTURAL RESPONSES TO HIROSHIMA

Creative artists of every variety have made incisive, satiric, or powerful statements about nuclear threat. Songwriters, sculptors and painters, choreographers, playwrights, and others have offered cautionary works that depict the horror of the bomb, or its meaning in our society. What these artistic statements share, however, with rare exceptions, is a general avoidance of the specific subject of Hiroshima.

In the pages that follow, we do not attempt an overview of nuclear culture but concentrate instead on three art forms—film, fiction, and poetry—that together reach a wide and varied audience, and in this way explore the overall cultural response to, and avoidance of, the atomic bombings.

Hiroshima on Film

Since September 1945, when *First Yank in Tokyo* brought the image of a mushroom cloud to the screen, hundreds if not thousands of "nuclear movies" have appeared. The nuclear genre spawned subgenres: survivalist fantasies, irradiated monster films, post-apocalypse thrillers. Many of the films have been of the exploitative variety, but at least one was a work of genius *(Dr. Strangelove)* and several others explored the issue thoughtfully (including *Fail-Safe* and Peter Watkins's *The War Game,* and the more recent *Testament* and *Desert Bloom).*

What is most striking, however, is that few of these films say anything directly about Hiroshima. Nearly all of them, in fact, are works of pure fiction, imagining nuclear attacks in the near or distant future, while ignoring the two instances when atomic weapons have already been used. Hundreds of films have explored the Civil War, the war against Hitler, and Vietnam. Yet only three Hollywood movies have emerged about the making or use of the first atomic bombs. This is surprising on one level. An epic saga of American achievement, the story is set in wartime, with larger-than-life characters and considerable drama, and it concludes on a triumphal note. Yet ambivalence or guilt are certain to be evoked by any cinematic treatment of Hiroshima.

Perhaps that is why films related to Hiroshima all grapple with the notion of American decency. The three Hollywood films have much else in common. Each was highly touted, and directed by talented filmmakers, but was an artistic failure. Each very much reflected the mood of its time—the first two raising few questions about the Hiroshima story, the third revisionist in outlook. Finally, each was subject to political pressure or scrutiny (also true, as we will see, of the television movie *The Day After*). That is why the making of the films is as revealing as the films themselves, perhaps more so.

THE BEGINNING OR THE END

Inspired by a scientist's letter to actress Donna Reed, this controversial MGM film emerged, after many revisions, as a Hollywood version of the Hiroshima narrative.

Early outlines and scripts raised doubts about the Hiroshima decision (as we observed earlier) and portrayed the effects of the atomic bombing in a way that would have shocked many viewers. In one scenario, General Thomas Farrell, guided by Japanese radiation expert Masao Tsuzuki, toured the ghostlike ruins of Hiroshima, where they encountered "a baby with a face burned . . . The death of the city lies heavily on the scene." The overall political message was alarmist and aligned with the scientists. A Robert Oppenheimer character would warn of "mistaken publicity surrounding the bomb." According to other scientists in the film, it would have been better to lose half a million American lives "than release atomic energy in the world" at Hiroshima.

Then something happened and the sensibility of *The Beginning or the End* shifted suddenly. The decision to use the bomb, in revised scripts, was viewed as not merely justifiable but admirable. Now, after the bombings, no victims appeared—just a burning landscape observed from the air. General Leslie Groves and an assistant who monitored the scripts played a vital part in the editing process. Activist scientists who agreed to be portrayed in the film were not able to secure the right of script approval, which the studio had granted to both Groves and Truman.

Further changes in the script, although ultimately deleted, reveal how thoroughly the outlook of the film had changed. One scene depicted a fictional German physicist delivering atomic secrets to the Japanese at a nuclear laboratory located in—Hiroshima.

MGM hired Norman Taurog to direct the film and Hume Cronyn to star as Oppenheimer. The studio jumped a major hurdle when it received word that Truman, after reviewing the script, had no objection to *The Beginning or the End,* subject to a few minor changes, which included deleting a reference to the president providing the title of the film. Many of the scientists impersonated in the film expressed concerns about the movie, but nearly all signed releases, even Einstein. Oppenheimer paid a visit to the movie set after being assured that his character (the film's narrator) would display "humility" and "a love of mankind." The Hollywoodization of the bomb had begun.

Leo Szilard felt the script was "lousy" and he was so worried that he traveled to Hollywood to rewrite scenes in which he appeared. The film, however, did not depict or even mention his attempts to prevent the bomb from being used against Japan. Activist scientists raised so many objections that MGM secretly recorded their telephone conversations with the studio's technical adviser.

Shooting of *The Beginning or the End* concluded in the summer of 1946. Even in minor details and lines of dialogue—some laughable—the film manifested the Hiroshima narrative:

- At a pre-Trinity briefing, General Groves makes light of fallout. When a scientist asks what to do if a radioactive cloud drifts their way, Groves replies, with a chuckle: "I don't know about you, but I intend to run!"

- The name of one of the four planes on the Hiroshima mission—in real life called *Bock's Car*—was changed in the film to *Necessary Evil.*

- The B-29s are pelted with heavy flak over Hiroshima, a fabrication that makes the attack more contested, the airmen more courageous.

- Witnessing the mushroom cloud, the crewmen are awestruck and grim, a reflection of American compassion and decency.

- The film makes no mention at all of Nagasaki.

Yet it was in the script's central melodrama that the true message of the film was conveyed. Matt Cochran, a young, good-looking scientist involved in the bomb project, repeatedly expresses qualms about where it all might lead. Finally, in arming the bomb at Tinian, an accident occurs, Matt prevents a chain reaction from blowing up forty thousand people on the island—thereby exposing himself to a fatal dose of radiation. "Maybe that's what I get for helping to build this thing," he observes.

But the film does not leave it at that. In the closing scene, one of Matt's friends delivers the customary "final letter" he wrote to his pregnant wife just before he died. In the letter, Matt recalls his doubts about the bomb but concludes that "God has *not* shown us a new way to destroy ourselves. Atomic energy is the hand he has extended to lift us from the ruins of war and lighten the burdens of peace. . . . We have found a path so filled with promise that when we walk down it we will know that everything that came before the discovery of atomic energy was the dark ages." The logical inconsistency of the final scene—just moments earlier, Matt had called his fatal accident a just punishment for his sins—reflects the filmmakers' equally sudden change of heart, under pressure from Washington, months before.

In October 1946, just as Henry Stimson started writing his *Harper's* article, *The Beginning or the End* was screened for a group of officials and scientists in Washington. Nearly every scene in the film now underscored the Hiroshima narrative, but trouble brewed. The White House felt uncomfortable about one key sequence, which Walter Lippmann found "shocking." It pictured Groves and Stimson informing Truman about the bomb after Roosevelt's death in April 1945. This was the only time the character of Truman appeared in the film.

The segment was filled with outrageous untruths, such as Groves telling Truman that there was reason to believe that the Japanese would greet a U.S. invasion with their own atomic weapons. But that isn't what displeased some of the viewers. They objected to the president deciding, after only a brief reflection, that the U.S. would use the weapon against Japan—because "I think more of our American boys than I do of all our enemies."*

Truman's secretary, Charles Ross, informed MGM that everyone "enjoyed very much" the screening. "This is a thrilling picture," he added. But "something needs to be done about the sequence in which President Truman appears." Truman himself wrote a letter to the actor portraying him (as we mentioned earlier), asserting that his "only objection to the film" was that it pictured his decision as a "snap judgment." Apparently the opinions of others had moved Truman to protest a scene he had approved months before.

Longtime MGM screenwriter (and conservative political activist) James K. McGuinness immediately went to Washington and met with the president's secretary. Then he deleted the offending scene and wrote a new one. McGuinness informed Walter Lippmann about the change, claiming to be "deeply impressed by your feeling that we were showing our country's Chief Executive deciding a monumental matter in what was a much-too-hasty fashion." Lippmann, in turn, assured James Conant that the crisis had passed, observing whimsically that "sufficiently drastic criticism does have its effect upon the producers."

The new scene placed Truman in Germany, talking to Charles Ross across a desk just after his secretary had handed out copies of the Potsdam Declaration to the press in July 1945. Truman was to be filmed from the rear in a darkened room (as the White House demanded), almost Godlike in his authority, as he finally told Ross about the bomb. Ross responded in the new script by exclaiming that if the Japanese had it, "they'd use it on us."

"That's a *persuasive* argument, Charlie—but not a *decisive* one," Truman replied. The president then explained that in his many consultations on this matter the "consensus of opinion is that the bomb will shorten the war by approximately a year." The scene concluded with this exchange:

* *Lippmann privately told John J. McCloy that this scene was an "outright fabrication," a "libel" that would "disgrace" Truman and America. It reduced the role of the president "to extreme triviality in a great matter," Lippman informed another friend. "Serious people abroad are bound to say that if that is the way we made that kind of decision, we are not to be trusted with such a powerful weapon. As you know, the decision was not made that way. . . ." McCloy agreed, asserting that "such a misrepresentation would greatly complicate some of the thinking which is now current about the bomb. . . ."*

The president: The Army has selected several Japanese cities as prime military targets—because of war industries, military installations, troop concentrations, or fortifications. We are going to shower all these places for ten days with leaflets telling the population to leave— telling them what is coming. We hope these warnings will save lives. . . . A year less of war will mean life for untold numbers of Russians, of Chinese—of Japanese—and from three hundred thousand to half a million of America's finest youth. That was the decisive consideration in my consent.

Ross: As President of the United States, sir, you could make no other decision.

The president: As president, I could not. So I have instructed the Army to take the bomb to the Marianas and—when they get the green light —to use it.

As drama the sequence succeeded, but it was faulty (as we have seen) on several factual grounds. In any case, McGuinness sent the draft to Ross, explaining that time was short and he was eager "to incorporate anything else you deem advisable."

Ross requested further changes on November 8. In the final draft the length of time the bomb would shorten the war increased from "approximately a year" to "at least a year." A reference to scientists calling for a demonstration shot was deleted. Added was a Truman quote predicting that in peacetime "atomic energy can be used to bring about a golden age —such an age of prosperity and well-being as the world has never known." But the most revealing revision found Ross sympathizing with Truman about the difficulty of his decision, by saying: "You must have spent many sleepless nights over it." Years later, of course, Truman would repeatedly insist that he *never* lost any sleep over the decision.

Apparently after learning of the latest revisions ordered by the White House, Vannevar Bush assured a friend that "history was not unreasonably distorted" by the film. But James Conant, who had just finished revising the Stimson article, was still concerned, and he made a last-ditch attempt to prevent the film from being released in any form. He told Bernard

Baruch, the U.S. nuclear arms negotiator, that *The Beginning or the End* could have a "bad effect" on how other countries might view America and urged him to take steps to keep the film out of circulation. Baruch agreed to look into it, but apparently nothing came of his efforts.

The Beginning or the End opened across the country in early March 1947 to mixed reviews. *Time* laughed at the film's "cheery imbecility," but *Variety* praised its "aura of authenticity and special historical significance." The liberal New York daily *PM* found the film's moral message "reassuring." Harrison Brown, who had worked on the bomb, exposed some of the film's factual errors—he called the showering of warning leaflets over Hiroshima the "most horrible falsification of history"—in the *Bulletin of the Atomic Scientists*. But in the far more influential *New York Times,* Bosley Crowther called the picture a fair and "creditable" reenactment and observed that MGM had "taken no obvious sides in the current atomic contentions." He praised how it handled the moral issue in portraying the bomb as "a necessary evil."

MGM invited scientists to a screening in Chicago. Most of them watched the film—which billed itself as "basically a true story"—in dejected or angry silence. A few days later Leo Szilard put the matter in perspective, with biting humor. "If our sin as scientists was to make and use the atomic bomb," he explained, "then our punishment was to watch *The Beginning or the End.*"

While it is tempting to find ridiculous the sometimes obsessive concern with the film displayed by the scientists, one factor must be recalled: *The Beginning or the End* was inspired by the activists, and the making of the film coincided with the emergence of the first sustained challenge to the Hiroshima narrative. And so the scientists struggled to preserve the initial spirit of the film. But, as historian Michael Yavenditti has observed, the battle over *The Beginning or the End* illustrated the same "perils of dependency" first raised in the scientists' work for the Manhattan Project. Scientists who felt uneasy about the bomb had trusted the nation's leaders to handle it wisely. Now, after their experience with the MGM film, Yavenditti explained, scientists "drew similar lessons from their wartime dependence on Washington and their postwar dependence on Hollywood."

In his review, Bosley Crowther found *The Beginning or the End* marred by a self-important tone. The filmmakers, he said, "actually think that they have made history." In a sense, however, the filmmakers—in exaggerating, glorifying, and even fabricating key events—*did* make history. Although the MGM movie did not become a box office sensation, it was seen by hundreds of thousands of Americans. *The Beginning or the End* reached a larger audience over the years via television and is still occasionally aired. Because of its quasi-documentary form, its depiction of history is probably accepted by most viewers.

There would not be another Hiroshima-related Hollywood movie for more than six years, and it too would adhere to the official narrative; and then another thirty-five years would pass before the next treatment. The movie industry's capitulation on *The Beginning or the End* reveals how Hollywood, no less than the press, eagerly served the official narrative, acting out of a perceived patriotic need to do what the military and their President desired. The movie industry's subsequent failure to re-examine the subject with a fresh eye contributed "to the larger cultural process," Paul Boyer has observed, "by which Hiroshima and Nagasaki gradually sank, unconfronted and unresolved, into the deeper recesses of American awareness."

ABOVE AND BEYOND

Like *The Beginning or the End,* the 1953 film *Above and Beyond* was something of an "official" production. The idea for the movie came from a close associate of General Curtis LeMay, then head of the Strategic Air Command. Paul Tibbets was a paid consultant, and the military cooperated fully with the production. *Above and Beyond,* like its predecessor, emphasized American decency. In the key scene, Tibbets, after releasing the Hiroshima bomb and surveying a city on fire, radios in a strike report. "Results good," he says. Then he repeats it, with grim irony. But this was not in the original script for the film. It was added later, presumably to show that the men who dropped the bomb recognized the tragic nature of their mission. Tibbets, who had never expressed qualms about dropping the bomb, criticized this scene when the movie came out.

In the initial film treatment, in fact, the sequence was closer to the historical truth. After Tibbets radioed "Results good," *without* irony, another crew member interjected: "What do you mean 'good'? It was perfect!"

Above and Beyond, like *The Beginning or the End,* did not focus on the Hiroshima mission but rather what led up to it, this time with pilots, not scientists, at its center. It may not have been a good movie, but it was an influential one, as it was one of the rare encounters millions of Americans would have with Hiroshima. Bosley Crowther of the *New York Times* criticized its sentimental aspects but—just as he had six years earlier with *The Beginning or the End*—praised the "substance and plausibility" of its handling of Hiroshima.

As with *The Beginning or the End,* what is most revealing in *Above and Beyond* are its fabrications. A key early scene in the movie shows a General Brent (a composite character based mainly on Leslie Groves) testing Paul Tibbets's suitability for the job of flying the first atomic mission. He hands Tibbets a buzzer attached to a cord and asks: "What if you could push that button and end the war, saving half a million Americans—but you'd kill 100,000 people in an instant?" Tibbets ponders a moment, then presses. With the question posed like that, one can easily imagine a theater of moviegoers pushing an imaginary button right along with Tibbets.

The film depicts marital discord, largely caused by the stress of extreme secrecy. When his wife confesses that she can't help thinking of children in other countries being killed by American bombs, Tibbets explodes. "Lucy, don't ever say that again!" he shouts. "Look, let's clear up one little piece of morality right now. It's war that's wrong, not war's weapons. Sure, innocent people are dying and that's horrible. But to lose this war to this gang we're fighting would be the most immoral thing we could do. . . . And don't you ever forget it!"

On Tinian, the night before the Hiroshima mission, Tibbets (played by Robert Taylor) can't sleep, so he writes a letter to his mother, the soon-to-be immortalized Enola Gay. He admits he's scared. He might foul up. He might get killed. A decent man, he doesn't like dropping a bomb that could kill thousands of people ("but it's part of my job, and I've got to do it"). But mostly he's worried about his children and the world they will inhabit if what he is about to unleash "doesn't stop this war, and all others."

After calmly dropping the bomb and surveying a city on fire—with special-effects footage borrowed from *The Beginning or the End*—Tibbets's crewmen appear awed, their hearts heavy. Back on Tinian, Tibbets is badgered by the press. One reporter shouts: "You've just dropped a bomb that's killed eighty thousand people. My readers want to know how you feel about it!" Tibbets replies: "How do *they* feel about it?" A perceptive question, to be sure, but given what the viewers had learned in this movie, their answer would almost certainly have to be: "Uncomfortable, but satisfied."

Above and Beyond ends with Tibbets's estranged wife rushing to the airport to meet his plane, ending the story with a hug and a kiss. Thus, as H. Bruce Franklin has pointed out, the film "presents a subtext urging civilians to accept secrecy, avoid meddling with military concerns, and be grateful for the bomb." In real life, unfortunately, there was no happy ending. Tibbets and his wife were divorced, and he pointed to secrecy as the primary cause.

FAT MAN AND LITTLE BOY

Subgenres of nuclear movies would come and go, but more than three decades would pass between *Above and Beyond* and the next Hollywood film to explore the Hiroshima decision, *Fat Man and Little Boy*. During the intervening decades a mass of new evidence about that decision had come to light, and *Fat Man and Little Boy* drew on it, at times effectively. It also reflected (and no doubt was inspired by) the antinuclear upheaval of the early 1980s.

Roland Joffe, who had earlier directed *The Killing Fields,* set out to make an artful, complex picture that questioned the official narrative, while emphasizing the decency of the scientists who made the bomb. To complicate matters, he cast Paul Newman, a longtime arms-control activist (who had served in the Pacific war in 1945) as Leslie Groves. With Newman in the starring role, Groves would dominate the film, bullying or cajoling Oppenheimer, played by little-known Dwight Schultz, at every turn. Groves's desire to use the bomb to bolster his own career is transparent. We are meant to believe that without Groves riding herd on the scientists, there would have been no decision for Truman to make in 1945. When Oppenheimer expresses doubts about using the weapon, Groves snaps: *"Give* me the bomb! Just *give* it to me!"

Joffe dramatized all sides in the brief debate over the decision to use the bomb, but perhaps because of the weighty dialogue, the film was only occasionally riveting, and it did not approach the popularity of *The Killing*

Fields. Its final scene, however, was memorable: Oppenheimer in a parade, celebrating the Trinity test, waving to the other heroes of Los Alamos as his smile grows tighter and tighter. The camera pulls in close to his haunted eyes, a familiar image for anyone who has seen pictures of the real Oppenheimer late in his life.

But the key scene, and the one that would—inevitably—prove controversial, concerned the death of a young scientist from exposure to radiation. Joffe obviously wanted one character to represent the thousands of Americans who would later suffer from their encounters with radiation, so he backdated the real-life Daghlian accident so it would fall within the time frame of the movie. The incident in the film (like the one in real life) is kept hush-hush. This provokes the camp physician to complain to Oppenheimer that the reason for all the secrecy at Los Alamos was not to keep vital information from the enemy, but from Americans. Then the doctor blurts out that physicians at Oak Ridge *were injecting patients with plutonium.*

This statement was contested even before the film's release. Scientific advisers and cast members belittled its accuracy, and soon the press was on the case. One authority on this subject questioned the plutonium reference when he read the script. "Everyone understood by the end of the Second World War how extremely toxic plutonium is when injected into the body," he told the *New York Times.* "And if they wanted to study the effects after the war, they had two whole cities in which to do so. I'm sure nothing like that happened during the war."

On the defensive, Joffe cut a scene that actually showed a plutonium experiment but otherwise stuck to his story, attributing his information to a congressional investigation. This was the Markey subcommittee probe that first uncovered evidence about the radiation experiments, some of which, as we have seen, *did* take place before Hiroshima (including, as it happens, at Oak Ridge). The Markey findings had been ignored so completely that the scene in *Fat Man and Little Boy* seemed like science fiction. Four years later Joffe would look like a prophet. But at the time, the film suffered the fate of any serious challenge to the narrative: It was politicized, and thereby tainted.

The film received a mixed reception from critics. Vincent Canby of the *New York Times* observed that Groves expressed his sentiments so much more persuasively than anyone else that the film was "stunningly ineffective" in promoting director Joffe's obvious anti-bomb views.

. . .

Although only three major Hollywood features have explored the first atomic bombs, American audiences have been exposed to several foreign films on this subject, including Akira Kurosawa's *Rhapsody in August* and Shohei Imamura's *Black Rain*. The foreign film that gained the widest American audience was Alain Resnais' classic 1959 drama, *Hiroshima, Mon Amour*. A love story, with Hiroshima as a physical and emotional backdrop, it contained photographs and film footage of A-bomb victims, images rarely if ever seen before in the United States—and certainly not part of any of the Hollywood atomic-bomb movies.

Hiroshima, Mon Amour, and several films on this subject by Japanese directors, are original or highly imaginative and contain striking images. American directors exploring this subject seem bound to the docudrama form, a literal approach so inappropriate for this revolutionary and psychologically ambiguous event—and one that makes few emotional demands on its creators and the audience.

Although rarely at the center of American films, Hiroshima has influenced every "nuclear" movie. Two of the best, *Fail-Safe* and *Dr. Strangelove,* may reflect a displacement of Hiroshima guilt: they both show the U.S. launching unprovoked atomic attacks. Many "nonnuclear" films made after 1945 also bear the mark of Hiroshima. The feelings of futurelessness that Hiroshima evoked provided filmmakers as diverse as Ingmar Bergman and Roger Corman with a bleak theme and alienated tone for countless movies in the cold-war era.

The well-intentioned but dangerously naive scientist has become a stock character in modern movies. This, of course, is nothing new; witness *Frankenstein* from the early 1930s. But whereas the creations of earlier inventors once merely threatened a village, after Hiroshima they endangered the entire world. The metaphors derive partly from Hiroshima even in "nonnuclear" films. In the recent *Jurassic Park,* for example, a scientist condemns colleagues who have brought to life a pack of flesh-eating dinosaurs. They were "so preoccupied with whether or not they *could* they never stopped to ask whether they *should,*" he observes.

Susan Sontag, in her 1965 essay, "The Imagination of Disaster," declared that "a mass trauma exists over the use of nuclear weapons and the possibility of future nuclear wars." Most science-fiction films "bear witness to this trauma and, in a way, attempt to exorcise it." Within these films "lurk the deepest anxieties about contemporary existence. . . ." She could have been writing about the postholocaust films of the 1980s, such as the Mad Max series—or, as we will now see, the television movie *The Day After*.

THE DAY AFTER

Many television movies of the 1980s explored present or future nuclear threat, and three focused on Hiroshima: *Enola Gay, Day One,* and *Hiroshima: Out of the Ashes.* The films all lacked high artistic merit, but the chronological sequence is interesting. The first film, which supported the official version of Hiroshima, appeared in 1980 just before the nuclear-freeze movement swept the country; the other two, which reflected revisionist views, arrived afterward. Obviously, an alternative cultural sensibility had been building, beyond the official narrative's control. In the 1980s that viewpoint could emerge—even on a major television network.

Of all the TV movies, however, one stands out—and not just because it made use of actual Hiroshima images. *The Day After* was the most controversial TV film ever made. It drew record ratings when shown over the ABC network in 1983, partly because it coincided with a surge in antinuclear attitudes, but mainly because it had become a cause célèbre.

Well before it aired, antinuclear activists learned that *The Day After* would present viewers with a graphic portrayal of the aftermath of a Soviet nuclear attack on America, centered on the Kansas City area. This film, too, recognized American decency—but showed that this would not necessarily prevent a nuclear war. Soon, activists were publishing educational guides and organizing viewing parties in cities across the country. Conservative groups smelled trouble and started pressuring ABC for revisions in the movie—a precursor of the Smithsonian controversy a decade later. But what they objected to most was that this type of movie would be shown at all, for it might imperil President Reagan's nuclear buildup. ABC officials forced the director to make changes, but conservative groups continued to pressure sponsors to cancel their ads, and several did. Once again, defenders of the official narrative would not allow even an indirect challenge to be presented without the taint of controversy.

There was only one verbal reference to Hiroshima in *The Day After,* but it was pivotal. Early in the film, as the superpower conflict intensifies but before the bombs actually hit, a physician reveals that residents were already fleeing Kansas City—but did they really think they would be safer outside the city? "We are not talking about Hiroshima anymore," he declares. "Hiroshima was *peanuts.*" Later, this statement echoes in another character's mind when he is stricken with radiation disease.

Although *The Day After* did not reopen the debate over Hiroshima, it filled a void that had existed for nearly forty years. It made available to a mass audience, probably for the first time, vivid images of the effects of the bomb on ordinary people. When the bombs went off over Kansas City we saw the usual firestorms but we also witnessed the horrifying spectacle of incineration in a flash (a kind of X-ray effect). It is significant, however, that despite all the talent and money that went into special effects, the filmmakers often relied on visuals from Hiroshima, utilizing footage of the rubble from Herbert Sussan's recently declassified color film shot in 1946.

But as hard as they tried, the filmmakers could not come close to duplicating the human effects of the bomb. *The Day After*'s survivors shuffled along the highways, but they were merely cut and bruised. Burns did not cover half their bodies, as they had in Hiroshima and Nagasaki; flesh did not hang from their arms in sheets. We did not see rivers clogged with hundreds of burned bodies floating on the surface like dead fish. Few corpses appeared in *The Day After*. Two brief shots of charred bodies appeared to be photographs from Hiroshima—nightmare images Hollywood makeup artists could not hope (or want) to match. As bad as this postattack Kansas City was, Hiroshima was much worse. Nuclear holocaust remains impossible to render fully and therefore continues not to be fully felt. The filmmakers seemed to recognize this, adding a postscript to *The Day After* warning that what viewers had just seen was "in all likelihood, less severe than the destruction that would actually occur in the event of a full nuclear strike against the United States."

The most striking use of Hiroshima in the film occurred near the end when the central character, a physician played by Jason Robards, climbed to the top of a hill overlooking Kansas City to see what, if anything, remained of the city. He was greeted by a vast landscape of nothingness, dotted with an occasional building. For this effect, the filmmakers borrowed a familiar photograph of Hiroshima, taken from a hillside shortly after the bombing, and doctored it by adding puffs of smoke rising from its surface. Once again, the only suitable image came directly from Hiroshima.

Although *The Day After* did not challenge the decision to use the bomb against Japan, it called into question what evolved from the Hiroshima narrative: the notion that nuclear weapons were our salvation, not our doom. At the conclusion of *The Day After,* the U.S. still had nuclear weapons, but everyone was dead, or dying.

As it turned out, that wasn't quite the end. Sensitive to protests from the Reagan administration and its allies, ABC televised a panel discussion immediately after the airing of the film, heavily weighted with Washington insiders like George Shultz and Henry Kissinger. They argued that the bleak message of *The Day After* was actually an appeal for modernizing our nuclear arsenal so the Soviets would not dare attack us.

And so, *The Day After*—attacked from the right, scorned by sponsors, and ultimately compromised by the very network that aired it—proved to have little political impact, despite high ratings. Opinion polls showed that it changed few fundamental attitudes about nuclear weapons. Yet, as we learned later, its psychological impact on many individuals was powerful. Many interviewed in a study at the Center on Violence and Human Survival told of having derived their images of what nuclear war would be like from that movie, and very likely from its Hiroshima-derived visuals—for *The Day After* was the closest most viewers had ever come to Hiroshima.

Hiroshima in Fiction and Poetry

Television and cinema have slighted Hiroshima, but fiction has virtually ignored it. There is no major American novel about Hiroshima. Indeed, few American novels of any stature explore the consequences of using the atomic bomb. Only a handful of fiction writers have utilized Hiroshima or Los Alamos as a setting, or explored the emotions and attitudes of the scientists, the policy makers, or the airmen who dropped the bomb. The few novels that have approached the subject have all been forgotten.

"Hiroshima has had nothing like the literary impact of other great military events," Paul Brians recently observed in his book *Nuclear Holocausts: Atomic War in Fiction.* Brians chronicles over eight hundred "nuclear novels," most of them science fiction. Less than a dozen explore the building or use of the bomb; few of them sold particularly well or remained long in print. In contrast, Brians notes, some people read a dozen Civil War novels *every year,* and he asks: Where are the Hiroshima "buffs"?

There are reasons for this, of course, including moral ambivalence. "Evil has no place, it seems, in our national mythology," asserts Tim O'Brien, author of the novel *The Nuclear Age.* Another factor is the technological nature of the atomic attacks. The bombing of Japan may have been efficient but it was hardly "stirring"; it involved only a small group of airmen, not vast armies; and it was uncomfortably one-sided. Still, it can be said that, as with cinema, Hiroshima is everywhere in postwar and contemporary fiction—in its themes of futurelessness and absurdity, and its predilection for violent or vengeful behavior by heroes and antiheroes alike. One critic has observed that the "usual place" for Hiroshima in Western literature is "the unconscious."

Like Hiroshima films, Hiroshima fiction often seems inappropriate to the subject, treating a revolutionary event far too realistically. What happened to Hiroshima is impossible to make explicit. (One recalls Walt Whitman's comment on the Civil War: "The real war will never get into the books.") Of the few published novels, most focus on the scientists—not the decision makers, the pilots, or the Japanese victims.

If there are any major novels exploring the decision to drop the bomb, or the *Enola Gay*'s mission to Hiroshima, no bibliographer has yet uncovered them. Many novelists of the postwar era seemed to follow the advice of William Faulkner's 1950 Nobel Prize acceptance speech. Faulkner lamented that "the young man or woman writing today has forgotten the problems of the human heart in conflict with itself which alone can make good writing because only that is worth writing about, worth the agony and the sweat." There were no longer "problems of the spirit. There is only the question: When will I be blown up?" Faulkner offered this advice to the modern writer:

> He must teach himself that the basest of all things is to be afraid; and, teaching himself that, forget it forever, leaving no room in his workshop for anything but the old verities and truths of the heart . . . Until he does so, he labors under a curse.

Others, however, believed that the "curse" itself must *not* be forgotten but rather addressed, directly or subversively. Alfred Kazin wrote: "I don't care for novelists who ignore what H. G. Wells himself called the 'queerness' that has come into contemporary life since the bomb." Kazin scored the "dimness," "flatness," and "paltriness" of many reputable novelists, calling them "ways of escape" from the nuclear reality.

AGEE AND THE ETERNAL FUSE

The work of fiction most directly related to, and inspired by, Hiroshima—and certainly reflective of Kazin's notion of "queerness"—is a short story written by James Agee called "Dedication Day." Significantly, it was conceived in the immediate aftermath of Hiroshima, before the event was covered over and it was easier for a writer to act as witness. Agee wrote in a feverish rage. The day after the attack on Hiroshima, he informed a *Time* colleague that it was "the worst thing that ever happened—so far: anyhow, that it pretty thoroughly guarantees universal annihilation, within not many years." As an American, he felt he was personally implicated in the killing of thousands of civilians. It was Agee who wrote the first *Time* magazine essay on Hiroshima, which brilliantly (as we have seen) rendered the splitting of American conscience no less than the atom. A few days later, he started work on what he called "a story . . . about the atomic bomb." This subject was "the only thing much worth writing or thinking about."

A satirical fantasy, "Dedication Day" (which was published in Dwight Macdonald's *Politics* in 1946) depicts the postwar celebration of the bomb in which any attempt to atone for Hiroshima must be viewed as evidence of madness.

The time is 1946. A great arch designed by Frank Lloyd Wright, made of fused uranium and meant to mark "the greatest of human achievements," is about to be dedicated in Washington, D.C., near the Capitol. Reporters, generals, statesmen (including Truman and Conant), and enthusiastic citizens gather. Agee spares no aspect of the American way of life: advertising, religion, science, the military, psychiatry, art. Vendors sell Good Humor bars. Church leaders offer prayers. The first major television hookup in history carries the event to New York City. But all is not well. A pregnant woman faints and miscarries. A bugler, assigned to play "Reveille," feels impelled to play "Taps."

An Eternal Fuse—which symbolizes America's growing nuclear-weapons arsenal—will feed a memorial flame. Made of cotton, it burns so swiftly that it must be manufactured on the spot, in an "irradiated work-shop" directly beneath the arch. These keepers of the flame toil in twelve-hour shifts, behind glass, always under the gaze of tourists. One shift is made up of disabled American veterans. The other is composed of Japanese survivors "of the experiments at Hiroshima and Nagasaki," who had "been forgiven." The survivors have become a popular tourist attraction because of "those strange burns which have excited, in Americans, so much friendly curiosity."

The dedication ceremonies, however, are marred by "a pathetic incident." One of the scientists who invented the bomb, and had been seeking atonement ever since Hiroshima—which struck his colleagues as "a little queer in the head"—now insists on joining the Japanese custodians of the flame. To humor him, officials oblige. Tourists, watching him among the survivors, tearing at his hair and beating his face with his fists, try to cheer him up by flashing the V for Victory sign. Officials, feeling that "the intended dignity, charm, and decorum of the exhibit" is threatened, decide to send the scientist to a sanitarium. This he accepts, in return for being allowed to throw the switch that starts the burning of the Eternal Fuse. General Groves, who was to have performed this task, agrees to step aside.

Alas, a few minutes after he throws the switch, the scientist is found next to the great spool of cotton, dead, by his own hand. Pinned to his laboratory coat is a note revealing that "he regarded his suicide as obligatory—as, indeed, a kind of religious or ethical 'sacrifice,' through which he hoped to endow the triumphal monument with a new and special significance and . . . once more (as he thought) to assist the human race." As the scientist is buried with full honors at the Trinity site, philosophers and clergymen embark on a campaign of "controlled ridicule," pointing to the scientist as an object lesson for anyone "liable to the grievous error of exaggerated scrupulousness." Yet the narrator of Agee's story concludes that this view of the scientist was too harsh:

> For misguided and altogether regrettable though his last days were—a sad warning indeed to those who turn aside from the dictates of reason, and accept human progress reluctantly—he was nevertheless, perhaps, our last link with a not-too-distant past in which such con-

ceptions as those of "atonement," and "guilt," and "individual responsibility" still had significance.

Richly symbolic, if erratic, "Dedication Day" makes plain the "intensity and bitterness of Agee's feelings about the atomic bomb," Paul Boyer
has observed. "The story's topographical structure—official celebrations
aboveground contrasting with strange and disturbed goings-on under-
ground—metaphorically suggests his sense of the complexity and partially
hidden nature of the American response to the bomb." Yet the story
would find only a limited audience, and Agee lamented his inability to
turn it into a more complete work, in the end dubbing it a "Rough
Sketch for a Moving Picture." More than anything, it offers eloquent
evidence, according to Boyer, "of Agee's difficulty in translating anguish
and dread into literature." Few have made this kind of attempt, regarding
Hiroshima, since.

VONNEGUT AND SURVIVOR MEANING

Agee fared no better with two other projects he began and then abandoned: a nonfiction book on the bomb and a treatment for a nuclear
holocaust film, starring his friend Charles Chaplin (entitled *Scientists and
Tramp*). Few serious writers shared Agee's passion and sense of personal
connection to the atomic bombings. One who did was Kurt Vonnegut, Jr.

His book *Cat's Cradle,* published in 1963 shortly after the Cuban
missile crisis, is probably the only widely read novel overtly related to
Hiroshima. Many who read *Cat's Cradle* years ago probably still recall how
it ends: with crystals of a substance called ice-nine destroying the world.
Many forget how the book begins: with the narrator interviewing Americans about what they were doing on August 6, 1945 (he's writing a book
on this subject). This leads him to the children of Dr. Felix Hoenikker,
one of the inventors of the A-bomb, who, as it turns out, also created ice-
nine. Dr. Hoenikker doesn't have much use for people. When confronted
with Oppenheimer's notion that the atomic scientists had "known sin," he
replies: "What is sin?"

Vonnegut, educated as a chemist, based Hoenikker on the famous
scientist Irving Langmuir, whom he met when he worked at General
Electric after the war. "I want scientists to be more moral," Vonnegut

once told an interviewer. The end of the world, or of distant planets, due to human greed or miscalculation would figure prominently in many of his novels.

This is not surprising, because Vonnegut is probably the only major fiction writer who personally experienced a near-apocalypse: the firebombing of Dresden, which he witnessed as a prisoner of war. This inspired his most acclaimed novel, *Slaughterhouse Five,* and surely influenced his lifetime obsession with nuclear weapons, global self-destruction, and human conscience. The parallels between Dresden and Hiroshima are obvious. Vonnegut has said that in response to Dresden he became a pacifist. Later, he instructed his sons that they were not to take part in massacres or work for companies that make "massacre machinery"; further, "the news of massacres of enemies" was "not to fill them with satisfaction or glee."

Another response to the bombing of Dresden: Vonnegut no longer believed what his government said. After all, the U.S. had claimed that it was not bombing civilians in the war; and later, when Vonnegut tried to obtain information on what had actually happened in Dresden, he ran into a government stonewall. Told that this information was still top secret, Vonnegut exclaimed: "Secret? My God—from whom?"

Vonnegut was "sickened" by Hiroshima. Having observed city bombings in Europe, he knew immediately "what bullshit it was" when he heard Truman's reference to Hiroshima as a military base. He compares his reaction to that of "being a devout Christian and then seeing some horrible massacres conducted by Christians after a victory." In *Slaughterhouse Five,* Vonnegut quoted the first six paragraphs of Truman's August 6 announcement in their entirety—probably the widest airing this text had received since August 1945—and followed it with quotes by two Allied generals justifying the firebombing of Dresden as a "military necessity." Later, a fictional character comments on the Dresden raid: "Pity the men who had to *do* it."

Slaughterhouse Five is a survivor's effort to make sense of a world dominated by the threat of holocaust and the reality of numbing. It is about feeling and not feeling, about remembering and not remembering.

Like *Slaughterhouse Five,* Joseph Heller's *Catch-22* has never been considered a "nuclear" book, but its themes of absurd death and amoral bureaucracy could not be more relevant to Hiroshima. Catch-22 itself represents the dilemma facing all Americans in a nuclear era of secrecy and powerlessness: "Catch-22 says they have a right to do anything we can't stop them from doing." This includes ordering the use of nuclear weapons. As Heller shows, the American airmen in World War II had as much to fear from their own generals as they did from the enemy: an apt metaphor for the nuclear age.

The essence of both *Catch-22* and *Slaughterhouse Five,* Alfred Kazin observed, is that though both are ostensibly about World War II, "they are really about The Next War, and thus about a war that will be without limits and without meaning, a war that will end only when no one is alive to fight it." In *Closing Time,* his recent sequel to *Catch-22,* Heller made this manifest. He portrayed General Leslie Groves engaged in a project to build an attack plane that flies so fast "you can bomb someone yesterday." An admiral asks arms merchant Milo Minderbinder if it can destroy the world. "I'm afraid not, sir," he replies. "We can make it uninhabitable, but we can't destroy it." "I can live with that!" the admiral replies.

This, in a sense, has been the grim message of countless postapocalypse novels: Ray Bradbury's *The Martian Chronicles* (1950), Nevil Shute's *On the Beach* (1957), Russell Hoban's *Riddley Walker* (1980), Bernard Malamud's *God's Grace* (1982), and Denis Johnson's *Fiskadoro* (1985), among others, as well as accidental nuclear war novels such as *Fail-Safe* (1962). By now, the publishing pattern is predictable: nuclear novels appear when the bomb appears most threatening (for example, the fallout scare and "missile gap" of the late 1950s and early 1960s) and virtually disappear when the terror subsides. "The all-time high point of nuclear war fiction," according to Paul Brians, was 1984—not coincidentally a time of antinuclear fervor. But that trend quickly collapsed. Not much prose on this subject has appeared since the mid-1980s. And even at its high-water mark, nuclear fiction evaded Hiroshima.

HIROSHIMA POETRY

In contrast, a number of major poets have written brilliantly on nuclear concerns, and they have invoked Hiroshima far more often than the novelists. This is especially significant when one considers that the tradition of political poetry in this country was "very, very thin" until Vietnam, as Galway Kinnell has observed. The subject of nuclear war is "inherently very difficult," Kinnell explains. "If a poem is to be useful, it has to give hope, but if it is to be realistic, it has to cause despair. Despair is built into the subject."

American poets have applied themselves to Hiroshima more imaginatively and persistently than filmmakers and fiction writers, perhaps because they are not constrained by the historical or documentary narrative common to those other forms of expression. They can attempt to get at the meaning of Hiroshima in a more personal, creative, imagistic, even fractured way—an approach the event practically demands. *Atomic Ghosts,* a 1995 anthology, includes more than one hundred "nuclear" poems, with many (written by well-known poets such as Philip Levine, Mary Jo Salter, and Denise Levertov) relating specifically to Hiroshima.

Shortly after Hiroshima, Randall Jarrell informed a friend that he felt "so rotten about the country's response" to the atomic bombings that he wished he could become "a naturalized cat or dog." That year (in "Losses") he wrote of men in "bombers named for girls" carrying out missions to burn cities to the ground. The following year (in "1945: The Death of the Gods") he pondered the end of the world "when rockets rise like stars." Robert Frost, in "U.S. 1946 King's X," observed the hypocrisy of those who "invented a new Holocaust" yet believed that no other country had the right to use the bomb. John Berryman (in "The Dispossessed") considered individual versus collective guilt for Hiroshima and Nagasaki.

Years passed, but prominent poets would not let go of Hiroshima. Robert Penn Warren's poem "New Dawn" rendered the flight of the *Enola Gay* in a dispassionate, documentary-like manner. Beat poets, on the other hand, railed angrily, vulgarly, against the bomb in the 1950s, but rarely invoked Hiroshima.

In the late 1980s, Marc Kaminsky created a cycle of poems about *hibakusha* called "The Road from Hiroshima." Campbell McGrath examined how the atomic bombings had psychologically affected his entire generation in "Nagasaki, Uncle Walt, the Eschatology of America's Century," noting that young people had "invested so much in World War III it seems a shame to miss it."

Also in the 1980s, two prominent poets, Galway Kinnell and Carolyn Forché, made highly significant visits to Hiroshima and Nagasaki. Already antinuclear in spirit, they achieved a more direct artistic witness in the two cities. Indeed, the subtle brilliance of the poems that resulted shows the value, even the necessity, of such witness in exploring what happened in Hiroshima. "One of the things I've learned," Kinnell said afterward, "is that if one doesn't feel despair, one has not really understood what's happened in the world. From now on, it is certain that a kind of despair has to be a component of hope." That sense is expressed in the powerful poem "The Fundamental Project of Technology," which grew out of his visit, marked by the memorable repetition of the phrase "a white flash sparkled."

"We are the poets of the Nuclear Age," Carolyn Forché exclaimed in 1984, shortly after returning from Hiroshima, "perhaps the last poets, and some of us fear what the Muse is telling us. Some of us are finding it harder to write. . . . There is no metaphor for the end of the world and it is horrible to search for one." Nevertheless, she would compose one of the most haunting poems about Hiroshima, "The Garden Shukkei-en." An American visits a place in Hiroshima with a survivor who "has always been afraid to come here." Forché writes:

> It is the river she most
> remembers, the living
> and the dead both crying for help.

The poem ends, however, with the hopeful line, "it is the bell to awaken God that we've heard ringing." Forché is telling us that Hiroshima can provide illumination, can "awaken God," and that the Hiroshima bell tolls for everyone. That is precisely the message Americans have resisted for so long and must now address after fifty years have passed.

NOTES

We conducted original research for this book at the Truman Library in Independence, Missouri; the National Archives in Washington, D.C.; the Columbia University Oral History Collection, The Museum of Television and Radio, and The New York Times Archives in New York City; the University of Southern California Cinema-Television Library and the UCLA Research Library (special Collections) in Los Angeles, California; and other libraries and archives.

Lengthy interviews conducted specifically for this book (during 1994) include those with McGeorge Bundy, Ted Conant, Gerald Holton, and Philip Morrison. We had briefer interviews with many other individuals, including prominent scholars, officials at the National Air and Space Museum in Washington, D.C., and representatives of veterans' groups. We also drew on many prior interviews from years of researching and writing about nuclear issues: with Erik Barnouw, Hans Bethe, Richard Garwin, Daniel McGovern, Herbert Sussan, Theodore Taylor, Paul Tibbets, and Herbert York, among others; with more than one hundred atomic-bomb survivors in Japan; and with various American and Japanese authorities on the atomic bombings. Oral histories consulted included those of Gordon Aneson, Eben Ayers, Harvey Bundy, James B. Conant, George Elsey, William L. Laurence, Henry Stimson, and Paul Tibbets. Particularly useful were the typed notes of interviews conducted by Lansing Lamont for his book *Day of Trinity* (now at the Truman Library). We also consulted the critically important diary of Henry L. Stimson, available on microfilm at the Truman Library.

A NOTE ON ABBREVIATIONS:
TL: Truman Library, Independence, Missouri. OF: Official File. PSF: President's Secretary's File. PPF: Post-Presidential File. PPFM: Post-Presidential Files, Memoirs (includes transcripts of interviews with Truman, drafts, and other material used in preparation of his 1953 *Memoirs).*

Groves Top-Secret: Files (on microfilm) labeled "Top Secret-Special Interest to General Groves," part of general records of Manhattan Engineering District (Manhattan Project) at the Modern Military Branch of the National Archives in Washington, D.C.

Introduction

xii George Will on ABC's "This Week with David Brinkley," 28 August 1994.

xiv "America was not": Barton Bernstein, "The Atomic Bombings Reconsidered," *Foreign Affairs*, January/February 1995, 152.

xv "Seldom, if ever": Edward R. Murrow radio broadcast, 12 September 1945, from Edward R. Murrow, *In Search of Light* (New York: Knopf, 1967).

xv "pride that begot blindness": Lewis Mumford, "Atom Bomb: 'Miracle or Catastrophe', *Air Affairs*, July 1948, 326.

xv McCarthy in her letter to *Politics*, November 1946.

xv Lapp, from Paul Boyer, *By the Bomb's Early Light* (New York: Pantheon, 1985), 182.

xvi "The world never": from his poem "Letter to Simic from Boulder." Gallup poll results: survey conducted in November 1994 for America's Talking cable network.

Part I—Chapter 1

3 At the White House, described in Eben Ayers oral history, Truman Library, 42–47.

4 Original text of Truman announcement in "Top Secret–Special Interest to General Groves," Manhattan Engineering District Papers, Modern Military Branch, National Archives.

4 Background on preparing the announcement in Vincent C. Jones, *Manhattan: The Army and the Bomb* (Washington: Center of Military History, U.S. Army, 1985). Also: Gordon Arneson oral history, Truman Library; Leslie R. Groves, *Now It Can Be Told* (New York: Harper, 1962); W. L. Laurence oral history, Columbia University Oral History Collection.

4 Sent to Potsdam: Arneson oral history, 14–16. The original statement was dated June 29, 1945, and named as the target "the Nagasaki Naval Base."

4 "The reason for the haste," from Stimson letter to Truman, 31 July 1945, with edited copy of announcement, TL-PSF 199. Truman approval in Stimson memo to Truman (from White House Map Room), 6 August 1945, TL-PSF, 199.

4 Groves's efforts, and Marshall, in Groves, *Now It Can Be Told*, 321–31.

5 Details added to original text in Groves Top-Secret.

5 Soldiers in Hiroshima and overall population documented in Committee for the Compilation of Materials on Damage Caused by the Atomic Bombs, eds., *Hiroshima and Nagasaki: The Physical, Medical, and Social Effects of the Atomic Bombings* (New York: Basic Books, 1981).

5 There is no record of Groves cabling the final changes to Truman for approval, but it may have happened.

6 "Grand Slam" inserted after final draft sent to Truman by Stimson on July 31.

Part I—Chapter 2

8 "an impenetrable cloud": *New York Times*, August 7, 1945.

8 "was essentially": Lang, *From Hiroshima to the Moon* (New York: Simon & Schuster, 1959).

9 Thomas, Goddard, Kaltenborn all quoted in Boyer, *By the Bomb's Early Light*, 4–5.

9 "We whooped" quoted in George Feifer, *Tennozan* (New York: Ticknor & Fields, 1992), 567.

9 Bradbury quoted in Boyer, 257.

9 Mumford reaction from Donald L. Miller, *Lewis Mumford: A Life* (New York: Weidenfeld and Nicholson, 1989), 431.

9 Maxwell Anderson quoted in *The Atomic Age Opens* (New York: Pocket, 1945), 45.

10 Fourteen releases listed in Groves Top-Secret. Apparently, only statements by Truman and Stimson were to be released on August 6, but Groves's usual enthusiasm could not be checked. Late on August 6, Stimson's office ordered a halt to the flow of releases "until they had been cleared." ("Memo for the Record," by "W.H.K.," from files accompanying Gordon Arneson oral history, Truman Library.)

10 "the birth of a new age" in report by General Thomas H. Farrell on Trinity test, included in War Department release, 6 August 1945, in Groves Top-Secret.

10 "most newspapers": Jones, *Manhattan: The Army and the Bomb*.

10 "unprecedented . . . ," in War Department press release on Trinity test, 6 August 1945.

10 "fabulous achievement": ibid.

11 "Grand Slam": *San Francisco Chronicle*, 7 August 1945.

11 Cartoon and power station in *New York Journal-American*, 7 August 1945.

11 "We didn't want MacArthur . . .": Lansing Lamont, *Day of Trinity* (New York: Atheneum, 1965), 305.

11 "suitable newspaperman": Groves memo to chief of staff, 26 March 1945, in Groves Top-Secret.

11 "the project will be," ibid.

12 "unquenchable": miscellaneous Catledge papers, New York Times Archives.

12 "the Atomic Age": War Department release on Trinity, 6 August 1945.

13 "long before it was more than a gleam . . .": William L. Laurence, oral history interviews by Louis M. Starr, 1956–57, and by Scott Bruns, 1964, Columbia University Oral History Collection. Unless otherwise indicated, the quotations and general information in this section come from this source.

13 "a revolutionary discovery" through "a frightened man": Laurence, *Dawn Over Zero: The Story of the Atomic Bomb*, (New York: Knopf, 1947), Introduction, vii.

13 "by direct order of Hitler . . . ,": *Saturday Evening Post* article, 7 September 1940, "The Atom Gives Up," reprinted in *The Atomic Age Opens*, 132–33.

13 "active war service" *through* "Thus began my journey. . . . no one had ever thought possible": *Dawn Over Zero*, Introduction, x, xii.

14 "The story is much bigger" *through* "provided eyewitness survives,": *Dawn Over Zero*, Introduction, xiii, xiv, 4, xii.

14 "And just at that instant . . ." *through* "to me, who saw . . . a new world": *Dawn Over Zero* (1946 edition), 10–11. 4, 271.

16 "Prometheus had broken . . . down to earth": *Dawn Over Zero*, 3, 11.

16 "I had a fairly good notion . . . first test in New Mexico": *Dawn Over Zero*, 3, 13, 271, 207.

16 "Being close to it . . . earth tremble for many miles?" *through* "watching the atomists working . . . or anyone else for that matter": *Dawn Over Zero*, 23–24.

17 "We are on our way to bomb . . . 4,000 B-29 superbombers": *Dawn Over Zero*, 228.

18 "the giant flash that . . . incredulous eyes . . .": *Dawn Over Zero*, 236–37.

19 "too detailed, highly exaggerated, even phoney": Hewlett and Anderson, *A History of the United States Atomic Energy Commission: The New World* (University Park: Penn State University Press, 1962).

19 "a new Promised Land . . . the world has never seen": original Lawrence draft, Groves Top-Secret.

19 "an emotional celebration . . . civic journalism far behind": Robert Karl Manoff, "Covering the Bomb: The Nuclear Story and the News," *Working Papers*, May–June 1983, 22.

Part I—Chapter 3

23 Report from *Augusta: New York Times,* 7 August 1945.

23 "The experiment": *Newsweek,* 20 August 1945, 31.

23 "This is the greatest thing," quoted in Peter Wyden, *Day One* (New York: Simon & Schuster, 1989), 289.

24 60 percent figure stated in *New York Times,* 7 August 1945.

24 Aerial photo published ibid, 10 August 1945.

24 Parsons and Tibbets: ibid, 8 August 1945.

24 Footnote: report of Joint Target Group, 1 September 1945, Groves Top-Secret.

24 "However much we deplore": *Washington Post,* 9 August 1945.

24 "Being merciless": *Chicago Tribune,* 11 August 1945.

25 "too numerous": *New York Times,* 9 August 1945.

25 Eyewitness account: ibid, 11 August 1945.

25 "trying to establish": ibid, 9 August 1945.

25 Cartoon in *New York Journal American,* 8 August 1945.

25 "crime against God": quoted in *New York Times,* 9 August 1945.

25 Hutchins quote: from *Atomic Age Opens,* 206.

26 Oxnam and Dulles call: *New York Times,* 10 August 1945.

26 "may yet reap": ibid, 7 August 1945.

26 This scene is documented in Eben Ayers's diary and oral history, both at Truman Library.

26 "showed his pleasure": Ayers's handwritten notes of meeting, TL-Ayers papers, Box 4.

27 "mentioned the terrible": Stimson's "Memorandum of Conference with the President, August 8, 1945": TL-Vertical File.

27 Text of speech in *New York Times,* 10 August 1945.

27 Drafts of speech in speech file, TL-PSF.

28 Punishing Hirohito described in Bar-

ton Bernstein, "The Perils and Politics of Surrender: Ending the War with Japan and Avoiding the Third Atomic Bomb," *Pacific Historical Review,* February 1977.

28 Murrow: 12 August 1945, radio broadcast, from Murrow, *In Search of Light.*

29 "I'd like to fly over there": quoted in *Time,* 20 August 1945, 22.

29 Russell to Truman, 7 August 1945; Truman to Russell, 9 August 1945, TL-OF 197.

29 "the growing feeling" cited in Lawrence S. Wittner, *One World or None* (Stanford: Stanford University Press, 1993), 248.

29 Barton Bernstein, "An Analysis of Two Cultures," *Public Historian* 12, no. 2 (Spring 1990), 10.

30 Response at Los Alamos and Oppenheimer from Wyden, *Day One,* 289–290. Groves-Oppenheimer call from Richard Rhodes, *The Making of the Atomic Bomb* (New York: Simon & Schuster, 1986), 735.

30 "One down" from Edward Teller with Allen Brown, *The Legacy of Hiroshima* (Garden City: Doubleday, 1962), 18.

31 Frisch recalled the scene in his *What Little I Remember* (Cambridge: Cambridge University Press, 1979), 176.

31 Frank Oppenheimer interviewed in the documentary film, *The Day after Trinity,* produced and directed by Jon Else.

31 Szilard letter from William Lanouette, *Genius in the Shadows: A Biography of Leo Szilard* (New York: Scribner's, 1992).

31 Bethe interviewed by Lifton.

31 Rhodes, *The Making of the Atomic Bomb.*

32 This proved: Bernstein, "The Perils and Politics of Surrender," 26.

32 Krock in the *New York Times,* 15 August 1945.

32 Footnote: Speech file, TL.

33 Ciardi in Studs Terkel, *"The Good War"* (New York: Ballantine, 1985), 197.

33 Styron article, "The Enduring Metaphors of Auschwitz and Hiroshima,"

appeared in *Newsweek*, 11 January 1993, 28–29.

33 Roper results in Boyer, *By the Bomb's Early Light*, 183.

33 Gallup results in *The Gallup Poll* (New York: Random House, 1971) 521–22.

33 Gallup: ibid, 527.

34 O'Neill from his *A Democracy at War* (New York: The Free Press, 1993).

34 Americans did not learn . . .: *New York Times*, 27 August 1945.

35 "relative to it": *Time*, 20 August 1945, 19.

35 "a primitive fear": *Saturday Review*, 18 August 1945, 7; "For the first time": the *New Yorker*, 18 August 1945, 13; "A single airplane": *U.S. News*, 17 August 1945; "a fresh page": *Life*, 20 August 1945, 17; "Man had been tossed": *Time*, 20 August 1945, 29.

36 "no answer": from *Nation*, 18 August 1945, 149.

36 "it could justly be argued" in *The New Republic*, 20 August 1945, 222.

37 "so fearsome": *New Yorker*, 18 August 1945, 13.

37 Macdonald in his magazine *Politics*, August–September 1945, 225, 257–60.

37 "What Hath Man Wrought!": in *U.S. News*, 17 August 1945. Lawrence was also editor (and would remain so for more than twenty-five years).

37 "A Curious Chronology": *U.S. News*, 31 August 1945.

38 "then, without warning . . .": *Commonweal*, 24 August 1945, 443; At the end of August: *Commonweal*, 31 August 1945; 468.

38 "Prometheus": *Life*, 20 August 1945, 32.

Part I—Chapter 4

40 "We know" and poll results in *Fortune*, December 1945.

40 Jacobson story appeared in *New York Journal American*, 8 August 1945, 1.

41 Pentagon response in "Memorandum for the Press," 8 August 1945, TL-PSF 227.

41 Military officials' visit described in *New York Times* and *New York Journal American*, 9 August 1945.

41 "Many of those": *New York Times*, 23 August 1945.

41 "ghost parade": ibid, 25 August 1945.

42 "Experts on Japanese propaganda": ibid.

42 *Philadelphia Bulletin* article censorship noted in Herbert N. Foerstel, *Secret Science* (Westport, Conn.: Praeger, 1993), 58.

42 "make certain" in Groves message to Marshall, 24 August 1945, Groves Top-Secret.

42 Radiation precautions described in Spencer Weart, *Nuclear Fear* (Cambridge: Harvard University Press, 1988).

42 Frisch in 1939: Rhodes, *The Making of the Atomic Bomb*.

43 "for radiological reasons": Oppen-

heimer memo to Farrell, 11 May 1945, Groves Top-Secret.

43 Pre-Trinity preparations in Wyden, *Day One*; Groves, *Now It Can Be Told*; Lamont, *Day of Trinity*; Rhodes, *The Making of the Atomic Bomb*.

43 Drifting fallout in Catherine Caufield, *Multiple Exposures* (New York: Harper & Row, 1991), 59–61.

43 "just damn lucky," quoted in Jonathan Weisgall, *Operation Crossroads: The Atomic Tests at Bikini Atoll* (Naval Institute Press, 1994), 209.

43 "We must keep": Lamont, *Day of Trinity*, 240.

44 Oppenheimer ordered secrecy, in Caufield, *Multiple Exposures*, 61.

44 Kodak discovery described in *New York Times*, 30 October and 1 November 1945.

44 Footnote: from K. D. Nichols, *The Road to Trinity* (New York: William Morrow, 1987).

45 Leahy's beliefs expressed in his *I Was There* (New York: Whittlesey House, 1950), 441.

45 Telex to Groves and reply in Wyden, *Day One*, 18–19.

45 Full transcripts of two Groves-Rea conversations, 25 August 1945, 9 A.M. and 10:50 A.M., in Groves Top-Secret.

46 "The atomic bomb": *New York Times,* 31 August 1945, 4.

46 "Any person with": Wyden, *Day One,* 16.

46 See Nichols's account in his *Road to Trinity,* 223.

47 MacArthur and censorship fully described in Monica Braw, *The Atomic Bomb Suppressed: American Censorship in Occupied Japan* (Armonk, N.Y.: M. E. Sharpe, 1991). Occupation files were not declassified until 1977.

47 Burchett trip to Hiroshima described in Wilfred Burchett, *Shadows of Hiroshima* (London: Verso, 1983); also Ben Kiernan, ed., *Burchett: Reporting the Other Side of the World* (London: Quartet Books, 1986), 13–40.

47 Hachiya account in his *Hiroshima Diary* (Chapel Hill: University of North Carolina Press, 1955).

47 "In Hiroshima": Burchett, *Shadows of Hiroshima,* 34.

48 Lawrence article in *New York Times,* 5 September 1945.

49 Lawrence's memoir was *Six Presidents, Too Many Wars* (New York: Saturday Review Press, 1972).

49 Footnote: Gay Talese, *The Kingdom and the Power* (New York: World Publishing, 1969), 127.

49 MacArthur orders reporters out: Braw, *The Atomic Bomb Suppressed.*

50 Weller account in anthology, David Brown and W. Richard Bruner, eds., *How I Got That Story* (Overseas Press Club, 1967), 209–27.

51 "Make us look": Michael Sherry, *The Rise of American Air Power* (New Haven: Yale University Press, 1987), 346.

51 Byrnes's "torture" report analyzed in *Time,* 17 September 1945.

51 "This might be": Ross memo to Lieutenant Colonel B. W. Davenport, 27 August 1945; reply: "Myrtle" to Ross, 28 August 1945, TL-Ross Papers.

52 Laurence account in *New York Times,* 12 September 1945.

52 "oddly reassuring": *New York Times,* 16 September 1945.

52 "Japanese in Hiroshima": *Life,* 24 September 1945.

52 Footnote: Stout's story was told in an NBC-TV documentary, "Footnotes on the Atomic Age," which is briefly described in Jack Shaheen, ed., *Nuclear War Films* (Carbondale: Southern Illinois University Press, 1978), 116–17; and in Thomas H. Saffer and Orville Kelly, *Countdown Zero* (New York: Putnam, 1982), 203–4.

53 Background on mission in Farrell memo to Groves, 27 September 1945, published in Anthony Cave Brown and Charles B. Macdonald, eds., *The Secret History of the Atomic Bomb* (New York: Delta, 1977), 529–39.

53 "our mission was to prove": Weisgall, *Operation Crossroads,* 210.

53 Morrison and Tsuzuki (and other details on the mission): Daniel Lang, "A Reporter at Large," *New Yorker,* 8 June 1946, 62–72; also: Wyden, *Day One,* 323–24.

54 "the number was": *New York Times,* 12 September 1945.

54 "an unusual mixture . . .": Lang, "A Reporter at Large," 62.

54 "alter ego": notes of Farrell interview, Lansing Lamont papers, Truman Library.

54 Farrell press conference covered by *New York Times,* 13 September 1945 and 16 September 1945.

54 Limits of survey revealed in Nichols, *Road to Trinity,* 218–19.

54 "any conclusions": Groves report to Colonel H. P. Gibson, 17 September 1945, Groves Top-Secret.

55 7 to 8 percent: Wyden, *Day One,* 325.

55 "told the truth": *New York Times,* 13 September 1945.

55 Burchett returns: Burchett, *Shadows of Hiroshima.*

55 Truman note to editors: A. D. Surles (War Dept.) to Charles Ross (White House), 13 September, and Truman statement, 14 September 1945, TL-OF 692-A.

55 Burchett's expulsion: Burchett, *Shadows of Hiroshima.*

56 American POWs cover-up: *New York Times,* 22 August 1979; Robert Karl Manoff, "American Victims of Hiroshima," *New York Times Magazine,* 2 December 1984; Wyden, *Day One;* Dan Kurzman, *Day of the Bomb* (New York: McGraw-Hill, 1986). Martin Sherwin and Barton Bernstein both played key roles in bringing the "cover-up" to light in the late 1970s.

56 Occupation censorship: Braw, *The Atomic Bomb Suppressed.*

56 "a maliciously false": Lawrence S. Wittner, *One World or None,* 47.

57 Background on filming: interview with Barnouw by G. Mitchell; Barnouw, "The Hiroshima-Nagasaki Footage," *Historical Journal of Film, Radio and Television* 2, no. 1 (1982); official documents furnished exclusively to G. Mitchell by McGovern.

57 McGovern advised, in his memo to Lieutenant Commander Woodward, 29 December 1945.

58 Headline in *New York Times,* 18 May 1967.

58 "It was a revelation": Barnouw interviewed by G. Mitchell in 1983.

59 McGovern interviewed by G. Mitchell in 1983.

59 *Herald-Tribune:* in 4 September 1945 issue.

60 Luce quoted in *Life,* December 1972, 128.

60 *Life* photos in 17 September 1945 issue.

60 Japanese soldier set on fire in *Life,* 13 August 1945.

60 Truman and photos: Arnold sent memo and package to Truman, October 25,

acknowledged by Truman, same day, TL-OF 692-A.

60 "The world": *Life,* September 29, 1952.

60 Matsushige interviewed by G. Mitchell in 1984. Also, G. Mitchell, "The Photographer and the Flash," *The Progressive,* August 1990.

61 "When Atom Bomb Struck": *Life,* 29 September 1952.

62 Background on Daghlian and Slotin in Richard L. Miller, *Under the Cloud* (New York: Free Press, 1986), 66–69. Also: *The Greenpeace Book of the Nuclear Age* (New York: Pantheon, 1989), 63–73; "The Strange Death of Louis Slotin," Stewart Alsop and Ralph Lapp, *Saturday Evening Post,* 6 March 1954; Clifford Honicker, "The Hidden Files," *New York Times Magazine,* 19 November 1989; interview with Philip Morrison by Lifton, 1994.

62 Insurance check offer from Daghlian file at Los Alamos National Laboratory archives.

62 "first peacetime victim": *Time,* 10 June 1946.

63 "as a symbol": interview with Morrison by Lifton.

63 Army release in *New York Times,* 25 May 1946, 30.

63 Eight days after the accident: Robert Jungk, *Brighter Than a Thousand Suns* (New York: Harcourt, 1958), 229.

63 "Hero of Los Alamos": *Time,* 10 June 1946.

64 Memo from Colonel O. G. Haywood, Jr. (Corps of Engineers) to "Dr. Fidler" of the AEC, 17 April 1947.

64 A study would later show: described in Caufield, *Multiple Exposures,* 63.

Part I—Chapter 5

65 Szilard comment in the *Nation,* 22 December 1945, 718.

65 "the people of": *New York Times,* 31 August 1945.

65 "pleasant way to die": Groves statement in transcript of Senate Hearings, "Atomic Energy Act of 1945," 37.

66 "frankly pleased": Alice K. Smith, *A Peril and a Hope* (Chicago: University of Chicago Press, 1965), 80.

66 "an intensely personal": ibid, 77.

66 Oppenheimer on the scientists: George L. Harrison, "Memo for the Files," 25 September 1945. TL-Arneson

files which accompany his oral history.

66 "assumed for themselves": Laura Fermi, *Atoms in the Family* (Chicago: University of Chicago Press, 1954), 241.

66 Best sources on the scientists' movement are previously cited books by Alice K. Smith, Boyer, and Wittner. Survey described in Smith, 79.

67 "water over the dam": Boyer, *By the Bomb's Early Light*, 193.

67 Szilard request in his letter to Compton, 6 August 1945. TL-PSF 199.

67 Response to Szilard from Lanouette, *Genius in the Shadows*.

67 Threats against Szilard: ibid; and Wittner, *One World or None*, 264–65. At the Interim Committee meeting of May 31, 1945, Groves stated that the bomb project had been "plagued" by certain scientists of "doubtful discretion and uncertain loyalty." According to the official minutes, "It was *agreed* that nothing could be done about dismissing these men until after the bomb has actually been used. . . . After some publicity concerning the weapon was out, steps should be taken to sever these scientists from the program. . . ."

67 Administration and activists: see A. K. Smith; *A Peril and a Hope*.

68 Baldwin in *New York Times*, 12 September 1945, 4.

68 Oppenheimer memo to secretary of war, 17 August 1945, Groves Top-Secret.

68 Byrnes's response in George L. Harrison, "Memo for the Record," 18 August 1945, TL-Arneson files with oral history.

69 "long and painful thoughts": Kai Bird, *The Chairman: John J. McCloy and the Making of the American Establishment* (New York: Simon & Schuster, 1992).

69 Stalin remark from David Holloway, *Stalin and the Bomb* (New Haven: Yale University Press, 1994).

69 Stimson memo found in TL-PSF 112. Discussed in (among other places) Richard G. Hewlett and Oscar Anderson, *A History of the United States Atomic Energy Commission: The New World*, 418–20.

69 Acheson's views in his memo to Truman, 25 September 1945, TL-PSF.

69 Allison incident in Smith, *A Peril and a Hope*, 88; Hewlett & Anderson, *A History of the United States Atomic Energy Commission*, 422.

70 "policy of abridging": Smith, *A Peril and a Hope*, 8.

70 "catch up with us" from *NY Times*, 9 October 1945, 1.

70 "armaments race is on": Gregg Herken, *The Winning Weapon* (New York: Knopf, 1981), 39. The friend was Fyke Farmer.

70 "atomic diplomacy": *New York Times*, 17 November 1945.

71 "they alone": Smith, *A Peril and a Hope*, 142.

71 "a profound grief": in Oppenheimer letter to Lawrence, 30 August 1945, published in Alice K. Smith and Charles Weiner, eds., *Robert Oppenheimer: Letters and Recollections* (Cambridge: Harvard University Press, 1980), 301.

72 Urey in *New York Times*, 30 November 1945.

72 "If atomic bombs": Peter Goodchild, *J. Robert Oppenheimer: Shatterer of Worlds* (New York: Houghton-Mifflin, 1980).

72 "I never saw a man": *The Price of Vision: The Diary of Henry A. Wallace* (Boston: Houghton-Mifflin, 1973).

73 Details on *One World or None*: Boyer, *By the Bomb's Early Light*.

73 *The Beginning or the End* background: production files, Cinema-Television Library, University of Southern California. Although others have written about this film, we had access to the earliest production notes and scripts, and uncovered new letters to and from the White House, and script fragments, at the Truman Library (see appendix).

73 Tomkins, Truman, Marx quotes: ibid.

74 Bush remark in his letter to Charles Ross (Truman's secretary), 20 May 1946, TL-OF, 73.

74 "always within the bounds": in Carter

Barron letter to Truman, 21 November 1945, TL-PSF Box 112.

74 Groves's demands in Nathan Reingold, *Science, American Style* (Rutgers University Press, 1991), 336.

74 *March of Time* review in *Time*, 12 August 1946, 23.

Part I—Chapter 6

75 de Seversky quoted in *New York Times*, 3 November 1945.

76 "a terrifying": *Newsweek*, 17 December 1945, 37.

76 All quotes from testimony: *New Republic*, 11 February 1946, 177–80.

76 Background on testimony: Morrison interviewed by Lifton in 1994.

77 "extraordinary document": *Time*, 11 February 1946.

77 "funeral processions": for complete Siemes text, see Brown and MacDonald, *Secret History*.

77 Mumford background in *Lewis Mumford: A Life*, 431.

78 Essay appeared in *Saturday Review*, 2 March 1946, 5–6.

79 "fear psychosis": quote from Boyer, *By the Bomb's Early Light*.

79 Article based on visit appeared in *New York Times* on February 25, 1946.

79 "American soldier good": *Time*, 15 July 1946.

79 Air show depicted in *Los Angeles Times*, 26 and 28 October 1945.

80 Footnote: Oxnam and Dulles letter to Truman, 22 August 1945, TL-OF 692-A.

80 Council report analyzed in *New York Times*, 6 March 1946; excerpts in *U.S. News*, 22 March 1946.

81 Compton from *New York Times*, 7 March 1946.

81 Conant-Niebuhr exchange drawn from James Hershberg, *James B. Conant: Harvard to Hiroshima and the Making of the Nuclear Age* (New York: Knopf, 1993), 284–85.

81 Sheen comment from *New York Times*, 8 April 1946.

81 Lawrence from *U.S. News* editorial, 1 March 1946.

82 Nitze's role in Strobe Talbott, *The Mas-*

ter of the Game (New York: Knopf, 1988), 37–39; and Paul Nitze, *From Hiroshima to Glasnost* (New York: Grove Weidenfeld, 1989), 40–45.

82 Galbraith describes his work in his book, *A Life in Our Times* (Boston: Houghton-Mifflin, 1981), 225–33.

83 Report reprinted in *U.S. News*, 5 July 1946.

83 Footnote: Gar Alperovitz, "Why the United States Dropped the Bomb," *Technology Review* (August/September 1990): 28.

83 Baldwin in *New York Times*, 3 July 1946.

84 "So we strive": R. G. Swing radio broadcast.

85 Laurence in *New York Times*, 1 July 1946.

85 Cousins: *Saturday Review*, 29 June and 10 August 1946.

85 "curiosity": *Time*, 5 August 1946.

85 Test Baker results from Weisgall, *Operation Crossroads*.

85 "It was Bikini" from Boyer, *By the Bomb's Early Light*.

85 Laurence in *New York Times*, 4 August 1946.

86 Hersey article in *New Yorker*, 31 August 1946.

86 "I felt I would": a rare interview with Hersey on this subject in *Antaeus Report* (Fall 1984): 2–4.

87 "terrified": ibid.

87 Ross's role in the article explained in *Time*, 9 September 1946.

87 Background and response to article from Michael J. Yavenditti, "John Hersey and the American Conscience," *Pacific Historical Review* (February 1974): 24–49.

88 "who has permitted": *New York Times*, 30 August 1946.

88 Benedict: the *Nation,* 7 December 1946.

88 Quotes from letters in Yavenditti, "John Hersey."

88 Einstein: *New York Times,* 19 August 1946, 1.

88 "I read": Yavenditti, "John Hersey."

89 "minority opinion" appeared in the newspaper on September 19, 1946.

89 Macdonald and McCarthy reactions in *Politics,* October 1946, November 1946.

89 "sensory": George Bataille, "Concerning the Accounts Given by the Residents of Hiroshima," reprinted in *American Image* 48, no. 4, 497–514.

89 "back into Japanese": Boyer, *By the Bomb's Early Light.*

90 Farrell reaction in Hershberg, *James B. Conant,* 295.

90 "We all exhausted": interview with Bundy by Lifton in 1994.

90 Leonard Lyons column: 7 October 1946 (syndicated in many papers).

90 "has not heard": letter from H. Ross to C. Ross, 9 October 1946; "magnificent": C. Ross to H. Ross, 14 October; "There is": H. Ross to C. Ross, 17 October; "glad to have": C. Ross to H. Ross, 22 October; "killed": H. Ross to C. Ross, 29 October. All TL-OF 692-A.

91 "exercise in power politics": *Saturday Review,* 15 June 1946.

91 "The Literacy of Survival": *Saturday Review,* 14 September 1946.

92 "I am considerably disturbed": from Hershberg, *James B. Conant,* letter reprinted in full in appendix of that book, 761.

Part I—Chapter 7

93 "had a toy" from *New York Times,* 11 September 1946.

93 Baruch response from Hershberg, *James B. Conant,* 296.

94 "professional pacifists": ibid, 761.

94 References to Conant letter to Harvey Bundy, including quotations: Hershberg, *James B. Conant,* 761–62. Most subsequent description of Conant's life also comes from this source.

95 "people, projects, and prospects" *through* "would be a vital . . . worker's houses": ibid., 148, 225–26.

95 "Well, would you rather . . . million men invading Japan?": interview by Lansing Lamont with Samuel K. Allison on April 28, 1964, TL-Lamont Papers.

96 "I'm sorry it worked": Periscope, *Newsweek,* 20 August 1945. (The article attributes this statement to "one of the leading scientists" and records of Matthew Connolly at the Truman Library show that Conant was the only scientist present at the meeting.)

96 hoped "the thing won't work"—but they had to "make sure": private Co-

nant papers made available by Theodore Conant.

96 "almost public hysteria" *through* "despondency might set in . . . with probably fatal consequences" from Hershberg, *James B. Conant,* 282, 281.

96 "if the American people . . . use of the bomb" *through* "the propaganda against . . . the atomic bomb": ibid., 298.

97 "deserted a post of danger" *through* "should have discouraged me for a lifetime": ibid., 38–39.

97 "to me . . . manufacturer of explosives and guns": James B. Conant, *My Several Lives: Memoirs of a Social Inventor* (New York Harper, 1970), 49.

97 Conant's fear of an attack on science *through* quotation "without understanding . . . why it was necessary": Lifton interview with Theodore Conant, 4 May 1994.

98 Two excellent sources on preparations of Stimson article are Hershberg, *James B. Conant,* 291–304, and Barton Bernstein, "Seizing the Contested Terrain of

Nuclear History," *Diplomatic History* 17, no. 1 (Winter 1993): 35–72.

98 the "victim": Hershberg, *James B. Conant,* 295.

98 McCloy involvement from Bird, *The Chairman,* 263.

99 "the product": Bernstein, "Seizing the Contested Terrain," 50.

99 Truman refers vaguely to having urged Stimson to write such an article earlier in his 31 December 1946 letter to Stimson, TL-OF.

99 Footnote: *The Gallup Poll,* 623.

99 Harvey Bundy, Groves, Arneson drafts are all in Groves Top-Secret.

99 Groves letter to M. Bundy: ibid., 6 November 1946.

100 Conant's comments detailed in Hershberg, *James B. Conant,* 296, and Bernstein, "Seizing the Contested Terrain," 49.

100 "history with a purpose": Bernstein, "Seizing the Contested Terrain," 36.

100 Menand comment in *New York Review of Books,* 14 July 1994.

101 Bundy from Hershberg, *James B. Conant,* 297.

101 "great deal of": ibid.

101 "I have rarely been": ibid., 295.

101 "the only one" from Bernstein, "Seizing the Contested Terrain," 51.

101 Frankfurter and Patterson: ibid., 50.

102 "I think you know the facts. . . .": Truman letter to Stimson, 31 December 1946. TL-Vertical File.

102 "Chicago scientists": Hershberg, *James B. Conant,* 300.

102 "the same ghosts": Bernstein, "Seizing the Contested Terrain," 51.

102 "the first sensible": Truman to Compton, 16 December 1946, TL-OF. Compton had submitted a report to Truman on his visit to Japan on October 4, 1945. TL-OF 182.

103 "The Decision to Use the Atomic Bomb," *Harper's,* February 1947, 97–107.

103 "historic article": from *Washington*

Daily News, 28 January 1947. One of the few dissenting voices was the *Christian Century,* 12 February 1947.

104 "whether their appearance": Bernstein, "Seizing the Contested Terrain," 36.

104 "So much for the past": *New York Herald-Tribune,* 28 January 1947.

104 AEC meeting in Hershberg, *James B. Conant,* 313.

105 Bundy: ibid., 300.

105 clarified "very well": Truman letter to Stimson, 4 February 1947, TL-Vertical File.

105 Compton: Bernstein, "Seizing the Contested Terrain," 55.

105 Acheson and Byrnes response: Wittner, *One World or None,* 263.

105 "if the propaganda": Hershberg, *James B. Conant,* 298.

106 Conant at the War College: ibid., 304.

106 "every human instinct": ibid., 302.

106 Conant and Oppenheimer: ibid., 303.

109 "History is often not": Henry Stimson and McGeorge Bundy, *On Active Service in Peace and War* (New York: Harper, 1947), xi.

109 "and a good many others": from Hershberg, *James B. Conant,* 300.

110 "wholly agreed": ibid., 626–29.

110 MacArthur made point: Norman Cousins, *The Pathology of Power* (New York: Norton, 1989), 71.

111 Bernstein, "Seizing the Contested Terrain," has an excellent account of the Kennan episode, 65–69.

111 "unnerving insights": ibid., 68.

111 Kennan's warning: ibid., 67.

112 "The crisis": Hershberg, *James B. Conant,* 303.

112 Opinion polls cited in Boyer, *By the Bomb's Early Light.*

112 Szilard, Mumford, Einstein: ibid., 97.

113 Groves and "less a stimulus": ibid., 96.

113 Footnote: polls cited, Wittner, *One World or None,* 354.

114 Stimson letter to Truman: 31 August 1945, TL-PSF 199.

Part II—Chapter 1

117 atrocity-producing situation: for general concept see Lifton, *Home from the War: Learning from Vietnam Veterans* (1973; reprint, Boston: Beacon Press, 1992), 41–42.

118 "statesmanlike insight . . ." *through* "within his horizons": Allan Nevins quoted in David McCullough, *Truman* (New York: Simon & Schuster, 1992), 949.

118 On the psychological field and flow of feeling leading to the bomb's use, Kai Erikson, "Of Accidental Judgments and Casual Slaughters," *Nation*, August 3/10, 1985, 84–85, speaks of "a force like gravity" and "complex fields of force."

119 "the decision was implicit in the project": Len Giovannitti and Fred Freed, *The Decision to Drop the Bomb* (New York: Howard-McCann, 1965), frontispiece.

119 "the thing" *through* "the secret": quoted in Elting E. Morrison, *Turmoil and Tradition* (Boston: Houghton Mifflin, 1960), 618; and Martin J. Sherwin, *A World Destroyed: The Atomic Bomb and the Grand Alliance* (New York: Knopf, 1975), 163.

120 "there wasn't anything I didn't interfere with": Lamont, *Day of Trinity*, 308.

120 For Groves's sense of mission, see Stanley Goldberg, "Groves and the Atomic West: The Making and the Meaning of Hanford," in *The Atomic West*, ed. Bruce Hevly and John Findlay (Seattle: University of Washington Press, forthcoming).

120 Groves's detailed memo taken from Gregg Herken, *The Winning Weapon: The Atomic Bomb in the Cold War, 1945–1950* (New York: Alfred A. Knopf, 1980), 13–14.

120 "collection of crackpots": Sherwin, *A World Destroyed*, 59–62.

120 "to its best effect" *through* ". . . center of [the] selected city": Leon Sigal, *Fighting to a Finish: The Politics of War Termination in the United States and in Ja-*

pan, *1945* (Ithaca: Cornell University Press, 1988), 188–89.

121 "a genius" who "knows about everything": Rhodes, *The Making of the Atomic Bomb*, 448–49.

122 Oppenheimer's susceptibility to anxiety and depression: Smith and Weiner, eds. *Robert Oppenheimer*.

122 Advocacy of Ernest Lawrence for a demonstration of the bomb: Wyden, *Day One*, 160; Sherwin, *A World Destroyed*, 214.

122 Groves's use of the Scientific Advisory Panel to stifle the protest of atomic scientists is discussed in Sigal, *Fighting to a Finish*, 199.

122 "brilliant . . . someone with a strong character to manage him": Lamont, *Day of Trinity*, 308.

122 Groves's determination to avoid any chance the war might end before the bomb could be used is discussed in detail in Sigal, *Fighting to a Finish*, p. 201.

122 "unusual haste" and "the greatest congressional investigation . . ." and discussion of Groves's motivations, see Goldberg, pp 60–66.

122 Philip Morrison's impression about relaxing safety measures: Lifton interview with him on August 4, 1994.

123 Groves's "abiding interest in showing off the bomb": Sigal, *Fighting to a Finish*, 201.

123 "the nexus was complete. . . . The link between making . . .": Ian Clark, *Nuclear Past, Nuclear Present* (Boulder and London: Westview Press, 1985), 37–38.

123 "most adversely affect . . . continue the war" *through* "the advantage of being of such a size . . ." (in footnote) and general discussion: Sigal, *Fighting to a Finish*, 183–89.

123 Groves and field commanders' leeway, and "I didn't have to have the President press the button on this affair": Giovannitti and Freed, *The Decision to Drop the Bomb*, 251.

124 "Atom-General" and "nothing less than . . . Pax Atomica": Herken, *The Winning Weapon*, 111–13.

124 Truman's comments on Roosevelt: Robert J. Donovan, *Conflict and Crisis: The Presidency of Harry S. Truman 1945–1948* (New York: Norton, 1977), 15–17, and McCullough, *Truman*, 352–55.

125 Roosevelt-Churchill memo and its withholding by Groves and Stimson: Sigal, *Fighting to a Finish*, 180–81 and 181n.

125 "a full debate . . ." *through* "Why did you spend . . . why didn't you use it?": ibid., 221.

125 Quotations on Truman's psychological state: Donovan, *Conflict and Crisis*, 15, and McCullough, *Truman*, 347.

126 "Boys, if you ever pray . . . all the planets had fallen on me": McCullough, 353.

126 "the old one-two to the jaw" ". . . Did I do right?": Robert L. Messer, *The End of an Alliance: James F. Byrnes, Roosevelt, Truman, and the Origins of the Cold War* (Chapel Hill: University of North Carolina Press, 1982), 76.

126 Wallace diary entry on Truman's premature decisiveness: John Morton Blum, *The Price of Vision: The Diary of Henry A. Wallace, 1942–1946*, 417.

126 "necessarily laboring with . . . allow him to control them": Sigal, *Fighting to a Finish*, 210–11.

127 1943 interaction between Stimson and Truman: McCullough, *Truman*, 289–91.

128 "The new President on the whole . . . I hope not": Donovan, *Conflict and Crisis*, 13, 16.

128 "It was a wonderful relief . . . and decided it": McCullough, *Truman*, 369.

128 "The President so far . . . to keep his balance": 2 July 1945 entry in Stimson diary (TL-microfilm).

128 "about a most urgent matter . . . destructive power" *through* "but have not urged it . . . you have been under": *Harry S. Truman Memoirs: Year of Decisions* (Garden City: Doubleday & Co., 1955), 10, 85.

129 Stimson on revolutionary device that "went right down to the bottom . . . morals and government" and Felix Frankfurter on Stimson's mind: Sherwin, *A World Destroyed*, 195.

129 Stimson on "the necessity" and "the possible use of S1 to accomplish this" from his diary entries of late August 1944, in preparation for a meeting with President Roosevelt, quoted in James MacGregor Burns, *Roosevelt: The Soldier of Freedom* (New York: Harcourt, 1970), 459.

129 "master card" *through* "was what turned . . . the use of the bomb": Sherwin, *A World Destroyed* 198–99.

130 "terrible and probably unnecessary" *through* "I believe the same rule . . . of any new weapons": Sigal, *Fighting to a Finish*, 173–75.

131 McGeorge Bundy quotations: Lifton interview with McGeorge Bundy, 17 March 1994.

131 Stimson quotations in footnote: Ronald Steel, "Doomsday," *New York Review of Books*, 25 November 1965, 8.

131 The weapon is to be used between now and. . . . will be a purely military one": Robert H. Ferrell, ed., *Off the Record: The Private Papers of Harry S. Truman* (1980; reprint, New York: Penguin, 1982), 55–56.

131 "could not concentrate on a civilian area . . . of the inhabitants as possible": Barton J. Bernstein, "An Analysis of 'Two Cultures': Writing About and Making and Using of the Atomic Bombs," *The Public Historian* 12, no. 2 (Spring 1990): 97. The quotation comes from Interim Committee Minutes of May 31, 1945. The words are identified with Stimson but it was added that "there was general agreement." Bernstein sees Stimson as having "succumbed" to this new ethic of war—the targeting of civilians. The statement also was an extension of Stimson's (and others') numbing and self-deception, coming as it did immediately after affirming the "vital war plant . . . workers' houses" principle.

132 (". . . a population of over a million

. . . war work") *through* "Aware of no factors. . . . tend to confirm it": Sigal, *Fighting to a Finish*, 193–95.

132 "military objectives . . ." *through* "a purely military": *Off the Record*, 55–56.

132 "a human content . . . did not find in Hiroshima" *through* "one [was] a great city . . . an army headquarters": McGeorge Bundy, *Danger and Survival: Choices About the Bomb in the First Fifty Years* (New York: Random House, 1988), 79–80.

133 "I told him. . . . said he understood": Sigal, *Fighting to a Finish*, 194–95.

134 "knew that the critical condition . . . would be preserved": ibid., 86.

134 For discussion of the doctrine of unconditional surrender see ibid., 89–93; and ibid. 94 and McCullough, *Truman*, 358, for Truman declaration of that policy to Congress. See also Charles B. Strozier, "Unconditional Surrender and the Rhetoric of Total War From Truman to Lincoln," The Center on Violence and Human Survival, John Jay College of Criminal Justice, Occasional Paper Number 2, 1987.

134 Grew and "the greatest obstacle . . . of the Throne" *through* "the real future which would govern the situation": Sigal, *Fighting to a Finish*, 112–115.

134 "war passion and hysteria that had seized the country": Stimson diary, 2 July 1945 (TL-microfilm).

135 McCloy's appeal to Stimson's "sense of moral statesmanship" *through* "even in that high circle . . . in good Yale society": Kai Bird, *The Chairman*, 244–47; James Reston, "McCloy on the A-Bomb," appendix of *Deadline*, 495–99; and Sigal, *Fighting to a Finish*, 120–22. McCloy's account verified in White House memo dated March 8, 1947, "Meeting with McCloy," by "JF," TL-PSF.

136 On Stimson's unclarity, see Sigal, *Fighting to a Finish*, 122ff.; and Barton Bernstein, "Seizing the Contested Terrain of Early Nuclear History: Stimson, Conant, and Their Allies Explain the De-cision to Use the Atomic Bomb," *Diplomatic History* 17, no. 1, 62–72.

136 "Stimson's torturous arguments with himself": Charles L. Mee, Jr., *Meeting at Potsdam* (New York: Evans, 1975), 153.

136 "older brother": Messer, *End of an Alliance*, 13.

137 "my able and conniving . . ." *through* "And he is an honest man": McCullough, *Truman*, 479.

137 "the bomb might well . . . end of the war" *through* "our possessing . . . manageable in Europe": Messer, *End of an Alliance*, 86.

137 "it would be capable . . . killing people wholesale": TL-PPFM.

138 Concerning Byrnes's influence on the Interim Committee and his overall nuclearism, see Messer, *End of an Alliance*, 87–88, 106–7.

139 "neither a gesture . . . to mere propaganda": Sigal, *Fighting to a Finish*, 130.

139 "seems to have given no thought to the moral implications": Messer, *End of an Alliance*, 104.

139 "crucifixion of the President": Barton J. Bernstein, "The Perils and Politics of Surrender: Ending the War with Japan and Avoiding the Third Atomic Bomb," *Pacific Historical Review* 46 (February 1977): 5.

140 "what might have been" *through* "I trusted him implicitly . . . over my head": *Off the Record*, 348–49.

140 "the worst thing that ever happened": Sigal, *Fighting to a Finish*, 178.

140 On ambiguities concerning Marshall and the bomb, see "Marshall, Truman, and the Decision to Drop the Bomb," a correspondence exchange in which Gar Alperovitz and Robert L. Messer comment on a previous article by Barton J. Bernstein, and Bernstein replies. *International Security* 16, no. 3 (Winter 1991–92): 204–21.

141 "struggle to retain the older code . . ." and "straight" military target: Bernstein, "The Atomic Bombings Reconsidered," *Foreign Affairs*, January–February 1995, 143.

141 "barbarous weapon" and what Leahy

said at the time, see Sigal, *Fighting to a Finish,* 209; and Bernstein, "Ike and Hiroshima: Did He Oppose It?" *Journal of Strategic Studies* 10 (September 1987): 387.

141 "he may have mistaken . . . for affirmation": Sigal, *Fighting to a Finish,* 208.

141 On Bard's dissent, see his memorandum on the use of "S-1 bomb" of 27 June 1945, TL-Vertical File; and Sigal, *Fighting to a Finish;* reprinted in Udall, *Myths of August,* 123, 205–6.

Part II—Chapter 2

143 "I'm here to make decisions . . . I am going to make them": McCullough, *Truman,* 384.

143 "seemed . . . eager to decide in advance of thinking": John Morton Blum, *Price of Vision,* 437; "air of decisiveness": Sigal, *Fighting to a Finish,* 211.

144 "an informal but clearly . . ." through *"firm* instructions": Bernstein, "Writing, Righting or Wronging the Historical Record: President Truman's Letter on his Atomic-Bomb Decision," *Diplomatic History* (Winter 92): 163–73.

144 "torturous atomic ride . . . about atomic issues . . .": Stewart L. Udall, *The Myths of August: A Personal Exploration of our Tragic Cold War Affair with the Atom* (New York: Pantheon, 1994), 96.

144 "various records . . . and even wise" *through* "can easily . . . frameworks and beliefs": Bernstein, "Writing, Righting or Wronging," 172–73.

145 "the most terrific experience of my life": McCullough, *Truman,* 132.

145 "he never forgets . . . button in his lapel": S. J. Woolf, "President Truman Talks About His Job," *New York Times Magazine,* 15 July 1945.

145 Autobiographical sketch including "a serviceman of my acquaintance" *through* "he must change now . . . planet will succeed him": McCullough, *Truman,* 518–19.

146 "just the same as artillery . . ." *through* "for military reason": TL-PPPM.

147 "I regarded the bomb . . . that it should be used": Bundy, *Danger and Survival,* 59–60.

147 "does not close the book": Robert L. Messer, "New Evidence on Truman's Decision," *Bulletin of the Atomic Scientists* 41 (August 1985): 50–56.

147 "why Truman often seemed so confused . . ." and "why Truman and other . . . overruled their subordinates": J. Samuel Walker, "The Decision to Use the Bomb: A Historiographical Update," *Diplomatic History* 14, no. 1 (Winter 1990): 110.

147 "he had been giving serious thought . . ." *through* "he was just as reluctant . . .": *NBC White Paper,* 5 January 1965.

148 Truman's diary entries from "machines are ahead of morals . . ." *through* "It seems to be . . . made the most useful": *Off the Record,* 52–53, 55–56.

149 "appeasement": Sigal, *Fighting to a Finish,* 127.

149 "be in Jap war . . ." *through* "fini Japs when that comes about": *Off the Record,* 53.

150 "I've gotten what I came for . . ." *through* "he must have realized . . . be used at all" from Messer, "New Evidence," 50–51.

150 "neither the President nor I . . ." *through* "it was important . . . came into the war": *NBC White Paper.*

150 Lines from Tennyson poem "Locksley Hall," McCullough, *Truman,* 64–65. See also H. Bruce Franklin, *Warstars: Superweapon and the American Imagination* (New York: Oxford University Press, 1988), 81–82, 153.

151 "I'm not working for . . . of the United States": *Off The Record,* 49.

151 "realized that the man . . . be the next President . . ." through "vivid nightmare": McCullough, *Truman,* 327, 308, 330.

151 "I had been afraid . . . after I became Vice President": Sherwin, *World Destroyed*, 146.

152 "he had bad headaches . . ." *through* "Both": Blum, *Price of Vision*, 475.

152 "hardly conducive to . . . information and options" *through* "fully appreciated . . . bombing called for": Sigal, *Fighting to a Finish*, 211.

152 "I made the only decision. . . . what I thought was right": quoted from a 1965 lecture in Margaret Truman, *Harry S. Truman* (New York: Morrow, 1972), 567.

153 "No man-made phenomenon. . . . witnessed to be realized": Groves, *Now It Can Be Told*, 437–38.

153 "immensely pleased" *through* "he now understood . . . felt the same way": Stimson diary entries of 21 July, 22 July, and 30 July 1945. TL microfilm.

153 "visibly jubilant" *through* "Byrnes and my fellows . . . on air": Messer: *End of an Alliance*, 103–4.

154 "the commencement of . . ." *through* "the callousness . . . seems ominous": Bird, *The Chairman*, p. 251.

154 "didn't know beans . . ." *through* "inevitable": Wyden, *Day One*, 170.

155 "the fact of the atomic bomb. . . . problems with the Soviets": Bird, *The Chairman*, 251–52.

155 Oppenheimer's later admission, and its being too late because "the whole mechanism . . . set in motion": Bernstein, "An Analysis of Two Cultures," 100.

156 "For what sane power . . . fortified mainland?": Erikson, "Of Accidental Judgments," the *Nation*, 3/10 August 1985, 83.

156 "began telling them . . ." *through* "the secret . . . could not discuss it with each other": McCullough, *Truman*, 453–54.

156 Revelations about atomic bomb to junior officers: Fletcher Knebel and Charles W. Bailey, "Secret: The Fight over the A-Bomb," *Look*, 13 August 1963, 19–23.

157 "This is the greatest thing in history!"

through "We won the gamble": McCullough, *Truman*, 454–55.

158 Footnote: *Newsweek*, 20 August 1945, 31.

158 "he always gives me the impression . . ." *through* "there was no . . . outstanding mind": Bird, *The Chairman*, 256.

159 "slow accretion of large fears . . . incremental decisions": Michael Sherry, *The Rise of American Air Power*. 363.

160 "I'll certainly have a hammer on those boys": Gar Alperovitz, *Atomic Diplomacy: Hiroshima and Potsdam,* (New York: Simon & Schuster, 1965), 130.

160 "I hoped that it would . . . expensive bit of explosive": TL-PPPM.

161 Concerning the uncertainty surrounding intra-Japanese conflicts and the persistence of military fanaticism, see extensive discussions in Sigal, *Fighting to a Finish,* and Robert J. Butow, *Japan's Decision to Surrender* (Stanford University Press, 1954). Butow, however, believed that a diplomatic approach through discreet political channels might have brought an end to the war in late July or early August without either use of the atomic bombs or Soviet participation (133–35).

161 July 25 order went from General Handy to General Spatz, TL-PSF 112.

162 Telford Taylor: in his *Nuremberg and Vietnam*.

162 "had never been explicitly endorsed": Clark, *Nuclear Past*. The account that follows draws heavily on the Clark book (54–70) and Groves's *Now It Can Be Told* (341–55), among other sources.

162 "decided that we should . . .": Groves, *Now It Can Be Told*, 342.

163 Account of casualties and other details about the bombing in Committee for the Compilation . . . (eds.), *Hiroshima and Nagasaki.*

163 "once you get your opponent reeling . . .": Lamont, *Day of Trinity*, 307.

163 Many years later: ibid.

164 Sherwin's comment from his *A World Destroyed*, 233.

164 Brewster letter quotations from TL-Vertical File.

164 Roosevelt discussion with Bush on the bomb: Bundy, *Danger and Survival,* 90.

165 Alexander Sachs's exchange with Wallace and comments about Groves: Blum, *The Price of Vision,* 499–500.

165 "tantalizing hints . . . successor never was": Bundy, *Danger and Survival,* 90.

165 "have it in his head . . . would have been heard . . . way up": Lifton interview with Bundy, 17 March 1994.

165 "to give public assurance . . . keep her Emperor" *through* "had envisaged . . . of the war": from Samuel Eliot Morrison, "Why Japan Surrendered," *Atlantic Monthly,* October 1960, 23.

166 "that President Roosevelt would have forbidden . . .": *New York Times,* 19 August 1946.

166 "they . . . would have talked and talked . . ." *through* "wiser things to say": Lifton interview with Philip Morrison, 4 August 1994.

Part II—Chapter 3

168 "Mr. President, I have blood on my hands" *through* "bring that son of a bitch around here again": Wyden, *Day One,* 349; and McCullough, *Truman,* 475; Peter Michelmore, *The Swift Years: The Robert Oppenheimer Story* (New York: Dodd, Mead, 1969), 121–22.

168 For Truman's retelling of "the cry-baby scientist" story see 7 May 1946 memorandum to Acheson and *The Journals of David E. Lilienthal,* vol. 2, *The Atomic Energy Years 1945–1950* (New York: Harper, 1964), 118.

169 "jubilant" and "happiest": Merriman Smith, United Press Report, aboard USS *Augusta,* 7 August 1945.

169 "the total destruction . . ." *through* "the terrible responsibility . . . here and himself": August 8 Stimson diary entry, TL-microfilm.

169 "no President of the United States . . . could kill innocent human beings": 8 August 1945 telegram from Lew Wallace; "the good feeling . . . new engine of destruction": Truman's 9 August 1945 letter to Wallace, TL-OF 692-A.

170 "total war" *through* "I certainly regret . . . is absolutely necessary": McCullough, *Truman,* 458.

170 "When you have to deal": Truman to Samuel Cavert of the Federal Council of Churches, 11 August 1945, TL-OF 692-A.

170 "purely a military base" *through* "we wished . . . killing of civilians": TL-speech file.

171 Oppenheimer's reservations about the tests, a letter to Truman of 3 May 1946; Truman's memo to Acheson, 7 May 1946. TL-National Security Council papers, 201.

171 "Get plenty of Atomic Bombs . . . set up a free world": Desk Note June 1946, in Monte M. Poen, ed., *Strictly Personal and Confidential: The Letters Harry Truman Never Mailed* (Boston: Little, Brown, 1982), 31.

172 "well imagine the emotional torture . . ." *through* "for not having . . . outside of the Hiroshima . . ." and suggestion that Truman himself played the role: 2 December 1946 letter from Roman Bohnen to Truman; "the talent to be a movie star" *through* "Americans could be saved . . . and it was": 12 December 1946 Truman letter to Bohnen. TL-PSF, Box 112.

173 "weapons of genocide": scientists' General Advisory Committee report of 30 October 1949, quoted in Herbert York, *The Advisors: Oppenheimer, Teller, and the Super Bomb* (San Francisco: Freeman, 1976), 156–57; "steamroller" effect: Lilienthal, *Atomic Energy Years,* 633. "It would have been preferable . . . closer examination": McCullough, *Truman,* 764.

174 "quick and unexamined," Bundy, *Danger and Survival,* 237.

174 "there actually was no decision to make

on the H-bomb": TL-Ayers diary, 4
February 1950.

174 "original program inaugurated by President Roosevelt. . . . at that conclusion in 1943": Truman letter to Harold Ickes, 1 February 1950, TL-PSF.

174 "I have directed the Atomic Energy Commission to *continue* . . .": Philip M. Stern, *The Oppenheimer Case: Security on Trial* (New York: Harper, 1969), 154 (italics added).

175 "We just *had* to drop the bomb": *Independence Examiner,* 8 April 1958.

175 "I didn't have any doubt at the time" and story about student in the history class: Eben Ayers description, TL-PPF.

175 "Monday-morning quarterback" *through* "Well, there's your answer" from TL-PPFM, 1953; *Independence Examiner,* 18 June 1956; George Carpozi, Jr., "Hiroshima Plus 20," *Pageant Magazine,* September 1965, 90; *Kansas City Star,* 12 July 1955.

176 People in Hiroshima angered by that kind of Truman statement: Lifton, *Death in Life: Survivors of Hiroshima* (Chapel Hill: University of North Carolina Press, 1991 [1968]), 333–35.

176 1959 statement "I never lost any sleep over my decision" quoted in Udall, *Myths of August,* p. 96.

176 "I lost plenty of sleep. . . . when just one of our soldiers, sailors or marines died": Carpozi, "Hiroshima Plus 20," 91.

176 "Don't you ever lose any sleep. . . . You had no choice": Tibbets, *The Tibbets Story,* 8.

177 "There has been. . . .": 1 August 1957 letter to Mrs. Cyril Smith, TL-PPF.

177 Scrawled note, "File. Know not very much about it": on 4 May 1960 letter from Eugene Rabinowitch, TL-PPF.

177 "in deep indignation" *through* "a gross defilement . . . their fallen victims": 1 March 1958 letter from Tsukasa Nitoguri, chairman of the Hiroshima City Council, to Truman, TL-PPF.

177 "courteous letter" *through* ". . . Japan as a great and prosperous nation": 12

March 1958 letter from Truman to Nitoguri, TL-PPF.

178 "Why don't you have conscience enough . . ." *through* "frank and thoughtful reply": 20 March 1958 reply to Truman from Nitoguri, TL-PPF.

178 "He could not understand why . . . first atomic bomb on the Japanese city": *Independence Examiner,* 8 April 1958.

178 "You write just like the usual egghead. . . . Our boys would all be dead": Poen, *Strictly Personal and Confidential,* 34.

179 "the Christian tradition of civilized warfare" *through* "it has always been . . . and never civilized": 30 November 1956 letter from Truman to Thomas E. Murray, TL-PPF.

179 "the Jap Bomb affair": mentioned in Box 39, TL-PPF. This may have been the actual name of the file or Truman's name for it.

179 "Your own letter. . . . save a half million lives . . .": 23 September 1963 letter to George A. Warmer, Vice President for University Affairs of Boston University. TL-PPF.

180 "I knew what I was doing . . . youngsters on both sides . . .": Poen, *Strictly Personal and Confidential,* 36.

180 Barton Bernstein figures of 20,000 to 46,000 *through* "half a million American lives" and Marshall agreement with estimate of 46,000 *through* suggestion of a "layman" of half million dead: Bernstein, "A Postwar Myth: 500,000 U.S. Lives Saved," *Bulletin of the Atomic Scientists,* (June/July 1986): 38–40.

180 Concerning figure of 500,000 given him by Marshall, Truman had originally said 250,000 but agreed upon the higher figure after an elaborate exchange on the matter involving the historian James L. Cate, who was writing an official World War II Air Force history, and White House aides Kenneth Hechler and David D. Lloyd. See accounts by Hechler (December, 1952), Truman (December 31, 1952), and Lloyd (January 6, 1953); TL-PSF. And also discussions by Bernstein in "A Postwar

Myth" and "Writing, Righting, or Wronging."

180 Footnote on informal oral history of military estimates from Charles B. Strozier, personal communication.

181 "were offered the terms. . . . the bomb caused them to accept the terms": 16 December 1946 letter to Karl Compton, TL-OF 692A.

182 "a commission consisting of . . . whose name I have forgotten" *through* "was sent to Japan . . . I can't remember which . . .": letter to Stimson, 31 December 1946, TL-PSF.

182 "an ultimatum to Japan . . . I forget which . . .": TL-PPFM.

182 "the Japs were much more vicious fighters. . . . the bomb would be better": TL-PPFM.

182 ". . . ordinary things like that": 21 July 1948 meeting described in Lilienthal, *Atomic Energy Years,* 391.

183 "German scientists in Russia did it": McCullough, *Truman,* 748.

183 "I know. Never": John Newhouse, *War and Peace in the Nuclear Age* (New York: Knopf, 1988), 73.

183 "It's very nice of you . . ." *through* ". . . was in the first place": "Transcript of the conversation between former President Harry S. Truman and Dr. Takuo Matsumoto, a spokesman for the Japanese Goodwill Ambassadors of the World Peace Study Mission," Harry S. Truman Library Auditorium, 5 May 1964," TL-Vertical File.

184 "quick suspicion" *through* "I'll go to Japan . . . but I won't kiss their ass": Merle Miller, *Plain Speaking: An Oral Biography of Harry S. Truman* (New York: Berkley, 1974), 247–48.

184 "with deep concern" *through* "where it began and should have ended": Truman letter of 20 October 1966 to Howard Willits, TL-PPF.

184 Talk with Tom Clark during which "He defended his dropping the bomb": Oral History interview with Tom C. Clark by Jerry N. Hess, TL.

185 "really did not want to know" *through*

". . . without knowing what was going on themselves": Blum, *The Price of Vision,* 530.

185 "a substantial amount for the Atomic Energy Commission" *through* "The military commander . . . as he always has": Robert J. Donovan, *Tumultuous Years: The Presidency of Harry S. Truman, 1949–1953* (New York: Norton, 1977), 307–9.

186 "devastatingly foolish . . . a fiasco": McCullough, *Truman,* 822.

186 "nonassembled bombs were secretly transported to a U.S. aircraft carrier": Joseph S. Goulden, *Korea: The Untold Story of the War* (1982; paperback, New York: McGraw-Hill 1983), xxv.

187 "If I had been in that frame of mind . . ." *through* ". . . and those were the cities that were bombed": TL-PPFM.

187 "every agreement" *through* ". . . or you will be completely destroyed": Ferrell, ed., *Off the Record,* 250–51.

187 "Truman never came close . . ." *through* ". . . it did *not* take the form of atomic diplomacy": from Bundy, *Danger and Survival,* 231–33.

188 "for peace, I took it upon myself . . ." *through* ". . . if it could conceivably be avoided": *New York Times,* 27 October 1948.

188 "small stag dinner" *through* ". . . the Prime Minister was acquitted": Margaret Truman, *Harry S. Truman,* 555–56.

190 "injury" to the "human order of being": Martin Buber, "Guilt and Guilt Feelings," in *The Knowledge of Man* (New York: Harper, 1966), 132.

190 Hiroshima survivors' difficulty in determining whom to blame: Lifton, *Death in Life,* 52, 333, 342.

190 "a price that had to be paid": TL-PPFM.

191 "inheritors of the mantle of Genghis Khan" *through* ". . . the mark of the beast": Hanson Baldwin, *Great Mistakes of the War* (New York: Harper, 1950).

191 Baldwin as "Monday-morning quarterback": 17 November 1958 letter from

Truman to Robert A. Goldwin, TL-PPF.

191 December 1947 Washington Gridiron Club speech and secretary of reaction through "put the atom back together so it can't be broken up": Donald R. McCoy, "Harry S. Truman: Personality, Politics, and Presidency," *Presidential Studies Quarterly* (Spring 1982): 217.

191 ". . . let me speak to the yet unknowing world. . . . On plots and errors, happen": Merle Miller, *Plain Speaking*, 248.

191 Footnote: G. Mitchell interview with O'Donnell, January 1995.

192 "the stakes in our search for peace" *through* ". . . not a possible policy for rational men": Bundy, *Danger and Survival*, 233–34.

192 "retirement syndrome" discussed by Lifton in Lifton and Richard Falk, *Indefensible Weapons: The Political and Psychological Case Against Nuclearism* (1982; reprint, New York: Basic Books, 1991), 96–98.

Part II—Chapter 4

193 "old man" not very likeable: Richard Lawrence Miller, *Harry S. Truman: The Rise to Power* (New York: McGraw-Hill, 1986), 10. See also part 1 of McCullough, *Truman*.

194 Studied careers of "great men" to be worthy of her: McCullough, *Truman*, 43. For childhood heroes associated with principles of "unconditional surrender," see Sigal, *Fighting to a Finish*, 89.

194 "I like being on the road": John Hersey, *Life Sketches* (Knopf, 1989), 236–39.

195 "His reading of history was often uncritical . . . substituting philosophy for history": McCoy, "Harry S. Truman," 217.

195 "The only thing new in the world is the history you don't know": Merle Miller, *Plain Speaking*, 69.

195 "Nothing but the lives of great men! . . . dope on the 20th century . . .": Hersey, *Life Sketches*, 244–45.

196 Communists were engineering the student sit-downs *through* ". . . the Kremlin is behind it": David Caute, *The Great Fear: The Anti-Communist Purge Under Truman and Eisenhower* (New York: Simon & Schuster, 1978) 35.

196 "I was afraid my eyes . . . too much of a rough and tumble play": Richard Miller, *Harry S. Truman*, 12.

196 "intended for a girl" *through* nicknaming him Horatio after Hamlet's staunch friend, McCullough, *Truman*, 46, 49.

197 "some of the old masters . . . a fairy goddess of some sort . . ." Richard Miller, *Harry S. Truman*, 26.

197 "I got the notion . . . a boy of that age a sissy": S. J. Woolf, "President Truman Talks about His Job," *New York Times Magazine*, 15 July 1945.

197 Escapade with the Independence Junior Militia: Richard Miller, *Harry S. Truman*, 34–35.

198 "that he might somehow fail . . ." *through* "go-along, get-along Harry": McCullough, *Truman*, 107, 160, 220.

198 "There . . . he struck his gait": ibid., 192.

198 "dogged determination to shoulder . . . beyond his personal capabilities": Alonzo L. Hamby, "Harry S. Truman: Insecurity and Responsibility," in *Leadership in the Modern Presidency*, ed. Fred I. Greenstein (Cambridge: Harvard University Press, 1988), 44.

201 "Truman moved with such celerity . . . to make decisions and act": Donovan, *Tumultuous Years*, 196.

201 "made it clear, from the moment . . . was the opening of World War III" *through* "the last thing Truman wanted was a war in Korea, or anywhere": McCullough, *Truman*, 775–76, 779. The Goering reference was originally from Roy Jenkins, *Truman* (London: Collins, 1986), 164.

202 "frankly, a great military disaster . . .
the wrong enemy": Goulden, *Korea,*
xv.

202 "I have hoped and prayed. . . . that's
out of my mind": Donovan, *Tumultuous
Years,* 199.

203 "by using nuclear weapons . . . they

were legitimate": Gerard H. Clarfield
and William M. Wiecek, *Nuclear America: Military and Civilian Nuclear Power in
the United States, 1940–1980* (New York:
1984), quoted in Walker, "Decision to
Use the Bomb," 111.

Part III—Chapter 1

209 "public memory" and quotes that follow: Michael Kammen, *Mystic Chords of
Memory* (New York: Knopf, 1991), 1–
13.

212 "I disliked seeing": *Crusade in Europe*
(Garden City, N.Y.: Doubleday, 1948),
443.

213 "because Stimson": from Bernstein,
"Ike and Hiroshima," 386.

213 "During his recitation": *Mandate for
Change* (Garden City, N.Y.: Doubleday, 1963), 312.

213 Groves investigated: Bernstein, "Ike and
Hiroshima," 380.

213 "It wasn't necessary": *Newsweek,* 11
November 1963, 107.

213 Bradley quoted in Bernstein, "Ike and
Hiroshima."

213 Ambrose in *Eisenhower, 1890–1952* (New
York: Simon & Schuster, 1987), 426,
596.

214 "couldn't quite make up his mind":
Reston, *Deadline,* 194.

214 Dulles: ibid, 230–32.

214 Film clip of Bentsen making statement
appears in the documentary film *The
Atomic Cafe* (1982), produced by Kevin
Rafferty, Pierce Rafferty, and Joyce
Loader.

214 Gore quotes in letter to Truman, 14
April 1951, TL-OF, 692-A.

215 "Surely no sane": Bundy, *Danger and
Survival,* 254.

215 "You boys": ibid, 270.

215 Inside account from Robert F. Kennedy, *Thirteen Days* (New York: Norton, 1971), 84–85.

216 McNamara: quoted in Bundy, *Danger
and Survival,* 376.

216 Dugger: from his *The Politician: The Life*

and Times of Lyndon Johnson (New York:
Norton, 1982).

217 The Hersey incident is described in
Eric Goldman, *The Tragedy of Lyndon
Johnson* (New York: Knopf, 1969).

218 "has made the world promise": *The
Meaning of Survival* (Hiroshima:
Chugoku Shimbun, 1983), 172.

218 "The Japanese are": *Time,* 29 July 1985,
48.

219 Interviewed by Rosenblatt: ibid, 48–53.

219 Bundy interviewed by Lifton.

219 "obsession" from Nixon, *1996* (New
York: Simon & Schuster, 1988), 18.

219 footnote: Haldeman, *The Ends of Power*
(New York: Times Books, 1978), 82–
83.

220 "made one of the few": Halperin, *Nuclear Fallacy* (New York: Ballinger,
1987).

220 "the Soviets know" statement by William Dyess on NBC *Newsmakers,* 3 February 1980.

220 "ended a great war": Robert Scheer,
With Enough Shovels (New York: Random House, 1982), 253.

220 "Yet we must remain": *Washington Post,*
7 August 1985, A3.

221 "the eyes are burned": Lou Cannon,
President Reagan (New York: Simon &
Schuster, 1991), 289.

221 Cheney on *This Week with David Brinkley,* ABC News, 3 February 1991.

221 "sent a crystal-clear" from Hershberg,
James B. Conant, 280.

222 Bush response from *New York Times,* 6
December 1991, and *San Francisco
Chronicle,* 2 December 1991.

222 Poll published and analyzed in *New York
Times,* 8 December 1991.

Part III—Chapter 2

224 Lamont interview found in Lamont papers, Truman Library.

224 "I understand why": ibid.

225 "I do not regret": Goodchild, *J. Robert Oppenheimer,* 274.

226 "I never regretted": *New York Times Magazine,* 1 August 1965.

226 "My first impression . . ." *through* ". . . time scale of years!" from James Hershberg, *James B. Conant,* 232.

227 Plan for microfilmed record of our civilization: ibid., 241–42.

227 "louse up the world still more" *through* ". . . from the United States point of view": ibid., 466, 474, 475, 484.

227 For discussion of nuclear backsliding, see discussion by Lifton in *Indefensible Weapons,* 96–98.

228 "the atomic bomb is a bad weapon . . ." *through* "I have no sense of accomplishment": Hershberg, 484, 605.

228 "heavy with grief" *through* ". . . barriers of science one millimeter": ibid., 571–75.

229 "haunted" *through* "verdict of history" ibid., 752, 755.

230 "I've got a standard": Tibbets interviewed by G. Mitchell in 1985. For similar comments see Tibbets oral history, Columbia University Oral History Collection.

230 "that if a thing": "Claude Eatherly's Dark Star," Ronnie Dugger, *Progressive,* August 1966.

230 Incident early in the war revealed in Glenn Van Warreby, *Looking Up, Looking Down* (Winona, Minn.: Apollo Books, 1985), 113–14. Van Warreby spent considerable time with many of the pilots and crew.

231 Nagasaki episode in Tibbets, *The Tibbets Story,* 9, 241–42.

231 Air show: ibid., 304–5; *New York Times,* 30 September 1977.

231 "You can only beat": Van Warreby, *Looking Up,* 40.

232 Beser in *Remembering the Bomb,* film documentary produced and directed by Steve York for KCTS-TV (Seattle) and York Productions, Washington, D.C., 1986.

232 Sweeney effort noted in *The Tibbets Story.*

232 Other crewmen: Merle Miller and Abe Spitzer, *We Dropped the A-Bomb* (New York: Crowell, 1946) 151–52.

232 "down there": Van Warreby, *Looking Up,* 99–100.

232 "So many of my comrades": ibid., 117.

233 "There was a job": ibid., 120.

233 *This Is Your Life* episode described in detail in Rodney Barker, *The Hiroshima Maidens* (New York: Viking, 1985).

234 Sculpture discussed in Van Warreby, *Looking Up,* 1.

234 Best look at Eatherly's background in Ronnie Dugger, *Dark Star* (New York: World, 1967).

236 Tibbets comment from Van Warreby, *Looking Up,* 39.

237 "Certain that only": Feifer, *Tennozan,* 568.

237 "The veterans": E. B. Sledge, *With the Old Breed at Peleliu and Okinawa* (San Francisco: Presidio Press, 1981).

238 Mailer recollections taken from his discussion with Lifton in 1994.

238 "Who the hell": Feifer, *Tennozan,* 570.

239 Cartoon in Boyer, *By the Bomb's Early Light,* 158.

239 *Nightline* transcript, 5 August 1985.

240 Truman's message to Congress, 3 October 1945.

240 Groves quotes from his letter to Kenneth T. Bainbridge, 28 September 1945, TL-Lamont papers.

241 Fussell article originally in the *New Republic,* August 22, 1981, 26–30. *Thank God for the Atom Bomb and Other Essays* (New York: Summit, 1988).

242 Walzer and Fussell response in the *New Republic,* 23 September 1981. Elsewhere, Walzer has declared that Truman "owed the Japanese people an experiment in negotiation."

242 Years later Fussell quoted in *Washington City Paper,* 3 April 1994.

243 "This is to miss": Clark, *Nuclear Past, Nuclear Present.*

Part III—Chapter 3

246 Agnew in *Time,* 29 July 1985, 45.

246 Alvarez in Luis Alvarez, *Alvarez* (New York: Basic Books, 1987), 141–52.

246 Teller's claim in his *Legacy of Hiroshima.*

247 "chief regret" in The *Nation,* 19 September 1994, 263.

247 Wilson interviewed in film documentary *The Day After Trinity.*

248 Neddermeyer quoted in Wyden, *Day One,* 366.

248 Rothblat article in *Bulletin of Atomic Scientists,* August 1985, 16–19.

248 "My Trial As a War Criminal": *University of Chicago Law Review,* Autumn 1949.

249 "walked the streets": *Bulletin of the Atomic Scientists,* January 1951, 3.

249 Letter published in the *New York Times,* 28 June 1971.

249 On another occasion: Wittner, *One World or None,* 33.

250 Three reactions from Bethe interview with Lifton.

250 Bethe on no first use: Wittner, *One World or None,* 65.

250 "You may well ask": documentary *The Day After Trinity.*

250 Morrison: interviewed by Lifton.

253 "divide our forces": Boyer, *Bomb's Early Light,* 193.

253 "confession and repentance": *New York Times,* 1 August 1955.

253 The Hiroshima Maidens segment is based primarily on three sources: Barker, *The Hiroshima Maidens;* Michael Yavenditti, "The Hiroshima Maidens and American Benevolence in the 1950s," *Mid-America,* April–July 1983, 21–39; and Lawrence S. Wittner, "The Menace of the Maidens," paper presented at the Conference of the International Peace Research Association, Malta, 2 November 1994, nine pages.

255 one historian: Yavenditti.

255 One sympathizer: John Leonard in the *New York Times,* 1 August 1976.

255 Footnote: Committee for the Compilation . . . , eds., *Hiroshima and Nagasaki.*

256 Spiegelman wrote the introduction to *Barefoot Gen: The Day After* (New York: Penguin, 1990), xi–xiv.

256 Japanese-Americans: "Unclaimed," Dan Ouellette and Evantheia Schibsted, *San Francisco Examiner Magazine,* 4 August 1991; interview with Jennifer Morozumi of Friends of Hibakusha by G. Mitchell in 1994.

257 "We walked into Nagasaki": Harvey Wasserman and Norman Solomon, *Killing Our Own* (New York: Delta, 1982), 4. Other background: Defense Nuclear Agency "Fact Sheet," 6 August 1980.

257 "closely resembles": Wasserman and Solomon, *Killing Our Own,* 7.

258 "In the back of our minds": Terkel, *The Good War,* 544.

258 Hatfield experience from Colman McCarthy column, the *Washington Post,* 20 September 1994, D21.

258 Bronowski: from his classic *Science and Human Values* (New York: Harper, 1959), 3–4.

259 Sussan segment based on interviews with Sussan and McGovern by G. Mitchell and Susan Jaffe and documents the two men provided to G. Mitchell in 1983.

260 "times fairly scream": Sussan letter to Truman, 25 September 1950. White House reply: Dallas Halverstadt to Sussan, 3 October 1950, TL-OF 73.

260 Warner Brothers: McGovern memo to General Orvil Anderson, 10 July 1946 (courtesy McGovern).

260 "Herb was frustrated": McGovern interviewed by G. Mitchell.

260 Curator: T. Iwakura interviewed by G. Mitchell in 1984 in Tokyo.

260 "I think our government": Beaver interviewed by G. Mitchell in 1984.

261 Background on doctors' movement from Paul Boyer, "Physicians Confront the Apocalypse," *JAMA*, 2 August 1985, 633–51. Other antinuclear background from Milton S. Katz, *Ban the Bomb: A History of SANE* (New York: Greenwood, 1988), and other sources.

Part III—Chapter 4

264 "and achieve": Kammen, *Mystic Chords of Memory* (New York: Vintage, 1991).

265 "There are official records": Michael Amrine, *The Great Decision* (New York: Putnam, 1959).

265 Footnote: Herter letter to John A. McCone (chairman AEC), 8 December 1960, U.S. Department of State Records, National Archives.

266 "rarely with": Herbert Marks, *University of Chicago Law Review*.

267 *White Paper* aired 5 January 1965 (tape at Museum of Television and Radio, New York, N.Y.).

267 Barnouw interviewed by G. Mitchell; Barnouw, "The Hiroshima-Nagasaki Footage," *Historical Journal of Film, Radio and Television* 2, no. 1 (1982).

268 Gould review appeared on August 5, 1970.

268 Footnote: Greenberg and Faye, "Sensitizing People by Making the Abstract Concrete," *American Journal of Orthopsychiatry* (October 1972) 811–15.

268 Special issues: *Time*, 29 July 1985; *Newsweek*, 29 July 1985.

268 "Great Invasion" appeared in *Life* special issue, "World War II," Spring–Summer 1985, 105–8.

269 Buckley from *National Review*, 5 September 1985, 54.

269 Fairlie: "Ban the Bombast," *New Republic*, 2 September 1985, 12–14.

269 Will: *Washington Post*, 14 July 1985.

269 *Today* show episode from Peter Goldman, *The End of the World That Was* (New York: New American Library, 1986), 98.

269 *Nightline* transcript of show, 5 August 1985.

271 Blackett book published in 1949 by McGraw-Hill.

271 *Atomic Diplomacy* published in 1965 by Simon & Schuster; updated edition published in 1985 by Penguin.

271 critics Thomas T. Hammond and Robert James Maddox cited in Walker, "Decision to Use the Bomb," 100.

272 Anderson in *New York Times Book Review*, 18 July 1965, 1.

272 Amrine in *New York Herald-Tribune*, 18 July 1965.

272 Steel in *New York Review of Books*, 25 November 1965, 8–9.

272 *A World Destroyed* published by Knopf in 1975, updated edition published in 1987 by Vintage.

272 "Potsdam diary": see Ferrell, ed., *Off the Record*.

273 "shaped the debate": Walker, "Decision to Use the Bomb," 97–114.

273 "centrally connected": *New York Times Book Review*, 16 December 1975.

273 Sherwin's growing belief: "Introduction to the New Edition," *A World Destroyed* (1987).

274 Casualties: Bernstein, *Bulletin of the Atomic Scientists*, June/July 1986, 38–40.

274 Bundy quote: *Danger and Survival*, 97.

274 Walker quote: "Decision to Use the Bomb."

275 Steel quote: *New Republic*, 10 August 1992.

275 Woodward comment: interview with Philip Nobile.

275 McCullough mistake probed in " 'Truman' Author Errs on Japan Invasion Casualty Memo," Tony Capaccio, *Defense Week*, 11 October 1994, 1.

Part III—Chapter 5

276 "intensify argument": *New York Times*, 29 January 1995.

277 "intellectual bloodletting": Barton Bernstein.

278 "focusing graphically": *National Journal*, 2 April 1994, 805.

278 "the toughest": *St. Louis Post-Dispatch*, 9 June 1994.

278 "It's one of those": *Baltimore Sun*, 24 March 1994.

278 Planning documents dated July 1993.

278 "the central subject": memo from Adams to Harwit, 17 July 1993.

279 Crouch memo: 21 July 1993.

279 "the importance of": *New York Times*, 29 July 1994.

280 Bernstein wrote comment to Harwit on May 23, 1994.

280 Hallion's "Comments on Script" submitted to curators on February 7, 1994, with handwritten notes.

280 Sherwin was interviewed by G. Mitchell in 1994.

280 Correll report issued by Air Force Association on March 15, 1994.

280 "politically correct curating": *Washington Times*, 28 March 1994.

281 "The blunt answer": *National Journal*, 2 April 1994.

281 "extensively": *Air Force*, 1 September 1994.

281 "like babies": *Washington City Paper*, 3 April 1994.

281 "I think what": ibid.

282 "There's real discomfort": Knight-Ridder article, April 1994.

282 "These issues" quote: Agence France Presse, 21 May 1994.

282 "The use of the weapon": William Detweiler statement, 22 September 1994.

283 "absolute nonsense" and "still pushing the thesis": *Washington Post*, 21 July 1994.

283 Hallion's handwritten notes on his "Comments on Script" submitted to curators on February 7, 1994.

283 "a poor script": *Air Force*, September 1994.

283 "don't want to hear": *Washington Times*, 11 August 1994.

283 "I think anybody": *National Journal*, 2 April 1994.

284 "divergent but widely": *Washington Post*, 7 August 1994.

284 "fifty years may not be enough": *Air & Space*, September 1994.

285 Lewis statement issued on August 10, 1994.

286 Sidey in *Time*, 23 May 1994; *Newsweek*: 29 August 1994.

286 *Washington Post*: Ken Ringle story, 26 September 1994.

286 *Wall St. Journal*: 29 August 1994; *USA Today*: 31 August 1994; 6 million: Tony Snow, 1 August 1994; Krauthammer: *Washington Post*, 19 August 1994.

287 *This Week with David Brinkley* show of 28 August 1994.

287 New script dated August 31, 1994.

288 "anti-American": Jonathan Yardley, *Washington Post*, 10 October 1994.

288 Sweeney on *Nightline*, 25 October 1994.

288 Jesse Brown letter dated September 6, 1994.

289 "surrender ceremony": Daniel Schorr in *Christian Science Monitor*, 14 October 1994.

289 "figured out": *Los Angeles Times*, 26 December 1994.

289 "misunderstood": *Asahi Shimbun*, 19 September 1994.

289 New script dated October 26, 1994.

291 Linenthal from transcript, ABC News *Nightline*, 25 October 1994.

291 "patriotically correct": letter by Sherwin and Kai Bird, 16 November 1994.

291 resolution dated October 22, 1994.

292 This is based on Mitchell's notes of meeting with Harwit held on November 17, 1995.

293 "We were told": *Washington Times*, 20 January 1995.

293 Detweiler letter to Clinton on January 19, 1995.

293 "look at future funding": *Washington Times*, 20 January 1995.

293 Dole and Stevens: *Washington Post*, 25 January 1995.

294 Gingrich: *Washington Times*, 28 January 1995.

294 "antinuclear": *Washington Post*, 20 January 1995.

294 "being hijacked": *New York Times*, 30 January 1995.

294 Legion spokesman was Phil Budahn, interviewed by G. Mitchell.

295 "They better not let": ibid.

295 "basic error": *Washington Post*, 31 January 1995.

295 "The president": transcript of briefing, 30 January 1995.

296 Detweiler released a personal statement at a press conference on January 30, 1995.

Part IV—Chapter 1

302 Cold-war fears: reflected most dramatically in a 1961 Gallup poll which found that if given a choice between "fighting an all-out nuclear war" or living under communism, Americans favored the war, by a margin of 81 to 6 percent. A Gallup poll taken at the same time in England found only 21 percent choosing nuclear war. In 1983, a Public Agenda poll found that 41 percent of Americans would "rather die in a nuclear war than see communism come to this country."

303 in an unsafe world, "we must arm . . . with the winning weapon": Gregg Herken, *The Winning Weapon: The Atomic Bomb and the Cold War 1945–1950* (New York: Knopf, 1980), epigraph.

303 Footnote: Gallup poll: November 1994 survey for America's Talking cable network.

303 "a national, psychological reaction . . ." *through* ". . . other types of weapons": by Ralph Lapp and Stewart Alsop, reproduced by Executive Office of the President, TL-PSF, 23 October 1952.

303 Seeking security: Lewis Mumford, 1950, quoted in Boyer, *By the Bomb's Early Light*.

303 "Atomic bomb yes, hydrogen bomb no": Lifton interview with Bethe, December 1987.

304 ". . . for most of the younger writers . . . they most fear": Leslie Fiedler, *Waiting for the End* (New York: Stein & Day, 1964), 156.

305 "nuclear sublime" from Frances Fergusen, "The Nuclear Sublime," *Diacritics* (Summer 1984): 4.

305 Gallup poll data: *The Gallup Poll* (New York: Random House, 1971).

305 Interviews at Center on Violence and Human Survival from Lifton, *The Protean Self: Human Resilience in an Age of Fragmentation* (New York: Basic Books, 1993), 47–48.

306 Mary Wollstonecraft Shelley, *Frankenstein: Or the Modern Prometheus* (1818; reprint, New York: Signet, 1963), 95.

306 "atomic bombs" that could destroy humankind: H. G. Wells, *The World Set Free* (1913; reprint, New York: Dutton, 1914).

Part IV—Chapter 2

307 "enthusiastic commentaries" *through* ". . . has every chance of being final": Albert Camus, "After Hiroshima: Between Hell and Reason," *Combat*, 8 August 1945, reprinted in a translation by Ronald E. Santoni in *Philosophy Today* (Spring 1988): 77–78.

308 "the first true residents of the atomic age" *through* ". . . to redeem to bomb": M. Susan Lindee, *Suffering Made Real: American Science and the Sur-*

vivors of Hiroshima (Chicago: University of Chicago Press, 1994), 4, 10, 134, 136, 14–15.

308 Footnote: Reuters news service summary of article, 21 August 1994.

309 "ripples of destruction" *through* "from the kingdom of hell" from David A. Hoekema, "Aftereffects—The Legacy of Hiroshima and Nagasaki," *Reformed Journal* 35, no. 5 (August 1985): 10–13.

310 "inhuman blasts . . . only against the vanquished in a lost war": Richard A. Falk, Gabriel Kolko, and Robert J. Lifton, eds., *Crimes of War: A Legal, Political, and Psychological Inquiry into the Responsibility of Leaders, Citizens, and Soldiers for Criminal Acts in War* (New York: Random House, 1971): 109, 126–7, 131.

310 Shimoda case from ibid., 57; and Falk and Mendlovitz, eds., *The Strategy of World Order: Toward a Theory of War Prevention* (New York: World Law Fund, 1966), vol. 1, 314–59.

310 "We have tried to make up for . . ." *through* "if anybody treads on the tail of its coat . . .": Edmund Wilson, *Patriotic Gore: Studies in the Literature of the American Civil War* (New York: Oxford University Press, 1962), Introduction, xxvii–xxx.

310 "Our knowledge, our genius. . . . bombs bigger and bigger . . .": Ann Druyan, in *Women on War: Essential Voices of the Nuclear Age,* ed. Dinniela Gioseffi (New York: Touchstone, 1988), 34.

311 "as an instrument of war . . .": Fred Kaplan, *The Wizards of Armageddon.* (New York: Simon & Schuster, 1983).

311 "How can I go to war . . ." *through* ". . . we've built some spares": Herman Kahn, *On Thermonuclear War* (Princeton: Princeton University Press, 1961), 641–42.

311 Colin Gray on "Armageddon Syndrome" in Gregg Herken, *Counsels of War* (New York: Knopf, 1985), 310.

311 "legacy of Hiroshima" *through* ". . . not try to limit the use of weapons": Teller, *Legacy of Hiroshima,* 209, 312.

311 Discussion of Cord C. Meyer and Thomas K. Finletter from Boyer, *By the Bomb's Early Light,* 34, 37, 44.

312 "real human horror such weapons can produce" and subsequent quotations from Joseph Nye, *Nuclear Ethics* (New York: Free Press, 1986) are from ix, 108, 52, 74, 63–64, 15; quotations from the Harvard Nuclear Study group (Albert Carnesale et al.), *Living with Nuclear Weapons* (Cambridge: Harvard University Press, 1983) are from 73, 63.

313 "great void . . . eviscerated, extirpated": Boyer, *By the Bomb's Early Light,* 182.

Part IV—Chapter 3

314 "at whatever expense . . . global environment": Michael Howard review of John Keegan, *A History of Warfare* (New York: Knopf, 1993), in *New York Times Book Review,* 14 November 1993.

315 "invoking the forces . . . tidy up the living room," Dwight Macdonald, "The 'Decline to Barbarism' " in *Memoirs of a Revolutionist* (New York: Farrar, Straus & Giroux, 1957 [reprinted from *Politics II,* August-September 1945]), 84, 86.

315 "potentially terminal revolution": Lifton, *The Broken Connection* (New York: Simon & Schuster, 1979), 337.

315 "the irreversible null point . . . comprehends them": Edith Wyschogrod, *Spirit in Ashes: Hegel, Heidegger and Man-Made Mass Death* (New Haven: Yale University Press, 1985), x.

315 Quotations from Mary Shelley's *Frankenstein* are from 40, 46, 50, 51, 52, 54.

316 more sympathetic and "human" than his creator: Harold Bloom, Afterword to *Frankenstein,* 215.

317 "this group love of science . . . scientific work only threatens us now": Thomas McMahon, *Principles of American Nuclear Chemistry: A Novel* (Boston: Atlantic/Little, Brown, 1970), 245.

317 "the antithetical halves of a single being" from Bloom, p. 213.

317 This process of doubling: Lifton, *The
Nazi Doctors: Medical Killing and the Psy-
chology of Genocide* (New York: Basic
Books, 1986), 418–29. For doubling in
weapons designers and strategists see
Lifton, *The Genocidal Mentality* (New
York: Basic Books, 1989), 148–55. For
Rank's division between mortal and
immortal self, see Otto Rank, *Beyond
Psychology* (1941; reprint, New York:
Dover, 1958), 62–101.

317 "America's century begins in fire . . .
jellied to magma . . .": "Nagasaki,
Uncle Walt, the Eschatology of America's Century," in *American Noise*
(Hopewell, N.J.: Ecco Press, 1993), 43.

318 "Praise/Our electrons. . . . between
the virus and the germ": from title
poem of Rodney Jones, *Apocalyptic Narrative* (New York: Houghton Mifflin,
1993), 29.

Part IV—Chapter 4

319 "nuclear-waste crisis" *through* ". . .
atomic waste dumps": *Newsweek*, 27
December 1993 17–18.

319 "environmental crimes . . . de facto
plutonium dump": Len Ackland, "A
Dump Called Rocky Flats," *Bulletin of
the Atomic Scientists* (November/De-
cember 1994): 12–13.

320 "the single most polluted place . . .":
Stewart Udall, Foreword to Michael
D'Antonio, *Atomic Harvest: Hanford and
the Lethal Toll of America's Nuclear Arsenal* (New York: Crown, 1993), xii.

320 knowledgeable Hanford engineer:
Chugoku Newspaper, *Victims of Radia-
tion Speak Out* (New York: Kodansha
International, 1992), 23.

320 "There's a job . . ." *through* "not on
the team": *Atomic Harvest*, 15, 18–19,
102.

320 "using sand filters . . . make things up
as we went along": *Exposure*, (New
York: Kodansha, 1992), 23.

320 "We don't have time . . .": *Atomic
Harvest*, 110.

321 "I find it impossible . . ." from *Exposure*, p. 23.

321 "How can they do that. . . . why not
use them . . .": Carole Gallagher,
*American Ground Zero: The Secret Nuclear
War* (Cambridge: MIT Press, 1993), 50.

321 "the most long-lived program . . ."
through ". . . OUTSIDE THE TEST
SITE": Udall, *Myths of August*, 229,
235.

321 "There hasn't been . . . any place to
put it": *New York Times*, 15 November
1994, dateline Spokane, Washington.

321 "Go ahead and tell the world" *through*
"Hiroshima and Nagasaki must be going through": *Exposure*, 28, 27.

322 Government agencies conducting radiation experiments from Interim Report
of the Advisory Committee on Human
Radiation Experiments, Washington,
D.C., 21 October 1994.

322 "The only thing I could think
of . . .": *Newsweek*, 27 December
1993, 15.

323 "I was over there fighting the Germans.
. . . conducting them on my mother":
Newsweek, 17.

323 "a little of the Buchenwald touch":
Arjun Makhijani, "Energy Enters
Guilty Plea," *Bulletin of the Atomic Scien-
tists* (March/April 1994): 26.

324 "I knew that the AEC . . ." *through*
"their bodies guinea-pigged on": Chip
Brown, "The Science Club Serves Its
Country," *Esquire*, December 1994,
124–26.

324 "has never sponsored . . . for experimental purposes": *Washington Post*, 6
July 1994.

324 "special hazard injuries" through "conference" on the matter from the Medicine, Health and Safety Claims folder of
the DOE archives of the Atomic Energy Commission.

325 Radiation effects at Trinity and "The

idea was to explode . . ." *through* "If it went east, I was sunk": Weisgall, *Operation Crossroads,* 209, 208.

325 Warren and radiation dangers at Bikini from "Medico-Legal Board" through "practically browbeat": ibid., 210–11, 227, 230, 232, 273–74, 277, 212.

327 Description of exposure of military personnel to atomic explosions from P. C. Murphy et al., "Atomic Veterans and Their Families: Responses to Radiation Exposure," *American Journal of Orthopsychiatry* 60, no. 3 (July 1990) 418–27; and Michael Uhl and Todd Ensign, *GI Guinea Pigs* (New York: Wideview, 1980).

327 "Green Run" through ". . . has a lot to answer for": *Exposure,* 22–25.

328 "men, women, and children . . . in the United States alone": Murphy et al., "Atomic Veterans," 418.

Part IV—Chapter 5

330 Definitions and derivations of "secret" and "concealment" from *Oxford English Dictionary.*

330 "We were shrouded . . ." *through* "Washington monuments" in footnote from John H. Cushman, Jr., "204 secret nuclear tests by U.S. are made public," *New York Times,* dateline Washington, December 7, 1994.

330 "Only a handful. . . . without even knowing they are doing it": Dwight Macdonald, reprinted in *Memoirs of a Revolutionist* (New York: Farrar, Straus & Giroux, 1957).

330 "Those who worked. . . . on a long mission at sea": Susan Griffin, *A Chorus of Stones: The Private Life of War* (1992; reprint, New York: Anchor, 1993), 88–89.

331 battle between the children of light and the children of darkness: Edward A. Shils, *The Torment of Secrecy: The Background and Consequences of American Security Policies* (Glencoe, Ill.: Free Press, 1956), 71. See also David Caute, *The Great Fear: The Anti-Communist Purge under Truman and Eisenhower* (New York: Simon & Schuster, 1978).

331 "All of our Presidents . . . released to the public": Morton H. Halperin, "Secrecy and National Security," in *Assessing the Nuclear Age,* ed. Lou Ackland and Steven McGuire (Chicago: Educational Foundation for Nuclear Science, 1986), 253.

331 1948 document from Gregg Herken, "Direct Hit, Soft Targets," *Deadline,* Center for War, Peace, and the News Media (New York University) January-February 1989.

332 For presidential conflict and frustration concerning nonusability of weapons, see Jonathan Schell, *The Time of Illusion* (New York: Knopf, 1976); "drove two Presidents into states . . . near-ruin of our political system" from p. 381.

333 Footnote, "a secret debate . . . no public discussion at all": Bundy, *Danger and Survival,* p. 000.

334 "For the last four years . . ." and "the bomb was to save mankind from itself": Sissela Bok, *Secrets: On the Ethics of Concealment and Revelation* (New York: Pantheon, 1982), 199, 200.

334 "shake mankind free from parochialism and war": Nuel Pharr Davis, *Lawrence and Oppenheimer* (New York: Simon & Schuster, 1968), 221.

334 "What does worry me. . . . appears to me full of danger": Oppenheimer letter to Conant quoted in Stanley A. Blumberg and Gwinn Owens, *Energy and Conflict: The Life and Times of Edward Teller* (New York: Putnam, 1976), 207.

334 For Michael Carey study see his "Psychological Fallout," *Bulletin of the Atomic Scientists* 38 (January 1982): 20–24; and discussion of it by Lifton in Lifton and Falk, *Indefensible Weapons: The Political and Psychological Case Against Nuclearism* (New York: Basic Books, 1982), 48–54.

Part IV—Chapter 6

338 Observations in Hiroshima from Lifton, *Death in Life*, 1–63, 500–510.

338 *"cordon sanitaire"*: Wyschogrod, *Spirit in Ashes*, xi.

338 "I knew what sort of bombs . . . the definition of infinity": Scott Russell Sanders, *At Play in the Paradise of Bombs* (New York: Simon & Schuster, 1987), 11.

339 "a solution that's the same . . ." *through* ". . . I wouldn't grow up": Sally Belfrage, *UnAmerican Activities: A Memoir of the 50's* (New York: Harper, 1994), 29–30.

339 "selective inattention." . . . what we are actually aware of": Helen Swit

Perry, "Selective Inattention as an Explanatory Concept for U.S. Public Attitudes Toward the Atomic Bomb," *Psychiatry* 17 (1954): 226.

339 Styron quote: from *Newsweek*, January 11, 1993, p. 29.

339 Alice Walker, "The trouble with numbness . . ." quoted from Mary Watkins, "In Dreams Begin Responsibilities," in *Facing Apocalypse*, Valerie Andrews et al. (Dallas: Spring Publications, 1987), 78.

340 "watching houses slide into the ocean . . . grander, more sweeping": Don DeLillo, *White Noise* (New York: Viking Paperback, 1985), 64.

Part IV—Chapter 7

341 "it has already left. . . . and it will find you": Sharon Doubiago, "Ground Zero," *New England Review/Bread Loaf Quarterly*, "Writers in the Nuclear Age" (Summer 1983) 459.

341 "Is it the death of zero. . . . how can we not?": *Credo*, "Writers in the Nuclear Age," 565.

341 "incapable of conceiving . . ." *through* ". . . and he lied about the future": Jeff Nuttal, *Bomb Culture* (New York: Delacorte, 1968), 13–14.

342 "The bomb that . . . punctuated history": Harry Stack Sullivan, "Editorial Notes: The Cultural Revolution to End War," *Psychiatry* 9, 81.

342 Fear has not disappeared: Gallup poll for America's Talking in March 1995 revealed 20 percent believed there would be a nuclear war in their lifetime.

342 "America when will we. . . . with your atomic bomb": Allen Ginsberg, "America," in *Howl and Other Poems* (San Francisco: City Lights, 1956), 31.

342 "I saw the best minds of my generation . . . in the machinery of night . . .": "Howl," in *The New American Poetry*, ed. Donald M. Allen (Grove: 1960), 182.

342 "our work is guided by . . . in the experiment with living": Todd Gitlin, *The Sixties* (New York: Bantam, 1987), 27.

342 "American existentialist . . . the rebellious imperatives of the self": Norman Mailer, *Advertisements for Myself* (Cambridge: Harvard University Press, 1992 [1960]), 339.

343 "Can't imagine how. . . . a hydrogen bomb?" from Allen Ginsberg, "Yiddishe Kopf," *American Poetry Review*, May/June 1994.

343 For an extensive discussion of the symbolization of immortality, see Lifton, *The Broken Connection*, especially 1–112.

343 The "protean self": Lifton, *The Protean Self* (New York: Basic Books, 1993).

344 "When there's no future . . ." through ". . . NO FUTURE FOR ME": Greil Marcus, *Lipstick Traces: The Secret History of the Twentieth Century* (Cambridge: Harvard University Press, 1989), 10–11.

345 "curse" *through* ". . . When will I be blown up?": William Faulkner Nobel Prize acceptance speech, Stockholm, 10 December 1950.

345 "The way back is lost. . . ." *through* "ask whose dream it is": Carolyn

Forché, "The Testimony of Light," in *The Angel of History* (New York: Harper, 1994), 72. Forché identifies the sentence "If Hiroshima in the morning . . . whose dream it is" as the question asked by Peter Schwenger in his book, *Letter Bomb.*

345 "there is no God, no Buddha" and principle of *akirame* from Lifton, *Death in Life,* 23, 185–86, 369–95.

346 "The bomb that fell on Hiroshima . . . like a knife": Henry Wieman, quoted by W. R. Bauckham in "Theology After Hiroshima," *Scottish Journal of Theology* 38, 583.

346 "an eschatological symbol of our age . . .": ibid., 583–84.

346 Pastoral letter: from Boyer, *By the Bomb's Early Light.*

347 Fundamentalism and nuclear threat discussed in Charles B. Strozier, *Apocalypse: On the Psychology of Fundamentalism in America* (Boston: Beacon Press, 1994); and in Lifton, *The Protean Self,* 160–89.

347 "the state may collapse . . . rivers remain": Lifton, *Death in Life,* 94.

348 On the connection between atomic destruction and environmental concerns, Spencer Weart *(Nuclear Fear,* 324–27) tells how both Barry Commoner and Rachel Carson, during the late 1950s and early 1960s, were largely motivated by nuclear threat and dangers of fallout. See also discussion in Lifton, *The Protean Self,* 218–19.

348 "It is not an exaggeration . . ." through "laboratory for atmospheric scientists": Michio Kaku, "War and the Environment," *Audubon Magazine,* September/October 1991, 91–93.

349 "beatific" through "glories of heaven": *Oxford English Dictionary.*

349 "I couldn't begin to count the versions. . . . an eternal Las Vegas of the soul . . .": Campbell McGrath, "Nagasaki, Uncle Walt, the Eschatology of America's Century," *American Noise,* 43–49.

Part IV—Chapter 8

351 "death event": Wyschogrod, *Spirit in Ashes,* xii.

351 "My birth sign": Sanders, "At Play," 2.

351 "double life" *through* "business as usual": *The Broken Connection,* 366.

351 Glover on world-destruction and "the capacity so painfully acquired . . . seriously weakened": Edward Glover, *War, Sadism, and Pacifism* (London: George Allen & Unwin, 1946), 274.

352 "doomed to die . . ." *through* "causeless as well . . .": Mailer, *Advertisements for Myself,* 338.

354 "retrieval of the apocalyptic tradition": Bauckham, "Theology after Hiroshima," 597.

354 "No one surfed the river Styx": Chris Offut, *The Same River Twice* (New York: Penguin, 1993), 84.

354 "disenthrall ourselves": Jerome B. Wiesner, "A Militarized Society," in *Assessing the Nuclear Age,* ed. Len Ackland and Stephen McGuire (Chicago: Educational Foundation for Nuclear Science, 1986), 227. Wiesner quotes Lincoln here but refers to nuclear weapons.

354 "added consciousness" and "a heightened . . .": Harold Bloom, Afterword to *Frankenstein,* 215.

354 "protean self" and "species self": see Lifton and Markusen, *The Genocidal Mentality,* 255–79; and Lifton, *The Protean Self,* pp 213–32.

355 "anyone who would seek . . . Hiroshima and Nagasaki" from Clark, *Nuclear Past, Nuclear Present.*

356 "who first produced and tested" *through* ". . . creating the situation we face today": George Kennan, *The Nuclear Delusion* (New York: Pantheon, 1982), 177–78.

Appendix

359 "Creative artists": notable is the artist known as "Jess," who as Burgess Collins worked for the Manhattan Project as a chemist at Oak Ridge and Hanford. He quit his job in 1949 after dreaming that the world would be destroyed.

359 First Yank review in Variety, 5 September 1945. An RKO melodrama, it is now available on videotape. Footage from Trinity test was grafted onto the end of the film.

360 Early scripts at Cinema-Television Library, University of Southern California library.

360 Background on film: ibid; Michael Yavenditti, "American Reactions to the Use of Atomic Bombs on Japan," Ph.D. dissertation, University of California-Berkeley, 1970; Yavenditti, "The Atomic Scientists and Hollywood: The Beginning or the End?" Film & History, December 1978, 73–88; Smith, A Peril and a Hope; Nathan Reingold, Science, American Style (Rutgers University Press, 1991), 334–47; Hershberg, James B. Conant.

360 Truman okayed: letter of Carter Barron to Charles Ross, 19 April 1946; reply by Ross (same day). TL-PSF 112.

362 Original scene labeled "Excerpt from 'The Beginning or the End,'" with "rejected" written across it by Charles Ross, two pages, TL-Ross Papers.

363 Footnote: Lippman and McCloy reactions in Hershberg, James B. Conant.

363 "enjoyed very much" in letter from Ross to Carter Barron, 29 October 1946, TL-Ross Papers.

363 Truman letter to Bohnen, 12 December 1946.

363 McGuinness, Lippmann, Conant from Hershberg, James B. Conant.

363 McGuinness trip to Washington revealed in his letter to Ross, 1 November 1946, TL-Ross Papers.

363 New scene: labeled "New Scene," five pages, TL-Ross Papers.

364 "to incorporate": 1 November 1947, TL-Ross Papers.

364 Ross's request in his letter to McGuinness, 8 November 1947, TL-Ross Papers.

364 Final draft, unlabeled, four pages long, TL-Ross Papers.

364 Bush, Conant, Baruch reactions in Hershberg, James B. Conant.

365 Time: 24 February 1947; Variety: 19 February 1947. PM: 21 February, 1947.

365 Brown: Bulletin, March 1947; Crowther: February 21, 1947.

365 Szilard quoted in Lanouette, Genius in the Shadows, 362.

365 Yavenditti quote from his "The Atomic Scientists and Hollywood."

366 "to the larger" from Boyer, By the Bomb's Early Light.

366 idea for the movie: revealed in The Tibbets Story.

366 initial film treatment: production files on Above and Beyond, Cinema-Television Library, University of Southern California.

367 Crowther in New York Times, 31 January 1953.

368 "presents a subtext": Franklin, War Stars.

369 Plutonium scene: New York Times (Arts & Leisure), 15 October 1989; National Review, 10 November 1989; Premiere, October 1989.

369 One authority was Richard Rhodes in New York Times, 15 October 1989.

369 Canby review appeared 20 October 1989.

370 Sontag: Against Interpretation (New York: Farrar Straus & Giroux, 1966).

373 Opinion polls: for example, see Susan T. Fiske, "Adult Beliefs, Feelings, and Actions Regarding Nuclear War," in The Medical Implications of Nuclear War (Washington, D.C.: National Academy of Sciences Press, 1986), 444–60.

373 "Hiroshima has had": Paul Brians, Nuclear Holocausts: Atomic War in Fiction

(Kent, Ohio: Kent State University Press, 1987).

374 O'Brien quote from his article "The Vietnam in Me," *New York Times Magazine*, 2 October 1994.

374 Faulkner address was 10 December 1950.

374 "I don't care": Boyer, *By the Bomb's Early Light*, 246.

375 "Dedication Day" was published in *Politics*, April 1946, reprinted in *New Directions* 10, 1948.

375 "the worst thing": Laurence Bergreen, *James Agee: A Life* (New York: Dutton, 1984), 294.

375 "a story": his letter to "Father Flye," 19 November 1945.

377 Agee and Chaplin relationship from Bergreen, *James Agee*, 302–24.

377 "intensity": Boyer, *By the Bomb's Early Light*.

377 "I want scientists": Kurt Vonnegut interviewed by G. Mitchell.

378 "massacre machinery": *Slaughterhouse-Five, Or The Children's Crusade* (New York: Delacorte, 1969).

378 "sickened" *and* "what bullshit": *Nation*, 2 August 1980.

379 "they are really about": Alfred Kazin, *Bright Book of Life* (South Bend: University of Notre Dame Press, 1971), 83.

379 "The all-time high": Brians, *Nuclear Holocausts*.

380 *Atomic Ghosts:* John Bradley, ed. (Minneapolis: Coffee House Press, 1995).

380 "very, very thin": Kinnell speaking at conference in Hiroshima, July 1983, reprinted in *Literature Under the Nuclear Cloud* (Tokyo: Sanyusha, 1984).

380 Kinnell and Forché remarks: *Literature Under the Nuclear Cloud*.

INDEX

ABOUT THE AUTHORS

ROBERT JAY LIFTON is an eminent psychiatrist and author. Among his many books are the National Book Award–winning *Death in Life: Survivors of Hiroshima; The Nazi Doctors,* which received the Los Angeles Times Book Prize for history; and *The Protean Self.* He is Distinguished Professor of Psychiatry and Psychology at John Jay College and the Graduate School of the City University of New York, and director of the Center on Violence and Human Survival. For more than two decades Lifton held the Foundations' Fund Research Professorship of Psychiatry at Yale University.

GREG MITCHELL is the author of *The Campaign of the Century: Upton Sinclair's Race for Governor of California,* winner of the 1993 Goldsmith Book Prize from Harvard University. His other books include *Acceptable Risks* and *Truth and Consequences.* For many years he served as the editor of *Nuclear Times* magazine, and his articles on the atomic bombings of Japan have appeared in *The New York Times, The Washington Post, the Los Angeles Times,* and more than a dozen other publications. Mitchell lives in Nyack, New York.